Business Ethics

Business
Ethics

Richard T. De George
The University of Kansas

Macmillan Publishing Co., Inc.
New York

Collier Macmillan Publishers
London

Macmillan Publishing Co., Inc.
866 Third Avenue, New York, New York 10022

Collier Macmillan Canada, Ltd.

Library of Congress Cataloging in Publication Data

De George, Richard T
    Business ethics.

    Includes bibliographies and index.
    1. Business ethics. 2. Business ethics—Case studies. I. Title.
HF5387.D38   1982   174'.4   81–492
ISBN 0–02–328000–X   AACR1

Printing: 1 2 3 4 5 6 7 8   Year: 2 3 4 5 6 7 8

Preface

Courses in ethics have long been standard fare in American colleges and universities. Courses in business ethics are of more recent vintage. The latter took root in the post-Watergate era, were nurtured by successive exposés involving bribes and kickbacks, illegal political contributions, airplane disasters, and the sale of defective tires, automobiles, and other products. Consumerism, the cry for increased governmental control, and a changing attitude of large numbers of people toward business and its social responsibility have made questions of business ethics topics of general and current concern.

This book is an attempt to cover the field in a systematic and reasonably comprehensive way. It deals first with the techniques of moral reasoning and argumentation that are needed to analyze moral issues in business. It then raises basic questions about the morality of economic systems, especially that of the United States. It next discusses a variety of current and pressing moral issues in business from worker's rights to trade secrets. Finally it discusses the moral obligations of nations to other nations, of peoples to other people geographically distant from them, and of one generation to later generations.

Since business ethics is a comparatively new field of scholarly endeavor, I should make clear some of my presuppositions and aims from the start.

This is not simply a book in general ethics that takes its examples from the business world. Ethics as a discipline has a long and venerable history. But students do not need to know that history, nor do they need to know the large number of disputed questions with which that discipline abounds in order to engage in moral thinking. Moral issues are pressing, and people must grapple with them using the best tools available to them at the time. I try, therefore, to introduce the student to as much of the technical aspect of ethics as is necessary for him or her to approach moral issues intelligently and to take part in the ongoing debate about the morality of certain social and business practices. The aim of my initial chapters is a practical one, and to achieve this end I necessarily ignore or pass over lightly some of the theoretical issues on which much of contemporary professional ethical thought is focused. Students, I assume, come to classes in business ethics with a good deal of moral baggage. They are not nonmoral beings who must be made moral but rather moral beings who can be helped to think through moral issues and to argue cogently and effectively for their moral views.

The traditional approach to ethics is an individualistic one. Our notions of morality, moral worth, moral praise, and blame have grown up primarily from consideration of the human person as a moral agent. We know what it means to call a person moral or his actions morally praiseworthy. Economic systems do not act in a way comparable to the way human individuals act; corporations and nations act only figuratively and through the agency of human intermediaries. Moral language must be used with care and caution when applied outside the realm of human individuals and their actions. Special problems arise when considering the morality of corporations, nations, and people—problems that concern the meaning of moral terms, and problems that must be faced and clarified if we are to be clear about our moral judgments in these areas.

I assume that there is little need to argue that murder is wrong, that stealing and lying are in general wrong, or that discrimination on the basis of sex, race, or creed is immoral in business as in other areas of life. There is no need therefore for a course in business ethics to arrive at or justify these conclusions. But many of the questions of business ethics that involve reverse discrimination, truth in advertising, whistle blowing, and disclosure, among others, are not clear-cut. They require careful analysis, and a weighing of appropriate facts and applicable principles in order to arrive at justifiable answers. Our society is clearer on some of these issues than on others. I have tried to present the complexities of each problem and to weigh the opposing views on an issue. When I have taken sides, I have given my reasons for doing so; if an argument is inconclusive, I have indicated where and why. On broad social issues no argument will be the final one, and my hope is that students using this text will by reading it be encouraged and emboldened to help continue and advance the public debate on these issues.

I do not think it is sufficient simply to identify moral problems in business, to determine what actions are right and wrong, and to demand that people be moral heroes in doing what is required of them. If practices are immoral and if people are faced with the obligation of sacrificing their jobs and their security to fulfill their moral obligations, then these practices should be changed. I therefore attempt not only to discuss what is morally required of a person in a firm—a worker, a manager, a member of the board of directors—but also what structures are conducive to a person's accepting moral responsibility and fulfilling his or her moral obligations. How firms can be reorganized so as to preclude the necessity for whistle blowing is as pressing (if not more pressing) a question as asking when a person is morally obliged to blow the whistle.

Business is a social activity and, like all social activity, could not function unless certain moral prerequisites were fulfilled. An analysis of these and of the social and business structures conducive to morality form, I believe, an important and frequently neglected aspect of business ethics. At each stage of investigation, therefore, I raise and attempt to answer not only the question of whether a particular practice is moral or immoral but also the question of what alternative can and should be pursued with respect to immoral practices. The morality of individuals should not be separated from the morality of business procedures and institutions, and in what follows I handle them together to the extent possible.

The daily newspaper carries ample current materials for analysis for those wishing case studies and specific, timely examples of moral issues in business. I have incorporated into my discussion some actual and some fictitious case studies to illustrate specific principles, to exemplify ways of analyzing moral problems, and to contrast varying approaches to an issue. Although the book is written so that it develops a total view through successive chapters, each chapter can be studied apart from the others. Those who wish to omit the analysis of some issues and concentrate on a selected few can do so without a loss of intelligibility. Those wishing to read further on a topic will find suggestions for doing so listed at the end of each chapter. These listed works include any book or article mentioned in the chapter and represent both sides of controversial questions.

R.T. DeGeorge

Contents

Business
Ethics

Introduction

1

Ethics and Business

"Business and ethics don't mix," goes the old adage. "Nor do heaven and businessmen," goes the wry reply. This adage, a piece of American folk-knowledge, forms part of a popular view which I shall call the "Myth of Amoral Business." The myth, as most myths, has several variations. Many people believe it; at least they more or less believe it. It expresses a certain truth and accounts for a surface phenomenon. At the same time it conceals a good deal of reality. The myth is to some extent descriptive. It describes how American business and American business men and women perceive themselves and are perceived by others. They are concerned with profit, with producing goods and providing services, and with buying and selling. According to the myth, people in business are not explicitly concerned with morality—they are amoral. This does not mean they are immoral. Rather they feel moral considerations are inappropriate in business. They are opposed to moralizing. They dislike being preached to by moralists, and they therefore are very reluctant to throw moral stones even at their fiercest competitors. Most people in business do not act immorally or maliciously. They think of themselves in their private lives as well as in their business lives as moral people. They simply feel that business is not expected to be concerned with morality. Even when a firm acts out of principle, it rarely boasts about it in moral terms or even presents its actions as such. Many outside the business world share the view that business is amoral.

One of the interesting variations on the theme is that since businesses are not concerned with morality, they often act immorally. Think of the many scandals which make newspaper headlines—the many unsavory accounts of bribery, misrepresentation, white collar crime, kickbacks, unsafe products, and insider manipulation of markets, not to mention a business's lack of concern for the environment, for company towns whose local plant is closed, and a lack of concern for the common good. According to the myth businesses act immorally not out of any desire to do evil but simply out of a concern for making profit and out of a disregard for some of the consequences of their actions on other people.

The Myth of Amoral Business not only represents the way many people in and out of the business world perceive business but also represents the way many would like to continue to perceive business. It is much easier to deal with dollars and cents than to deal with value judgments. It is more comfortable to discuss a problem in terms of a bottom line which represents profit or loss than one which does not. It is not only easier for those in business. It is also easier for those not in business to judge a firm by its financial bottom line. This is what concerns investors, the myth continues. This is what directly affects the workers in a company. This is what consumers expect.

As with most popularly held myths, the Myth of Amoral Business captures a popular truth. Yet it also conceals or hides a good deal of real life. This book and the general topic of business ethics concern what has for a long time been covered, concealed, and ignored. Scandals, environmental problems, and energy problems have all helped the reality surface now and then. They have not yet given rise to a Myth of Moral Business. What, then, is the reality which lies hidden? What is the true relation of ethics to business which is only slowly coming into general view and consciousness? What are the indications of its emergence?

Let me address the last question first. The breakdown of the Myth of Amoral Business has been signaled in three fairly obvious ways: by the reporting of scandals and the concomitant public reaction to these reports; by the growth of popular groups such as the environmentalists and the consumerists; and by the concern of businesses expressed in conferences, articles, the burgeoning of codes of ethical conduct, and so on. How does the reporting of scandals in business and the popular reaction to them signal a breakdown of the Myth? Consider what the Myth implies if it is taken seriously. If it were true that business is viewed as amoral, that it is not expected to behave according to moral rules, and that it is appropriate for it to do whatever is necessary in order to increase its profit, then there would be no surprise, shock, or uproar when a business acted immorally. The uncovering of bribes and kickbacks would not be news. Revelations about unsafe products and white collar crime would be routine, expected, and unexceptional. The fact that such events *do* make news, *do* cause public reaction, *do* adversely affect a company's image, and *do* cause scandal is an indication that the Myth of Amoral Business is not unambiguously held. More people daily expect companies to act morally, at least in certain instances and within certain limits. It is no longer true that anything goes.

Even though the Myth does not say that anything goes, some of its variations imply this. Contemporary reactions provide evidence that if the Myth describes the way things are, there are many people who feel things should be otherwise, that business should behave morally. At least two groups—the environmentalists and the consumerists—articulate their demands and try to force businesses to consider values other than those that are reducible to sales figures and ledger sheets. The issues raised by these groups are not stated in terms of dollars and cents but in terms of other values, such as the beauty of the land, the preservation of certain species of animals and fish, and the right of people to adequate information about the goods they purchase. These demands have a new moral dimension which has forced even those firms reacting negatively to the environmentalists and consumerists to consider the claims which these groups and others are making. If the Myth of Amoral Business were the whole story, the environmental and consumer movements would make no sense, and business would not respond to them. Since the movements do make sense, and since business does respond, the Myth is at best only part of the story.

The reaction of business to the above movements has been significant. In some ways it has been one of annoyance and puzzlement, some businesses have even tried to ignore the claims being made in the name of the environment, consumers, and morality, and have tried to act as if the Myth of Amoral Business were true. Others have seen that ignoring the demands will not make them go away. One reaction has been to seek counsel from other groups and to share their perplexity about how to respond to the increasing public demands. One result has been the convening of a surprising number of conferences, meetings, and symposia either sponsored by business or attended by those in business. The themes are most frequently related to values, to questions of business ethics, and to the ways of handling what has become known as the social audit. In the past, business as a whole has thought of itself according to the Myth of Amoral Business. It is not structured to handle moral questions and its managers are typically not trained in business schools to do so. Experience has supplied even less training along these lines. Hence many businesses have faced a new dilemma. They are now beginning to feel they should respond to moral demands and should take moral issues into account in their deliberations, but don't know how to. Nonetheless, conferences, meetings, and new ethical codes in businesses prove that the Myth of Amoral Business is slowly waning.

The Relation of Business and Morality

Business and morality are related in a number of significant ways which are ignored by the Myth of Amoral Busines. Some of these relations are obvious. They are so obvious that we take them for granted, and hence we tend to ignore them. Others are subtle. They are so subtle that again we tend to ignore them. But whether obvious or subtle they form part of the makeup of our daily lives and experience. We can illuminate them, focus on them, bring them into the open, and so articulate the relation of business and morality. I shall consider five aspects of this relation under the following headings: The Moral Background of Business; The Business of Business; Business and the Law; Business and Values; and The Foundations of Property.

1. The Moral Background of Business

Business is an important part of contemporary society. It involves all of us in one way or another. We all purchase goods that we need for survival and comfort. We all rely on the availability of electricity and gasoline. We buy food, clothing, and services. People supply these for us. Manufacturers make goods that we need and want. Other people transport them to stores where still others sell them to consumers. Business is therefore not something separate from society or imposed upon it—it is an integral part of society and its activities. Morality consists of rules of human behavior and specifies that certain actions are wrong or immoral and that others are right or moral. We can take the moral point of view to evaluate human action. Some actions such as murder are considered immoral. Others, such as helping one's neighbor, are generally considered moral. Still others, such as tying one's shoe, are, at least in the abstract, morally indifferent. They assume moral character only in particular circumstances, for instance, when used purposefully to annoy someone, or to cause someone harm. Any action can be viewed from a moral perspective. Hence it is difficult to imagine what people mean when they say that morality and business do not mix or are antithetical. Since business activity is human activity, it can be evaluated from a moral point of view just as any other human activity can be so evaluated. The relation of business to morality goes even deeper than this. Business, like most other social activities, presupposes a background of morality and would be impossible without it. For instance, employers expect their employees not to steal from the firm; parties to a contract each expect each other to honor an agreement; those who buy a product expect it to be as advertised when they take it home and unpack it; and people who work with others expect them generally to tell the truth, to respect rather than assault them, and to do the job for which they are paid. In most cases their expectations are met. If everyone in business—buyers, sellers, producers, management, workers and consumers—acted immorally or even amorally (i.e., without concern for whether their actions were moral or immoral), business would soon grind to a halt. Morality is the oil as well as the glue of society and business. It is only against the background of morality that immorality can not only be profitable but even possible. Lying would not succeed if most people were not truthful and did not tend to believe others. A breach of trust requires a background of trust. Business does not really operate according to the dictum of "let the buyer beware." Business generally values its reputation. We therefore really do not live in a "dog-eat-dog" business would be-cause such a world would not be tolerable.

People, of course, do act immorally in business as well as in other spheres of life. There are numerous cases of fraud, misrepresentation, inflated business accounts, and so on. But there is no proof that people are more immoral in their business lives than in their private lives. It is not clear that the structures of business are more prone to immorality than any other structures of society—those of government, family, education, or religion. Nor is it clear that large, impersonal businesses are either more or less moral or immoral than small, individually owned businesses.

Business is a part of society and therefore, the actions of people in business are subject to moral rules. The point is probably so obvious as to be generally forgotten. It is forgotten by those who practice the Myth of Amoral Business. Most adults do not need to be told that lying and stealing are wrong, or that murder is wrong. These actions are wrong whether done in or out of business. It is because the ordinary person does not need to be told that these things are wrong that they form part of the background of business. It is assumed by those in business. The thesis that business and morality do not mix, consequently, cannot be convincingly maintained. The point of business ethics is not necessarily to change anyone's moral convictions but to build upon them.

2. The Business of Business

A famous cliché maintains that "the business of business is business." The business of business is not government, charity, or social welfare. Nor, the cliché implies, is it morality. But what does it mean to say that the business of business is business, and who is to decide? To get some perspective on the question we can look beyond our own society. What we find is that what is considered both business and its business varies from society to society. In Japan the business of large corporations is not only to produce goods but also to care for the firm's employees—in effect, guaranteeing them lifetime employment. Paternalism is thus part of the business of business in Japan in a way that it is not in the United States. In the Soviet Union private ownership of the means of production and ownership of companies and factories is prohibited by law. There are of course still factories, offices, stores, and goods. But business is a state affair, not a private affair. Therefore, what constitutes business varies from society to society. The question of what business is and what it is properly concerned with is a social question which is answered socially, not individually.

In the United States the mandate to business was initially rather simple. People wanted goods to be as plentiful, good, and cheap as possible. Those interested in producing them were given relatively free rein under competitive conditions. Some businesses succeeded and grew. Others failed. As problems developed regulations were introduced by law regulating working conditions, protecting children, preventing monopolistic practices, and preserving the environment. The regulations frequently represented moral concerns on the part of the American people. The business of business was and is decided by the people of each society. What practices are and are not to be tolerated are not eternal givens; nor are the determinations of what is and is not acceptable to a society. The mandate to business to some extent also sets limits to its proper activity and to what is and is not socially tolerable. The limits are not set by business or by those who run the business, even though some of them act as if they were. The limits imposed on business and the demands made upon business are frequently moral ones. A business may ignore the moral demands of an individual but it can hardly ignore the moral demands of a whole society since it is part of that society and dependent on it at the same time that it serves it. There is increasing evidence that the mandate to business in the United States is changing and that businesses are increasingly expected to weigh more factors in their actions than only financial ones. What the business of business is, in fact, is itself a moral decision and one that is socially made and implemented. Insofar as business is a part of society, it rightfully has a voice in arriving at the social determination of what its business is. To do so effectively, it must be able to enter into the moral social discourse which is debating its future. Business ethics helps clarify some of the issues and provides the techniques for effectively entering into the debate.

3. Business and the Law

Business is a social enterprise. Its mandate and limits are both set by society. The limits are often moral, but they are also frequently written into law. The history of the development of business in America is an interesting one, as is the history of the relation of business and morality, and business and law. In the early days of our history most American businesses were small. The Protestant work ethic was a strong influence. It provided both motivation and justification for the businessman's activity. The good, the elect, and the hardworking were blessed with riches. The lazy and incompetent suffered. Rugged individualism was both an ingredient in the work ethic and a secular moral value as well.

In contemporary society the work ethic has changed to some extent. Society, through welfare, attempts to take care of some of the poor and needy. Small businesses have for the most part given way to giant corporations. Individuals who own their own businesses are relatively rare. The large firms are owned by stockholders and are run by managers who are paid wages, even if they be handsome wages. The feeling of private ownership is no longer appropriate for those people who run a big business and the old virtues are also no longer appropriate. Since they are hired managers, these people run the companies not for themselves but for the stockholders; they run the company not necessarily as they choose but to some extent as they must. They are subject to a board of directors and therefore have a certain distance from the workers of the company. They cannot impose their own morality on company policy but run it in a somewhat neutral way.

The dissociation of management from ownership took place at the same time that laws regulating business proliferated. It was natural, as a result, for those running firms to feel that what society and stockholders of their company required of them was only compliance with the law. If they complied with the law, they fulfilled their social obligations. As a result, they began to feel that morality was personal, that it varied from person to person and from group to group, and that all that could be expected of the managers of business, as well as of business itself, was fulfillment of the law. The law prohibits theft, enforces contracts, sets limits to advertising, and reinforces many moral norms. Equating what is required of business with what is required by law became a convenient and easy norm to adopt. It made clear one's duty and limited what one had to consider. It provided a convenient rationale for ignoring moral demands and for living by the Myth of Amoral Business.

This view fails to consider closely the relation of law and morality. Many laws prohibit immoral practices. Immoral practices for the most part are socially harmful practices. Some such as murder, stealing, and perjury are so harmful that to moral sanction is added the sanction of law. Hence, one of the ways to argue that a law should be passed is to argue that the conduct which the law governs is immoral and seriously harmful to society. For instance, discrimination was immoral before it was made illegal.

Nor are all laws themselves morally defensible. The laws requiring discrimination are a case in point. To abide by the law in practicing discrimination was in fact to act immorally. The danger of equating law with what one is morally as well as legally required to do is that it denies the possibility of arguing from a moral point of view that either a law should be passed or a bad law repealed. Finally, not everything that is immoral can be made illegal. If, for instance, it is immoral to lie, that does not mean that all lying should be made illegal. The reason is that such a law would be unenforceable. Nor would it be worth the time and effort to try to enforce it to any considerable extent. Yet it does not follow, even for those who claim that they are only bound by law, that it would be right for them to lie whenever they felt like it within the company, to those with whom they do business, and so on. In most cases it would be considered bad business as well as immoral.

The retreat to law as the sole norm by which to guide business is in part a reflection of the fact that most managers do not know how to handle many moral issues in business. Having equated morality with personal opinion, they understandably find it difficult to defend their moral judgments in objective terms. A correct perception of the status of morality and a knowledge of the techniques of moral argumentation are necessary to handle moral values and moral issues in business. Part of the task of business ethics is to supply the appropriate perception and knowledge.

4. Business and Values

The social mandate to business is not only given in law. The general mandate to provide a plentiful supply of high quality goods at a cheap price is in fact a social mandate. It arises from the need of the general public and is expressed in many ways. The mandate to business today is more complex. Demands are made on it from many quarters. Businesses have responded to some and not to others. Frequently they do not know how to evaluate conflicting demands—we have already noted the retreat to law on the part of some firms. Some businesses choose to ignore the background of morality with which and in which they operate.

The retreat to law together with a disclaimer concerning moral demands is frequently not a reflection of bad will or a desire to be immoral; rather, it often reflects the lack of internal structures within a firm to consider and weigh moral as well as financial considerations and a lack of confidence in the ability of those within a firm to engage in public, moral reasoning. Even those forms which are exemplary from a moral point of view are reluctant to defend their positions in moral terms.

This is in part a reflection of the Myth of Amoral Business. The economic system is thought by some to be value-free. Each person within it seeks his or her own good. Buyers contract with sellers to the mutual benefit of both. The marketplace becomes the neutral ground of common activity and general good is achieved without its being intended by anyone. This view, which is a simplified form of how the free enterprise system is sometimes presented, does not correspond to the way any economic system works. But it is certainly clear that it corresponds even less to the economic system of America today than it did in nineteenth-century America.

The nation and the world have come to see that there are limits to available natural resources, that industrialization has been purchased at a certain price, and that the ecosystem is so delicately balanced that each change we produce in it triggers other, sometimes deleterious changes, which we do not necessarily intend. As a result we now collectively know that many of our actions involve value judgments. For instance, do we want more electricity? If so, are we willing to risk the dangers involved in nuclear reactors? When oil is scarce, we know that we must sometimes choose between having gas for our cars or fuel for heating our homes. If we want a strong military force we cannot have it unless we raise through taxes the money required to support it.

Individuals in business can no longer act simply as they choose. Government regulations, decisions, and guidelines temper the moves of the marketplace. In addition corporations are being asked, if not forced, to consider the impact of their decisions and actions on the environment, the public, and on the common good. Air and water are no longer goods to be freely used. The safety of workers and consumers of products is no longer something any manufacturer can ignore. Businesses are for the most part not structured to handle moral demands or to weigh values in nonmonetary terms. How can they do this? They can do so by considering what structures promote moral responsibility and facilitate the weighing of moral and other values—topics appropriately raised in business ethics.

5. The Foundations of Property

Private property is a cornerstone of capitalism or of the free enterprise system, and socially owned property is the cornerstone of socialist economic systems. But what is property? What makes property private? By what right do I call property mine? These are not economic questions. Legally, property is defined in terms of rights. If something is mine, I have the right to use it, to destroy it, to sell it, or to protect it from your taking or using it. But rights may be moral as well as legal. The question of property can therefore be put in terms of morality as well as legality.

In order to produce, human beings need raw materials with which to work. Who then owns nature? John Locke, the British philosopher whose theory influenced the American Founding Fathers, argued that every man is allowed to use what nature provides. He may make it his own if he can use it and if other people have as much and as good remaining for their use as well. The initial partition of the earth is a fact. Some people own diamond mines; others own oil fields; still others own iron and coal mines, and so on. By what right do certain people claim the exclusive right to the earth's resources simply because they happen to have been fortunate enough to have been born in the country where the resources existed? Do one people have a right to resources and the riches they bring while other people who happen to inhabit barren land without resources are doomed to poverty and starvation? Can one argue plausibly that the resources of the world are for the benefit of all people and not just for the lucky few? The less developed countries of the world are asking Americans these questions. Eight percent of mankind uses forty percent of the earth's natural resources; we are being forced by the other ninety-two percent to answer by what right we have so much more than others.

Similar questions are being raised within our own country. Can we justify the wealth and opulence of a few together with the poverty of large numbers of others? A negative answer can result in a demand for the transfer of wealth from those who have wealth to those who do not. These transfer payments in the United States are carried on primarily through taxation. Taxation, therefore, is a means of transferring property—namely money—from one person and group to another. By what right is this done? The answer requires not only legal reasoning but also moral reasoning and argument. Once again, the topics appropriately addressed by business ethics surface as we investigate the foundations of business and property.

Business Ethics

Thus far we have referred to business ethics but we have not seen in any detail what it is. Since business ethics is part of an ongoing philosophical enterprise, we can start with a general notion of philosophy, then proceed to that portion which is called ethics, and then finally proceed to business ethics. These three notions are closely related. Philosophy in its broadest meaning is a systematic attempt to make sense out of our individual and collective human experience. As opposed to theologians, philosophers use reason to interpret experience and do not rely on divine revelation. Traditionally philosophers have engaged in two types of rational activity. One is analytic. The philosopher analyzes or investigates in detail the meaning of terms, the validity of arguments, and the nature and status of presuppositions by discerning their components. The philosopher looks at basic questions such as the nature of reality, the meaning and reliability of knowledge, the foundation of values, and so on. The philosopher differs from the scientist in a number of ways. The questions he asks are sometimes broader than those of the scientist, and the techniques he uses are not laboratory techniques. But if he examines the theoretical foundations of physics or the foundations of induction he does something that some scientists also do. The philosophy of science is therefore a meeting point for philosophers and scientists.

Synthesis is the second type of rational activity in which the philosopher engages. He constructs a unified view which brings together, integrates, and makes all the parts of our experience as intelligible as possible. He attempts to relate the findings of the sciences, the arts, and human experience in general into a comprehensible whole. The endeavor is an ongoing one, which has been more favorably perceived in some periods of history than in others.

Ethics is a part of philosophy. Those people who study ethics engage in analysis and synthesis just as those in other branches of philosophy do. The two activities, moreover, are related and it is not always easy to separate them. Ethics, as a part of philosophy, is related to the other parts. Whether we can have knowledge of the subject matter of ethics and how sure that knowledge can be are questions related in general to the question of what human knowledge consists of, the limits of such knowledge, the laws of valid reasoning, and also the status of values and norms. Yet, though related to philosophy, ethics is usually considered to have at least a relative independence in that it can be pursued in its own right.

The object that ethics studies is morality. *Morality* is a term used to cover those practices and activities that are considered importantly right and wrong, the rules which govern those activities, and the values that are imbedded, fostered, or pursued by those activities and practices. The morality of a society is related to its mores or the customs accepted by a society or group as being the right and wrong ways to act, as well as to the laws of a society which add legal prohibitions and sanctions to many activities considered to be immoral.

Ethics in general can be defined as a systematic attempt through the use of reason to make sense of our individual and social moral experience in such a way as to determine the rules which ought to govern human conduct and the values worth pursuing in life. The attempt is systematic and hence goes beyond what each reflective person tends to do in his daily life in making sense of his moral experience, organizing it, and attempting to make it coherent and unified. Since it uses reason and does not use revelation, it can be distinguished from a religious or theological approach to morality. Insofar as it attempts to ascertain what rules and *values* ought to be followed and pursued, it can be distinguished from anthropology, psychology, and sociology. Those disciplines describe how peopple behave but usually do not prescribe how they should or ought to behave. Ethics concerns itself with human conduct, taken here to mean human activity which is done knowingly and, to a large extent, willingly. It does not concern itself with automatic responses, actions done in one's sleep or under hypnosis, and so on.

The above definition defines ethics as the study of morality. The term ethics is, however, used in a variety of ways by different people. Sometimes ethics is used for morality—an action which is morally right is called an ethical one. I referred earlier to the work ethic, since that is the common phrase, though I could have called it the work morality. Codes of moral conduct adopted by professions are frequently called ethical codes. Although philosophically speaking business ethics is a branch of general ethics, some people understand by business ethics business morality. They interpret this either descriptively as the morality followed in business, or normatively, as the morality which ought to be followed. We cannot legislate the use of terms. It is wise, however, to be conscious of divergent uses.

Those engaged in ethics as a branch of philosophy do analysis and synthesis. There are three related phases of ethical study which are known commonly as descriptive ethics, normative ethics, and metaethics. The three constitute what is sometimes called general, as opposed to special, ethics.

Descriptive ethics is closely related to anthropology, sociology, and psychology and leans heavily on them. It consists of studying and describing the morality of a people, culture, or society. It also compares and contrasts different moral systems, codes, practices, beliefs, principles, and values. Descriptive ethics provide basic material which normative ethics must account for, and it provides a touchstone of the considered morality of a people or society with which the normative theory must more or less coalesce.

Normative ethics systematically attempts to supply and justify a coherent moral system. Typically it seeks to uncover, develop, and justify the basic moral principle or principles or the basic moral values of a moral system. The system itself consists both of the basic moral principle(s) and values and the particular moral rules that govern people's behavior in the sense of prescribing those actions that are right or moral and proscribing those that are wrong or immoral. These rules and values constitute the moral norms of the society. The task of normative ethics is threefold. First, it attempts to form into a related whole the various norms, rules, and values of a society's morality. It tries to render these as consistent and coherent as possible, with perhaps some hierarchical arrangement of norms. Secondly, it attempts to find the basic principle from which the particular norms can be derived. Thirdly, it attempts, in a variety of ways, to justify the basic principle of morality.

A society can hold various moral norms that may or may not be consistent. In forming a system the moral philosopher attempts to make the various norms consistent with one another. This system constitutes a theory of morality. If the basic principle is powerful enough, it should provide the means for deriving the set of consistent norms accepted by a society as well as for making norms explicitly held that were previously held only implicitly. The basic principle should also provide a procedure by which conflicting norms can be adjudicated and particular cases decided. A moral theory interacts dynamically with the norms of a society in that both remain open to correction. A moral theory which resulted in the injunctions to murder, steal, lie or commit other actions a society considered immoral would be properly suspect. It is difficult to imagine why society would accept or adopt such a theory. In general, a society is more certain of the bulk of its traditional norms of morality than it is certain of any theory of morality. Exceptions may be possible, for instance, when a society undergoes a conversion and adopts a religion together with its moral code; but this is not the general rule.

Metaethics, the third portion of general ethics, is closely related to normative ethics. To some extent, both normative and descriptive ethics involve some metaethical activity. Metaethics is the study of normative ethics. It is sometimes called analytical ethics because it is concerned with analysis. Metaethics deals with the meaning of moral terms and with the logic of moral reasoning. It asks, for instance, what the terms "good" and "bad" mean in the moral sense, what "moral responsibility", "moral obligation", and other similar phrases mean. Meaning, of course, is closely related to linguistic usage. Some people think meaning is identical with such usage. To say what "good" means may be distinct from saying what things or actions are good. The former is generally considered a metaethical concern, the latter a normative ethical concern.

The analysis of moral reasoning involves clarifying and evaluating presuppositions and investigating the validity of moral arguments. A famous and still not completely resolved metaethical dispute concerns the question of whether a moral ought or duty can be derived logically from a statement of what is, exclusive of normative premises. General ethical theory provides a careful and systematic approach to morality which finds parallels in ordinary life and discourse. It develops and analyzes the type of moral arguments that are used in ordinary language, in everyday life, in newspapers and magazines, in books and articles on moral problems that confront society and individuals. Hence it is a practical discipline with practical import. Like science, ethics constitutes a continuing social endeavor. It is not a completed discipline but a developing one in which there are a number of disputed issues. The presence of these disputes, however, does not indicate that there is no agreement nor does it indicate that ethics has produced no usable results. Some results are negative; certain theories that were initially plausible have been shown to be mistaken and some popular approaches to morality have proved untenable; however, the last word has yet to be written on this. Mastery of ethical theory, however, provides the necessary tools to engage intelligently in personal and social analysis of moral issues.

Special ethics applies general ethics first, to solving particular problems, and second, to investigating the morality of specialized areas of human endeavor. The first of these is sometimes called casuistry. *Casuistry* is the art of solving difficult moral problems, cases, or dilemmas through the careful application of moral principles. Casuistry uses the principles and norms which have been developed and justified in general ethics. It is an important art or skill, but one which has sometimes been held in low repute. For instance, it can easily degenerate into the technique of seeing how close one can come to the line that separates a moral from an immoral action. A moral person, its critics maintain, is more interested in pursuing a moral course of action than in seeing how he can minimally fulfill what is morally demanded. The attempt to determine the latter has frequently led to all-too-subtle rationalizations of questionable actions.

The second area of special ethics involves the application of general ethics to specialized fields. This yields business ethics, medical ethics, engineering ethics, professional ethics, social ethics, and so on. Each of these, however, involves more than just the application of general principles to particular areas. Business ethics also has a descriptive, normative, and a metaethical aspect. The techniques of moral reasoning developed in general ethics are appropriate here. But many descriptive, normative, and metaethical questions arise in the business context and require special analysis. In some cases, it is difficult to decide whether an issue is one of general ethics raised by a business problem or an issue that is particular to business ethics itself. But since the division between them is rough and not exact, the question of whether or not an issue is one of general or business ethics need seldom, if ever, be decided. We shall investigate, for instance, whether moral terms generally used to describe individuals and the actions they perform can also be applied to organizations, corporations, businesses, and other collective entities. Do they have consciences in the same way individuals do? Does moral language appropriately apply to them, and if so, does it apply in the same way as it does to individuals?

I shall take business to include any and all economic transactions between individuals, between individuals and profit-making organizations, and between profit-making organizations and other such organizations. It will include the various activities carried on in producing, selling, and buying goods and services for profit. This is broad enough to include the business activities of people in the professions and so includes part of what is considered professional ethics. The delimitation of these domains, however, is not at all sharp and great precision in delimiting them is not necessary.

One of the aims of philosophy is to analyze presuppositions, and one of the aims of analytical ethics is to analyze ethical presuppositions. Part of what constitutes business ethics is the analysis of the presuppositions—both moral presuppositions and the presuppositions from a moral point of view—of business. Since business operates within an economic system, part of the proper task of business ethics is to raise questions about economic systems in general and about the morality of the American economic system in particular. This in turn raises questions about the appropriateness of using moral language to evaluate these systems. The structures of business shall also be analyzed and evaluated. In addition to determining how people should act within given business structures, the questions shall be raised whether and how the structures themselves promote or impede moral action and the acceptance of moral responsibility.

Business ethics can help people approach moral problems in business more systematically and with better tools than they might otherwise approach them. It can help them to see issues they might normally ignore. It can also impel them to make changes that they might otherwise not be moved to make. But business ethics will not by itself make anyone moral. Business ethics, just as ethics in general, presupposes that those who study it already are moral beings, that they know right from wrong, and that they wish to be even better, more thoughtful, and more informed moral beings. Business ethics will not change business practices unless those engaged in the practices that need moral change wish to change them. Business ethics can produce arguments showing that a practice is immoral, but obviously only those in a position to implement the changes will be able to bring them about. Business ethics is a practical discipline with practical import, but it is up to those who study it to put what they learn into practice.

The Case of the Collapsed Mine

The following case illustrates the sorts of questions that might arise in business ethics and various ways to approach them. Consider the case of the collapsed mine shaft. In a coal mining town of West Virginia, some miners were digging coal in a tunnel thousands of feet below the surface. Some gas buildup had been detected during the two preceding days. This had been reported by the director of safety to the mine manager. The buildup was sufficiently serious to have closed down operations until it was cleared. The owner of the mine decided that the buildup was only marginally dangerous, that he had coal orders to fill, that he could not afford to close down the mine, and that he would take the chance that the gas would dissipate before it exploded. He told the director of safety not to say anything about the danger. On May 2nd, the gas exploded. One section of the tunnel collapsed, killing three miners and trapping eight others in a pocket. The rest managed to escape.

The explosion was one of great force and the extent of the tunnel's collapse was considerable. The cost of reaching the men in time to save their lives would amount to several million dollars. The problem facing the manager was whether the expenditure of such a large sum of money was worth it. What, after all was a human life worth? Whose decision was it and how should it be made? Did the manager owe more to the stockholders of the corporation or to the trapped workers? Should he use the slower, safer, and cheaper way of reaching them and save a large sum of money or the faster, more dangerous, and more expensive way and possibly save their lives?

He decided on the latter and asked for volunteers. Two dozen men volunteered. After three days, the operation proved to be more difficult than anyone had anticipated. There had been two more explosions and three of those involved in the rescue operation had already been killed. In the meantime, telephone contact had been made with the trapped men who had been fortunate enough to find a telephone line that was still functioning. They were starving. Having previously read about a similar case, they decided that the only way for any of them to survive long enough was to draw lots, and then kill and eat the one who drew the shortest straw. They felt that it was their duty that at least some of them should be found alive; otherwise, the three volunteers who had died rescuing them would have died in vain.

After twenty days the seven men were finally rescued alive; they had cannibalized their fellow miner. The director of safety who had detected the gas before the explosion informed the newspapers of his report. The manager was charged with criminal negligence; but before giving up his position, he fired the director of safety. The mine eventually resumed operation.

There are a large number of issues in the above account. The tools for resolving them are part of what we shall have to develop in later chapters.

The director of safety is in some sense the hero of the story. But did he fulfill his moral obligation before the accident in obeying the manager and in not making known either to the miners, the manager's superior, or to the public the fact that the mine was unsafe? Did he have a moral obligation after the explosion and rescue to make known the fact that the manager knew the mine was unsafe? Should he have gone to the board of directors of the company with the story or to someone else within the company rather than to the newspapers? All these questions are part of the phenomenon of worker responsibility. To whom is a worker responsible and for what? Does his moral obligation end when he does what he is told? Going public with inside information such as the director of safety had is commonly known as "blowing the whistle" on the company. Frequently those who blow the whistle are fired, just as the director of safety was. The whole phenomenon of whistle blowing raises serious questions about the structure of companies in which employees find it necessary to take such drastic action and possibly suffer the loss of their jobs. Was the manager justified in firing the director of safety?

The manager is, of course, the villain of the story. He sent the miners into a situation which he knew was dangerous. But, he might argue, he did it for the good of the company. He had contracts to fulfill and obligations to the owners of the company to show a profit. He had made a bad decision. Every manager has to take risks. It just turned out that he was unlucky. Does such a defense sound plausible? Does a manager have an obligation to his workers as well as to the owners of a company? Who should take precedence and under what conditions does one group or the other become more important? Who is to decide and how?

The manager decided to try to save the trapped miners even though it would cost the company more than taking the slower route. Did he have the right to spend more of the company's money in this way? How does one evaluate human life in comparison with expenditure of money? It sounds moral to say that human life is beyond all monetary value. In a sense it is. However, there are limits which society and people in it can place on the amount they will, can, and should spend to save lives. The way to decide, however, does not seem to be to equate the value of a person's life with the amount of income he would produce in his remaining years, if he lives to a statistically average age, minus the resources he would use up in that period. How does one decide? How do and should people weigh human lives against monetary expenditure? In designing automobiles, in building roads, in making many products, there is a trade-off between the maximum safety that one can build into the product and the cost of the product. Extremely safe cars cost more to build than relatively safe cars. We can express the difference in terms of the number of people likely to die driving the relatively safe ones as opposed to the extremely safe ones. Should such decisions be made by manufacturers, consumers, government, or in some other way?

The manager asked for volunteers for the rescue work. Three of these volunteers died. Was the manager responsible for their deaths in the same way that he was responsible for the deaths of the three miners who had died in the first mine explosion? Was the company responsible for the deaths in either case? Do companies have obligations to their employees and the employees' families in circumstances such as these, or are the obligations only those of the managers? If the manager had warned the miners that the level of gas was dangerous, and they had decided that they wanted their pay for that day and would work anyway, would the manager have been responsible for their deaths? Is it moral for people to take dangerous jobs simply to earn money? Is a system that impels people to take such jobs for money a moral system? To what extent is a company morally obliged to protect its workers and to prevent them from taking chances?

The manager was charged with criminal negligence under the law. Was the company responsible for anything? Should the company have been sued by the family of the dead workers? If the company were sued and paid damages to the families, the money would come from company profits and hence from the profits of the shareholders. Is it fair that the shareholders be penalized for an incident they had nothing to do with? How is responsibility shared and/or distributed in a company, and can companies be morally responsible for what is done in their name? Are only human beings moral agents and is it a mistake to use moral language with respect to companies, corporations, and businesses?

The decision of the trapped miners to cast lots to determine who would be killed and eaten also raises a number of moral issues. Our moral intuitions can provide in this case no ready answer as to whether their decision was morally justifiable, since the case is not an ordinary one. How to think about such an issue raises the question of how moral problems are to be resolved and underscores the need for some moral theory as guidelines by which we can decide unusual cases. A number of principles seem to conflict—the obligation not to kill, the consideration that it is better for one person to die rather than eight, the fact noted by the miners that three persons had already died trying to rescue them, and so on. The issue here is not one peculiar to business ethics, but it is rather a moral dilemma that requires some technique of moral argument to solve.

The case does not tell us what happened to either the manager or the director of safety. Frequently the sequel to such cases is surprising. The managers come off free and are ultimately rewarded for their concern for the company's interest, while the whistle blower is blackballed throughout the industry. The morality of such an outcome seems obvious—justice does not always triumph. What can be done to see that it triumphs more often is a question that involves restructuring the system.

Business ethics is sometimes seen as conservative and is also used as a defense of the status quo. Sometimes it is seen as an attack on the status quo and hence viewed as radical. Ideally it should be neither. It should strive for objectivity. When there are immoral practices, structures, and actions occurring, business ethics should be able to show that these actions are immoral and why. But it should also be able to supply the techniques with which the practices and structures that are moral can be defended as such. The aim of business ethics is neither defense of the status quo nor its radical change. Rather it should serve to remedy those aspects or structures that need change and protect those that are moral. It is not a panacea. It can secure change only if those in power take the appropriate action. But unless some attention is paid to business ethics, the moral debate about practices and principles central to our society will be more poorly and probably more immorally handled than otherwise.

Further Reading

Baumhart, Raymond, S.J. *Ethics in Business.* New York: Holt, Rinehart and Winston, 1968.

Business and Professional Ethics; A Quarterly Newsletter/Report. Center for the

Study of the Human Dimensions of Science & Technology, Rennsselaer Polytechnic Institute. Troy, N.Y. (Carries a continuing bibliography.)

Dam, Cees van, and Stallaert, Lund, eds. *Trends in Business Ethics.* Boston: Martinus Nijhoff Social Sciences Division, 1978.

De George, Richard T., and Pichler, Joseph A., eds. *Ethics, Free Enterprise and Public Policy.* New York: Oxford University Press, Inc., 1978.

Dworkin, Gerald; Bermant, Gordon; and Brown, Peter G., eds. *Markets and Morals.* New York: John Wiley & Sons, Inc., 1977.

McGuire, Joseph W. *Business and Society.* New York: McGraw-Hill, Inc., 1963.

Purcell, Theodore V., S.J. "Do Courses in Business Ethics Pay Off?" In *California Management Review,* XIX (Summer, 1977), pp. 50–58.

Moral Reasoning
in Business

2

Conventional Morality and Ethical Relativism

Many people in business as well as in other areas of life feel that morality is personal, that each person has his or her own moral views and that no one should force such views on others. According to this position, each person is entitled to his or her own moral opinion. All the members of a society must abide by the law. But beyond that each person is to be guided only by his or her own individual conscience. Many people hold a similar position with respect to different countries and cultures. Each, they maintain, has its own views of what is moral and immoral. No one country or culture is better than the other. If someone is doing business in a different culture, then that person should adopt the local ways. If bribery is the common practice in a given society, then it is proper to engage in bribery in that country. It is arrogant to think that the morality of one's own country is better than that of another country or to think the morality of one's own country is binding when doing business in another country.

The above view is a popular form of moral and ethical relativism. It is a popular position that deserves careful attention. Is morality simply a matter of individual choice? Is it culturally determined? Is the claim that there is a universal morality applicable to all people and at all times defensible? This chapter will deal with these questions.

The Levels of Moral Development

An American psychologist, Lawrence Kohlberg, has done extensive work on moral development and has generalized the findings based on his studies. The results of his investigations coincide with what many people experience in their own moral development and therefore his position, at least in its broad general outlines, is widely accepted. Kohlberg identifies three major levels in the moral development of an individual. Not everyone advances to the third level; and no one operates only on the third level. Most people operate sometimes on one level and sometimes on another. Yet the levels of development are characteristics of the moral development of individuals and serve as handy classificatory devices.

Kohlberg not only identifies three levels but subdivides each of the levels into two stages. He calls Level I the preconventional level. As infants start to grow up, they go through a phase of development which is not yet moral. In the first stage of the first level of their moral development, they react to punishment. The toddler does not have any sense of moral right or wrong, but he soon learns that if he writes on the living room wall with a crayon, he will get spanked or scolded. What keeps him from writing on the wall is his desire to avoid a spanking, a scolding, or whatever other punishment he has come to associate with the action. The second step in this level reflects his desire to receive a reward. Here he seeks the praise of his parents. He acts so as to maximize his pleasure, though of course he does so unwittingly. This reaction to punishment and reward teaches children that certain behavior is undesirable and other behavior is permissible. Children thereby learn what to do and what not to do. But they do not yet understand that they are obeying rules or doing an action *because* it is right—they do not yet have a developed sense of what morality means.

All of us to some extent react to pleasure and pain and reward and punishment. Hence all of us sometimes act on the preconventional level.

Kohlberg calls the second level of moral development the conventional level. The morality practiced here is the morality of conventional role conformity. He calls the first stage of this second level Good Boy/Nice Girl Morality. In this stage a person reacts to the expectations of parents or peers. We conform to the norms learned at home, in school, or in church. The motivation for action is more subtle than in Level I—we come to understand what moral norms and rules are. We learn how a good boy or a good girl is supposed to act. The norms we get from our family, school, and peers may not all coincide. In a homogeneous society they will probably coincide more than in a less homogeneous one; they will also tend to coincide more closely in a more traditional society than in a more dynamic one. But in all cases, the morality we accept is a morality which we learn from others. We learn what is expected of us in our role as a devoted child, adolescent, and as a student. Conventional role conformity in its first stage is a reaction to peers, parents, or other similar persons or groups. In its second stage, it usually develops into conformity with the laws of one's society. Kohlberg calls it the "law and order" stage. The individual becomes acculturated. He understands what a good citizen is supposed to be and do, and he lives in accordance with the role he has in society and with the conventional rules that govern that role.

Most adults live at the level of conformity morality. Some—probably many—never get beyond it. All of us spend a good part of our lives on this level. Murder is wrong, lying is wrong, stealing is wrong. Why? Because everyone knows those actions are wrong. And though it is impractical to have laws against all lying, lying in important circumstances is illegal (e.g., perjury), and murder and theft are both against the law.

Many adults never reach the third level of moral development. Yet some do. This third level interests philosophers the most. Kohlberg calls Level III the post-conventional, autonomous, or principled level. This is the morality of self-accepted moral principles. At this level one accepts moral principles not because society says they are right and acceptable, but because one knows what it means to say that principles are right and understands what makes them right. The first stage is the level of contract and individual rights. One speaks of and understands morality based on the rights of individuals and on agreements made between consenting adults. At the final and highest stage, one is able to give a rational defense of the moral principles which guide one's actions. The moral agent is conscious of the moral law and acts in accordance with it, not because of reward or punishment, and not because others tell him he should, but because he understands why the moral law is binding on him. He accepts the principles as his own and not as a foreign constraint imposed on him by others.

The third level is the most interesting to philosophers because at this level one raises questions about the justification of the moral norms one holds. Most people simply accept the morality of their society. But it is possible to ask: Is what my society holds to be right *really* right? Might the people of my society be mistaken? Why should I accept what my parents told me is right or wrong, or why should I accept what legislators tell me is right and wrong? How do they know? They certainly cannot make actions right or wrong; or, if they can, so can I. If none of us can, then there must be reasons why some actions are right and others wrong independent of people classifying them in this way. What are those reasons? These are the questions which ethics seeks to answer, and it is at this third level that moral philosophy operates. Of course, what conventional morality holds to be immoral may well be immoral. The difference between levels two and three is not necessarily in content; rather, the difference is in the reasons for holding actions as right or wrong.

The description of the levels of development helps us to understand a good deal about business ethics. We noted earlier that people in business frequently claim that they are bound only by the law and not by moral norms which they see as personal. Since most people like to operate at the second level of morality, it is not surprising that most businesses operate at this level too. Certainly some business practices are held to be moral and proper and others are held to be improper. It is possible simply to accept these conventional norms. But it is also possible to ask whether these norms should be held, whether some of them may in fact be improper, and whether there are other activities in which businesses do not but *should* engage.

At one time in the United States large numbers of people in the South accepted slavery. We now generally think that slavery is immoral. Was it always immoral? We might answer that according to the conventional morality which was held in the South at that time, slavery was moral. That reply is consistent with the claim that if one were to rise to the third level it would be seen to be immoral then as well as now. In fact many argued that it was immoral despite the fact that it formed part of conventional morality.

Somewhat closer to our own time, significant numbers of Americans held that the Viet Nam War was immoral despite the belief of the majority, at least in the beginning of the war, that it was moral. The division of levels of morality makes intelligible the attacks on conventional morality and makes clear what sort of evaluation is appropriate to it.

The description of the levels of moral development does not imply that everyone always acts morally. This is of course not the case. People break the laws of the land. But this does not mean that there are no laws. They could not break them if there were no laws. Similarly, people break the moral law. But this does not mean there is no moral law. Rather, since they could not break moral law if there were none, it shows that there are moral laws.

Subjective and Objective Morality

When we speak of morality we refer to our judgments of right and wrong, good and bad. Three characteristics are usually associated with such judgments. First, moral judgments about the rightness or wrongness of an action are held to be universally applicable. If an action is right for me, it is also right for anyone else in the same circumstances. If it is wrong for you, it is also wrong for anyone else similarly placed. Something of the notion of universality is captured by the injunction to do unto others as you would have them do unto you.

A second characteristic of morality is that moral judgments are important. They are so important, in fact, that they override other considerations. We are morally bound to do what we sometimes may not want to do; it is wrong to steal even when we would like to steal. If we say that it is our moral duty to do an act, that means we have an obligation to do it which can only be overridden by a stronger moral consideration. Convenience, personal gain, and even legal requirements fall before moral obligations.

The third characteristic is that moral praise can properly accompany the doing of morally right actions and moral blame can properly accompany acting immorally. If we say that someone in a business transaction acted immorally, this means that it is appropriate for us to blame him from a moral point of view. For instance, if taking bribes is immoral, then those involved in bribery deserve moral blame or censure.

The vocabulary of morality is rich, and it is applied to a variety of objects in a number of ways. We can be clearer if we keep the various uses of the terms separate.

We call individual persons moral or immoral; we call actions moral or immoral; and we call economic systems, social institutions, and business practices moral or immoral. What we mean in each of these cases is not identical, though each has something to do with conformity or lack of conformity to the moral law or to morality.

When we speak of persons being moral or immoral we may mean at least three different things. It is not always clear which meaning an individual has in mind when he says of someone that he is moral. In a first sense, a person may be considered moral if he habitually acts in accordance with his conscience. We may speak of him as more or less moral, depending on how frequently, within tolerable levels, he acts contrary to his conscience. What we mean is that he tries to do what he thinks is right. Sincerity is the keynote of morality here. But whereas each of us knows his own conscience, we do not know the conscience of others and cannot be sure when they are acting in accordance with their beliefs.

In a second sense, if we hold that certain actions are immoral, then we might call someone a moral person if he acts in conformity with the moral law, or if he does what the moral law requires, or if he does not do what the moral law forbids. The third case is a combination of the previous two. We may reserve the term moral to describe only that individual who both acts in conformity with the moral law and does so because he knows what that law requires. He acts in accordance with his conscience, but his conscience also is correct in its judgments of right and wrong.

The third case is the one that a moral individual expects of himself. He knows that he should do the right thing and that he should act in accordance with what his conscience tells him to do. Only then is his action fully praiseworthy from a moral standpoint. But none of us can be sure we know in all situations what is right. We are all fallible. Hence, the best we can do is try to determine as carefully as possible what is right and so act. We can follow our conscience and hope that our efforts to form a correct conscience have been successful. The distinction between what one believes to be right and what is actually right is an important one. We can make the distinction by referring to subjectively right (and wrong) and objectively right (and wrong) actions. What we are judging from a moral point of view is actions, not persons. An action is subjectively right if a person believes that the action is moral. An action is objectively right if the action is in conformity with the moral law.

If I believe that telling the truth is right and it is right, then telling the truth is both subjectively and objectively right. If I believe that bribery is wrong and in fact it is immoral, then bribery is both subjectively and objectively wrong. An action may be subjectively right and objectively wrong. If I am mistaken about the morality of bribery, for instance, I may believe it to be moral for me to take a bribe, even though it is actually immoral. An action can be subjectively wrong and objectively right. This again involves a mistake on my part about the morality of the action. Suppose that in taking candy from a box I think that I am stealing; in fact, however, the candy was part of a display and was there for anyone who wanted to take it. I did not objectively steal, even if I thought that I was stealing. Finally, an action may be both objectively and subjectively wrong; for instance, when I believe bribery to be wrong and it is in fact immoral.

One of the pitfalls in the study of morality is that we typically operate on two levels—the personal level at which we wish both to judge the action and to act in accordance with our conscience, and the third-person level in which we wish to judge the actions of others from an objective point of view but do not wish to know or cannot know the subjective state of the one performing the action.

Reluctance on the part of some people to judge the internal state of others sometimes leads them to refuse to judge the actions of others. The two judgments, however, can be kept distinct. We can judge the crimes of Hitler without knowing whether or not he *thought* he was doing something moral when he performed or ordered others to perform immoral acts. Attitudes and intentions make up a part of what is properly the object of moral evaluation, but many actions can be considered in their own right, in abstraction from the intent of the agent, and can be evaluated from a moral point of view. This in fact is how we typically judge such actions as stealing, bribery, murder, lying, and so on. Obviously, when we speak of an economic system as moral or immoral, or of business practices as being immoral, we are also judging them without reference to whether those involved in them believe them to be moral.

The facts that we are fallible in our moral judgments, that we sometimes believe an action to be right when it is objectively wrong, that people disagree in their moral judgments, and that in a pluralistic society the norms of conventional morality are sometimes not clear lead some people to adopt a moral tolerance toward others. They refuse not only to judge others but also refuse to judge their own actions. Since they cannot give reasons why actions are right or wrong, they often retreat into a position which says that there is no objective morality, or that morality is purely subjective. They feel they are personally moral when they act as they believe they should. But others may act differently and still be moral if they believe that they are acting morally. This position confuses subjective guilt and blame with objective guilt and blame. Pushed to its conclusion it denies the objectivity of moral judgments and claims that whatever anyone holds is moral is thereby moral. It abandons the universal characteristic of morality. When made explicit, this position is known as ethical relativism.

Cultural Relativism

Anthropologists and sociologists have documented the fact that people in different cultures, as well as people within a given culture, hold divergent moral views on particular topics. The ancient Greeks believed that infanticide was not immoral, although we believe that it is. Some members of our society believe that abortion is immoral whereas others believe that it is morally permissible. These differences exemplify transcultural and intracultural relativity. We should, however, distinguish descriptive cultural relativism from normative cultural relativism, and distinguish both of these from normative ethical relativism.

Given the fact that a practice is held to be moral in one society at one time and wrong at another time or in another society, and given the fact that people within a society in any given time differ in their moral views, we can draw no conclusions about cultures or about a society other than that the differences described above exist. Consider a class of twenty third-graders given a long addition problem. Suppose that each child in the class comes up with a different answer to the problem. Because of our knowledge of mathematics, we can say that no more than one of them has the right answer. None of them may have the right answer. But we would be mistaken if on the basis of the reported differences we concluded that there was no right answer to the problem.

Anthropology and sociology supply data to be considered and explained. Starting with the differences between societies concerning what is viewed as moral, we can appropriately ask about the extent of the disagreement and about the basis for the disagreement. In some ways it may be more interesting to inquire as to the extent of the agreement rather than the extent of the disagreement. For surely the agreements as well as the disagreements deserve consideration and explanation.

Differing views regarding the morality of a given action or practice may be the result of a number of factors. Two societies may basically and ultimately disagree on moral principles. But the disagreement may also be on many other levels. For instance, two societies may adhere to the same basic principle that what helps the society flourish is moral and what hinders it is immoral. Yet, if one society lives in a warm climate and has an abundance of water, it will have a different view of clothing and use of water than will a society that lives in a very cold climate and has little water. A country with many men and few women will probably not look upon monogamy in the same way as a society with an approximately equal number of men and women. Differing conditions, therefore, provide a reason for holding differing actions to be moral or immoral. A society's beliefs also affect what it holds to be moral or immoral. A society which believes in volcano gods that demand human sacrifice will treat this practice as a moral one, one that is demanded by higher authority and necessary for the preservation of the society. A society which does not believe in volcano gods will not consider the practice either necessary or morally justifiable. Factual beliefs are an important ingredient in the morality of any society and differences in these beliefs lead to differences in what is considered moral or immoral. Nor is it improper to admit that some societies believe what is false. This is probably true to some extent of all societies. Most societies, moreover, are aware of the fact that they obtain more and more factual knowledge as they develop and progress. Just as a society may be mistaken about facts, so it may be mistaken about some of its moral judgments. We know historically that members of a society frequently hold that one or more of the moral beliefs of that society are erroneous. There is no reason in principle why members of another society cannot make and defend similar claims about a society other than their own.

Descriptive transcultural relativism describes differences between cultures. In some cases the differences are such that the terms right and wrong or better and worse are not applicable to the differences noted. All cultures have a language. Some languages are more intricate than others. But it makes little sense to say that one language is in some absolute sense better than another. Similarly, many aspects of one culture will differ from aspects of another; but they are not necessarily contradictory and both can be equally good. Is the same true when we consider questions of morality?

Many people dispute anthropological reports of the morality of primitive tribes and foreign cultures because what the anthropologist describes as a society's morality may actually be an imposition of his own categories and interpretations on unfamiliar practices. Yet it is true that the ancient Greeks believed that infanticide was morally permissible and we do not. The same is true when viewing the South before the Civil War; many people thought slavery was morally permissible whereas many in the North held it to be immoral. Do the differences in beliefs show that morality is relative?

Ethical Relativism

Normative ethical relativism claims that when any two cultures or any two people hold different moral views of an action, both can be right. An action may be right for one person or society and the same action taken in the same way may be wrong for another reason, and yet, both persons are equally correct. What are the claims of those who hold this position? A first interpretation says that neither of the conflicting moral judgments is right and neither is wrong because moral judgments are not right or wrong—they are simply the statement of opinion or of feeling. A second view holds that judgments of right and wrong are culturally determined and that transcultural judgments make no more sense in questions of morality than they do in judgments about whether one language is better than another. A third interpretation claims that we should not say that either judgment is right or wrong because we have no way of deciding which is which. One judgment may be right and the other wrong; but since we have no way of proving this, it is better, more prudent, and more cautious not to claim either is right or wrong.

These views deserve some attention since they bear directly on such questions as which morality a businessman in a foreign country is supposed to follow—his own or that of the country in which he finds himself. Their importance is also clear if we are to be able to judge the actions of businesses. Whose morality are they to follow? The various forms of moral relativism all hold that there is a close connection between the fact of moral diversity and the claim that there are many moralities, each equally valid or good. The connecting link between cultural relativism and normative ethical relativism is usually some theory or view about morality.

The obvious forms of normative ethical relativism, however, do not stand up well to analysis. Take the first view—moral judgments are neither true nor false, right or wrong because they are simply statements of feeling or emotion. A number of consequences follow from this position which do not cohere well with the moral experience of most people. One of the results of adopting this view is that a moral judgment about an action, for example the judgment that stealing is immoral, is not a judgment about stealing at all. It is simply the expression of one's feeling about stealing. Suppose A feels negatively about B's taking his wallet and A says that B's taking A's wallet is immoral. B replies that B feels no guilt about taking A's wallet; therefore, according to B his action is moral. If both are simply reporting or expressing their feelings, then each is speaking about himself. If each is speaking about himself, they are not speaking about the *action* of B taking A's wallet. That they have different reactions is perfectly possible and involves no disagreement between them. Hence they each express their emotions and if the emotions happen to differ, they differ. Nor does it change matters to say that when someone makes a moral judgment he not only expresses his emotions or feelings but he also adds that others should feel as he does. For once again, different people can each have different emotions. each can feel that others should feel as he does. It may be said that each is simply saying something about himself and none of them is judging the action.

A second consequence is that no one can ever disagree with anyone else about the morality of an action. For if a moral judgment is simply a statement about oneself, his reactions or an expression of his emotions, then when someone expresses his emotions and they happen to differ from someone else's, each person is appropriately saying that he has different emotions or is expressing differing emotions. But emotions are not true or false; therefore, since each person is not making claims of truth or falsehood or claims of right or wrong, they are not disagreeing with each other.

A third consequence of this view is that people can never be mistaken in their moral judgments because if someone feels negatively about an action today and feels positively about the same action tomorrow, then he will have had or expressed different emotions. But expressing one emotion today is not incompatible with expressing a different one tomorrow. Since in neither case does the individual make a factual statement or claim, there is nothing to be right or wrong about, and hence no way to be mistaken.

A fourth consequence is that people can change the morality of an action by taking or expressing a different emotion concerning it. If a moral judgment is only the report of an emotion or the expressing of an emotion, then by changing his emotion a person changes the morality of the action.

These four consequences do not correspond well with the moral experience of most people because in their lives they do make judgments about actions, at least that is what they intend to do. They do find that they disagree with others in some cases about the morality of an action. They do change their minds and conclude that they were mistaken in the past in judging an action right, whereas today they know it is wrong. And they do not think they can change the morality of an action simply by changing their emotions or by expressing different emotions. What reason do they have for giving up the common sense beliefs that form part of their experience? So far we have not been given any evidence which is stronger than ordinary experience. What we have been given is a theory of what moral judgments supposedly are. But why accept that theory? We certainly do express our moral feelings when we make moral judgments. We do wish people to have feelings similar to ours when we express our emotions relative to an action. But that is not all we do. We also judge the action, disagree with those who judge it differently, and so on.

Consider next the view of the defender of normative ethical relativism who argues that judgments of right and wrong are culturally determined. He may be claiming that one society holds some act to be right while another society holds a similar act to be wrong because the circumstances in which the act is performed make the acts different. What appears as brutal in one society may appear as kind in another. The practice in a society where the aged leave the society to die alone might appear heartless to someone who comes from a society in which the moral thing to do is to care for the aged, keeping them alive as long as possible and by whatever means possible. But both actions might be construed as showing respect for the aged, though the respect is shown in very different ways. So interpreted, however, we do not have normative ethical relativism; we simply have differing instantiations on the level of practice of a similar higher moral norm shared by both societies.

Another interpretation of normative ethical relativism might maintain that what each society means by the term "moral" is that the action is held to be right in that society. "Moral" then means "is approved by this society". In this case it would follow that no two societies disagree on the morality of an action, because what each society means by the term moral is different. By judging an action to be moral, a member of society A is reporting that the people of his society believe the action to be moral. By judging the same action to be immoral, a member of society B is reporting that the members of his society believe it to be immoral. Each report can be correct. But a consequence of this view is that no two societies can disagree on the morality of an action. All anyone can do is report what his society thinks about the action. A second consequence is that no member of the society can disagree with his society about the morality of an action. By saying that an action is immoral all he is really saying (according to this view) is that his society believes it to be immoral. And if his society actually believes the action to be moral, then he is simply mistaken in asserting what they do not believe. Yet a fact of moral life is that people do disagree in some instances with what the other members of the society believe in moral matters; and societies do disagree with one another on moral matters. Hence once again there is more reason for denying the doctrine than there is for holding it.

Some cultural differences are matters of taste which offer no basis for deciding that one is right and another wrong. Nor is there any need to do so. For instance, if one culture likes fried food and another dislikes it, each can have its own way without harm. If one person likes chocolate ice cream and another strongly dislikes chocolate but likes vanilla ice cream, we are not tempted to say one is right and the other is wrong. Cultural and individual differences exist. In many instances there is no claim of truth or falsehood, and no basis or need for deciding one is right and the other wrong. Why is it not so in the moral realm?

The argument from moral experience claims that we do judge actions to be moral or immoral, and that in making these judgments we are saying something about the actions and not just something about ourselves. It claims also that people do disagree on moral issues. Since they believe that they are making statements that are true or false, right or wrong, they are not satisfied if they are told that they are not doing this at all. Their protest is not sufficient to show that they are correct in their assertion. But more is needed to show them that they are mistaken than simply someone's theory which asserts the contrary.

A closer look at what many people consider they are doing when they make moral judgments shows part of the reason why moral disputes occur. In making the judgment that murder is immoral, the ordinary person means that murder is immoral for everyone. He is not making the judgment that it is immoral only for him, but that others, if they feel differently, may be acting morally if they kill him arbitrarily. He is claiming that the action is immoral for everyone. Nor is he restricting his judgment only to the members of his society. Murder is immoral in his own country and in other countries as well, whether or not the people of that country realize or admit it. In making his moral judgment, therefore, he is making a claim about the nature of an action and it is a claim with universal import. This is what he means by saying murder is immoral: that no one should do it and that it is wrong for anyone to do it.

A society may morally judge actions only for its own members because it ignores all other societies, or because it considers all other people barbarians and not worthy of respect. The domain of people to which a society extends may be restricted because of the belief of that society about other people. But in making a moral judgment in such a society, the judgment still has universal import in that it applies to all those within the moral community. If one's view of the moral community includes all human beings, then the moral judgment of an action is made in the name of all. If in addition one's moral community includes animals as well, then the judgments apply to them as well.

Yet it does not follow that simply because people make universal moral judgments they do so correctly. Nor does it follow that simply because people disagree in their moral judgments it is possible to determine which one is correct. The third interpretation of ethical relativism stated that we should not say disagreements on moral issues are right or wrong; because no one can show he is right and someone else wrong, there is no way of deciding such disputed issues. According to this view it is arrogant to claim that one is right and another wrong in moral disputes. At best we can discuss our differences to determine whether they rest on the differing facts. If so, we can try to determine which are the correct facts. We can also see if we have different beliefs. Once again we can try to adjudicate our differences. But if we finally find that we agree on the facts and have the same beliefs but still differ on the morality of an action, then this view claims there is no way to show that one of us is right and the other wrong. The view implies that moral principles are not right or wrong and cannot be rationally defended. Yet moral principles have been and are frequently given rational defense, and disagreements on moral issues are argued in rational as well as emotional terms. It is worthwhile looking at these debates. But we should be clear about what can and cannot be claimed for them.

If the arguments presented here against normative ethical relativism are sound, what follows? What follows is neither a completed moral system nor even the claim that somewhere there is a completed moral system waiting to be found. Rather what follows is that moral judgments are judgments which can and should be defended but for which better or poorer arguments are often given. If we are faced with contradictory judgments about an action, only one of them can be right. The way to determine which one is right is to see which judgment is best supported by the facts and arguments presented in its defense. We may eventually arrive at high level, abstract, moral principles. If they clash, we will then have to decide which of the alternative principles or approaches is better defended. Upon investigation we may conclude that no theory investigated is completely defensible or completely satisfactory. In that case more work is necessary. The conclusion that there is no satisfactory theory is not a valid conclusion based on the evidence. We do not conclude that there is no satisfactory unified theory of physics because we have not yet found one. In both cases the appropriate response is to continue the search, to continue to make improvements, and to continue to use what we presently have available, despite the deficiencies.

Moral Absolutism

One alternative to ethical relativism is moral absolutism. A moral absolutist holds that there are eternal moral values and eternal moral principles which are always and everywhere applicable. But there are degrees of absolutism. Some absolutists, for instance, hold that the most general principle of morality is absolute, but that as it is applied in differing circumstances, certain lower level norms may vary. Other, more extreme absolutists, claim that all moral norms are everywhere and always the same. Between the two positions is a third position which holds that the most general principle of morality is everywhere and always the same, and that moral norms are everywhere and always the same, but that these norms have exceptions which are also everywhere and always the same. There is a difference between holding that the principles of morality are universal and eternal and holding that one knows with certainty what the principles are. A person might hold that there are eternal moral principles without being able to produce them. What he might produce instead are various approximations of those principles, which he is willing and ready to modify when he sees they are not exact in their formulation. There is an alternative to absolutism, however, which does not fall into the category of relativism. This position claims that morality is not eternal. It is an attempt by human beings to adopt principles to govern human society and the lives of those within society which will help them live together and abide by rules that all of them in their reasonable and objective moments would accept. Unlike the absolutist, someone holding this position need not claim that some final, ultimate, eternal moral principle exists somewhere, for instance in the mind of God. He need only claim that the idea of such a principle forms an ideal towards which ethics strives. He is then content to examine the various moral principles which have been suggested during the history of mankind and the various ethical theories which men have produced. He can see which ones stand up best to rational scrutiny, which ones are most helpful to him, and which ones correspond most closely to the values he perceives. This is not only an individual endeavor but also a collective one, for we can build on the accomplishments of others as well as on their mistakes. I shall follow this alternative in the succeeding chapters. No claim of infallibility or privileged eternal knowledge shall be made. Rather, the most successful traditional approaches to morality and the types of moral arguments currently used in our society will be explained.

Moral Pluralism

American society is in many ways diverse, combining various cultures and traditions. It is heterogeneous in composition, containing many ethnic and racial groups. Dynamic and changing, it is pluralistic in many ways. It is culturally pluralistic. It is also, to some extent, morally pluralistic.

We can distinguish four levels of moral pluralism: radical moral pluralism, the pluralism of moral principles, the pluralism of moral practices, and the pluralism of self-realization. Radical moral pluralism describes that state of affairs in which people hold mutually irreconcilable views about morality such as what the terms "right" and "wrong" mean, and about which actions are right or wrong. People holding such radically divergent views, however, do not form a society. To be a society, a group must accept certain basic practices and principles. At a basic level, for instance, there must be general agreement that life is worth living, that the lives of the members of the society should be respected, or that people will respect existing differences to the extent that they do not interfere with each other. If someone does not care whether he lives or dies and believes it is his moral duty to kill others, it may not be possible to convince him he is mistaken. But people with such a view cannot form a society. To the extent that society and morality go together, the morality of a society must be a shared morality and not a radically pluralistic set of opposing moralities. Yet a society may be morally pluralistic on the other three levels.

A plurality of moral principles within a society does not necessarily mean irreconcilable diversity. Pluralism on the level of moral principles is compatible with social agreement on the morality of many basic practices. Such agreement does not necessarily involve agreement on the moral principles different people use to evaluate practices. The vast majority of the members of our society, for instance, agree that murder is wrong. Some members of our society operate only at the level of conventional morality and do not inquire further as to why murder is wrong. Some may believe it is wrong because God forbids such acts; others because it violates human dignity; others because so acting has serious bad consequences for society as a whole; and so on. Each of these constitutes a different moral principle. These different principles are compatible with similarity of moral judgments.

On the level of specific actions, we encounter a variety of moral opinions about some of them. This pluralism of moral practices may stem from differences of moral principles. But it may also stem from differences of fact or perception of facts, differences of circumstances, or differences in the weighing of relevant values. Not all moral issues are clear even when there is basic agreement on principles. In a changing, dynamic, and developing society there is certainly room for moral disagreement, even if there is unanimous agreement that what helps the society's survival is moral. For new practices might be seen by conservatives as threatening the society's survival, while the same practice might be championed by others as the necessary means for survival. Pluralism of practices, however, is compatible with areas of agreement, and this is usually the case.

The fourth level of moral pluralism is the pluralism of self-realization. As long as the members of a society abide by the basic moral norms, they are allowed in such a pluralistic society to choose freely their other values and their lifestyles. This constitutes a kind of moral pluralism because self-development and fulfillment, according to some views, are moral matters. A society which allows divergence of self-development within the basic moral framework tolerates a great many differences that would neither be allowed nor found in a homogeneous society.

Moral pluralism of the second, third, and fourth kinds are found in the United States. They do not imply normative ethical relativism, and in fact they presuppose a wide common background of moral practices. The diversity we encounter is often so striking that it tends to make us forget the similarities. But respect for human beings, respect for truth, and respect for the property of others are all commonplaces found in America making business possible. With this background we have adopted laws to enforce common moral norms, to define proper areas of toleration, and to provide adjudicatory functions in cases of moral disputes on socially important issues.

The contrast between the cohesiveness, despite its pluralism, of American society, and the absence of a cohesive society on the world level helps us understand the difficulty of making moral judgments on the international level. There are certainly some basic similarities in all the moral codes and views held in each country of the world. In every country the murder of members of the society is prohibited, otherwise no society would exist. In all of them lying is immoral; otherwise, there would be no secure social interaction. There is respect for property, however defined, otherwise no one would be able to count on having what he needs to live. Yet the way in which the nations of the world form a society is at best a tenuous one. National sovereignty limits the extent to which any nation wishes to abide by a tribunal higher than itself. On the international level, law cannot serve the same mediating and adjudicating role it does in the United States, for instance, because there is no general acknowledgement of a body qualified to pass and enforce such law. The differences that divide nations are much deeper and more profound than the differences that divide members of the same society. The notion of a common morality for all in the world, pluralistic in nature but providing a basic framework within which all can work, is a goal still to be achieved, not a present reality. There is sufficient agreement among societies for business to be carried on internationally. But even in business there are a host of unresolved problems. The moral intuitions, feelings, and beliefs of most people have been primarily focused within their own society and on the level of personal morality. Their moral views on an international level of obligations among nations are less well formed, partly due to the fact that people in general have not given it much thought. We find, therefore, few ready answers to questions on this level and more puzzles and problems.

Before leaving the topic of moral pluralism, however, we can put to rest the question which some people raise when speaking of morality in business. The question is: whose morality? This question is a bogus one. Moral pluralism presupposes a society, and if a society is to function, it must have a large core of commonly held values and norms. These norms form the common morality of the society. They are yours, mine, and ours. We hold them applicable to everyone. In areas of serious differences—which were described as the third level—the clash of moral views must be decided by public debate, and perhaps even by legislation. Moral arguments are raised and countered until clarity emerges, or until a way of resolving the problem while recognizing differences is worked out. It is not true, therefore, that when faced with moral claims against me or my business practices I need merely shrug and dismiss them as being your moral views and not mine. Moral claims are universal.

Approaches to Ethical Theory

In describing the plurality of moral principles we saw that though people may all agree that murder is immoral, they may arrive at that judgment on the basis of different moral principles. Ethics is a theory of morality which attempts to systematize moral judgments, and establish and defend basic moral principles.

We need not describe here the great many different ethical systems that have been developed in the history of philosophy. But through the centuries two basic approaches to moral reasoning have prevailed. One approach argues on the basis of consequences. This approach to ethical reasoning is called a teleological approach. It states that whether an action is right or wrong depends on the consequences of that action. A common form of teleological ethics which is very strongly represented in our society is utilitarianism, a theory which we shall examine in the next chapter.

The second basic approach is called the deontological approach. This states that duty is the basic moral category, and that duty is independent of consequences. An action is right if it has certain characteristics or is of a certain kind, and wrong if it has other characteristics or is of another kind. The traditional Judeo-Christian approach to morality is deontological. The German philosopher, Immanuel Kant, gave a classical philosophical statement of the deontological approach which is currently influential in our society. Most of the discussion on questions of business ethics as well as on questions of social ethics, e.g., welfare, on the morality of governmental practices or of laws, is conducted by people who use—knowingly or unknowingly—a utilitarian, a Judeo-Christian, or a Kantian approach to ethics.

Philosophers, and others who wish to be consistent, often attempt to use only one of the ethical approaches to questions. Those interested in ethics as a theoretical pursuit attempt to construct the approach they choose in such a way that it can handle difficulties and objections and can be defended and rationally justified. Those who are willing to mix their approaches are sometimes called ethical pluralists. They hold one primary approach or set of principles but join them with another approach or set of principles at certain times and for certain reasons. One charge often brought against utilitarianism, for instance, is that it cannot provide a satisfactory account of justice. Hence some philosophers join a deontological notion of justice to their utilitarian ethical views. The mixing of approaches has advantages. It obviously also has disadvantages, since one needs some rule to decide when to use one principle rather than another. If someone always knew which principle to use by the way he solved the problem he faced, he would know the solution to his moral problem independently of his ethical theory and so would not really need the theory.

Yet while philosophers argue, both they and the other members of society must act. In the absence of definitive ethical theories we make do with the best we have. In our society the moral arguments are basically the three types previously named. We therefore need to be familiar with them, know how to employ them, and be conscious of their strengths and weaknesses. To a large extent our country is ethically inarticulate. The members of our society make moral judgments and hold moral values. But most members are poorly trained in the art of defending their moral views and of using moral reasoning in a focused way on public policy, social issues, and business practices. That art is an important part of business ethics.

Further Reading

Ayer, A.J. *Language, Truth, and Logic.* 2nd ed. New York: Dover Publications, Inc., 1946. Chapter VI.

Blanshard, Brand. *Reason and Goodness.* New York: Macmillan, Inc., 1961. Chapter V. "Subjectivism."

Foot, Philippa. *Moral Relativism.* Lindley Lecture. The University of Kansas, 1978.

Ginsberg, M. *Essays in Sociology and Social Philosophy.* Vol. I, *On the Diversity of Morals.* New York: Macmillan, Inc., 1957.

Kohlberg, Lawrence. "The Claim to Moral Adequacy of a Highest Stage of Moral Judgment." In *The Journal of Philosophy,* LXX (1973), pp. 630–646.

Moore, G.E. *Ethics.* London: Oxford University Press, Inc., 1912. Chapters 3 and 4.

Piaget, Jean. *The Moral Development of the Child.* Glencoe, Ill.: The Free Press, 1948.

Stace, W.T. *The Concepts of Morals.* New York: Macmillan, Inc., 1937. Chapters 1 and 2.

Stevenson, Charles L. *Ethics and Language.* New Haven: Yale University Press, 1944.

Sumner, W.G. *Folkways.* Boston: Ginn & Company, 1907.

Wellman, Carl. "The Ethical Implications of Cultural Relativity," In *Journal of Philosophy,* LX (1963), pp. 169–184.

Westermarck, E. *Ethical Relativity.* New York: Harcourt Brace, Inc., 1932.

3 Utility and Utilitarianism

Businesses seek to make a profit. They engage in accounting and attempt to have their income exceed their costs. This is a rational procedure, one we all understand, and one which we all utilize in our own lives. For instance, a family has an income and it sets limits on what it can spend. The members of a family need a great many different kinds of goods. People also want things which they do not absolutely need. Typically, they apportion their funds to take care of immediate needs first and then decide how to allocate the remainder, taking into account both present and long-range needs and desires. A budget helps individuals plan the wise use of their money. Though it is difficult to weigh the desirability of a music lesson as opposed to a movie, and to weigh that against one's desire for new clothes or a vacation, we know that people make these comparisons and choices. We also know that occasionally we forego earning more money in order to have more leisure time or more time to devote to members of our family. Though we can place a price tag on many things we desire, we cannot calculate the value of all of them in terms of money.

This common practice of calculating what we want, balancing wishes with our resources, and comparing present versus long-range desires forms the basis of the utilitarian approach to ethics. *Utilitarianism* is an ethical theory which holds that an action is right if it produces, or if it tends to produce the greatest amount of good for the greatest number of people affected by the action. Otherwise the action is wrong.

Utilitarianism does not force on us something foreign to our ordinary rational way of acting. It systematizes and makes explicit what its defenders believe most of us do in our moral thinking, as well as in much of our other thinking. It is reasonable for rational beings, who are able to foresee the consequences of their actions, to choose those actions which produce more good than those which produce less good, with other things being equal. Businesses traditionally reduce "good" to money and calculate costs and benefits in monetary terms. Since the aim of a business is to make money, those actions which tend to help it make money are considered good, and those that tend to make it lose money are considered bad. A rationally operated company tries to maximize the good and minimize the bad so that when income and costs are balanced out, there is a profit. The bottom line of the ledger sheet, which shows a profit or a loss, is the final accounting in which business is traditionally interested.

This cost-benefit analysis is a form of utility calculation. People in business theory use utility curves to plot the results of various actions, choosing those which maximize whatever it is that they wish to achieve. This utilitarian approach is not foreign to most people. It is widely used in many forms of general decision making and can be applied to moral issues as well as to strictly business issues. Its defense as an ethical theory is that it describes what rational people actually do in making moral decisions. Hence, it explicitly formulates for them the procedures they intuitively and spontaneously use in moral reasoning. The theory renders explicit what is implicit in the ordinary moral reasoning and argumentation that we find ourselves using, that we see displayed in newspapers and in discussions of public policy, that we read in the opinions of the Supreme Court, and that we encounter in debates on moral issues with our friends.

Utilitarianism adopts a teleological approach to ethics and claims that actions are to be judged by their consequences. According to this view, actions are not good or bad in themselves. Actions take on moral value only when considered in conjunction with the effects that follow upon them. Actions by themselves have no intrinsic value. They are simply means to attain things which do have value. But what things do have value? To answer this we must distinguish those things which have value as the means towards something else and those things which have value in themselves. A few examples might help.

Businesses seek to make a profit. But what is the point of having money? Is there anything intrinsically valuable in the pieces of paper which we use as money? The paper in itself is not intrinsically valuable. But it can be used to buy goods that we want. It is valuable as a means to an end. The more money we have, the more goods we can buy. But are goods valuable in themselves? Food, shelter, books, and clothing are in turn only a means to satisfy our needs and wants. The stopping point in this progression seems to be ourselves and others. People are the centers of value and what satisfies their needs is what they consider valuable. Basically, then, it is human satisfaction that is valuable in itself; money and goods are the means to produce this satisfaction. Dissatisfaction, harm, pain, or unhappiness are terms of disvalue.

Utilitarianism claims that an action is good if it produces or tends to produce the greatest amount of good for all those affected by an action. We evaluate an action by looking at its consequences and then weighing the good effects against the bad effects on the people affected by it. If the good outweighs the bad, it tends to be a good action. If not, it tends to be a bad action.

In trying to state and use utilitarianism a number of complications arise which have been discussed at length in the philosophical literature. We need only note a few of these. One question which surfaces immediately is how can we calculate consequences which are radically different one from another. In a business calculation everything is typically reduced to dollars and cents. This makes calculation relatively easy. But how are we to evaluate actions from a moral point of view? Is there some least common denominator in terms of which we can and do calculate? A number of answers have been proposed to this question. One, which is called *hedonistic utilitarianism,* holds that the basic human values are pleasure and pain (sometimes defined simply as the absence of pleasure). According to this view, everything that people desire, want, or need can be reduced in one way or another to pleasure. Hence the calculation, though not easy, is possible because we are dealing with units of the same kind.

The advantage of this approach, however, has been challenged by those who claim that not all intrinsically valuable goods can be reduced to some uniform pleasure and pain. What is intrinsically valuable, they maintain, is not simply pleasures—which may differ in quality as well as quantity—but happiness. This second view is called *eudaimonistic utilitarianism,* since the basic value in terms of which the calculation is made is happiness, not pleasure.

A third approach is called *ideal utilitarianism.* This position maintains that what has to be calculated is not only pleasure or happiness but all intrinsically valuable human goods, which also include friendship, knowledge, and a host of other goods valuable in themselves.

The differences among these utilitarians are subtle with interesting and strong arguments on all sides. But we need not settle the dispute here because the debate does not actually call into doubt whether such things as knowledge, beauty, or friendship are valuable; rather, it questions whether they are valuable for their own sake or because they produce pleasure or happiness. The majority of calculations will come out the same whether we use the ideal utilitarian approach which allows a plurality of intrinsic values, or the hedonistic approach which reduces all values ultimately to pleasure, or that of the eudaimonistic utilitarians which reduces them to happiness. The hedonistic calculation may seem to be more straightforward than the others since we deal with the same units—i.e., pleasure and pain. But the problem of trying to reduce the multiplicity of goods and values to pleasure and pain is not an easy one. How do we decide the amount of pleasure we receive from a drink of our favorite beverage when thirsty as opposed to the amount of pleasure we receive from learning a new theorem in geometry or reading an exciting novel or giving a gift to a friend? Whether we face the problem of comparison as we weigh the various goods and values, we must face it at one stage or another. Thus the dispute about the differing approaches to the interpretation of good in the utilitarian formula, though interesting, is not as crucial as it may seem in deciding actual cases.

There are several assumptions made by utilitarianism that it is well to make explicit. In carrying out the calculation of good and bad consequences of an action, the utilitarian rule tells us to. consider all the persons affected by the action. The assumption is that our good counts for no more than anyone else's good. Nor does anyone else's good count for more than ours. The approach is neither egoistic nor altruistic—it is universalistic. The defense of this approach is that it captures what we actually do when we make moral judgments. Moral judgments are judgments we make concerning actions, and we believe that the actions are right not only for oursevles but also for anyone else similarly situated. From the moral point of view, which is impartial, my good counts no more than anyone else's. Nor does anyone else's good count more than mine. Each person is equal and each person's good is as important and worthwhile as is each other person's good. Our moral calculation, thus, is a calculation made from an impersonal point of view. It should come out the same whether made by me, or by you, or by any other rational person adopting an objective point of view. What is weighed is the good or bad resulting to each person affected by an action. This is an objective state of affairs. Though pleasure, happiness, or other goods may be subjectively experienced, the experiences are considered and weighed objectively with each given its due.

Jeremy Bentham, who was a hedonistic utilitarian, argued that in attempting to evaluate the pleasure or pain produced by an action there are various aspects of the pleasure and pain which we should consider. We can generalize his analysis to any value or good we are taking into account. We should consider the intensity, duration, certainty or uncertainty, propinquity or remoteness, fecundity, and the purity of the value in question. A more intense pleasure, for instance, might have to be weighed against a less intense but longer-lasting pain. In making our calculation we give greater weight to the pleasure or other value which we are more certain of attaining and less weight to less certain values. Similarly we weigh differently those goods which we will get immediately from those which we will only acquire in a more distant time. Frequently, we are willing to undergo immediate discomfort and unpleasantness because these are necessary in order to achieve something that is worthwhile in the future and that makes the present unpleasantness worth suffering through. Fecundity refers to whether the action will produce more of the same kind of value we achieve in the first instance. The pleasure we get from learning a new skill, for instance, may be followed by other instances of pleasure as we utilize that skill. If a value is followed by its opposite, then it is impure. For instance, the pleasure of a glass of beer which makes one intoxicated is frequently followed by the pain of being sick or having a hangover.

In each case we consider the good and the bad produced by an action in the first instance and, in later instances, for those most directly affected by the action. We sum this up. We then consider all the others who will be affected by the action less directly. The number may be very large, but the intensity of the effect quite small. The good and the bad done to all of these people must be totaled. Many of our actions affect society as a whole. When I break a contract, I not only affect myself and the person with whom I made the contract, but I also affect a great many other people—all those, for instance, who hear about it. Many will be more cautious in making contracts not only with me but with others. Some will worry more than they otherwise would have. Still others may refuse to make contracts for fear of others breaking them as I did. All these are real consequences which must go into the calculation. After considering all the persons affected, we sum up the good and bad. We then sum that up together with the calculation we made concerning the effects on those more directly affected by the action. The final result of our calculation determines the morality of the action. If the action produces more good than bad, then it tends to be a morally right action.

But our calculation is not yet over. The utilitarian principle tells us that the action to be right must produce the greatest good for the greatest number of those affected by it. To know whether the action produces the greatest good, we need to compare it with alternative actions. In some cases this will be simply the opposite action. If we are considering the morality of breaking a contract, we should calculate the effects of breaking it; but we should also ask what the alternative action is. It is keeping or not breaking the contract. Hence we would sum up the results of that alternative in a way comparable to the way we did the first sum. When we compare the two, the morally right action is the one that produces the greatest net amount of good.

We can add several dimensions to the calculation. For purposes of determining whether a certain kind of action is moral or immoral, we need only calculate the action and its opposite. If the action in general produces more good than harm whereas its opposite produces more harm than good, then the action is generally a moral action. If more than one action and its opposite are available to us, we can calculate the results of all the alternatives. A stringent application of utilitarianism would lead to the conclusion that the action that produces the greatest amount of good is the desired moral action. A less stringent interpretation of rule utilitarianism would simply require that we choose one of the actions that tends to produce more good than harm, but would not require that we always choose only that action among good actions which is best. On any interpretation of utilitarianism, if two actions produce equal net amounts of good, then both are equal from a moral point of view and we may morally do either. If we have only two alternatives and both of them produce more bad than good, then we are morally obliged to do the one which produces the least amount of badness. We thereby choose the lesser of two evils.

Act and Rule Utilitarianism

Two versions of utilitarianism are compatible with the utilitarian principle stated above. They are known as act utilitarianism and rule utilitarianism. *Act utilitarianism* holds that each individual action in all its concreteness and in all its detail is what should be subjected to the utilitarian test. When faced with the temptation to break a contract we are always concerned with a particular contract in a particular set of circumstances. To determine the morality of the action we should calculate the effects of breaking this particular contract. The effects will be in part similar to breaking any contract, but in part they also will be different. If we believe that what is true of breaking contracts in general will not be true in this case, we should investigate the effects in this case.

When faced with the temptation to break a contract we may know that the bad consequences will outweigh the good ones, based on our knowledge of what the results of breaking contracts are and also our knowledge that this case has no special qualities. The act utilitarian emphasizes, however, that breaking contracts is generally immoral because the vast majority of such past cases have resulted in more bad than good. We hence arrive at a rule of thumb about the morality of breaking contracts. The rule of thumb, however, is a generalization of past instances, and some particular future instance may prove an exception to the rule. In that particular case, breaking the contract is the moral thing to do.

Those who defend rule utilitarianism object to this act utilitarian approach. *Rule utilitarians* hold that utility applies appropriately to classes of actions rather than to given individual actions. Thus, by looking at the consequences in general of breaking contracts, we can determine that breaking contracts is immoral. It is immoral because the bad consequences arrive at rules which state that certain actions are morally right and others morally wrong. Thus a rule utilitarian can say people should not lie, steal, break contracts, or murder. Each of these injunctions is the result of having observed the consequences of those acts as performed in the past, together with a certain assurance that the consequences in the future will be similar.

Why favor the rule utilitarian rather than the act utilitarian approach? The answer is that we cannot know all the consequences of an act nor can we know in advance with certainty even many of the consequences of a particular act. In act utilitarianism the temptation is always present to think that this instance will be the exception to the rule. If we are the primary beneficiaries of breaking a particular contract we may tend to discount the harm done to others, to diminish its seriousness, to guess that the consequences will not be as serious for them as they usually are for those affected by broken contracts. We will assume that no one will find out, if finding out is what will cause others to be reluctant to make contracts. We will be tempted to project what we would like to have happen, since we cannot know what will happen.

The rule utilitarian approach does not require guesswork as to what will happen. The history of mankind provides the sourcebook. If we wish to see the results of murder, lying, stealing, or breaking contracts, we can easily recall the consequences in many past cases. We know that most criminals think that they will get away with their crime. We also know that many, if not most, do not; and we know that even some of those who are not caught suffer pangs of conscience. We need not be prophets to foresee that the consequences of certain kinds of actions are on the whole bad rather than good. We can learn from human experience how people have come to hold the general moral rules that they do.

Rule utilitarianism provides a technique for determining the moral value of actions—both those on which society has already made a moral determination and those on which it has not. In addition to generalizing on the basis of past experience, the technique of utilitarianism enables us to determine whether conditions have changed to such an extent that what was once immoral because it produced more bad than good is now moral because in changed circumstances the action produces more good than bad. It also enables us to see whether we have been mistaken in our past calculation concerning certain practices. If we miscalculated as a society, we can now recalculate, and correct our past error. By making explicit the principle which we implicitly used before, we have the means to check our prior moral judgments, challenge those that are mistaken, and evaluate actions the moral values of which change because of new circumstances.

In our own society there are a number of disputed moral questions. In part the disputes hinge on the consequences foreseen as likely by one group and denied as likely by another. To some extent business is facing questions which are truly new and for which we have no easy way to determine the real consequences. I have indicated that act and rule utilitarianism are used to decide the morality of actions. They may also be used to decide the morality of laws, social practices, social structures, political systems, and economic systems. Does the adoption of free enterprise produce more good than bad? Does it produce more total good over bad than the adoption of socialism? The answer is not an easy one to formulate because the consequences are so complex. There is also no clear way of knowing what the consequences of adopting an economic system really will be in any given case. The adoption of an economic system is not like the performance of particular social acts which are very similar one to another and for which we have an abundance of information as to the consequences. When dealing with legislation, utilitarian arguments are also frequently used. A moral political system is one which produces an abundance of good over bad for the members of the society. At the least, this is one of its functions. A policy is morally justified if it produces more good than bad, and is optimally justified if it produces more good than any other alternative would. But since we cannot know that we have considered all the alternatives, and since we cannot know what all the consequences of any alternative will be, we cannot have certainty on the morality of policies. In some instances we can foresee that they will produce more harm than good, and we can morally attack them. In some instances we think they will produce more good and only after implementation do we find that we are mistaken. In still other instances, we may choose what appears to be the better alternative, only to find out that it may not have been better; but sticking with it may produce more good than trying to start all over. These are all parts of our ordinary experience. The utilitarian is not surprised that they are. For utilitarianism is simply the result of making explicit the ways we ordinarily argue about policies, laws, and actions.

Because some immoral actions seem at times to produce more good than bad, utilitarians promote penal legislation. A thief who sometimes gets away with his action may come to believe that theft produces more good consequences on the whole than bad. If, however, theft is made illegal and the penalty is serious, then the fear that accompanies stealing is increased and therefore the pain from stealing is made greater than the pleasure. One purpose of legislation, according to this view, is to add legal sanctions so that the calculation of the consequences becomes more obvious than it might otherwise be. Society protects itself by passing laws against those acts which tend to harm it and the people in it. It reinforces the calculation of the bad effects of those actions.

The application of this approach to business activities is no different from its application to actions in general. If we adopt the utilitarian perspective, we can evaluate certain business practices on the basis of their consequences. If they tend to produce more bad than good, they are immoral. If the harm done to society by these practices is sufficiently serious, then legislation might be passed subjecting the action to legal as well as moral sanctions. The sanctions must outweigh the good that the perpetrator of the action hopes to gain. For example, the usual punishment imposed on a corporation for breaking a law is a fine. If the fine is to serve as a deterrent, the amount of the fine should be greater than the amount the company would gain by doing the action. Law is used to protect the members of society when moral means do not suffice. The justification for such law is utilitarian, just as the evaluation of the action is. Law can provide an incentive to act morally for those who would not otherwise do so.

Utilitarians also consider moral and other sanctions in their calculations. If an action does more harm than good to society, then the members of society can impose a number of sanctions on the wrongdoer short of legal measures. If a merchant overcharges, people can stop patronizing him and spread the word to others to do the same. They can stop speaking to him and ostracize him from various social activities. They can chastise him, vent their moral indignation on him, and so on. All of these are sanctions that those who perform certain harmful actions can and should expect. It is because they should expect them that they can consider them when they calculate the results of an action.

Some people claim that the results will be the same whether one employs rule utilitarianism or act utilitarianism. Part of the argument hinges on the broad consequences of adopting the act utilitarian approach. One result of adopting it is that many people no longer know how a moral individual will act. An action which can be justified as an exception tends to do damage to the general good of having the rule. This is a negative consequence which must always be taken into account in any calculation from a utilitarian point of view. And this calculation will tend to outweigh the marginally good consequences of most exceptions. Hence, the argument goes, in the vast majority of cases and if not demonstrably in all, the person who adopts the act utilitarian approach will end up justifying the same thing as the person who adopts the rule utilitarian approach. Whether or not this is the case, if we do use the act utilitarian approach we must be scrupulously certain that we are not giving ourselves any undue advantage, that the results we calculate are not simply wishful thinking, and that we consider all the results of the action, including the effect that it will have on society. To be morally justifiable the results must be such that the action would be right not only for me but for anyone in similar circumstances. If they are, then we already have the basis for generalizing an exception to the rule, or for changing the rule to include the exception, resulting in a slightly different rule.

Objections to Utilitarianism

One of the classic statements of utilitarianism was given by John Stuart Mill in his work *Utilitarianism,* first published in 1861. In it he answers a number of arguments against utilitarianism. One of these objections is that utilitarianism is ungodly since it proposes utilitarianism as a basis for moral judgments rather than the Bible or God. His reply was in some ways a charming one. He indicated that since God was benevolent and loved his creatures, he would wish them to be happy. Hence what he commands are those actions which tend to produce the greatest amount of good or happiness for the greatest number. What he forbids are those actions which tend to produce more harm than good or happiness. Hence, Mill argued, the actions commanded and forbidden by utilitarianism are the same as the actions commanded and forbidden by God. The advantage of adopting utilitarianism is that we have a technique for deciding moral questions on which we have no direct information from God. Even the Ten Commandments require interpretation. Utilitarianism gives us the tool necessary for deciding those acts of killing, e.g., self-defense, which are compatible with the commandment "Thou shalt not kill," and those which are not.

A second objection frequently brought against utilitarianism is that no one has the time to calculate all the consequences of an action beforehand. This is frequently true. But utilitarianism does not require that we actually calculate all the consequences before we act any more than the religious person must reread the Bible each time before he acts. As we saw with rule utilitarianism, we have the history of mankind on which to build. We know that murder is wrong and need not calculate the results of murder every time we get angry at someone. We know that the bad results of murder outweigh the good. This is both obvious and a part of our general knowledge. But if we are ever questioned as to why murder is wrong, or if we ever seriously want to consider whether murder is wrong, we have in utilitarianism the means for arriving at a decision about the morality of murder together with the knowledge of why it is wrong. Similarly with other actions. If we are ever uncertain about the morality of an action, we know how to think about resolving the issue. We are not always in a moral quandary. But when we are faced with difficult moral choices, we should stop and consider the consequences, weigh them, and arrive at the best conclusion we can.

Another answer to the objection to utilitarianism is that the calculation is frequently a fairly simple one. For instance, when we are tempted to lie to gain some advantage, the temptation presents itself in the form of a calculation in which we focus on the advantage to ourselves and play down the harm done in the long run to either ourselves or to others. Frequently, the way we resist temptation is to quickly produce a more accurate calculation of the consequences using a rule utilitarian approach in which the disadvantages appear more clearly.

A third objection is that we cannot carry out the calculation which utilitarianism requires both because we cannot know the results of any action fully and because we cannot weigh different kinds of good and evil which result in any accurate fashion. The calculation is artificial and not practical.

The reply to the first part of the objection is twofold. First, as we have already seen, in judging most actions we have the benefit of evaluating the consequences of similar actions done in the past. Second, we can frequently foresee a large number of possible, if not actual, consequences and among these some that are so important as to dominate the calculation. This observation applies to the second part of the objection as well. For instance, we are not required by the utilitarian approach to perform a mathematically precise operation. If it were possible to do so, then we could and, if appropriate, should. But there is no way to get mathematical precision in most calculations dealing with the morality of actions. In the more standard cases the consequences are sufficiently obvious; the good or the bad predominates so clearly that great precision is not necessary. In difficult cases where the calculation is not clear, we cannot be sure we are correct in our moral assessment, and we should be ready to revise it if we find our calculation is mistaken. This is not a defect of the theory but a statement of the human condition and the nature of morality. In reply to the claim, moreover, that we cannot compare different values and weigh them, we need simply to point to the fact that we all make such calculations everyday. We weigh present against future good and one value against another all the time. The claim that it cannot be done is therefore simply false and flies in the face of our ordinary experience.

A fourth objection consists of the interpretation to be given to the utilitarian principle itself. The principle claims that an action is right if it tends to produce the greatest good for the greatest number of persons affected by it. But, the objection goes, the formulation is ambiguous. Are we to put our emphasis on the greatest aggregate of good or are we to concern ourselves with the good of the greatest number? Suppose, for instance, we had to choose between two cases. Action A resulted in 1,000 units of good for 100 people and 10 units of good for 9,900 people. Action B resulted in 19.9 units of good for each of the 10,000 people. In both cases we have a total of 199,000 units of good. If the good at issue was the standard of living in a community, utilitarianism would have us conclude that there is no moral difference between the two cases. A society in which a few live at a very prosperous level and the many live at a very much lower level is no better than another society in which all the people live at a level almost twice as high as the latter group in the first community. Such a result, to the critics, seems clearly mistaken. To make the case even stronger, we can add one unit of good to the privileged group in the first society; then, since that society has more good than its alternative, Action A is morally better than Action B. This, the objection continues, runs counter to our moral intuitions. Nor can we remedy the situation by putting the emphasis on the number of people rather than on the greatest good because the problem will still remain.

The utilitarian counter to the objection takes two forms, usually offered jointly. The first is that the objection, though theoretically possible is in real life implausible. The case is a fabricated one, the product of a philosopher's imagination, and not one that can be filled out in any concrete, historical detail. If one ever had such a choice, we should choose what produces good for more people rather than maximizing the greater good of a small number because this choice maximizes good in the long run. This fact has to be added to the calculation. The above case trades on an obvious discrepancy between the few and the many. But this discrepancy itself has negative consequences which the calculation does not take into account. The case seems to work because it is manipulated in such a way that the bad consequences which result from the great discrepancy between the two groups are not fully considered. If our moral intuitions tell us the calculation is mistaken, this is an indication that we have miscalculated and are ignoring some negative component in the case. Once this has been said, the utilitarian is then content to claim that there may well be cases in which equal good is produced by two different actions and that in such a case one may choose either alternative. We saw this earlier in the explanation of utilitarianism. Hence this observation is not a criticism of the position but a result which is accepted by the utilitarian.

Utilitarianism and Justice

Even if the utilitarian's answers to the previous objections are accepted, some critics claim that the theory cannot account for justice and in some instances runs counter to it. The claim is not a new one, since it was raised and answered by Mill in *Utilitarianism*. But the criticism has persisted and remains a live issue today. The typical argument goes as follows. Suppose we consider a small town in western United States during the nineteenth century. Law and order are newly established. Jim James is caught with a stolen horse and accused of being a horse thief. He claims he bought it from a passing stranger. The penalty for stealing horses is to be hanged. The judge in the town, unbeknownst to anyone, happened to be passing by and actually witnessed the purchase. He was hidden by trees and was therefore not seen by Jim. The judge, it turns out, was in the vicinity only because he was buying some illegal whiskey. The town is outraged by the horse theft and wants an example made of Jim. If the judge comes forward as a witness he will have to say what he was doing out in the woods; he will then be dismissed by the town. Another judge will not be available for some time, and the town will suffer. In addition, the people of the town are so convinced that Jim is guilty, that they will probably hang him anyway. Innocent people may well be killed in trying to prevent this. Taking all this into account, the judge decides it is better for him not to come forward with his information. He should condemn Jim and have him hanged. Jim will be killed no matter what. And more harm than good will come to the town if he tries to defend him.

The utilitarian calculation, its critics maintain, would be that the right thing to do here is to condemn an innocent man. But condemning an innocent man is obviously unjust. Hence it might be said that utilitarianism results in saying that to do what is obviously unjust is the morally right thing to do. The conclusion is that utilitarianism cannot be an accurate account of morality nor can it be an appropriate way to make moral judgments.

In its generalized form the argument maintains that justice does not depend on consequences. Justice consists of giving each person his due or treating people equitably. Such considerations do not depend on consequences. It is unjust to condemn an innocent person regardless of whether doing so produces better consequences than not doing so. Since consequences are irrelevant, justice is not based on utility and utilitarianism is therefore inadequate as a foundation of justice.

The objection has not convinced all utilitarians. The standard reply is that in the above example or in any other situation like it the objection is plausible only because not all the results are considered. The case does not end with the hanging. We must consider the consciences of the judge and of the people of the town, the reaction when the truth is discovered, what happens to the notion of justice when the judge tries to guess the consequences in each case, and so on. When we consider all these effects, we see that in the long run more good is done than harm by not condemning an innocent man than by condemning him. This is the practice, the results of which must be considered, not some isolated, hypothetical action whose results are arbitrarily cut off at a convenient point for the objector.

Many critics have not been satisfied by the reply. Nor have they been convinced by attempts to give a utiliarian account of justice. As a result, some people have advocated using two conjoint principles in moral evaluation—the principles of utility and justice. In most cases the principle of utility will take precedence. But in those cases in which the principle seems to go against justice, then the principle of justice takes precedence. The justification for this approach is itself utilitarian, namely, that it produces the best results or the greatest amount of good on the whole.

Despite the debate between the utilitarians and their opponents regarding the issue of justice, in most cases both sides will agree on which actions are just. If a case involves condemning an innocent man, most utilitarians will admit that such an action is morally wrong and will show how such an action is not in fact required by utilitarianism. For practical purposes this observation is important. It indicates that whether or not utilitarianism can be so formulated as to give an adequate theoretical account of justice, both sides can agree on which actions are just. Since, from the practical point of view, we are interested in rendering moral decisions about cases, we can do so without having to resolve fully the theoretical issue. It is only when the two approaches—the utilitarian and deontological—actually result in divergent moral judgments that we will have to choose between them. But if such cases exist, they can be treated separately and as special cases. In most instances the utilitarian and deontological approaches to justice as well as the moral evaluation of actions and practices will result in similar moral judgments. Nor should this conclusion be surprising, since both utilitarianism and deontological theories are attempts to systematize and provide the reasoned ground for our moral judgments. Both have as their starting points the large number of actions which we agree are morally right and morally wrong.

Utilitarianism and Bribery

Most people in the United States readily acknowledge that bribery is immoral. Bribery in business is an interesting kind of action to examine from a utilitarian point of view because those who engage in bribery frequently justify their actions by something similar to utilitarian grounds.

Consider an airplane manufacturer who has spent enormous amounts of money developing a new airplane. The company badly needs cash since it is financially overextended. If it does not get some large orders soon, it will have to close down part of its operation. Doing that will put several thousand workers out of jobs. The result will be not only disastrous for the workers but also for the town in which they live. The president of the company has been trying to interest the government in a large purchase. He learns that one of the key people in charge of making the final decision is heavily in debt due to gambling. He quietly contacts that person and offers him $100,000 in cash if he awards the contract to his firm. The contract is awarded, the money is paid, and the business is saved.

When justifying his action, the president of the firm points out all the benefits that result from the bribe—an important government official is much better off financially than he would otherwise be; the government purchases planes which are of good design and workmanship; the airplane company gets the contract and stays in business; the workers at the plant are kept on and they and their families do not have to suffer the way they would have if they had lost their jobs. The town in which they live also benefits. The president therefore concludes, that the results are on the whole positive. The only negative aspect is that an action which some people would not approve of took place. But that is the way of business, he claims.

The argument is a utilitarian one to the extent that it seeks to evaluate the results of the action, weighs the good against the bad, and argues that the good outweighs the bad. The alternative would have been not to give the bribe. But if it had not been given, then the contract may not have been awarded. If it had not been awarded, then all of the bad consequences indicated above would have taken place. No good would have been achieved, and the result would clearly have been worse.

The argument may sound plausible. Yet we know that bribery is immoral. Does utilitarianism not work in this case? The reply is that it works, but it has not been properly used here. The above account is obviously a one-sided version of the situation. It describes the thinking of the president of the company, his point of view, and his concerns. That is not the moral point of view. The moral point of view is an objective point of view which considers all of the consequences of an action on all of the people affected by it. We must therefore consider much more than we have considered so far. Broaden the picture and look more closely at the effects on the principles already mentioned, and then open your vision to those whom we have so far ignored.

Consider first the effects of the bribe on the public official. What are the consequences? The only consequence we have considered so far is that he gets the money he needs and gives a contract to the company in question. What are the chances that the bribe will be discovered, and what are the consequences if it is discovered? Bribery is illegal. If the public official's action is discovered, he would in all likelihood be charged with a felony, lose his job, and, if convicted, be heavily fined and/or go to jail. Will his life be better? If he is not found out, he could be subject to blackmail. He may also be tempted to live beyond his means and end up in a similar situation again. He will have to explain where he got the money to his wife and perhaps to others. He will not report it on his income tax and thus be liable for not reporting income. We can continue to consider what might happen to him and try to put some evaluation on how likely these things are to occur, how seriously they will affect him, and so on.

The good done to the workers, plant, and town have to be given their due weight. But the story does not mention competing firms. What is their situation? Will their workers be out of jobs? Will their town be depressed? Consider the president. How will he manage to pay $100 thousand? Where will it come from? How will he pay it without its being recorded and reported to the Internal Revenue Service and to the company auditors? For this project to succeed, it is clear that the president will have to break more laws than simply the one against bribery. These actions will all have their effects. If his actions are found out, he will be held liable, may lose his job, and may be imprisoned.

Consider next the effects on the general public. The government official is spending their money. If he is not buying the best equipment at the best price he can get, then he is misusing public funds, and hence harming the taxpayers. If the airplanes he contracted for were the ones he would have purchased anyway, then what was the point of the bribe? But even if he would have placed the order with that firm without a bribe, the $100,000 he received had to come from somewhere. Either it was added to the cost of the planes he purchased and thereby came from the taxpayers, or it came from the company's profits, and thereby came from the shareholders. In either case the money was taken from those who had legitimate claim to it, and they will be negatively affected to that extent.

The bribe also has an effect on the general system of bidding, on the practice of competition, and on the integrity of those engaged in these practices. Once bribery is an accepted way of doing business, then people will no longer get the best for their money. Does the good done to the person who receives the bribe and to the person who gives it outweigh the harm possibly done to them if they are caught, and the harm certainly done to those who have to pay more or receive less in the way of profit, and to the system as a whole?

If there is some doubt about whether the practice does more harm than good, we need only consider why bribery is not done openly. Why isn't the giving of a bribe considered part of doing legitimate business and engaged in aboveboard the way other business practices are? The obvious reason is that only a few people benefit from the practice at the expense of a great many other people and of society and business in general.

The argument is a utilitarian type argument. But it did not attempt any close calculation of good and bad results such that one could give each a number and then perform a numerical calculation. It is possible to be so exact only in rare instances. But the kind of reasoning did consider consequences to all those involved and attempted not to cut off the consequences considered at some convenient point. The account first presented by the president did not consider all those affected by the action. The use of the utilitarian calculation does not provide an automatic guarantee of morality. If it is to produce a morally justifiable result, it must be used by someone who truly wishes to find out what is right and who is willing to take into account all the consequences, both short- and long-range, for all concerned.

Someone might object that some important considerations have been omitted in the above calculation. This is always possible. If we omitted something important, then we must also take that into account and see whether this omission changes the final outcome. This is not an infrequent occurrence in using the utilitarian approach. In questions of public policy and public morality, in fact, the argument frequently takes place in just this way. Different sides bring out further consequences or argue that insufficient weight was given to one of the consequences discussed, or that an outcome which was considered unlikely was actually very likely.

The mid-seventies witnessed a major international scandal concerning bribes, kickbacks, and illegal campaign contributions both in the United States and abroad. Lockheed Corporation, among others, was involved in giving twelve and one-half million dollars in bribes and commissions in connection with the sale of four hundred thirty million dollars worth of TriStar planes to All Nippon Airways. Carl Kotchian defended his payments in an article in the *Saturday Review.* He was forced to resign from his position after the news of the payoffs broke. One claim was that it was common practice to give bribes in Japan and that this was expected. Nonetheless, the news rocked Japan even more than it did the United States. The Prime Minister of Japan, Kakuei Tanaka, and four others were forced to resign from the Government and were brought to trial. A wave of legislation attempting to control bribery was proposed, and some of it was passed both in the United States and Japan. The results of the bribery were far-reaching. But the Lockheed case was not a simple one. Lockheed did not offer a bribe; rather, the Japanese negotiator demanded it. Are those who accede to bribery equal in guilt to those who demand bribes? Are one's obligations in dealing with a corrupt government the same as one's obligations in dealing with an uncorrupt one? If the people of a country tolerate bribery among their officials, does this amount to consent to the system? If the paying of such commissions is the sine qua non of doing business with the government, does this justify such payments? These are all knotty questions which are compatible with the general claim that bribery is immoral. These are questions that have been raised and that are still discussed. Some attempts have been made to control bribery by legislation. Other forms of payment sometimes approach extortion and are not under the control of American laws since they are carried on abroad. How should American companies react? Some, such as Gulf Oil, having once been stung, have decided not to make any such payments and have been pleasantly surprised to find that their new policy has not decreased their sales or led to the threatened nationalization of their plants. A great many fears have been discovered to be unfounded. The people of some nations have been less tolerant of questionable practices than was thought. And there have been attempts to bring order into the international marketplace by firms in many countries that would prefer to compete on the merit of their products rather than on their skill at secret payments.

All of this provides additional information for the utilitarian calculation of the moral response to difficult problems. The utilitarian technique of arguing is a common one worth mastering.

Further Reading

Bentham, Jeremy. *An Introduction to the Principles of Morals and Legislation.* Oxford: The Clarendon Press, 1879. (First published, 1789.)

Brandt, Richard B. "Toward a Credible Form of Utilitarianism," In *Morality and the Language of Conduct.* Edited by H.N. Castaneda and G. Nakhnikian. Detroit: Wayne State University Press, 1963, pp. 107–140.

Jacoby, Neil H.; Nehemkis, Peter; and Eells, Richard. *Bribery and Extortion in World Business.* London: Collier Macmillan Publishers Ltd., 1977.

Kotchian, A. Carl. "The Payoff: Lockheed's 70-Day Mission to Tokyo." In *Saturday Review,* July 9, 1977, pp. 7–12.

Mill, John Stuart. *Utilitarianism.* New York: The Liberal Arts Press, 1957. (First published, 1863.)

Moore, G.E. *Ethics.* London: Oxford University Press, Inc., 1912.

Moore, G.E. *Principia Ethica.* London: Cambridge University Press, 1903.

Rawls, J.B. "Two Concepts of Rules." In *Philosophical Review,* LXIV (1955), pp. 3–32.

Shaplen, Robert. "Annals of Crime: The Lockheed Incident." In *New Yorker,* LIII (January 23, 1978), pp. 48–50 (January 30, 1978), pp. 74–91.

Sidgwick, H. *The Methods of Ethics.* London: Macmillan, 1874.

Smart, J.J.C. *An Outline of a System of Utilitarian Ethics.* Melbourne: Melbourne University Press, 1961.

4 Formalism and Justice

The deontological approach to ethics denies the utilitarian claim that the morality of an action depends on the consequences. Deontologists maintain that actions are morally right or wrong independently of their consequences. Moral rightness and wrongness are basic and ultimate moral terms. They do not depend on good and the production or failure to produce good. One's duty is to do what is morally right and to avoid what is morally wrong, irrespective of the consequences of so doing.

The deontological position is a commonly held one with a long history. In contemporary American society it is associated both with the Judeo-Christian tradition and with a philosophical tradition which goes back to the Greek Stoic philosophers. It includes the formalistic theory of Immanuel Kant and the theories of many contemporaries who present moral arguments in terms of justice and rights.

Judeo-Christian Morality

The Judeo-Christian tradition has nurtured the morality of the West for centuries and of our country since its inception. It is still an extremely powerful and potent force. Judeo-Christian morality includes not only a body of moral rules but also a view of what it means to be a human being and to have a set of values. The moral rules, the view of man, and the values have to a large degree been absorbed into the secular life of the West in general—and the United States in particular. The morality taught in the pulpits is fairly close to the morality taught in the public schools and conventional morality found in our society.

We can separate those aspects of the Judeo-Christian moral heritage having to do explicitly with religion and with man's duty to God from the other aspects of the morality having to do with man's relations to his fellow men. Primarily the latter has been taken over by Western society, absorbed, and to a large extent secularized.

The Ten Commandments, at least after the first three, are still widely held to sum up actions which we morally should do (e.g., honor thy father and mother) or not do (e.g., thou shalt not kill). To these are joined the Christian injunction to love your neighbor, together with all that it implies. The Christian virtue of charity is added to the Hebraic virtue of justice. The other virtues follow. Because the morality of the Judeo-Christian tradition rested for so many centuries on a foundation of faith, there was great fear that as religious faith diminished, immorality would increase. What has tended to happen, however, is that as religious faith diminished the virtues and commands which it had sustained found different, secular, philosophical underpinnings. We have already seen how utilitarians have been quite ready to accept and explain Christian morality using the utilitarian approach. Philosophical deontologists have also provided a secular foundation for the content of Christian moral norms and virtues.

Is there a Judeo-Christian ethics or theory of morality as well as a Judeo-Christian morality? The question is open to several interpretations. If ethics is taken as a *philosophical* attempt to forge morality into a defensible system based on principles, then we must ask whether there is a Judeo-Christian philosophy. If there is no Judeo-Christian philosophy, there can be no Judeo-Christian ethics as opposed to Judeo-Christian morality. If there is a Judeo-Christian philosophy, then there can be a Judeo-Christian ethics. But if ethics is not restricted to philosophy and religious or theological ethics is not considered a contradiction, then there can be a Judeo-Christian ethics.

A theological ethics is based on theology and hence on the acceptance of divine revelation. There are two dominant positions in this approach. One holds that divine inspiration took place not only in ages past through the prophets, Christ, and the authors of the New Testament but that it continues even now and is available to all believers. With this view, conscience is God's word and those who are in tune with Him know what is right and what is wrong. Viewed as an ethical theory, it simply means that what is right and what is wrong is determined by God and communicated by Him to His followers. The second position holds that God determines what is right and what is wrong, that He revealed it through His prophets, Christ, and the authors of the New Testament, but that this revelation requires interpretation. The interpretation may be done by each individual or by special persons in a particular Church, depending on one's religion.

According to either of these two interpretations, morality is first of all personal, governing one's actions vis-à-vis God. For those who find morality interpreted through a church, the morality preached therein is binding on them and on fellow members of the church. In both cases, however, the morality rests ultimately on God and is held because of revelation. Though members of our society frequently guide their lives by such an ethics, a religiously-based moral argument is frequently discounted by those not practicing the same faith as the person who puts forth the argument. Since the argument has as a central feature belief in God and in a certain kind of revelation, those who do not believe in God or who believe in a different kind of revelation are not logically compelled by such an argument.

Ever since the ancient Greeks, moreover, some people have asked whether an action is right because God says it is, or whether God says an action is morally right because it is morally right. In the former case God could make murder, theft, or lying moral if He chose to do so. In the latter case, He could not. He knows those actions are morally wrong, and helps us know this through His revelation. But the rightness or wrongness of the actions are not subject to His whim. By making us in certain ways, the moral rules by which we should live were built into our nature as human beings. Ultimately they depend on God; but we need not constantly ask or wonder whether He has changed His mind and whether what He once said was immoral is today moral.

Three points should be made clear. If one believes that he knows directly through divine intervention which actions are right and which are wrong, then he has no need of a philosophical ethical theory unless he wishes to defend his moral judgments to those who disagree with him or who do not believe as he does in God's direct intervention. Secondly, those who do not believe in God's direct personal intervention for all people must interpret the Ten Commandments and the injunction to love one's neighbor. What specific actions do these prescriptions and proscriptions command or forbid? Is killing in self-defense a justifiable form of killing? Is killing in defense of one's property defensible? Both actions are forms of killing. The Commandment "Thou shalt not kill" does not come with any exceptions built into it. How, if at all, do we justify exceptions? The rules by which we arrive at and justify exceptions make up part of a theory of morality and therefore part of an ethical system. If they are defended only on the basis of scripture, then they are designed only for the religious believer.

The third point is that what is demanded by religiously-based morality might in fact also be justifiable on nonreligious grounds. The content of religious morality might be acceptable, at least in large part, to nonreligious people and might find philosophical grounds adequate to support at least the portion that is not specifically religious. Many in the history of philosophy have defended this position, including such major figures as Saint Thomas Aquinas. As mentioned earlier, both Mill and Kant thought they were supplying a philosophical ethical theory which could support a Christian morality.

Individual people engaged in business may of course be religious and may govern the practices they engage in by their religious convictions. But defenses of business practices are not usually appropriately given in religious terms to those not practicing one's own religion; nor are public policy questions argued convincingly in religious terms. If the arguments are intended to be convincing to large segments of the population, they are characteristically put in such terms that the premises are acceptable to all human beings, and not just to believers.

The Ten Commandments and the commandment to love your neighbor have a deontological form to them. They are commandments to do certain actions and to refrain from others. The commands do not instruct us to look at the consequences of the actions before deciding whether or not they are right. Hence, they command without concern for consequences. Whether they could be derived by looking at consequences, as utilitarians maintain, is another issue. The present point is that the form they have is not consequentialist, does not indicate that we look at consequences, and hence is deontological.

Ethical Formalism

The standard deontological approach in contemporary ethical theory received its classic formulation in the writings of the German philosopher, Immanuel Kant. Both the contemporary deontological approach and Kant's are compatible with the Ten Commandments. But why should we obey these commands or why should we do what our parents, peers, or our society tell us to do? God, our parents, our peers, and our society may all correctly inform us what the right thing is to do. But the reason that the actions are right is not because they command them. Morality and moral obligation cannot be imposed upon us by others. We are the only ones who can impose them on ourselves. If we are moral we impose a certain way of acting on ourselves because we understand what it means to be a rational being and what sorts of actions are appropriate. For someone in the Kantian tradition, to be moral is the same as being rational. Just as no one can force us to be rational, no one can force us to be moral. If we choose to be rational, however, we at the same time choose to be moral. No reason can be given why we should be rational prior to our deciding to be so; to give reasons, to ask for them, or to be convinced by them are all rational activities and so presuppose the acceptance of reason.

If we wish to see more clearly what it means to be moral and what morality demands, we must analyze closely what it means to be rational and what the implications of being rational are for our actions. Since morality consists in acting rationally, it only applies to rational beings; the source of morality is to be found in ourselves and our reason and not in anything external to us. Since reason is the same in each of us, what is rational and moral is the same for all of us. We act morally according to this view when we knowingly choose to act in the way reason demands. The statement of what reason demands in the realm of action is the moral law. By analyzing reason as applied to action, which we can call practical reason, we find the key to morality.

The deontological tradition holds that what makes an action right is not its consequences but the fact that it conforms to the moral law. The test of conformity to the moral law which an action must pass is a formal one. An action is morally right if it has a certain *form*; it is morally wrong if it does not have that form. The moral law states the form which an action must have to be moral. The moral law, or the highest principle of morality, does not state what content an action must have to be a right action. It states only the form the action must have. This approach is therefore called a formalist ethical approach.

What is the form an action must have to be moral? How can we state the moral law? The answer lies in the nature of reason. Since being moral is the same as acting rationally, we can determine the moral law by analyzing the nature of reason itself and analyzing rational activity and what it means to be a rational being.

Consider what we know of reason from our examination of the reasoning we engage in when we do mathematics. Take the simple process of adding two plus two and getting four. Two plus two does not equal four only because our teachers said so. Two plus two equals four independently of our teachers. They equal four for everyone—for all rational beings. If we uncover the foundations of mathematics we come to understand why two plus two equals four. But even without such an understanding we know that two plus two equals four for everyone and that the validity of this addition does not depend on our experiencing two things and two other things equaling four things but that the mathematical operation is a self-consistent one.

Since the moral law is the statement of the form of a rational action, it will make explicit some of those characteristics which are central to reason. One of these is consistency. Moral actions must not be self-contradictory and, to the extent that we have a system of morality, moral actions must not contradict one another. A second characteristic is universality. Since reason is the same for all, what is rational for me is rational for everyone else and what is rational for anyone else is rational for me. A third characteristic of reason which we found exemplified in mathematics and which we also find characterizing the moral law is that it is a priori or not based on experience. It applies to experience but it is not derived from it, nor is its truth dependent on it. This is the reason why the morality of an action does not depend on consequences.

Since the moral law is a law, it issues a command or states an imperative—something which must be done. The imperative is an unconditional one. It states what everyone is to do because it is a command of reason. Following the somewhat technical terminology of Kant, the moral law commands categorically, not hypothetically. A hypothetical imperative states that an action should be done if, or on the hypothesis that, one wishes to achieve a certain end. Thus, "If you wish to do well in school, study!" is a hypothetical imperative. Not everyone is required to go to school and not everyone is required to study. The moral law, however, is not stated in hypothetical form. It is not something we can choose to follow or not, depending on whether we wish to achieve this or that end. We are bound by the injunction to be moral no matter what else we wish to do. The moral law binds unconditionally. Kant called the statement of the moral law, or of the supreme principle of morality, the Categorical Imperative. We noted that the Ten Commandments are also stated in categorical form. "Thou shalt not kill" states a moral norm or principle, applicable to all and binding on all unconditionally. But it is an imperative with content. It is therefore, according to the formalist approach, not the highest moral principle; rather, it is a principle, an imperative, a norm that is *a* moral principle because it is in accord with the moral law, but it is not *the* principle of morality. The highest moral principle—the Categorical Imperative—states the *form* which moral actions have and provides the criteria against which we can test whether an action or a principle is moral. Kant gave three formulations of the Categorical Imperative. These state three aspects of it or three formal conditions which an action must have if it is to be a moral action.

For an action to be a moral action: it must be consistently universalizable; it must respect rational beings as ends in themselves; and it must stem from and respect the autonomy of rational beings. These three conditions are all derivable from an analysis of reason and of what it means to be a rational being.

1. Universalization

Actions, strictly speaking, are specific intentional bodily movements that human beings do in a context and for a purpose. An action itself, therefore, cannot be universalized. It is what it is. Similarly, an action cannot contradict another action. We can avoid this difficulty, however, by speaking of a rule of action, a principle of action, or of the maxim of an action. It is the rule, principle, or maxim of an action that we test when we wish to determine whether an action is moral.

The a priori products of reason are universal and self-consistent. If an action is to be a moral action, it must have a rational form which means that the rule, principle, or maxim of the action must be capable of being consistently universalized. If an action is moral for me it must be moral for everyone. Since we are all commanded to do what is morally right, any action we are all commanded to do must be such that in doing it, none of us interferes with or precludes the other's doing it. An action which does not have this form is an immoral action. Note, moreover, that in asking whether the action can be consistently universalized we are not asking, from a consequentialist point of view what the results of everyone's doing that action would be. We need not suppose that everyone would do the action. We are inquiring whether the rule, principle, or maxim of the action can be consistently universalized.

Consider some examples to see how we can test the morality of an action. Is murder wrong? Is lying wrong? Let us define murder as the killing of a human being without a justifying reason. Defining it in this way, of course, characterizes it as unjustifiable from the start. So let us consider instead the action of killing another human being out of anger. Put as a rule it would read: "Kill others whenever you are angry at them." Can this rule be made consistently universal? The test is whether there is internal consistency within the rule when it is applied to everyone. Since it is likely that everyone gets angry at someone at some time, and since it is likely that everyone has had someone angry at him at some time, if everyone followed the rule, we would all kill each other off. It is not this consequence that makes the action immoral. Rather, if we all followed this rule none of us would be alive to continue following it. The rule, therefore, when made universal leads to its own demise. Therein lies its inconsistency. On the other hand, consider the action of respecting human life. The rule reads: "Respect human life." Make it universal. If made universal everyone would respect everyone else's life. The rule is consistent, for we can respect human life indefinitely. Following the rule does not lead to the rule's demise.

Now let's consider lying. The rule is: "Lie!" Can it be made consistently universal? The answer is that it cannot. If everyone lied then no one would believe anyone else. But if no one believed anyone else the possibility of lying would disappear. Hence lying cannot be made consistently universal. "Tell the truth!" however, is a rule everyone can always follow. If we all tell the truth we can all believe one another. We can indefinitely tell the truth. There is no inconsistency in the rule when it is made universal. Hence, it is a moral rule.

The formation of the Categorical Imperative which Kant gave concerning this condition of consistent universalization was: "Act only according to that maxim by which you can at the same time will that it should become a universal law" (*Foundations of the Metaphysics of Morals,* p. 44).

2. Respect for Rational Beings

A rational being can understand the need for consistency in action. A rational being is also conscious of himself as a person, as an entity who is valuable in himself, and as a being who is an end in itself. Because of this a rational being is worthwhile, has dignity, and is worthy of respect. Hence each person should be treated by every other person as an end, with respect and dignity.

We all use objects for our own purposes as means to our own ends. We also use people as a means to an ends when, for instance, they serve us in a store or restaurant or when we hire them to do what we want done. But even when we treat people as means we should not forget that they always remain ends. Thus, Kant formulated a second version of the Categorical Imperative as: "Act so that you treat humanity, whether in your own person or in that of another, always as an end and never as a means only" (p. 44).

This formulation of the Categorical Imperative, according to Kant, is simply a different statement of the supreme moral law contained in the first formulation. Consequently, it commands and forbids the same actions as the first formulation. Consider the two actions we examined earlier. If we kill people out of anger or to get them out of our way, we clearly do not treat them with respect. We use them exclusively as means to what we want and not as ends in themselves. When we lie to them we intend to deceive them, denying their right to the truth, and we wish to achieve our own ends at their expense. We treat them as the means by which we get what we want, or to avoid unpleasantness or punishment. Lying, theft, and murder all involve treating people as means only and not as ends, and therefore do not treat them with the respect they deserve as rational beings.

The kind of treatment which rational beings deserve as ends in themselves is sometimes put in terms of rights. People thus have the right to life, and this right imposes obligations on others not to take their life and, in certain conditions, to help them preserve it. A person's right to his property imposes the obligation on others not to take that property. This approach to rights maintains that people have rights because of the kinds of beings they are and denies that rights are dependent on consequences.

3. Autonomy

Since being moral is the same as acting rationally, morality is not imposed on persons from the outside. It is part of their nature. The moral law is recognized by them insofar as they recognize that they are rational beings and belong to the kingdom of beings who are ends in themselves. Moral law is self-imposed and self-recognized. This position does not deny that many people act only on the level of conventional morality. They may act in conformity with what the moral law commands when they act in conformity with conventional morality. But to have true personal moral worth their actions should be not only in conformity with the moral law but done with consciousness of the moral law and the fact they are obeying it.

There are three aspects of morality that are captured in the notion of autonomy: freedom, the self-imposition of the moral law, and the universal acceptability of the moral law.

Rational beings are the only entities that can be full-fledged members of the moral community because morality requires both the possibility of conceiving and understanding the moral law, and the possibility of knowingly and willingly acting in accordance with it. Animals are not moral beings because they fail in both these respects. They are not able to conceive the moral law, and they are not able to choose whether to act in accordance with it. Animals act from instinct and in reaction to immediate sensations. Human beings are able to inhibit and control their instincts, passions, and drives and are able to examine their actions before performing them. Their reason enables them to do so. The ability to so act carries with it the obligation to do so. This ability constitutes the freedom of the rational being. Nonrational entities that act only instinctively and in response to present stimuli are not free. They are determined by their instincts and stimuli. The ability to override instincts and stimuli constitutes the freedom of the human being. This freedom, which we can call the rational freedom of self-determination, becomes moral freedom when we choose to act in accordance with the moral law. This moral freedom can be called the rational freedom of self-perfection. The first type of freedom is a human being's ability to choose to act morally or immorally. But he acts morally only when he acts in accordance with the demands of reason. In acting this way he exercises his moral freedom and perfects himself from the moral point of view.

The second aspect of autonomy emphasizes the fact that moral beings give themselves the moral law. As ends in themselves, moral beings are not subservient to anyone else. Each determines the moral law for himself in accordance with reason. Each imposes it upon himself and accepts its demands for himself. This is simply a function of the rational being's freedom and of his dignity as an end in himself. But though each person gives himself the moral law he cannot prescribe anything he wants. He is bound by reason and its demands. Since reason is the same for all rational beings, we each give ourselves the same moral law. The Categorical Imperative is the same for all of us, though imposed by each of us and recognized by each of us for ourselves. Kant's third formulation of the Categorical Imperative is: "Act only so that the will through its maxims could regard itself at the same time as universally lawgiving (p. 59)."

The third aspect of autonomy, the universal acceptability of the moral law, is a function of the fact that each moral being gives himself the moral law. This aspect provides a test of moral rules or principles. If we wish to see whether a rule, principle, or maxim is a moral law we should ask if what the rule commands would be acceptable to all rational beings acting rationally. Hence in considering murder, lying, theft, and so on, we must consider the action not only from the point of view of the agent of the action but also from the point of view of the receiver—the person who is murdered, lied to, or stolen from. Rational beings will all see that they do not want murder, lying, and theft to be universal moral laws. They do not want to be murdered, lied to, stolen from. It is not simply a matter, however, of their own good being violated, though it is also that. As rational beings they also accept limitations on what they permit themselves to do, for they understand that they live in a community. Each sees the necessity of restricting his own actions as he expects others to restrict theirs. The test of the morality of a rule is not whether people in fact accept it. The test is whether all rational beings, thinking rationally, would accept it regardless of whether they were the agents or the receivers of the actions.

Application of the Moral Law

The moral law, or the ultimate principle of morality according to the dominant deontological position, requires that any moral rule or principle must be capable of being consistently universalized, must respect the dignity of persons, and must be acceptable to rational beings. Any action ruled out by one of these criteria should be ruled out by the other two. But sometimes one of the tests is clearer and leads more obviously to a moral evaluation than another. In testing whether the principle of an action is moral, therefore, it is prudent to apply all three tests. If the principle passes all three, it is moral; if it fails any one of the three, it is immoral.

There are two difficulties in attempting to apply this test to actions. One involves determining the level of generality of the principle on which we are acting; the second involves a clash between the actions which two moral principles command.

1. The Level of Generality

Consider once again the case of the airplane manufacturer who wishes to save his company and feels that in order to do so he must bribe a potential foreign purchaser. What is the principle on which he is acting? We might consider the principle to be: "Bribe!" If we attempt to universalize this principle, we quickly see that it is self-contradictory. If bribery were made a universal principle it would no longer be bribery but a universal way of doing business. Bribery only works when there is a background of nonbribery. For it is a way of gaining special advantage. If everyone always gained advantage in this way, the advantage would no longer be special. Universal bribery is self-contradictory. Hence it is immoral. Bribery also fails the second and third tests. However, one failure is enough to make clear its immoral status.

The airplane manufacturer, however, might protest that he was not acting on the principle "Bribe!" He would not advocate everyone always bribing everyone else. Rather, he advocates bribery only in certain select circumstances. The principle might be: "Bribe only when necessary to keep your company from going bankrupt!" Hence the test of universality requires only that all companies threatened with bankruptcy engage in bribery, not that all companies do so. Since the other companies do not engage in bribery, they form the necessary background for the bribery to be successful. Consider this principle. Would rational beings accept this principle as reasonable? Would everyone agree that a company facing bankruptcy should act in this way? Why should a company which is so managed as to be facing bankruptcy be allowed to gain special advantage? No company competing with other companies is likely to accept such a principle; nor are the people of a society who will eventually pay for the bribe in higher prices. The principle clearly fails the third test, and hence is immoral.

The point of the airplane manufacturer, however, is partially correct. We can construe the principle of actions more or less broadly. When we considered the injunction: "Kill other human beings!" we saw that it could not be made universal without contradiction. But does this mean that self-defense is immoral? Most people would argue that it is not. Hence, "Kill an unjust attacker if that is the only way you can defend innocent life whether in your own person or that of another!" can be made universal. It respects innocent life above that of the unjust attacker and and would be accepted upon rational consideration by everyone. It is an exception, therefore, to the general injunction: "Do not kill!" The injunction we should ultimately test is the injunction not to kill, together with all its exceptions. That would be a full statement of the principle concerning killing. It is sufficient, however, to test portions of it in considering particular cases. It is not always easy to state accurately the principle of an action or to test it. It is also not always easy to be completely honest with oneself in stating the principle on which one is really acting. We are frequently tempted to fabricate a maxim which will allow us to do what we wish rather than stating the maxim or principle on which we are actually acting.

2. The Clash of Moral Rules

The Categorical Imperative or supreme principle of morality involves in itself no conflict, and principles or maxims of actions which are in accord with it can each be made universal without contradiction. But there are circumstances in which two moral rules or principles, each of which is self-consistent, clash. Such clashes pose a moral dilemma. If we cannot follow either of the rules without violating the other rule, we necessarily violate one of them. We do what we should not do. Are we in such cases forced to do what is immoral? We cannot have a moral obligation to do what is immoral. This would be a contradiction; for we would both have the moral obligation to do and to refrain from doing the action. How can we escape the dilemma?

Suppose that in a slaveholding society we are hiding a runaway slave. The slave-owner comes to the door and asks if we are hiding the slave. Should we lie and oppose the immoral institution of slavery or tell the truth and cooperate in that immoral institution?

In attempting to resolve this and similar cases we should first make sure that we are really facing a dilemma. Is there some third way of acting by which we can avoid performing any action that violates the Categorical Imperative? Could we, in response to the question not answer but faint? Would fainting preclude the necessity of answering the question and still protect the slave? If it would not solve the problem and no other strategy would, then we must face the dilemma head-on and attempt to resolve it.

There are two standard ways of resolving such dilemmas. One is to construct the principle of an action in such a way that it allows the exception needed in the resolution of the given case. We construct the principle allowing us to lie and we construct the principle allowing us to participate in slavery. We then ask which can be made universal, which respects human beings and which would be universally acceptable to rational beings? The answer is not always clear. Hence arguments must be given, for instance, about how lying in this case respects human beings, and if it does not respect them why it is permitted. Someone might argue that the slaveholder has no right to knowledge of where his slave is since slavery is immoral. Hence, in not giving him the information he requests we are not denying him anything he rightfully deserves as a person. We are thus not denying him respect and so not treating him as a means only.

A second approach to such a problem views each moral rule as a prima facie moral rule. A prima facie rule is one which is in general binding. But when several prima facie moral rules apply, and when we cannot fulfill all of them, then they are not all morally binding. Our actual moral duty is to obey that prima facie moral rule appropriate in the given case. How are we to decide which prima facie duty is our actual moral duty? One answer, defended by some philosophers, is that when we carefully compare conflicting duties we come to see which takes precedence. Reasons, however, can and usually should be given as to why one rule takes precedence over another. These reasons constitute the justification for breaking a prima facie moral rule. In doing so we are not acting immorally, since prima facie rules do not express binding moral obligations but rather, simply state rules that are generally moral and are our actual moral obligations in those cases in which there is no conflict of moral rules.

In the example of our hiding the runaway slave we are faced with two prima facie moral rules. One is "Do not lie." The other is "Do not engage in or abet slavery." Each rule is one we should follow. But if they conflict, and if we cannot follow both, then we must decide which one takes precedence in this case. The one which takes precedence states our actual moral duty. In weighing the two rules we can argue that slavery is a greater evil and does more violence to the respect due human beings. Hence, using the criterion of respect for persons in evaluating both rules, we see that our obligation to prevent someone from being a slave is greater than our obligation not to lie to a slaveholder seeking his slave.

Using the notion of prima facie obligations we can incorporate much of utilitarianism into a deontological ethical position. The command "Produce the greatest amount of good for the greatest number of people affected by an action" can be considered a prima facie moral obligation. It states a rule or principle which can be universalized, which respects people as ends, and which can be rationally accepted by all. However, from a deontological point of view, this rule or principle is not the highest moral principle. Hence, if what it commands comes into conflict with some other moral principle, (e.g., that of justice), it might have to give way. This approach will not satisfy the utilitarian since he argues that utilitarianism states only the highest moral principle. Yet it does satisfy many people who feel that utilitarianism states a moral principle, while admitting there are others as well. It is often difficult, when moral principles clash, to decide which takes precedence. In these cases both individuals and society should very carefully and objectively consider the various arguments in support of opposing positions. When a clear decision is not available and one is forced to act, he should act on the basis of the strongest arguments available.

Justice and Rights

Deontologists claim that justice and rights are not derivable from a utilitarian calculation and that they do not depend on weighing the consequences of actions. Giving people what they deserve or what is their due may not be the best use of resources from the point of view of utility; however, this fact does not lessen their right to what they deserve nor the justice of giving them what they deserve.

Justice consists, in one of its formulations, in treating equals equally and unequals unequally, and in giving each person his due. There are various ways of construing what each person is due, however. Each person might be given what he is due according to his work, his ability, his merit, his need, or according to some other criterion. Each criteria might be appropriate for certain purposes and in certain conditions. When the male head of a household was the typical wage earner in society, it was generally considered just to pay him more than a single male or a female for the same work. The rationale was that the male head of the household had more mouths to feed and therefore needed more money. But as the social structure changed and women entered the workforce in greater number, the just thing to do became to pay people equally for equal work, regardless of their personal obligations to support a family.

There are also different kinds of justice.Compensatory justice consists in compensating someone for a past injustice or making good some harm he or she has suffered in the past. Retributive justice concerns punishment due a law-breaker or evil-doer. Procedural justice is a term used to designate fair decision procedures, practices, or agreements. Distributive justice involves the distribution of benefits and burdens, usually by the state.

The contemporary American philosopher John Rawls has formulated an influential theory of justice. The technique by which he defends it is Kantian in its approach. He attempts to arrive at principles of distributive justice which are acceptable to all rational persons. The principles would thus be universal, would respect all persons, and be rationally acceptable to all. In order to find such principles, he suggests we perform a thought experiment. Let us imagine that all people are behind a "veil of ignorance." Behind that veil we would know that we are rational human beings and that we value our own good. But we would not know whether we are rich or poor, members of the upper or lower class, talented or untalented, handicapped or physically and mentally fit, white, black, or a member of some other race, male or female, and so on. The question we are to ask ourselves is: what principles would we call just or fair if we did not know what place we would have in society? This technique is a useful one if we wish to achieve objectivity in our moral judgments. It is a technique which we can generalize beyond the use to which Kant puts it. It can help us apply the test of autonomous acceptability to any principle or rule we wish to consider, though to determine our answer we must sometimes build in more knowledge on the part of those behind the veil of ignorance than Rawls allows in his consideration of the basic principles of justice arrived at from what he calls the "original position" behind the veil of ignorance.

Rawls argues that behind the veil of ignorance people would agree to two principles of justice. In their simplest formulation in *A Theory of Justice* Rawls states the two principles as follows:

"First: each person is to have an equal right to the most extensive basic liberty compatible with similar liberty for others.

Second: social and economic inequalities are to be arranged so that they are both (a) reasonably expected to be to everyone's advantage, and (b) attached to positions and offices open to all" (p. 60).

The first principle guarantees the equal liberty of each person at a maximal level compatible with the same liberty for everyone else. Everyone wants as much freedom to achieve his ends as possible; freedom is a function of rationality and respect for it is respect for people. Each person under this rule is to be treated equally. Hence the first principle fulfills the requirements of the moral law, is morally justifiable, and would be accepted by all rational people. In the political realm this principle guarantees each person equal political freedom, protection by law, and equal treatment before the law.

The second principle is more controversial. It has an egalitarian thrust, which some critics deny justice requires. The second part of this principle requires equality of opportunity and access to positions and offices. This is generally accepted. But the first part allows for inequalities of wealth and income, influence and prestige. It claims that such inequalities are acceptable to all only if the least advantaged group is better off as a result of them. For instance, if given the choice between two societies, one of which had a standard of living of 100 for all members of the society and another of which had a standard of living ranging from 150 to 200 for all members of the society, it would be rational for everyone to choose the latter. Although all are not equal in that society—some live better than others—all are better off. Though the second part of the principle demands equal opportunity, the first part allows for inequalities of success, providing all are better off because of it. The justification for capitalism is sometimes framed in this way. Since all are free to compete, some fare better than others. But the competition increases productivity, raising everyone's standard of living. Hence all are better off than they would otherwise be.

The second principle is attacked both by those who claim the condition is too strong and by those who claim it is too weak. The former say that as long as there is equal opportunity, there is no injustice in some benefiting from their skill, work, ingenuity, or from the risks they take. They deserve more than others, and their benefit need not be conditioned by its also producing benefit for the least advantaged group in society. Those who claim the principle is too weak argue that the inequalities allowed may be so great as to be obviously unjust. The principle, they argue, allows the very, very rich to get very much richer as long as the very, very poor get only a little less poor. This, they claim, is unacceptable.

Exactly which principles or practices people would agree to behind the veil of ignorance can be and is disputed. But there are some principles rational people would agree to, and using the veil of ignorance is a useful technique for choosing principles.

The two principles of justice do not handle all questions of justice, but they do suggest an approach and provide a framework for a fruitful social discussion of justice.

If we are faced with the question of whether discrimination in hiring is just, we can step behind the veil of ignorance and ask if we did not know whether we would be male or female, black or white, would we prefer a system in which there was discrimination or in which there was none? The strategy is to ask if we were to be assigned our place in society by our worst enemy, would we pick one or the other system. The point does not hinge on whether or not we are gamblers and risk-takers. Rather, the point is whether we would all accept the system or structure as just, prior to knowing which place we occupied in it. If all rational people would accept the system or practice, then it would be just.

The notion of moral rights is another important and currently debated topic within the deontological approach to ethics. Moral rights are said to be important, normative, justifiable claims or entitlements. The right to life or the right not to be killed by others is a justifiable claim based on our status as rational beings and as ends-in-ourselves. Does our status as rational beings confer other rights on us? What are these and how can they be defended? The American Founding Fathers spoke in the Declaration of Independence of the natural rights of life, liberty, and the pursuit of happiness. John Locke had earlier spoken of the natural right to property. Today we speak of human rights, rather than natural rights. Some of these are rights vis-à-vis government; some vis-à-vis other people. Legal rights are rooted in law and protected by it. Moral rights are rooted in morality and in the nature of the members of the moral community.

The language of rights is frequently abused. People have claimed a wide variety of rights. Whether they can be justified is the crucial question. The way moral rights are justified is by presenting moral arguments of the type we have seen in this and the preceding chapter.

Moral argumentation and reasoning are frequently difficult and our conclusions on particular disputed issues are often tentative. The process of moral reasoning is a continuous individual and social endeavor, applicable to business as well as to all other spheres of life. The tools applicable in this endeavor are knowledge of ethical principles and mastery of the techniques of utilitarian and deontological moral argumentation. For most practical issues of business ethics, we need not resolve all the philosophical disputes between the utilitarians and the deontologists. Despite their differing approaches in the great majority of cases, either method, if carefully, subtly, and conscientiously applied, will produce the same moral conclusions with respect to the morality of the practice or act. This should not be surprising, since there is general agreement on the morality of most acts. Sometimes one approach is easier to apply than another or yields clearer results. Some people prefer one approach to another. When different approaches lead to different moral evaluations, care should be taken to review the accuracy and completeness of each analysis. If the conclusions still diverge, we must ultimately decide on the basis of which argument is stronger or clearer and which result coheres better with our other moral judgments. If forced to act, we should do so with the realization that we may be mistaken. Despite possible disagreements both a deontological approach and a utilitarian approach to moral issues provide powerful and widely used techniques of moral argumentation useful in resolving an individual's moral problems and in reaching a consensus on public policy.

Further Reading

Aristotle. *The Nicomachean Ethics.* Translated by Sir David Ross. London: Oxford University Press, Inc., 1961.

Daniels, Norman, ed. *Reading Rawls: Critical Studies of A Theory of Justice.* New York: Basic Books, Inc., 1974.

Kant, Immanuel. *Foundations of the Metaphysics of Morals.* Text and Critical Essays edited by Robert Paul Wolff. New York/Indianapolis: The Bobbs-Merrill Co., Inc., 1969.

Martin, Rex, and Nickel, James. "Recent Work on the Concept of Rights." In *American Philosophical Quarterly,* XIX (1980), pp. 165–180.

Nozick, Robert. *Anarchy, State, and Utopia.* New York: Basic Books, Inc., 1974.

Olafson, Frederick A., ed. *Justice and Social Policy.* Englewood Cliffs, N.J.: Prentice-Hall (Spectrum Books), 1961.

Paton, H.J. *The Categorical Imperative.* Chicago: University of Chicago Press, 1948.

Rawls, John. *A Theory of Justice.* Cambridge, Mass.: Harvard University Press, 1971.

Ross, W.D. *The Right and the Good.* Oxford: The Clarendon Press, 1930.

5

Moral Responsibility

Obligation and responsibility are closely related. In general we have an obligation or a duty to fulfill our responsibilities and we are responsible for fulfilling our obligations. Yet duty and responsibility are not the same.

There are many kinds of responsibility. Parents are responsible for their children—for raising them, feeding them, and caring for them. Hence we speak of parental responsibility. There are responsibilities of citizenship—the responsibility which goes with public office and positions of trust. Certain responsibilities also go with one's job and with one's place in an organization. Some of these responsibilities are legal responsibilities, some are moral responsibilities, some are both, and some are neither.

In a general sense each of us is responsible for all of his or her actions. For instance, if I drop and break a friend's expensive vase, I am responsible for breaking it. If, while I am driving a car, a child suddenly dashes out in front of me and I hit him before I can apply the brake, I am responsible for hitting him. In neither case may I be morally responsible; yet if someone asks who broke the vase or who hit the child, the answer is that I am responsible. In what sense am I responsible? I am *causally responsible* in each case. I was the cause of the broken vase and I was the cause of the injured child.

Causal responsibility is an ingredient in both moral and

legal responsibility. The causal chain sometimes is a long one. If I give a command which a number of people transmit until it is finally carried out, both the one who carries out the action and the one issuing the command are responsible for it, though each is responsible in a different way in the causal chain. Usually we are most concerned with the proximate cause in the chain, with the person doing the action in question. Sometimes, especially in questions of agency, the originator of the chain also bears responsibility for the action.

For an action to be a moral action it must be done knowingly and willingly. For instance, though I am causally responsible for things I do in my sleep, I am not morally responsible for them. Actions I do in my sleep are neither moral nor immoral. When we say that I am *morally responsible* for an action, then we mean both that I did the action, (i.e., that I am the cause of the result of the action), and that I did the action knowingly and willingly. Instead of saying that I did the action knowingly and willingly, we might say that I did it intentionally. The important point is that I was not forced to do it, that I had a choice, that I knew what I was doing, and that I did it deliberately. There are degrees of knowledge and degrees of deliberation; there are accordingly degrees of moral responsibility also.

Excusing Conditions

Moral responsibility may be lessened or mitigated in a number of ways. The conditions which diminish moral responsibility are known as *excusing conditions*. These conditions provide the reasons for lessening or cancelling moral responsibility and are related in one way or another to the conditions necessary for a moral action. Excusing conditions fall into one of three categories: those conditions which preclude the possibility of the action; those conditions which preclude or diminish the required knowledge; and those conditions which preclude or diminish the required freedom.

1. Conditions Precluding the Possibility of Action

To be morally obligatory, an action must be possible. We do not have an obligation to do what is impossible. Likewise, we cannot be morally responsible for doing what is impossible. We are relieved of moral responsibility in those cases in which we cannot fulfill what is demanded of us. The impossibility of doing an action may be a function of the type of action in question, of particular circumstances, or of my lack of ability. I am excused from moral responsibility if: (a) the action in question is an impossible one to perform; (b) if I do not have the ability required in the given case; (c) if the opportunity for my performing the action is absent; and (d) if the circumstances are beyond my control.

For instance, assuming that I had been driving carefully, observing the speed limit and with due attention (i.e., assuming that I had been driving responsibly), I am not morally responsible for running over the child who darts in front of my car if it was impossible for me to stop the car before hitting him. If I do not know how to swim, I cannot be morally responsible for letting someone drown if the only way I could possibly have saved him was by swimming out to him. Nor, if I knew how to swim, could I have the moral responsibility for saving him if I were not at the scene of the drowning and there was no reason why I should have been there. Likewise, if as I swam out to him he was attacked and killed by a shark, that is a circumstance beyond my control, and it excuses me from moral responsibility for his death. These are just four examples of excusing conditions related to the possibility of performing the action.

2. Conditions Precluding or Diminishing Required Knowledge

Since knowledge and will are necessary for moral actions, moral responsibility is lessened or removed when these aspects are less than fully present or when they are entirely absent. With respect to knowledge we can distinguish two excusing conditions: (a) excusable ignorance, and (b) invincible ignorance. Both are failures of knowledge. We are morally responsible for our actions and for the consequences of the things we do. But we cannot possibly know all the consequences of our actions. Which ones are we morally responsible for? We are morally responsible for the immediate and obvious consequences of our actions, as well as for the other reasonably foreseeable consequences of them. Our lack of knowledge may be either about the circumstances giving rise to a particular responsibility or about the consequences of our actions. Lack of knowledge is excusable if through no fault of our own we did not know the circumstances or the consequences. Ignorance, however, does not excuse us from moral responsibility if we could have and should have known the circumstances or consequences. A common test of whether ignorance is excusable is whether the average person of good will would have known the circumstances or considered the possibility of the consequences in question. Invincible ignorance is an excusing condition since we cannot be morally expected to know what it is impossible for us to know.

Is everyone who was involved in the production of the atomic bomb responsible for it and for the uses to which it has been and might be put? The atom bomb was developed in such a way in the United States that many people did not know what they were working on. Different people were responsible for working on different portions of its development frequently without any knowledge of the nature of the project as a whole. Many people working in laboratories were responsible for only particular portions of the bomb. They were told that their work was secret and that they would not know the type of end product to which their work was contributing. In many cases they had assurances that what they were working on would help the United States win World War II. Though we can say they were partially responsible for producing the atom bomb in a causal sense, they were not responsible in a moral sense. Adequate knowledge was lacking and its absence was morally acceptable. What about the leaders of the project? Should we hold the scientists who developed the atom bomb responsible for its use? Could they reasonably have foreseen the uses to which it would be put? They certainly knew that once developed it could be used to destroy both cities and the people in them. In wartime that might have been a legitimate use. But suppose tomorrow some country which has developed the bomb uses it to attack and destroy a neighboring country or uses it as a means of extortion. Were the scientists who originally developed the bomb responsible for its immoral use later on by others? Could they and should they have foreseen such uses? These questions are not easy to answer. Many scientists have pondered their moral responsibility in this area. We can say that those who were ignorant of the nature of the project are free of moral responsibility for its production. We can also say with some confidence that no one could have foreseen all the uses to which the development of atomic bombs would be put. The moral responsibility for the use of these weapons in immoral ways is much greater for those who decide to use them immorally than for those who originally developed them. We do not hold those who invented gunpowder morally responsible for all the harm that has been done with it, most of which they could not possibly have imagined. The degree of moral responsibility is a function of our knowledge, and an absence of knowledge may diminish or remove our moral responsibility.

3. Conditions Precluding or Diminishing Required Freedom

The third set of excusing conditions has to do with impairments or impediments to our freely choosing the action in question. We can distinguish four: (a) the absence of alternatives; (b) lack of control; (c) external coercion; and (d) internal coercion.

(a) If there is only one possible action that I can perform and there are really no other alternatives, not even that of nonperformance of the action, I cannot be said to have chosen the action, though I may or may not consent to it. By extension, if there is no reasonable alternative to the action that I perform, then my moral responsibility for it is lessened.

(b) Lack of control extends to a number of different kinds of cases. In some instances it removes all moral responsibility; in others it diminishes it. For instance, actions which I do in my sleep are actions over which I have no control and for which I am not morally responsible. Similarly, if I faint, and in the process knock over a lamp which starts a fire, I am not morally responsible for starting the fire.

(c) External coercion or compulsion either diminishes moral responsibility or removes it, depending on the coercion and the alternatives. If I am a bank teller and a bank robber puts a gun to my head and tells me to hand over the money in my cash drawer, I am giving him the money under compulsion and am not morally responsible for giving away the bank's money. There are various more subtle types of compulsion, however, which pose difficult problems. Suppose my boss tells me to falsify a report and also tells me that unless I do so, I shall be fired. Suppose further that I am deeply in debt due to the illness of my wife, and that I am unlikely to be able to find another job that pays as well as this one. Am I morally relieved of my responsibility not to falsify documents because of the coercion applied by my superior? The details of the case must be more fully examined before we can answer the question satisfactorily. But even with this sketchy information, if I do sign as commanded, I am less morally guilty than if I had falsified the documents without any outside compulsion. External compulsion may involve the use of physical force, the threat of death or violence to one's self or to others, or the threat or use of other kinds of pressures. Not all such pressures constitute excusing conditions. The kind and degree of external compulsion must be carefully considered and the criterion of what the ordinary rational person of good will would expect and demand of himself is the best we sometimes have to work with.

(d) Internal compulsions can be divided into two kinds. One is the clinically abnormal, and the other is the normal. Let's suppose we are told that a kleptomaniac is forced to steal by some inner compulsion over which he has no control. If he is actually forced to steal and has no choice, he is not morally responsible for his action. Other abnormal psychological conditions that drive a person to do what he does diminish his responsibility. Normal people are also sometimes overcome by passions which they say they cannot or could not control such as a sorrow or rage, lust or hate. Each person is morally obliged to control his passions and dominate them. But there are possibly cases in which through no fault of the person in question passions dominate him and lead him to perform some immoral action. Such internal compulsion provides an excusing condition and mitigates the agent's moral responsibility. The law also recognizes such conditions as excusing to some extent; for instance, a murder of passion is a less serious crime than a premeditated one.

Excusing conditions supply reasonable ways for lessening or precluding moral responsibility. But they must be used with care if we wish to assess accurately the moral responsibility of ourselves and of others. For instance, if I drive recklessly and I run over a child, does the fact I was drunk lessen my moral responsibility for hitting the child? If I got drunk knowingly and willingly, the answer is no. For though in my drunken state I had less control over the car than I would have had otherwise, and though in a sense I could not help hitting the child, I should have foreseen that one of the possible consequences might be such an accident when I decided to both drink and drive. I am morally responsible for the foreseeable results of my actions. How far people are reasonably expected to foresee the results of their actions in business and the use to which their products might be put is not always an easy question to answer. Many engineers and scientists have appropriately worried about the possible bad uses to which their research, discoveries, and inventions, might be put. They are responsible for the products they create even though they will not control the uses to which they are put. The problem of how much moral responsibility a manufacturer has for the use to which his product is put is a similar question. If a handgun is used to kill a shopkeeper during a robbery, the gunman is responsible for the death. Is the person who sold him the gun, the company that manufactured the gun, and the person who designed the gun also responsible? How far back do we go in the causal chain? What about the steel company which provided the metal to the gunmaker and the iron ore company which provided the iron to the steelmaker? Obviously the further back we go, the more remote the cause and the less likely that the person could have reasonably foreseen that particular consequence or could reasonably be held responsible. For instance, thalidomide caused a large number of birth deformities, and many parents sued the manufacturer. We assume that the doctors who prescribed the drug did so in ignorance of the drug's bad consequences, as did the druggists who sold it and the women who took it. If they acted in invincible ignorance, they are absolved of moral blame. Whether the drug company could have and should have known of the bad effects is a question we cannot answer without detailed investigation, though the company was equally liable for the effects of the drug.

The doctrine of excusing conditions is used by some people in such a way as to remove moral responsibility entirely for certain immoral acts or to remove moral responsibility entirely from everyone. In defense of those accused of murder, for instance, some argue that anyone who commits a murder must be at least temporarily insane. They are not responsible for their actions because they did not know what they were doing or had no control over their actions. Others who believe that people are completely determined in all their actions sometimes argue that all of us act from internal compulsions of such a kind that we never really choose between actions. We are determined to do whatever actions we perform, our feeling of choice is an illusion, and we are as truly compelled to do whatever we do (i.e., the kleptomaniac is compelled to steal). Such a view does not take adequate account of our common human experience and of our ability to distinguish between acts of kleptomania and those of purposeful stealing. Such distinctions are sufficient to sort out different kinds of cases, varying degrees of consent and knowledge , and hence varying degrees of moral responsibility.

Liability and Accountability

Moral responsibility is closely connected to a number of other concepts besides duty and obligation, possibility, knowledge, freedom, and choice. These include liability, accountability, agency, praise, blame, intention, pride, shame, remorse, conscience, and character. Liability for one's actions means that one can rightly be made to pay for the adverse effects of one's actions on others. Automobile liability insurance for drivers, for instance, is intended to cover the costs of damage to other persons or property. We are liable for such payments as long as we are causally responsible for the damage. If we accidentally run into another car, we do not do so intentionally. Yet we are liable for the damage we do. Liability, therefore, does not necessarily involve moral responsibility for the action. We may be morally (as well as legally) liable to make good the damage we do to others even if we are not morally responsible for the action. In many cases, however, the excusing conditions which apply to moral responsibility also apply to moral liability. We may be liable to punishment, blame, or censure, for an action we do knowingly and willingly but not for similar consequences which we produce unwittingly or accidentally.

Legal liability can be fit into a similar pattern of analysis with respect to individuals. Businesses, however, are often bound by laws of *strict liability*. Strict liability means that no excusing conditions are accepted or applicable. For instance, several people recently died of food poisoning. The cause was botulism that developed in cans of seafood which had tiny holes in the can cover. The packer did not intend to poison anyone, and no one intentionally punctured the can covers. Yet the packer was legally liable under rules of strict liability and was successfully sued for damages by the relatives of those killed. Corporations are formed, among other reasons, to limit the liability of owners or shareholders to the amount represented by their shares. The personal assets of the shareholders are not liable to seizure.

Accountability is the obligation of giving (or of being prepared if called upon to give) an account of one's actions. The account should explain the reasonableness, appropriateness, correctness, legality, or morality of the action. Accountability might be moral, legal, or other. One is accountable for one's actions and the consequences thereof. One is accountable to oneself and one is properly accountable to others for actions which affect them. An agent acting for others is also accountable for the actions and failures to act with respect to the domain covered by his agency. Financial accounting is one familiar way in which an agent justifies or accounts for his actions with respect to a business.

Moral accountability consists in being prepared to render a moral account of an action done either for ourselves or as agents for others. We appropriately give an account of those things for which we are responsible. A moral account of our actions is not always given explicitly in moral terms. For instance we might give an account in financial terms through a financial report in which we list income and expenditures (which we can justify if called on to do so). The report is an account of our handling of the funds on the assumption that it is accurate, contains all income and expenditures, and balances.

Within a firm or organization moral accountability may be structured or unstructured. Organizational accountability is frequently structured hierarchically with those below accountable to those above, but not vice versa. Moral accountability is not determined only by organizational structure, however. Each person is morally accountable to those whom his actions affect. Only rarely will he be called to account. For most actions fall within an acceptable range. They need no special justification because they form part of the large class of generally acceptable actions.

We are morally responsible in the sense of being liable and in the sense of being accountable for our action and failures to act. Broadly speaking we are morally responsible for all our actions; more narrowly, we are responsible for fulfilling our obligations. We are responsible to ourselves, since we are rational agents and follow the moral law. Hence we appropriately hold ourselves morally responsible, and if we wish to be moral we appropriately assume moral responsibility. We may also take on particular moral responsibilities as a result of contracts, agreements, special relationships, or prior commitments. If we act immorally, we appropriately feel moral guilt. Since, when we act immorally we do not act in accordance with our true ends, we appropriately feel moral shame. Moral remorse is the feeling of sorrow for our immoral actions together with an intention not to perform similar actions in the future. These emotions result from self-evaluation.

Because we all belong to the moral community, we can also ascribe moral responsibility to others, hold them morally liable, and appropriately demand a moral accounting of their actions insofar as they affect us, the organization or group to which we jointly belong, or society as a whole. Though we ascribe moral responsibility, it may not be assumed by the one to whom we ascribe it, and he may not agree to render an account. We can ascribe moral praise and blame for the actions of others and attempt to induce moral guilt, shame, or remorse.

As human beings develop, they tend to adopt patterns of actions and dispositions to act in certain ways. These dispositions viewed collectively are sometimes called character. A person who tends habitually to act as he morally should has a good character. If he resists strong temptation, he has a strong character. If he habitually acts immorally, he has a morally bad character. If despite good intentions he frequently succumbs to temptation, he has a weak character. Since character is formed by conscious actions, in general people are morally responsible for their characters as well as for their individual actions.

Conscience is the ability to reason about the morality of an action, together with a set of values, feelings, and dispositions to do or avoid certain actions. Conscience is something that every rational being has insofar as he is rational. But we can act against our conscience and can stifle it, as well as act in accordance with it. Though we give ourselves the moral law, we are all fallible, and so conscience must be informed, developed, trained, and corrected. We are morally responsible or obliged to act in accordance with our conscience; but we are equally responsible or obliged to develop an objectively correct conscience.

Failure to fulfill one's responsibilities sometimes leads not only to blame, shame, and remorse but also to punishment. We are liable to punishment if we do certain actions and are not able to provide any sufficient excusing conditions. The threat of punishment is a means of motivating people to act morally and responsibly, and to accept their responsibility. Yet justice demands that punishment be meted out only to those responsible for the actions in question. The innocent, or those not responsible for actions, should not be punished for them. Those more responsible deserve more punishment than those less responsible. Diminished responsibility because of excusing conditions rightfully diminishes the severity of the punishment appropriate for an action.

Agent Moral Responsibility

We saw earlier that the causal chain in an action may sometimes be a long one. If one person acts for another person, we can often correctly say that the second person is acting as an agent for the first person. We can accordingly speak of agent responsibility. Such responsibility is frequently found in business; it is often complex and it raises a number of special types of problems.

Consider first the simple case of agency in which one person acts for another.

A lawyer draws up a contract for a client. He acts as agent for the client, doing what the client wishes but is unable to do for himself. The lawyer draws up the kind of contract the client wants with the provisions he desires. The client is morally responsible for the contents of the contract, since they represent his desires. The lawyer is simply an agent for the client. But the lawyer also has moral responsibility for his actions which he cannot dismiss simply because he acts as an agent for another. He cannot morally do what is immoral simply because he acts for another.

In a large organization the chain of agency frequently involves many people hierarchically related to one another. This raises problems of moral responsibility both for those at the top of the ladder and for those lower down the chain.

Suppose the president of a corporation tells his vice-president that costs have to be cut in a certain division of the corporation. He does not say how the cuts are to be made. He leaves that up to the vice-president. The vice-president in turn decides that the cuts have to come from a certain section of his operation and tells the manager below him that certain cuts have to be made. The chain continues until finally, at the end of the line, corners are cut, endangering people's lives. Those near the end of the line feel that they are forced to do what they do. They have received their orders and the options open to them are limited. They may not want to cut the corners they cut; but they feel that the responsibility for their actions belongs to those above them. They did not initiate the action or the practice; they are just following orders. The president of the company in his turn does not see the specific results of the order he gave to the vice-president. He is far removed from its concrete implementation. He feels that those below him should be given the authority to make decisions, and he does not feel he should second-guess them as long as they perform well. He did not intend to cause the particular dangers to which people at the receiving end might be exposed. He did not intend that anything immoral or unjust take place. Hence, at both ends of the chain, the people involved feel that the actions are actions for which they are not morally responsible. Those at the bottom claim they had no other choice, were simply following orders, did not initiate the policy, and hence are not responsible for its effects.

The absence of the feeling of moral responsibility, however, does not indicate an absence of it. The delegation of authority to carry out a command or policy does not relieve the delegator of the moral responsibility for how the command or policy is carried out. We are morally responsible both for our actions and for the foreseeable consequences thereof. The diminished feeling of moral responsibility is psychologically understandable but it is not therefore excusable. Similarly, those near the bottom of the chain may find themselves forced to do what they would not on their own choose to do. They may wish to deny moral responsibility for their actions and feel that they are not morally responsible for them. Yet they remain moral agents and therefore cannot deny moral responsibility for their actions.

Agency moral responsibility, especially in large organizations, poses a variety of problems, some of which we shall investigate more closely in later chapters.

The Moral Responsibility of Nations
and Formal Organizations

Moral responsibility is usually both ascribed to and assumed by individuals. Does it make any sense to speak of the moral responsibility of nations, corporations, and of other formal organizations? If it does make sense to do so, do we mean the same thing by the terms "moral responsibility" in these cases as we do when referring to human individuals?

If we start from ordinary usage, people clearly refer to the actions of some nations as immoral; they speak of the moral responsibilities of rich nations vis-à-vis poor ones; they claim that corporations which sell unsafe or harmful products act immorally. Yet there is a strong position adopted by people like Milton Friedman, and by organizational theorists like John Simon, who seem to hold that corporations and other formal organizations are not moral entities. They are legal beings at best. They can be held legally liable, and they can be bound by laws. But, according to them, only human beings are moral agents and only human beings have moral responsibility. Some people may speak as if corporations or businesses had moral obligations; but they are simply confused. Moreover, the view continues, when individuals work for a company, they act for the company and in the company's name. When so acting, their actions are part of the actions of the firm. Hence they should not be evaluated from a moral point of view. When they act contrary to the interests of the firm or when they break the law, steal from the company, or embezzle funds, then they act in their own right and are properly judged from a moral point of view. The conclusion is that businesses are not moral agents, have no moral responsibilities, and should not be morally evaluated.

This view, which I shall call the Organizational View, is a variant of the Myth of Amoral Business. It developed in part as a reaction to a number of moral demands made by environmentalists and consumer groups concerning the social responsibility of business. Milton Friedman's reaction to such claims is to assert that the business of business is to make profits and that social reform, welfare, and the like are the proper concern not of business but of government.

The Organizational View has been widely attacked. Yet it cannot be dismissed out of hand. It makes the valid point that organizations, corporations, and nations are not moral entities in the same sense as are individual human beings. Hence, if we are to consider them as moral agents, we must be careful how we use our terms. We must make clear what we mean by them.

The argument against the claim that formal organizations are not moral beings is fairly simple. Morality governs the action of rational beings insofar as they affect other rational beings. Formal organizations, for instance corporations, act. Ford Motor Company produces cars; it also builds factories, hires and fires people, pays them wages, pays taxes, recalls defective models, and so on. Not only do businesses act, they act rationally according to a rational decision-making procedure. Their rational actions affect people. Hence these actions can be evaluated from a moral point of view. If it is immoral for an individual to discriminate, it is also immoral for a corporation to discriminate. If it is praiseworthy for an individual to give to charity, it is praiseworthy for a business to give to charity. If it is wrong for people to steal, it is wrong for businesses to steal. Actions, whether done by an individual or by an entity such as a company, or a corporation, or a nation, can be morally evaluated. The alternative would be to say that though murder is wrong for individuals it is not morally wrong for businesses; or that though exploitation of one person by another is morally wrong, exploitation of a person by a corporation is morally neutral. This is clearly unacceptable because murder, stealing, exploitation, and lying are wrong whether done by a human being, or by a corporation, or by a nation. The action is wrong whoever the perpetrator of the action is.

The dispute need not end here, however. For part of the point of the Organizational View is that formal organizations do not act. Neither do corporations, clubs, companies, nor nations. People within them act but the organization itself is nothing more than an organization. It does not do anything. People within it do whatever it is that gets done. Obviously there is something correct about the assertion that only people act and that formal organizations do not act. Yet we noted above that we often speak of firms and nations acting. Who is correct and how do we decide?

The answer to both questions can be found through a closer analysis of our use of language. When we say that Ford makes cars we do not mean that the cars are made by magic. We know that no car will get made unless someone makes it. A great many people, using a variety of tools and machines, contribute to any Ford car. Yet we can use the name "Ford" to mean all of the people and their relations and activities together. We know that there are workers and managers, a president of the firm, a board of directors, and shareholders. Yet without any knowledge of who does what within the firm, we can speak of Ford making cars. This is a perfectly understandable statement made from outside the corporation and referring to it as a whole. If Ford recalls defective cars someone must make the decision to recall them, and either the same person or other people must send out the notices. They act not in their own names but as employees or agents of the firm.

The use of the name of the firm to refer to all those associated with it, to refer to the products which those associated with it produce, or to refer to the entity which is liable to suit is a proper and common use of language. Hence when we make a moral judgment about the actions of a firm or of a nation, we need not know who within the firm is the person or persons responsible. We can hold the firm as such responsible from a moral as well as from a legal point of view. But granted that we can make moral judgments about the actions of a firm or nation, why should we? The answer can be found in what we wish to accomplish by such judgments. In making moral judgments about the actions we attribute to a firm or nation, we do many things. We express our emotions, evaluate an action, and encourage other people to react to the action as we do. In expressing our moral evaluation we either praise or blame. If we morally condemn an action we might wish to encourage others to impose moral sanctions or bring pressure to bear to rectify the wrong or to change the policy in question.

A case in point is the Nestlé Boycott. The Nestlé Company was charged with causing a great deal of misery by promoting in a number of questionable ways the use of its powdered milk product for infants in underdeveloped countries. The charge was that the powdered milk was being mixed with polluted water under un-hygienic conditions, resulting in disease and death in large numbers of infants. In order to put pressure on the company to change what was seen as an immoral prac-tice, a coalition was formed calling for people to boycott all Nestlé products. The purpose of the boycott was to produce a change in the company's policy. Those who called the boycott may not have known who within the company was respon-sible for the questionable practices, and they may not have cared. The boycott may have resulted in a cutback in production by the company with a consequent laying off of workers who were not involved in setting policy or implementing it in any way. The boycott was called, however, not to lay off particular people but to change the company's policy. From the outside it was a matter of indifference who was responsible for the practice and who carried it out. The intent of the coalition was to identify the practice as immoral, call it to people's attention, and unite them to create moral pressure to stop the practice.

Whether or not the attribution of an action to a corporation is strictly speaking correct, or whether it should be more appropriately attributed to the person or people within the corporation who make the decisions in question and carry them out, attribution of an action to a corporation is both intelligible and, from a prac-tical point of view, may be effective.

A similar analysis can be applied to nations. When the United States condemned the Soviet invasion of Czechoslovakia and the intervention in Afghanistan, spokes-men for the United States did the condemning. Although we say that the Soviet Union invaded Czechoslovakia, we obviously mean that Soviet soldiers invaded it. We see them as agents receiving orders from the heads of government. But the heads of government do not themselves physically invade. In some cases we distinguish what the leaders of a country do from what the ordinary people do. In other cases we do not. If one country blockades another, members of the armed forces of the one country prevent the exportation or importation of goods from or to the other country. One country may declare war on another. They do so through their gov-ernments; but war is not declared only against certain people. As with talk about businesses, the collective term serves many functions, even if we admit that no nation acts unless people act for it.

From within a formal organization or a nation, actions may also be ascribed by an individual to the organization or nation as a whole. Actions are more usually seen, however, as being done by certain people. The workers on an assembly line know that the cars they produce will not be produced unless they or others like them perform certain tasks. Policy will not be changed unless those capable of changing policy take the actions necessary to produce the changes. Moral responsi-bility may be assumed by various members within a firm. It may be assumed by the members of the board of directors, the president, various levels of management, or by the workers. Each person may hold himself morally responsible for doing his job, and he may hold others morally responsible for doing theirs; or moral responsibility may be refused by some or all of them.

Moral charges made from the outside and moral responsibility ascribed to a corporation or nation from the outside may be rejected, rebutted, refuted, or ignored. This happens when no one within the corporation or nation accepts the responsibility ascribed to it.

Corporations are not human beings. The differences between human individuals and corporations, other formal organizations, and nations are significant from a moral point of view and from the point of view of moral responsibility. A corporation as such has no conscience, no feelings, and no consciousness of its own. It has a conscience only to the extent that those who make it up act for it in such a way as to evince something comparable to conscience. Since corporations only act through those who act for it, it is the latter who must assume moral responsibility for the corporation. It may not always be clear who within the corporation should assume this responsibility.

When harm is unjustly done to an individual by a firm, the firm has the moral obligation to make reparation to the individual. For example, it matters little whether the particular person who systematically paid women employees less than men for the same work is still with the firm. If the women deserve compensation for past injustice, the firm has the moral obligation to make good. Someone who had nothing to do with perpetrating the past injustice but who is now employed by the firm may have the moral obligation to take action to make up for past wage discrimination. If a firm is morally responsible for wrongs done, it is morally obliged to make good on those wrongs. But exactly who must do what within the firm can often only be appropriately decided by an analysis of individual cases.

In dealing with human individuals we speak of their moral character. Do nations, firms, and formal organizations have moral character? There are some people who maintain that a firm that takes its moral responsibilities seriously, tries to be fair in dealing with its employees and customers, and takes into consideration the effects of its actions, and so on, is correctly called a moral firm. It can be said to have a moral character in a sense analogous to that used with respect to individuals. Its character is formed by its habitual actions in the past. It develops within it certain structures and patterns of acting. It molds those who join it into thinking and acting in certain ways. Tradition develops, a pride in the policies of the firm takes root, and each member of the firm helps form and mold the others in the firm to its tradition. In this sense, then, a firm or a nation can be called moral or immoral, can be said to have a moral or an immoral character, and can be thought of as having, or as not having, a conscience. But the sense is an analogous one and is not identical with the meaning of these terms when used with respect to individual persons.

We can and do use moral language with respect to the actions of businesses, formal organizations, and countries. But in any analysis we should be aware of the differences in meaning and application of the terms as we shift from individual human beings to organizational entities.

Collective Responsibility

Assigning or assuming responsibility within a firm or a nation can properly
raise questions of collective responsibility. There are differences, however, between
speaking of the collective responsibility of: a random group of individuals; a non-
freely joined group or organization such as a nation, family, or race; and a freely
joined organization. One cannot dissociate oneself from one's family, race, or
country in the same way that one can from freely joined organizations, including
corporations and other businesses.

We can describe five models for assigning collective responsibility. In the first
model, each member of the collective is assigned and/or assumes full responsibility
for an action. Cases of collusion or of conspiracy are typical of this model. All the
members of a conspiracy are fully responsible for the actions of any one of them. If
a group of armed bandits robs a bank and one of them kills a bank guard, all the
bandits are guilty of murder. For, in forming the conspiracy, they all intend the
same end and are guilty of the results that any one of them produces in attempting
to achieve it. If a firm decides to close down a plant without regard for the workers
who will be let go, and if the action is immoral, then all those who decided the
action have responsibility for it. If the action was decided by the board of directors,
all members of the board are equally responsible, even though each had only one
vote.

The second model assigns only partial responsibility either to all members of a
firm or country, or as a variant, to those involved in any decision or action taken by
the firm or country. Joint actions frequently require the participation of many
people; some play a larger role than others, though all contribute to the total act;
therefore all are partially responsible.

The above two models break down collective responsibility into individual responsibility. The third model holds the firm or nation fully responsible with responsibility assigned to individuals as in the first model. Thus, for instance, a worker
who had no part in making a decision which leads to the immoral action of his
company judges the firm to have acted immorally and imputes responsibility to
those who made the decision. Does he have, he may ask, the moral obligation to
leave a firm that acts in this manner? Should he assume responsibility for the firm's
actions simply because he works for it and thus helps it to act immorally?

The fourth model assigns full responsibility to the firm or nation with individual responsibility assigned as in the second model.

The fifth assigns responsibility for the firm or nation's action only to the firm
or nation as such, not to any of its members individually. Each member within the
firm or country may have acted morally; yet the outcome of their joint actions may
be morally wrong.

Other models are possible, including mixes of the models described above. One
view might place moral responsibility on the board of directors for all the actions a
firm may take. Another might place it on management, even though neither the

members of the board nor the managers did anything themselves which was immoral. A third view might put the responsibility .on the shareholders, who are in fact penalized if a firm is fined and if it cannot pass the fine on to either the public in the form of higher prices or to the workers in the form of lower wages.

Which of these models is correct? How should we assign or assume moral responsibility when dealing with corporations or nations? Who really has responsibility for their actions? The answer is that moral responsibility may be appropriately assigned and assumed in all of these ways. The proper way cannot be decided a priori but only after examining a particular case. The idea that a part-time janitor working for a firm should be held fully and morally responsible for the immoral actions of that firm might sound extreme. In most cases it undoubtedly would be an extreme view. But in others, if the actions of a corporation were truly morally heinous, and if working for the firm in any capacity might be viewed as condoning its actions, then the janitor might be held morally responsible for the firm's actions. Obviously we would want to know what it means to condone its actions, and whether the janitor's responsibility was of a lesser or greater degree than others in the firm. We would want to know what difference it makes to hold him partially or fully responsible and the considerations which lead us to one or the other view. If the janitor is morally responsible, we might expect him, upon realizing it, to quit. If the president is morally responsible we might expect him, upon realizing this, to change the firm's policies, assuming it is possible for him to do so. Ascribing responsibility and assuming it might imply responsibility to act in differing ways, depends on one's position.

To hold an entire race morally responsible for what some of its members does and in which the others have had no part is unjust. And if guilt by association is taken to be an integral part of collective responsibility, then we should not adopt the notion. But neither of these interpretations of what it means to speak of collective responsibility forms a necessary part of the concept.

The notion of collective moral responsibility is a fuzzy one because it can be interpreted in so many different ways. Our moral intuitions are frequently not clear when we are asked to decide who really is responsible for some actions taken by a firm or country and which of the models really applies. There is room for disagreement in many cases. When we encounter such cases we must do our best to analyze the situation, see the results of adopting this rather than that interpretation of responsibility, take into account the consequences of using one rather than another of the models, see which can best be justified in the given case, which makes more sense, whether any make sense at all, and what difference it makes if we adopt or employ one rather than another.

The nature of the internal collective responsibility of a firm or nation should be pursued by those within each, attempting to clarify, assign, and assume responsibility as appropriate. Only when all those within such entities assume appropriate moral responsibility can the full moral responsibility of a firm, formal organization, or country be met. Ultimately moral responsibility, as morality itself, must be self-imposed and self-accepted.

Further Reading

Blau, Peter M., and Scott, W. Richard. *Formal Organizations.* San Francisco: Chandler Publishing Co., 1962.

Cooper, D.E., "Collective Responsibility." In *Philosophy,* XLIII (1968) pp. 258–268.

Feinberg, Joel. *Doing and Deserving: Essays in the Theory of Responsibility.* Princeton: Princeton University Press, 1970.

Feinberg, Joel. "Collective Responsibility." In *The Journal of Philosophy,* LXV (1968), pp. 674–688.

French, Peter, ed. *Individual and Collective Responsibility: The Massacre at My Lai.* Cambridge, Mass.: Schenkman Publishing Co., Inc., 1972.

Friedman, Milton. "The Social Responsibility of Business Is to Increase Its Profits." In *The New York Times Magazine,* September 13, 1970.

Glover, Jonathan. *Responsibility.* New York: Humanities Press, Inc., 1970.

Held, Virginia. "Can A Random Collection of Individuals Be Morally Responsible?" In *The Journal of Philosophy,* LXVII (1970), pp. 471–481.

Ladd, John. "Morality and the Ideal of Rationality in Formal Organizations." In *The Monist,* LIV (1970), pp. 488–516.

Lewis, H.D. "Collective Responsibility," *Philosophy,* XXIII (1948), pp. 3–18.

Myles, Brand, ed. *The Nature of Human Action.* Glenview, Ill.: Scott, Foresman, & Company, 1970.

Silverman, David. *The Theory of Organizations.* New York: Basic Books, Inc., 1971.

Simon, Herbert A. *Administrative Behavior.* 2nd ed. New York: The Free Press, 1965.

Walsh, W.H. "Pride, Shame and Responsibility." In *The Philosophical Quarterly,* XX (1970), pp. 1–13.

Moral Issues
in Business

6 Justice and Economic Systems

Consider two neighboring slaveholders in the American South before the Civil War. The first slaveholder treats his slaves reasonably well. He beats them only when they do not do the jobs they are supposed to do or when they break the rules he sets. He feeds them fairly regularly. He does not expect them to work more than twelve or fourteen hours a day. He knows them by name and speaks to them on occasion. The other slaveholder beats his slaves whenever he gets angry at his wife or children. He gives his slaves swill to eat, and does not worry if sometimes they are not fed. When there is work to be done, he is not above making them work sixteen or eighteen hours a day. He is capricious in his dealings with them, arbitrary in the punishment he metes out, and surly in his attitude toward them.

Of the two slaveholders, which is the more moral? The temptation to call the first slaveholder the more moral is a strong one. For clearly he is kinder, fairer, and more just in his dealings with his slaves. Yet to call either one moral has an odd ring to it. If holding slaves is immoral—if it is wrong to own another human being—then there is a fundamental injustice in the practice. A slaveowner's treating his slaves kindly is better than his treating them unkindly, but such treatment does not justify or make up for his engaging in the practice of slavery. Both slaveholders are involved in an immoral practice, even if one is more kind than the other.

Yet, we may reflect, probably neither of the slaveowners believes slavery is immoral. That may be true. But their belief that slavery is moral does not make it objectively right. It is immoral whether or not subjectively speaking they believe it is.

Now we can approach our own society in a similar way. Consider two employers. One discriminates against women and blacks, does not care about the safety of his employees, pays them subsistence wages, and replaces them as they wear out just as he would replace his machines. The other employer does not discriminate, introduces safety devices where possible, pays his employees well above the subsistence level, and has a retirement plan. Which of the two is more moral? The answer is obvious and simple. But we can ask the question which we do not often ask, and that is whether the employers in our system are comparable to the slaveholders in the slave system. Is something comparably wrong with the economic system in the United States today as with the economic system in the Southern United States before the Civil War? The fact that most of us do not feel that there is anything wrong with the wage system or with the economic system in general says something about us. It does not necessarily say anything about the morality of the system in which we live. Is it moral? As we struggle with the question of whether reverse discrimination is the proper way to make up for past discrimination, whether whistle blowing is morally defensible, and whether advertising aimed at small children takes unfair advantage of them, are we questioning the morality of practices within a system when we should be questioning the system itself? Is the system basically just?

The Immorality of Slavery

Usually we speak of people or actions as being moral or immoral. Can we also describe an economic system as immoral? The answer seems to be clearly yes, since the overwhelming majority of Americans—as well as of most other people—would readily admit that slavery is immoral. And slavery constitutes an economic system. Yet we would do well to look a little more closely at the question and at our answer.

In characterizing the system of slavery as immoral we use the term "slavery" in two different senses. In the first sense we mean the practice of slavery. This defines a relation between people and a way of treating people. We can analyze both the relation and the actions that follow as a result of the relation. In the second sense by "slavery" we mean the economic system in which the slave relation is the fundamental productive relation. Because it is fundamental, we characterize the system by that relation. The system would not be that particular system if that relation were not present in a fundamental, constitutive way. If, for instance, we had an economic system that was basically capitalist or socialist but a few people within the system had slaves, we could say that the practice of slavery was immoral. But that would not mean that the system within which it was found was immoral, since slavery was not a fundamental or defining relation of the system.

We can evaluate the economic system of slavery in two different ways. One involves evaluating the morality of the fundamental economic relation on which it is built, and by extension analyzing the actions which follow as a result of that relation. This is a structural analysis. It involves looking at the basic structures and practices of the system, since the system is defined by its structures and practices. These are necessarily seen as relations among people and as practices which involve transactions among people. Are these fair and just? The second way of evaluating economic systems is an end-state approach. It involves looking at what the system as a whole does to the people affected by it. Does the system help them fulfill themselves and realize their potential as moral beings? Does adoption of the system produce a kind of human society that exemplifies or fulfills the moral aspirations of human beings? Both the structural and the end-state evaluations may be made from either the utilitarian or the deontological points of view.

Let us consider the economic system of slavery. We define it as a system in which the fundamental productive relation is the owning of one human being, the slave, by another, the master. The slave works for the master and produces the basic goods needed by the society. These include the food that the members of the society eat, the clothes they wear, the utensils they use, the tools they employ, the buildings they inhabit, and whatever else is necessary for their way of life. The masters may produce art or literature, philosophy or other human products which typically require leisure and time for reflection. The slave not only works for the master but belongs to the master as property belongs to a property owner. The slave, insofar as he is a slave, is not considered a person with rights or worthy of moral consideration. He or she is an object to be used, much as animals are objects to be used. The primary function of slaves is work, even if some slaves may not be used for work but for other purposes, just as the primary function of work animals is work, though some may be kept as pets, for breeding, or for other purposes.

This fundamental productive relation as we have described it may be defined by and circumscribed by law. But it is the economic, not the legal relation that is the center of our concern. We can look at the moral quality of the relation itself. We can also morally evaluate the actions which typically follow as a result of the relation.

First, let us consider the moral quality of the relation itself. Is it a moral relation? The obvious answer from the deontological point of view is clearly that it is not. The relation denies that the slave is an end in himself, worthy of respect. The maxim implied in the relation, namely, "Treat human beings who have the status of slaves as possessions," is in direct opposition to the second formulation of the categorical imperative which requires that we treat all rational beings as ends in themselves, not as means only. If we were to go behind the veil of ignorance, not knowing whether we would end up as a slave or as a master when we emerged, and if we wished to protect ourselves in case we were assigned our place by our worst enemy, would we choose a slave society or one in which all were free? Clearly we would choose the latter. Slavery violates the first principle of justice developed by John Rawls (see p. 67), and hence, according to that criterion, it is unjust. A utilitarian approach would require that we examine the results of actions, and not simply relations. Yet even from the utilitarian point of view it does not take much imagination to realize that the status of the slaves is such as to make them less human despite the fact that they are human beings. They will necessarily suffer loss of dignity in their status as slaves, which is a loss that cannot be compensated for even by kind treatment. Since a slave society is one in which the slaves dominate numerically, the pain they suffer as a result of their status is enormous, and clearly greater than the pleasure or good of the slaveholders. In general, therefore, the relation in itself has a tendency to produce more harm to those affected by it than good.

Second, let us consider the actions which follow as a result of the slave relation. Are they moral or immoral? The answer, of course, depends on which actions we choose. The productive work of the slave is not immoral, nor necessarily is the giving of commands by the master. But work and the giving of commands are not peculiar to slavery. Are there actions which follow from slavery as such? We need not deny that slaves might be treated kindly by masters. But if they were treated by masters in all ways as masters treat free men, then we would not in fact have the practice of slavery. The actions we must morally evaluate are those in which masters treat their slaves as property, as animals, as beings who are not ends in themselves. The analysis from both the deontological and utilitarian points of view would parallel the ones we just gave, except that the utilitarian would have actions, the results of which he could evaluate. The results would be similar. The conclusions which we can defensibly draw are that the practice of slavery is immoral and that an economic system which is dependent on the practice of slavery is inherently immoral. It cannot be made moral without changing the fundamental practice of slavery on which it is based. A slave system might be more tolerable to slaves in one society than in another, and one master might be kinder to his slaves than another. But neither of these considerations changes the moral character of slavery.

The results are similar if we take an end-state approach to slavery. The deontological evaluation will not differ significantly from the previous analysis. Slavery will still exist. Since that is the central ingredient in the system, the system remains immoral. But might slavery be only prima facie immoral? Might it be unjust but preferable to the other real alternatives? From the utilitarian perspective, might it not be possible that the results of adopting slavery are actually better than the results of adopting some other system?

Suppose that as a result of a worldwide nuclear war the population of the world is decimated. Those who remain have been affected by radiation poisoning of a type that affects their brains, making them dull witted and devoid of initiative. There are a few lucky people who were shielded by lead walls in bank vaults, or who were deep underground. When they emerge and assess the situation they realize that if the human race is to survive, they must reproduce. They cannot handle all of their needs. But the masses can be corralled and forced to work. In being so forced they will each be better off than they would otherwise be, because the alternative is that they would die. In being forced to work they will both keep themselves alive and keep alive those who have the capacity to develop the human race again. Hence the fortunate few institute what we call slavery. They argue that all the people in the society will be better off with slavery than any of them would be without it. The alternative is death for all. Hence, though slavery is prima facie immoral, when compared with the even worse alternative of extinction of mankind and the dreadful suffering those who die would go through, it is the lesser of two evils and so morally justifiable.

What are we to say of the argument? The first reply is that it is a flight of fancy—a philosopher's puzzle and not a real state of affairs. Morality, we can insist, is concerned with real alternatives. We have little basis for judging what might be right or wrong in the conditions described, which are far beyond our ordinary experience. But we need not stop with this reply. Take the example on its merits. It states that the people affected by the radiation are dull witted and without initiative, and if left alone would die. How dull witted are they? Can they think enough to consider consequences? Are they rational and able to decide between alternatives? Do they have a desire to live and do they see life as worthwhile? How can we explain the fact that they can be forced to work under slavery but not otherwise? How can the claim be defended that there is really no other alternative? Who decided that? The example makes too many vague and dubious claims. It concludes, if all the claims are admitted, that slavery, though prima facie immoral, is the least of the possible evils and therefore morally justifiable. Given our knowledge of human history, it is difficult to believe that there are really no other alternatives, that the few who become the masters do so for the good of all, that the slaves are better off than they would be if some other means of impelling them to action were employed. Nor is there much reason to think that the system of slavery once adopted would not tend to degenerate, that people would be treated worse instead of better, and that the masters would become more and more reluctant to give up slavery as the practice continued. We cannot settle the argument, since it is speculative. But we should not be forced to admit more than is plausible.

History might provide a better example. We know that as a great many societies emerged from primitive tribal conditions they developed slavery. The great pillars of Western civilization, Greece and Rome, were built on slavery. If slavery was historically necessary for us to emerge to the state of society in which each person is free, was not ancient slavery justified by its necessity, as well as by its results?

It is very difficult to settle counter-factual issues. How can we know what else was available in the times of Greece and Rome and what would have happened had slavery not developed? To say that slavery was a reality in ancient societies, however, is not to say that it was unthinkable that there be ancient societies without slavery. To claim it was historically necessary is to make an ambiguous claim. Certainly it was not logically necessary. It may have developed because of a natural inclination on the part of some people to dominate, or because of the weakness of others in comparison with the strength of the few, or because of the desire for luxury or ease on the part of those who would be masters, or for any number of other reasons. None of these is a justification for slavery, though in some sense they provide an explanation of why and how it arose. Historical necessity, if it is taken simply to mean that whatever happened historically happened necessarily, renders everything moral. More accurately, it renders everything morally neutral. Because if everything that happened happened necessarily, then one of the conditions for morality is denied, namely, the possibility in some sense of choosing freely. If Hitler's murder of millions of Jews in our century was historically necessary, simply because it happened, then we can justify anything. The result would be that there is no basis for evaluating anything. All we could do is state what happened.

The other historical rationale is to claim that slavery was necessary, but only up to a certain time. Thereafter it was no longer necessary and should have been given up. Slavery in the United States was not necessary. Mankind had found ways to organize society productively without slavery. It was an anachronism, which was finally uprooted by the Civil War. But ancient slavery, the argument contends, was a step on the road to feudalism, which in turn led to the development of the world as we know it. We could not have developed our productive capacities unless we had gone through the stage of slavery. Hence it was justifiable then, even though it is not justifiable now. Even if the argument is taken to be a type of utilitarian argument, it still remains questionable. The central issue is whether there was no real alternative to ancient slavery. How that claim can be substantiated is the crux of the issue. We can concede that *if* there actually was no better alternative, then slavery was justifiable as the least bad of bad alternatives; but this is different from accepting the claim that actually there was no alternative available.

Whatever our conclusion about ancient slavery, we can be certain that in today's world slavery is immoral. There are clearly alternatives and there is no justification for choosing an immoral system when moral systems are available.

We can generalize on the basis of our analysis, however. Since we have been able to argue conclusively that slavery is immoral and that today it is an immoral alternative, we have shown that it is possible, at least in the case of slavery, to give a moral evaluation of an economic system. We have seen how the question of the morality of economic systems can in general be approached and how specific arguments can be advanced. What of contemporary systems?

The Moral Evaluation of Contemporary Systems

In considering slavery we discussed a homogeneous economic system, characterized by the dominant productive relation of master and slave. We did not investigate the kind of political system to which it was joined. The political system of the Greek city-states was different from that of the Roman Empire, and both of those were different from the political system of ancient Egypt. But whatever the political system, it could not make up for the immorality of slavery. Nor was there any way that slavery could be changed internally so as to be moral and still be slavery.

The moral status of contemporary economic systems is not so easily settled. It is tempting to think simplistically about two great contending economic systems: capitalism and socialism. But we should remember the differences between nineteenth century capitalism in England and capitalism as it exists in the United States today. As we consider contemporary capitalism, we should consider not only its structure in the United States, but also in other countries, such as Japan and South Africa. In the latter case it is joined with apartheid, a radical form of racial segregation and discrimination; in the former two it is not. In Japan capitalism is joined with a kind of paternalism absent from its American counterpart. Nor are all socialistic systems identical. Socialism in the Soviet Union is closely linked with a centralized and dominant Communist Party. In England socialism is mixed with a democratic form of government. In Yugoslavia socialism exists with a Communist Party which allows a great deal of decentralization. Capitalism and socialism in each case is changed to some extent by the kind of political system and structure within which it operates. Moreover, pure capitalism and pure socialism do not exist in any country. Every country has something of a mixed kind of economic system, though some can be characterized as more clearly capitalistic and others as more clearly socialistic. Communism, as an economic system, has yet to be achieved, though countries with communistic governments claim to be developing toward it.

Since apartheid is present in South Africa but not in the United States, apartheid is not a constituent of capitalism. It is something added to capitalism or an ingredient part of a particular kind of capitalism. Socialism in the USSR under Stalin was founded together with totalitarianism. But socialism in England is not. Hence, totalitarianism is not a necessary part of socialism. Though economic and political systems are intertwined, we can distinguish them to a considerable degree for purposes of analysis. The way any specific contemporary economic system actually works, however, cannot realistically be separated from a consideration of the political and legal system with which it is found. Some of the moral deficiencies of an economic system, for instance, might be compensated for by the political system. Conversely, the political system might interfere in an immoral way with the workings of the economic system.

For purposes of analysis let us briefly consider capitalism and socialism as economic systems, floating free from any particular political system. The analytic technique useful for this purpose is the construction of a model. We can develop a model of capitalism and a model of socialism. We can then investigate the models to determine their necessary components. Once we have isolated the necessary components we can evaluate them from a moral point of view. If we find any structural immoral elements, then we can see if we can change those elements and still retain a system which we wish to call capitalism. If we do not find any structurally immoral elements, we can see if adoption of the system would result in an end-state product we would call either moral or morally neutral. We can do the same with socialism. The conclusions we reach as a result of this analysis will pertain only to the model. We need then see to what degree, if any, the model is actually instantiated in any really existing society. Obviously we are interested in models which bear some relation to existing societies. To the extent that we find the model defective or deficient from a moral point of view, we should see whether it can be made moral while still keeping its basic structure. If this is not possible, then the system is inherently immoral. If we find such a system in a particular country, the appropriate approach is to replace the system with a moral one. Whether that can be done while retaining the existing form of government is a question we cannot decide without investigating particular cases. Such replacement frequently involves a drastic and dramatic social change, usually called a revolution, whether it be violent or peaceful.

Economic Models and Games

Some people consider economics a kind of game. By pursuing the analogy we can see some of its strengths and weaknesses. Consider chess. To play chess you need a chess board and a number of pieces of a certain kind. They can be considered two sides or armies. Each side has a king and a queen, two knights, two bishops, two rooks, and eight pawns. Is the game fair? One obvious reply is that it is fair because both sides have the same number and kinds of pieces and both sides are bound by the same rules. This is to look at the game from the point of view of the players. But what if we looked at it from the point of view of a pawn. Think of the pawn standing in front of the queen. Within the game the queen can make many different kinds of moves, while the pawn moves one square at a time. Is that fair? My reply is that it is inappropriate to look at the game of chess from the point of view of the pieces. If you want to play chess, then you must follow the rules of the game. Fairness consists in following the rules, not in changing the possible moves.

But if you prefer equality, you might prefer the game called Chinese checkers. In it all sides have the same number of marbles. All the marbles are of equal value and can all make the same moves. We thus achieve equality within the system as well as fairness for the players.

Consider now the game of economics. In one system we have slaves and masters. In another we have rich owners of industry and factory workers. In another we have commissars and workers. If each one of these is considered a type of game with its own rules, we can describe how each operates. If each taken as a whole were considered a model, we could describe it in detail. We could talk of the place and role of each person in the economy. We could describe how prices rise and fall; how supply meets or fails to meet demand and what this does to prices; what happens when taxes are increased, the money supply is diminished, or interest rates are raised; and how full employment might be achieved. We could describe all this with some precision in our model, and possibly we could predict with some certainty the reactions of certain parts of the economy to certain actions in other parts of it.

According to this approach, economics is not something we morally evaluate. It is a game. Chinese checkers is one game and chess another But it is silly to try to say that one is more moral than another. The rules are different; the players are different. Chess is more complicated and interesting due to the different kinds of pieces and moves allowable. Chinese checkers is less complicated; all the pieces are equal; and it is comparatively dull. But some people prefer chess because of the skill it requires while others prefer Chinese checkers because of its simplicity. Similarly, some people feel that a free enterprise system is more challenging and interesting than a system of radical equality. From an economic point of view different systems can be described and the laws or rules governing the variables within the system detailed. Each can be modeled. But models are not moral or immoral, just as most games are neither moral nor immoral.

Though economics might be considered a game, economic systems are not games. Frequently, economics is studied as if it had nothing to do with people, as if it was simply the study of abstract concepts such as supply and demand, money, price, and profits. Economic systems, however, ultimately are ways in which people are related. Their relations are mediated by money and commodities, by prices and wages, by supply and demand. But all of these relations in the end are descriptions of how people interact. Their lives are shaped and seriously affected by the system in which they find themselves and by the rules according to which that system operates. Hence ultimately economic systems are not morally neutral and should be closely examined from a moral point of view. A chess piece is not a person. But a soldier fighting for a king is a moral being, an end in himself, and not simply a pawn to be used. We can therefore plausibly evaluate an economic system by an end-state evaluation as well as by an analysis of the fairness, justice, or morality of its structures and operative rules. What is interesting in the analogy with games, however, is that we consider them fair when both players start out equally and abide by the same rules. We allow one to win and the other to lose. In fact, that is the object of the game. Do we feel the same about the game of life? Should all start out the same and abide by the same rules? If they do, is it right that some win and some lose?

A Capitalist Model

A model may not correspond to any social reality. A model of capitalism may also not correspond to any socially existing economy. But a model can help us get conceptual clarity on some issues.

Capitalism in its long history has gone through a number of phases and stages. What I shall call classical capitalism is a model that is frequently both attacked and defended. It does not exist in its pure form anywhere in the world today, and may never have represented an actual economy. Yet its main features are commonly used and understood.

All economic systems produce and exchange commodities, use money as a medium of exchange, and pay labor. What are the specific defining features of the model of classical capitalism? We shall consider three which are necessary to it. Although each of the three features may be found in other kinds of economic systems, it is the combination of the three that makes the model different from other models. The three are: an available accumulation of industrial capital; private ownership of the means of production; and a free market system.

1. Available Accumulation of Industrial Capital
Capitalism derives its name from the fact that it is a system based on accumulated industrial capital. In a barter economy there is no accumulation of capital.

Goods are exchanged for goods of equal value—there is no residue left over. Capital, which we can think of in terms of large amounts of money that can be put into the production of goods, must be accumulated. Before capitalism, kings might accumulate fortunes; but they did not typically use their fortunes in the production of goods. Merchants and tradesmen might accumulate some wealth (though rarely in very large quantities) but typically did not use their wealth for the production of goods.

Several features are built into our model of capitalism which correlate closely with its historical development. The accumulation of large amounts of wealth available for productive purposes is one such feature. Large sums of money alone, however, are not enough. We must also have industrialization. Capitalism did not exist prior to the industrial revolution. Hence industrialization on a large scale is a necessary element of our model.

Neither the availability of wealth for productive purposes nor large scale industrialization are unique to capitalism. Any large, modern society, whatever its economic system, needs both of these. But industrialization carries with it certain problems, such as pollution. Industrialization involves the use of machines which in case of accidents can be dangerous; they wear out, become obsolete, and need replacing. Industrialization typically demands a large degree of division of labor. Some of the work required in using machines efficiently is routine and dull. Some requires great specialization and training. All of these aspects and functions of industrialization are not peculiar to capitalism. Any industrial society faces these potential problems and difficulties. But industrialization also has definite advantages. The greatest is that it multiplies human productive capacity and so makes possible a much larger number of goods than would otherwise be the case.

The model of classical capitalism includes industrialization and capital. It does not question where capital comes from or how it was developed. Since the model is not an historical account but an analytic tool, presence of capital is a given, a prerequisite of a capitalist model. The same is true of a model of some other contemporary economic systems, which includes capital and industrialization. Where did the capital present in that system come from?

The question of how capital was initially accumulated as well as the question of how it is increased within a system raises moral considerations. While from a moral point of view we can examine the transactions within the model of the system, we cannot examine the process of the antecedent capital formation and accumulation if the presence of such capital is assumed by the model and if such formation and accumulation are not part of the model.

2. Private Ownership of the Means of Production

The distinguishing characteristic of capitalism is sometimes said to be private ownership of the means of production. This is a distinguishing feature, however, only when joined with the first and third parts of the model. In a slaveholding society or in a feudal society there may also be private ownership of the means of production. The characteristic feature of capitalism is that there is private ownership of the means of large industrial production.

Private ownership of the means of production should not be confused with private ownership of property. Personal property, for instance, might be privately owned in a socialist economy. Personal property is owned by an individual and is not generally used for the production of commodities, though personally owned tools may be so used. But personally owned tools are not the dominant type of productive instrument in capitalism. In speaking of private ownership of the means of production we mean private ownership of factories, plants, corporations and businesses, transportation and communication facilities, raw materials, and large, commercially farmed land.

Private ownership in this model is opposed to social or state ownership. There are a number of difficulties which we can avoid by defining the components of our model clearly. Some people claim that there is something called state capitalism in which the state carries on all the functions generally attributed to private owners in a nonstate capitalist system. For our purposes, state capitalism is a different model. In our model, ownership by the state is not private ownership; private ownership is contrasted with state ownership. Private ownership is also contrasted with social ownership. But private ownership is not to be contrasted with public ownership. A firm may be owned outright by an individual or by a small group of individuals. Such ownership is private ownership. A firm may, however, be owned by many people each of whom owns a small portion of it represented by shares of stock in the firm. The owners of the stock may be individuals or may be other firms, or may be groups investing pension plan money or the like. Such firms, whose stock is publicly sold and held, are publicly owned. But since the public members hold their shares privately, such firms are also privately owned. Social ownership, for our purposes, would mean ownership by members of the society in general, insofar as they are members of the society. Co-ops or firms owned by the workers are for our purposes privately owned, but, because of the second ingredient of private ownership, they are a marginal case. They do not represent the dominant mode of ownership.

The second ingredient of private ownership characteristic of capitalism is that not everyone owns the means of production. The majority of people in our model of capitalism do not individually own the means of production which they use. They are employed by others and work for wages. Wages are the dominant source of income for the vast majority in our capitalist model. Workers sell their labor in order to earn money to keep themselves and their families alive and to buy whatever else they wish with their disposable income.

Private property in our model is compatible with both private and professional management of firms. A firm which is privately owned may be run by those who own it. They may both own and manage the company or business, whatever it may be. The owners, however, may hire professional managers to run their businesses. The separation of ownership from management raises special problems for moral consideration. But in looking at the model in general we need make no hard and fast decision on this issue. If, for analytic purposes, it would be helpful to distinguish the two cases, we could simply use two models. In one of them ownership and management would go together. In the other they would be separate. Our model is a third alternative and includes both of the others.

Private ownership of the means of production raises a number of moral issues. One is whether private ownership of the means of production is itself moral. By what right, some ask, do some people, either individually or collectively, claim the right to natural resources? The world is the home of all mankind. Its goods—coal, iron, copper, oil, and other resources—should be available to all and used for the good of all. It is unfair for certain people, simply because they or their forebears happened to have settled in an area, to claim the exclusive right to the resources of that area. Such questions form one part of the moral analysis of private property.

A second group of questions bearing on private property concerns the social nature of knowledge and culture. Each people inherit a store of knowledge—knowledge of how to make iron and glass, or how to make engines and tools, and so on. Industry depends on a large store of accumulated information and know-how, inventions and discoveries which no individual owns. They have been socially developed. The modes of production are also social. No individual produces cars by himself or with knowledge he individually developed. Private ownership uses for private profit what society has developed. The knowledge, techniques, and processes are all social. By what right are they individually appropriated and used for individual rather than for social good?

A third group of questions relates to the workers in our model. In our capitalist model the vast majority of people do not own the means of production and earn their living by working for others. Their livelihood is dependent on others. By what right do some have such power of life and death over others? The workers work for a wage. What constitutes a fair or a just wage? What constitutes exploitation? If goods are exchanged at their value, does profit for the owner of private property come from stealing from the worker by not paying him what is his due? How is the owner-worker relation to be construed? We have already seen that the slave-master relation is immoral. What is the moral status of the owner-worker?

3. A Free Market System

The third characteristic of our capitalist model is a free competitive market system. A market-type of system can be shared with other types of economic models. In our model the free market system is the dominant type operative within the system.

A free market is one that is not controlled either by government or by any small group of individuals. In a free market government does not set the price of any goods. It controls neither prices nor wages. It also does not control production. Absence of government control and intervention is matched by absence of control by any small group. This rules out monopolies (exclusive ownership or control of supply) and monopsonies (exclusive control of demand, i.e., only one buyer).

Competition is a necessary component of our model. Free competition involves the possibility of any who so choose entering into the market structure as buyers or sellers. Access is not artifically limited by any power, government, or group. Free competition is driven in part by the profit motive. In order to achieve greater returns on investment, resources must be free to move from within the system to whichever portion of it will bring the greatest return. This is true of natural resources, capital, and labor. Workers are free to move to whatever employment they choose and to seek to earn as much as they can.

Prices and wages in our model are determined by the mechanism of the market. They are a result of supply and demand. Skilled labor, if it is in short supply, will bring higher wages than if it is not in short supply. In general, unskilled labor will be in greater supply than skilled labor, and skilled labor will be paid more. Prices are also determined by supply and demand. Competition encourages many people to produce goods in great demand, since there is a ready market for such products. Since buyers prefer to pay less rather than more for goods of the same quality, competition encourages efficiency among producers and competition encourages competing firms to lower their prices to acquire a larger share of the market.

The free market system, in our model, can claim several virtues. It promotes efficiency—the efficient production and use of resources. Even more importantly, it values freedom. Each individual within the system makes free choices in each transaction into which he enters. Competition tends to lower the cost of goods to consumers who decide what will be produced by how they spend their money. The market responds by not producing what is not sold and by producing what is in demand. As demand changes, the market mechanism responds by encouraging the appropriate changes in the allocation of capital and the allocation of resources. Workers are free to negotiate the conditions of their employment and the kind of work they will do. If the conditions under which each individual transaction takes place is fair, then each party freely enters into such a transaction to achieve his own good and his own ends. All benefit thereby.

Many moral issues arise in considering a free market system. Each transaction entered into must be fair and free. What constitutes fairness and what are the prerequisites for a transaction to be free? One condition of fairness is that both sides have all the appropriate knowledge. Only if both parties know what they are doing can they properly evaluate the transaction. Is the doctrine of caveat emptor, or "let the buyer beware," a part of our system? Does freedom involve the possibility of one party taking advantage of the other party, or of one party gaining advantage of another party? If fairness is built into the system, then only fair transactions are allowed in the system; but efficiency or initiative, the willingness to take risks or some other quality may well give one party an advantage over another. Can a worker be said to enter into a wage contract freely if he has no other alternative to accepting the wages offered than to starve? Do consumers acting as individuals enter into transactions on an equal footing with large corporations?

In addition to questions about the fairness and freedom of transactions, some people ask from a moral perspective what competition does to people. Does it treat them as ends in themselves? Does it undermine their inclination to be helpful? Does it divide them from each other into opposing classes and groups? Does it impede social cooperation? Does it make people selfish, self-serving, mean, and inconsiderate of others?

Are there natural tendencies of the market that push it towards monopoly, or that encourage people to attempt to gain unfair advantage in order to improve their competitive chances for success? If there are such forces, can they be remedied within the system, or must they be handled by other forces, for instance, by the political and legal system with which the model is joined?

A Socialist Model

There is no classical model of socialism as an economic system. Historically, we have a number of very diverse societies which have been or are called socialistic. To the extent that socialism involves government ownership, it is very difficult, if not impossible, to separate socialism as an economic system from socialism as a political system.

A partial model of socialism which is restricted to socialism as an economic system could be characterized by three features, each of which parallels to some extent our model of capitalism. The three features are: an industrial base; social ownership of the means of production; and centralized planning. This is only one of many models. It does not correspond to all socialist societies, but it does correspond in part to some of the more important ones.

1. An Industrial Base

Socialism as a modern phenomenon appears later on the historical scene than capitalism. In Marx's writings, it is the stage that follows the stage of capitalism. The French socialists of the nineteenth century saw it as an alternative to capitalism. It is possible to speak of socialism in an agricultural society. But the model we shall use restricts socialism to industrial societies. This means that the major form of production is industrial. All the problems of industrialization must therefore be faced by socialist economies as well as by capitalist ones. Industrialization carries with it problems of waste and pollution which must be handled. In some cases the solutions may be the same as under capitalism. In others the solutions may be different. Problems of worker satisfaction, of tedium and boredom at work, and other problems resulting from the productive process, from specialization, and from the division of labor are problems to be solved in socialist economies as well as in capitalist ones.

2. *Social Ownership of the Means of Production*

Social ownership of the means of production is the most frequently mentioned characteristic of a socialist economy. Such social ownership does not deny private ownership of personal goods. Personal property is compatible with socialism. The form of social ownership in our model may be either state ownership or worker ownership. A model may be constructed with only state or with only worker ownership. Both are allowable in our model. Social ownership in the sense that the means of production are owned by all the people is not part of our model. The reason for excluding it is that there is no socialist society to which such ownership is applicable. It is neither clear what such ownership would mean nor how it would function in any detail on a large scale applicable to a whole society. State ownership involves control by the government. The government of the society may represent the people, and it may act in their name. The government, even if legitimate, is not the people.

The relation of government to people is the central moral question of socialism. The government is the employer of all. Is it possible for the government to pay people less than the value they produce? Is it possible for the government to exploit people? Is it possible for government to be inequitable in its allocation of goods and to give preference to some at the expense of others? It is certainly possible for all these things to happen. Government ownership does not preclude them. Equality of opportunity is not necessarily guaranteed, nor will people's desires necessarily be fulfilled or weighed seriously. On the other hand their desires may be weighed, their needs may be taken care of, and they may be treated fairly and equitably. There is no guarantee that government ownership will necessarily produce such a society, however, unless we build such virtues into the system. The difficulty with building these virtues into the model is that the model will not apply to an actual society unless the virtues are also present. Socialism as a model is frequently presented with such benefits built into it. Our model, however, is neutral on this score.

Worker ownership is a relatively new phenomenon and is usually joined to some extent with government ownership. Worker ownership is comparable with co-ops. What makes them different is the total system or model in which they are found. If factories, for instance, are all owned by the workers, are they run competitively or not? Is competition between worker-owned factories to be considered a part of socialism or not? Since worker-owned factories are possible under capitalism, what would differentiate this portion of the socialist model from the capitalist model is that worker ownership would be the dominant form of ownership rather than a marginal one.

3. *Centralized Planning*

Centralized planning is a necessary part of our model of socialism, at least with respect to heavy industries, transportation and communications. Total centralized planning is of course allowable under the model. But it is not a necessary component. Without centralized planning at least in essential sectors, however, it would be difficult to distinguish the model of socialism from the model of capitalism. If worker-owned factories, for instance, were allowed to compete freely for resources and in what and how they produced, they would not differ significantly in most respects from similar factories in the capitalist model.

Centralized planning involves government. It is the government that typically does the planning in a socialist society. The task might be done by some other group. But that group would in the final analysis be equivalent to a government. Its job is to allocate resources and to guide the production and allocation of resources and goods. Its ideal is to end the anarchy and wastefulness of the marketplace.

Centralized planning precludes free market decisions of many types, though not of all types. The market might still be the indicator of what people want. Central planners can take into account such information as unfulfilled demand and a supply that exceeds demand. The point of centralized planning, however, is to replace competition. Hence, the competitive aspects of the market would not be allowed. For the system to work, the central planners obviously need an enormous amount of information in time to use it in making decisions about the allocation of resources and the goods to be produced and distributed. They need some way of knowing the needs of the people and of the society, some way of determining which goods and needs to give preference over others. Typically this involves a large government apparatus, usually of a bureaucratic nature.

Can government know all it needs to know in such a system? The more centralized and encompassing the control, the more difficult it is to succeed. The fewer industries controlled, the more likely the success.

The Comparison of Models and Systems

Though we have raised some of the moral issues involved in the capitalist model and in the socialist model we have not determined whether either is or both are inherently immoral. If a moral analysis revealed that there were structural elements in either model that were immoral, then the system depicted by the model would be immoral. To the extent that the model was instantiated in a society, people of that society would have to see what was necessary to remove the immorality, what other system might be adopted, and how the change might be best achieved.

We have not discussed in any detail how the economic models intertwine with political and legal systems. Do particular legal and political systems mitigate the negative tendencies of capitalism or of socialism? Do they interfere with the positive tendencies? Can the mix be modelled and morally evaluated? Specific cases, of course, require specific analyses.

In the abstract, the proponents of capitalism frequently put forth the following values: it promotes individual freedom; it promotes and rewards initiative, innovation and the taking of risks; and it results in the efficient production of multitudes of goods, increasing the productivity of society and so benefiting all members of the society. Capitalism is attacked for exploiting the workers, for producing false wants, for waste, and for allowing gross inequalities.

Champions of socialism emphasize equality, security, and the absence of exploitation. The gross inequalities of wealth and income are mitigated under socialism, though some differences in both still exist. Workers are guaranteed work and all are guaranteed that their basic needs will be taken care of—food, shelter, medicine, clothing, education. The lack of exploitation is premised on the fact that no individual employs other individuals. The state is the major if not the sole employer and the state does not exploit its workers for profit as private employers are tempted to do. The absence of complete equality, the difficulties of proper allocation of resources and markets, and the lower productivity on the whole of workers, to the extent that they exist, are seen not as defects of the system but as remediable deficiencies.

During our century different countries have opted for different models. The newly emerging countries of Africa have frequently followed the model of socialism found in China, which is a primarily agricultural socialist model. Other countries have followed the model of socialism in the Soviet Union. Others have taken Sweden as the socialist model to follow. Still others, for instance Japan after World War II, have followed something like the model of the United States. In each case the economic models have been joined with a variety of political systems and have been adopted by people with a particular history and tradition, with certain natural resources, and with various international friends and enemies. Though the moral problems in each case vary to some extent, some basic ones are common to all. Some of these are a function of the economic systems with which they operate.

Economic Systems and Justice

We cannot morally choose or espouse an inherently immoral economic system. But on the assumption that there is more than one economic system that is not inherently immoral, there is no moral imperative mandating that we choose one rather than another. If we assume for the sake of an example that neither the capitalist nor the socialist model presented is inherently immoral, the choice of one rather than the other involves a choice of certain values over others. The mixture of freedom, security, and risk is very different in the two models. Which is the best mixture from a moral point of view? Since neither is immoral, either one, providing it is freely chosen, is morally acceptable. Immoral practices might develop in either system. If they do develop, such practices should be avoided and if possible rooted out. Each society can improve and should attempt to do so. There is no one best society.

Yet any economic system as well as any political system should embody justice to a considerable degree. Distributive justice, justice in the social allocation of benefits and burdens, is frequently thought to be the most important moral component of any economic system. Is justice a function of each system? Is there a capitalist conception of justice and a socialist conception of justice, each appropriate to the system? Is there an eternal or system-neutral conception of justice in terms of which we can evaluate any economic system?

In our discussion of justice we noted that it consists in giving each person his due, in treating equals equally and unequals unequally. We also saw that distributive justice could be formulated in a variety of ways.

In the capitalist system, justice demands equality of opportunity. It does not demand equality of results. The best way to tell who is the fastest runner is to have all runners compete under the same conditions. Someone will finish first, someone will finish last and others will finish somewhere in between. The capitalist system rewards some people who take risks while penalizing others. That is what is involved in risk taking. The rewards are frequently proportional to the risk. Capitalism also rewards a number of other attributes—work, initiative, energy, intelligence, and similar qualities applied to the marketplace. Within the system some may be lucky and others unlucky. But as long as there is equality of opportunity and as long as rewards are sufficient to generate productive activity, justice has been served. If we need a formula, each is rewarded in accordance with his input into the economy. "From each as he wishes to participate, to each as his participation is successful" might be its slogan.

Justice in a socialist system consists not only of equality of opportunity but it also allows proportionality of differential rewards. It guarantees that all receive some reward but tends to limit the amount of the reward anyone may get. A common slogan used to describe socialism is "from each according to his ability, to each according to his work." Lenin, among others, noted that this was not the social ideal. The social ideal which embodies justice is the slogan descriptive of communism, "from each according to his ability, to each according to his need."

We have already seen the suggestion of John Rawls that we choose our principles of justice behind a veil of ignorance. The two principles of justice thus derived, he claims, are compatible with both capitalism and socialism.

Obviously a view of justice which demands equality of results will not be compatible with capitalism. Nor will a view of justice which requires that differential rewards according to merit, work, or input be compatible with a system requiring equality of rewards. A variety of formulations of justice are possible and appropriate for various circumstances. It would be inappropriate in a race, for instance, to require that everyone be given first place. If we want a race, then the honor of first place should go to the one who wins. If we are not interested in seeing who is fastest, but we feel that other conditions should be taken into account, then we may assign handicaps, equalizing weight, size, training, or other differentials. But once these are established, we will still expect one person to win. Justice does not preclude our playing that game. Nor does it require that when we play it we not reward the winner. However, it may, for a variety of reasons, require that we not award him certain kinds of prizes, prizes out of proportion to the fact that the race is a game or a sport. But the consideration of justice here is different from the consideration of justice in having all the runners run under the same track conditions or in having some run with a handicap.

A similar approach can be taken with respect to justice in economic systems and the justice of economic systems. There is not just one notion of justice applicable; there are several different formulations and one of them may be appropriate for one purpose and kind of activity and another for another kind of event and activity. Each formulation of justice may be taken as a prima facie formulation. If its application is appropriate, it should be applied. If two or more different approaches seem to apply and if their application is mutually contradictory, then we must see what arguments can be mustered in defense of each in the particular case. What are the claimed injustices? How do they compare with the other claimed injustices? Is there some way to reconcile the differing claims? How are the claims supported? Which arguments prevail in the given case?

This solution may be unsatisfactory to some who claim to have the final, true, or applicable view of justice. But faced with competing claims, we can resolve the conflict in this instance only by trying to sort out the claims and arguments in support of them. We may not reach a solution with which everyone agrees. The debate may not be settled. All this is true. But all this neither means that we should not continue to strive to achieve justice in our economic systems nor that we should rest contented that the view of justice which we have is the last word on the topic. We should be constantly prepared to recognize injustice where we did not previously perceive it, and should be ready, if the argument demands it, to reevaluate the justice of the economic system in which we find ourselves.

Further Reading

Acton, H.B. *The Morals of Markets: An Ethical Exploration.* London: Longman Group Limited, 1971.

Arthur, John, and Shaw, William H., eds. *Justice and Economic Distribution.* Englewood Cliffs, N.J.: Prentice-Hall, Inc., 1978.

Brandt, Richard B., ed. *Social Justice.* Englewood Cliffs, N.J.: Prentice-Hall, Inc., 1962.

Boulding, Kenneth E. *Beyond Economics: Essays on Society, Religion, and Ethics.* Ann Arbor: The University of Michigan Press, 1968.

Dalton, George. *Economic Systems & Society.* Baltimore: Penguin Books, 1974.

Hare, R.M. "What Is Wrong With Slavery," In *Philosophy and Public Affairs,* VIII (1979), pp. 103–121.

Harrington, Michael. *Socialism.* New York: Saturday Review Press, 1972.

Nozick, Robert. *Anarchy, State, and Utopia.* New York: Basic Books, Inc., 1974.

Rawls, John. *A Theory of Justice.* Cambridge, Mass.: Harvard University Press, 1971.

7 American Capitalism: Moral or Immoral?

American capitalism from its inception to the present day has grown, developed, and changed. An attempt to reduce it during this whole period to the model described in the last chapter would be a gross oversimplification. Central to the changes that have taken place in American capitalism are its varying relations to government. The American economic system does not exist in a vacuum. It is closely tied to the political, cultural, and social system of the United States, and an adequate moral evaluation of it must take these relations into account.

The central component of the American economic system is sometimes called free enterprise. In terms of our earlier model, free enterprise emphasizes the absence of government ownership, control, regulation and planning, and the freedom of individuals to enter into transactions of their own choosing. This freedom is significant from a moral point of view. An argument in defense of free enterprise trades heavily on the maturity, intelligence, and responsibility of those operating within the economic system. Each person wishes his own good. Each person, it is further assumed, knows what he wants better than anyone else. He is respected as an autonomous adult and a responsible moral being when he is allowed to make his own decisions and choose his own way of life. We can reasonably assume, following John Rawls, that each person desires maximal freedom and that as a competent, adult, moral being he deserves it, providing it is compatible with like freedom for all.

Adam Smith in his classical defense of capitalism claims that each person in pursuing his own good indirectly and unknowingly also promotes the public interest. The general good is better served in this way, he contends, than by any group directly attempting to promote the general welfare through some means of overall planning and control.

For free enterprise to be morally defensible, however, the transactions between adults must be fair. Fairness can here be specified in procedural rather than substantive terms. A transaction is fair if both parties to it, typically the buyer and the seller, engage in the transaction freely (without coercion) and if both parties have adequate and appropriate knowledge of the relevant aspects of the transaction. If one of the parties hides relevant information, misrepresents the transaction in some way, or intimidates the other party, then the transaction is not a fair one. In such transactions one party takes unfair advantage of the other. A transaction is not defined as fair in terms of the value of the product or service that is transferred because some people may value one product or service more than another. If they are willing to buy a product at a higher price—providing they know what they are doing and are not coerced—the transaction is not unfair. This is the way the market works.

The Relation of the Economic System to a Free-Enterprise Government

What is the relation of the system to government? The economic system can operate only in a broader social system of reasonable security and stability. Government has traditionally provided security and stability for the people of a country by arranging for the means of common defense, protecting the person and property of the members of a society from incursion by other members, and by enforcing contracts and facilitating conditions for the exchange of goods and services. Thus a national government typically provides armed forces for the protection of the country, making the people secure from outside invasion. Through its laws, police force, court and penal system, it protects individuals in the society in their person and property. People can thus feel secure in acquiring goods and safe in their use of them. A nation's laws and courts make possible and enforce legally binding contracts and make available acceptable procedures for the peaceful adjudication of disputes. The government also prints and mints money, the generally acceptable medium of exchange which facilitates transactions within the economic system.

The relation of government and the economic system in the United States did not stop with these considerations. At least five other needs arose that the government sought to meet.

1. Distribution of Economic Rewards

Even if the system of free enterprise works as its defenders argue it should, it rewards only those who contribute to the economy and only in proportion to their contribution. It does not reward those who make no contribution to the economy. If someone can not contribute, he is simply ignored or left out of the activities of the marketplace. No one is forced to enter the marketplace, and those in the marketplace are not forced to consider those who do not enter it. But what does the capitalist system say and do for the sick, disabled, incapacitated, or those unable to take care of themselves? From the point of view of the economic model, they are simply not considered. Yet clearly a nation should not ignore the plight of some of its citizens. They should not starve or die from lack of care simply because they cannot contribute to the economy. The other members of the society, from their largesse and kindness, might help such people through charity. But historically such charity has been both inadequate and frequently demeaning. Hence, the government has been called upon or has taken upon itself to provide for those unable to care for themselves. Has governmental aid been administered wisely and sufficiently? Have people taken advantage of the systems of welfare the government has set up? These and similar questions can be investigated, debated, and possibly answered. But it seems clear that a society has a moral obligation to prevent its members from starving and dying from lack of basic needs when the wherewithal to provide them is available. If capitalism as a system does not consider those who do not contribute to the economy, society as a whole clearly must in some way make up for this deficiency; it acts immorally if it does not.

2. Government in the Marketplace

Government entered the marketplace to provide common goods which perhaps could not be (and in any event were not) provided adequately by the participants in the economic system. The United States highway system is an example of a type of common activity undertaken by the government. As in so many other areas, however, the United States government does not actually build the roads. It finances their building by private contractors. In the past, it assisted in the development of railroads, rather than building, owning, and operating them itself. It limited the liability of those who wanted to build nuclear power plants, enabling private producers to undertake a venture they felt involved too much risk to pursue otherwise. National, state, and local government has provided public education, public parks, reservoirs, and dams. Government has sought to consider and protect the common good where it was threatened by the transactions of private individuals and firms.

3. Cyclical Development of Capitalism

Capitalism historically suffered from cyclical development. It experienced periods of great expansion and productivity, followed by periods of recession and depression. The cyclical nature of capitalism seems to be part of its natural tendency. But the periods of decline and depression carry with it great pain and distress for many affected by it. As demand decreases, factories produce less. As they produce less they need fewer workers. People are laid off and are unable to find work elsewhere. Unemployment grows and with it comes misery for the unemployed and their families. Such a situation may be one that defenders of the capitalist system are willing to accept as part of the natural mechanisms of the market, which tends to be self-correcting. But such booms and busts take their toll on the members of a society, who clearly would prefer a system with more security and less drastic cycles. The government entered the economic realm both to alleviate the plight of the unemployed and to help set limits on the cycles through which the free market tends to go. It has attempted to keep the cycles from rising or falling too sharply. The task is a complicated one that government has not yet mastered. But it attempts to do so through its fiscal and monetary policies, through control of its spending, and other similar devices. In fulfilling this function government in America has entered substantially into the economic system.

4. Morality and the Free Enterprise System

The premise of the morality of the free enterprise system was that each party enter the transaction freely and with adequate knowledge appropriate to the transaction. Several tendencies of capitalism, however, have historically tended to undermine the fairness of transactions. In each of these cases government has been called upon to regulate the conditions of the transaction in an attempt to keep the transactions fair.

Antitrust legislation is one example of such an attempt. In capitalism, capital tends to accumulate in the hands of a few who become rich and powerful. If they can successfully dominate an industry, they can prevent free entry into that industry and they can set the conditions under which goods will be sold and persons hired. Such power clearly renders the transaction no longer one between equals who freely enter the transaction for mutual gain. The one holding the monopoly is able to restrain trade and free enterprise in the area he dominates and is able to set the conditions for the transaction. The other member, if he wants the product, has no alternative but to enter into the transaction with the monopolist on the latter's terms. The transaction is not free if the former needs the product or the job to live. To prevent such a situation from occurring, to preserve the conditions of a free and fair market, antitrust laws make restraint of trade illegal.

Regulated industries such as communications and the electric power industry provide a second example. In many countries these industries are owned and operated by the government and are seen as a common good. In the United States communications and power companies are privately owned. But clearly it has been in the general interest not to have competing telephone companies and many small producers of electric power. A single telephone system and large producers of electricity in a given area, tied in with other producers, can achieve economies of scale and efficiency. Monopolies are allowed in these areas. But the government regulates these industries to prevent them from taking unfair advantage of their customers.

Government also operates in a third area—that of food and drugs. In most transactions a buyer can decide on inspection whether he wishes to buy a product and whether he wants to pay the price asked. But the ordinary person can hardly be expected to know the effects of many drugs or to have a chemical laboratory in his home which he uses to analyze a drug before he takes it. He is at a great disadvantage with respect to his knowledge when he engages in a transaction involving the purchase of drugs. A transaction is fair only if both sides have adequate appropriate knowledge. The buyer can easily be fooled and taken advantage of, much to the detriment of his health. People have sought, therefore, to protect their interests and guarantee the fairness of the transaction by having the government intervene. The government tests the effects of drugs, or forces drug firms to test the effects, and then regulates the sale of drugs. It also regulates the contents of food products, mandates clear labeling, and determines what other information the manufacturer must supply to the purchaser in order to make the transaction fair.

5. Taxation

The fifth type of government intervention in the system is a function of the previous four and of other similar activities. Through taxation, the government redistributes income, regulates business activity, and finances its own activities. It funnels money to the private sector through welfare-type programs and through contracts. It is also a giant employer in its own right, supporting vast numbers of people in the armed forces and in the large government bureaucracy required to run its many programs.

The model of American capitalism is not a static one. Its entanglement was justified at various stages to keep the conditions of the market's operation fair and just, to make up for deficiencies of the system, and to supplement the system.

Taking all of this into account, what moral evaluation can we make of present-day American capitalism? Is it inherently immoral? If not, does it contain any immoral aspects which can and should be remedied? Many Marxists claim that capitalism is immoral, and we shall look at their charges first. A number of non-Marxists have also morally condemned capitalism and we shall investigate their claims next. Finally, we shall consider the moral alternatives to American capitalism proposed by critics from several points of view.

The Marxist Critique

Karl Marx analyzed nineteenth century capitalism, primarily as he found it in the England of his time. Though Marx frequently uses moral language in describing the ills of capitalism, commentators disagree about whether he actually condemned capitalism from a moral point of view. Capitalism, for Marx, was a necessary stage of economic and social development, but a stage which was to be superseded by the higher stage of communism. Yet many of Marx's followers have put his condemnation of capitalism into moral form and have claimed that capitalism is inherently immoral.

We shall examine three of the major claims such Marxists make. Capitalism is inherently immoral because it cannot exist without robbing the worker of his due. Capitalism is inherently immoral bcause it necessarily involves the alienation of human beings. Capitalism is inherently immoral at the present time because it protects the vested interest of the few and prevents the many from achieving a better, more just, more equitable society.

1. Exploitation of the Work Force

The first charge states that capitalism is based on exploitation of the worker—that is, not paying him what he truly deserves. Slavery, we have already seen, is inherently immoral. According to the Marxist critics, capitalism involves wage slavery. Capitalism cannot exist without exploiting the worker. Hence there is no way of remedying this evil while preserving the system. Since capitalism is inherently immoral, it should be replaced by socialism and eventually by full communism.

The basis for the claim of necessary exploitation is Marx's labor theory of value. According to this theory, commodities are exchanged at their real value. If this were not the case, then what one gains as a seller, he would lose as a buyer. Since commodities are exchanged at their real value, the question which must be answered is where profit comes from. Profit, in Marxist terminology, is called surplus value, or the money which a commodity brings a seller over its cost of production. Profit is accumulated as capital and allows the producer to expand and produce more. The producer would not produce if he did not get profit. But if we assume that all commodities are sold at their real value there will be nothing left over, and hence there will be no profit. We are forced to conclude that something is not sold at its real value. That something is human labor.

What all commodities have in common, according to the Marxist analysis, is that they are the products of human labor. Human labor finds raw materials and makes them available for transformation by further human labor into commodities. If I wish to trade what I have for what you have, I also wish to know the comparative value of each. The basis for comparison is something which is a common measure for both. This is the labor embodied in each. The total human labor that goes into a commodity is the basis for determining its value. For comparative purposes, moreover, we use the socially necessary unskilled labor time required to make a product as our least common denominator. Once again, if I trade my product for yours and if we trade equally, there is no profit left over. Profit must come from someone not being paid the value which he contributes to a commodity. It comes, according to the Marxist analysis, from workers not being paid the value which they contribute. The owner of the means of production systematically exploits his workers or steals from them by paying them less than the value they produce. Unless he did, he would get no profit and have no capital to invest.

But why do workers sell their labor for less than it is worth? The answer is that they are forced to do so in order to live. This is why the system is said to be a type of slavery; namely, wage slavery. Workers do not own the means of production. Hence they are forced to sell their labor power in order to live. They have no choice, unless they wish to die of starvation. Nor are they free to seek employment where they will be paid the full value they produce. Every employer exploits his workers; he must in order to make a profit. If a worker has a choice of jobs it is simply a choice of whether he will be exploited by company A or company B. The system makes all employers exploiters and exploits all workers.

Since an employer makes his profit by paying his workers less than the value they produce, he will tend to increase his profit by paying them as little as possible. If he pays them by the day, he will wish them to work twelve rather than ten hours, and ten rather than eight hours. If he pays them by the hour, he will wish them to produce during that hour five rather than four objects and four rather than three. As long as there is not enough work for everyone who wants it, there will be a buyer's market and workers will have to work for lower wages than they would otherwise. It is in the interest of the owners of the means of production to have a surplus work force, or for there to be a pool of unemployed. A higher unemployment rate is to their advantage rather than a lower one or no unemployment at all. The worker, on the other hand, will seek to work shorter hours, or to work less hard during the hours he does work. He will also seek more pay rather than less, so that he can improve his standard of living. The war between management and labor stems from the fact that management wishes to pay as little as possible for labor in order to increase its profits, while labor wishes to receive as much of what it deserves as possible.

In the nineteenth century Marx perceived certain trends in capitalism. He described the tendency of the owners to pay workers less and less, forcing women and even children to enter the labor force in order to help support their families. He described a growing army of the unemployed and more and more blatant exploitation until the workers finally would be forced to seize the means of production, take over the factories, put an end to exploitation and capitalism, and form a new social order—communism (the first stage of which he termed socialism).

The scenario has not taken place according to the Marxist script. The workers united and formed unions, in part, ironically due to the efforts of Marx. As a result, the workers were able to gain more pay, shorter hours, and better working conditions. The impetus for them to revolt and seize the factories diminished. Their interests became identified with the continuation of the system rather than with its overthrow. Contemporary Marxists asked how this was possible and did it mean that capitalism is no longer immoral?

Lenin gave an answer to both questions. According to him, the workers in the West were appeased by the increases they received in higher earnings and the goods they were able to buy with those earnings. Their standard of living rose so that the American worker lived better than any large number of people in human history.

But this does not mean that the worker is no longer exploited. He is still exploited, even if he does not realize it. Profit still comes from paying the worker less than the value he produces. But productive capacities have increased to such an extent that the worker can enjoy the fruits of productivity even while being exploited. Furthermore, the worker is no longer as grossly exploited as he was in the nineteenth century. This is not a result of the generosity of management. It is a result of capitalism's advance to the stage of imperialism. American corporations are able to exploit people in other countries, primarily in the underdeveloped countries of the world.

The upshot for Marxists is that capitalism still involves exploitation and hence is still inherently immoral. The American workers are still exploited, even though they have achieved a higher standard of living. They could be better off than they are. Part of the reason they enjoy the standard of living they do, however, is the fact that American companies are exploiting other peoples of the world. Capitalism, the Marxists claim, necessarily involves exploitation.

What are we to say of the claim? The claim depends on the validity of Marx's labor theory of value. This is an economic theory which attempts to explain not only profit but also prices, wages, economic cycles, and the variety of economic phenomena with which economics deals. Most western economists have not accepted Marx's version of the labor theory of value. It does not give due weight to creativity in the productive process or to the place of invention in expanding the economic pie which is to be divided. It fails to take into account the role of risk and the entrepreneur. It is inadequate as an analysis of contemporary American capitalism because it is vastly different from the system Marx described. Through pension plans and insurance policies American workers are in fact the owners of the means of production to a considerable extent. The workers are not oppressed. There may be some exploitation, but exploitation consists of paying the worker less than the productivity of a worker at the margin. It is not built into the system.

Nor does the claim that American capitalism survives because it exploits the underdeveloped countries carry much weight. There was a time during which many European countries had colonies; however, this time has passed. There are also many countries now which are not capitalist—they are socialist, and some of them have communist governments. But the underdeveloped countries do not sell the United States goods or raw materials at lower prices than they sell the same items to socialist countries. American companies pay workers of a country with a lower standard of living less than what American companies pay American workers. Is this exploitation? The question is a complex one, involving comparisons of buying power, skill, and comparative wage structures. But the major point is that there are alternatives for such countries. They can refuse American industry, and they can deal with other countries if they think it is not to their advantage to deal with the United States.

The conclusions we can draw from this brief analysis is that there are plausible replies to the Marxist charge of exploitation. The replies have not satisfied the Marxists; nor have attempts at updating Marx's theory satisfied most Western economists—the attack is at the least inconclusive if not definitely false.

2. Alienation of the People

The second claim is that capitalism is inherently immoral because it alienates human beings. It does not treat them as ends in themselves; separates them into antagonistic camps and sets them one against another; it stultifies the workers; it involves domination of some by others; and it produces other negative effects on all those who live within the system.

Alienation is a negative term. It describes the state of a person who is wrongfully separated from something to which he should be united, or who is dominated by something of his own making. The state or condition of alienation may be a conscious one in which a person feels alienated; but someone may be alienated without feeling so.

There are various kinds of alienation. People may feel alienated from their government. Government is something created by people to serve their needs. When they have no control over it and when government dominates them instead of responding to them and serving them, they are alienated from it. Religious alienation might be described by a believer as separation from God through sin; by an unbeliever as man being dominated by God, a creature of man's own imaginative making. Marx claims, however, that basic to all the other kinds of alienation is economic alienation. He describes it as the alienation of the worker from the product of his labor, from the productive process, and from other men.

Under the capitalistic system, Marx observes, objects come to dominate men. People are judged by what they have, not by what they are. People work and live for possessions. The possessions come to dominate them, rather than being objects which they use to satisfy their needs.

Under capitalism, work is typically stultifying, noncreative, and routine. Instead of expressing oneself through one's work and developing all the sides of one's personality, work limits, cramps, and dulls the worker. People live when they are not working, and when they are working they can hardly be said to be living. They look forward to their leisure time, weekends, vacations, and coffee breaks when they can be themselves. They are separated from their labor, which they have sold to their employer. They are alienated from their labor, which they must sell in order to live.

Finally, the capitalist system, built on competition, divides men from each other. Instead of all mankind living together in harmony and peace, capitalism pits workers against employers. It pits competitors against each other, just as it forces workers to compete against each other for jobs. Capitalism is built on the division of society into classes, the owners of the means of production on one side and the workers on the other. The society is divided, and the state, laws, courts, police, schools, churches, and the media are all controlled by the ruling class. The ruling class uses all these social institutions to dominate the workers, keep them subservient, and insure the continuation of the institution of private property. The workers are thus alienated in many aspects of their lives. The owners of the means of production also live in an alienated society, they are also evaluated in terms of what they have, and they are also separated from other men and dominated by what they have.

Marxists maintain that capitalism necessarily produces alienation since it is a function of private property and the division of labor. Alienation cannot be eliminated without eliminating private property, and this cannot be eliminated without at the same time eliminating capitalism. Hence capitalism is inherently immoral.

Defenders of capitalism have given various replies. One is to claim that the picture that Marx draws is a caricature of capitalist society. In America, they claim, the worker is freer than in any other society in the world. He has a strong voice in government, which frequently protects his rights and defends him against employers. Though there is still dull work to be done, automation has taken over much of it and has freed peple to do more creative work. Dull work that is a function of manufacturing, moreover, is not peculiar to capitalism, but is present wherever there is industrialization. A second response points out that Marx's description of capitalist society as a society of class conflict may have been true of nineteenth century England. The history of the United States, however, has been one of great class mobility. In fact, it is sometimes difficult for people to know which class they belong to. Classes are not obvious, and the division of people into proletariat and bourgeoisie is not clearly applicable to the people of the United States. Marx's description also ignores the spirit of cooperation which is present in many aspects of American life. The emphasis on goods undoubtedly characterizes many Americans. It has been somewhat tempered in recent times by large numbers of young adults who revolted against the emphasis on goods that typified their parents' values.

A third approach to the Marxist charge of alienation has been to see whether alienation has actually been eliminated in those countries which have done away with private property. The Soviet Union is the prime example of such a society. But clearly, the defenders of capitalism argue, during the reign of Stalin the Soviet people were more oppressed and alienated from their government than Americans have ever been. The claim that private property is the cause of alienation is therefore disproven.

There are other replies as well. The ones we have given exemplify the line they take. The replies have not convinced the Marxists. But they have a certain validity. Marx's description of the alienation of the worker in the nineteenth century is not an accurate picture of the worker in present-day America. Yet there are also aspects of the Marxist attack that are valid. Many people in America complain that government is out of control and that they have no real say in how they are governed; others complain about the emphasis of Americans on material goods; and still others speak in terms of alienation. Still, no one has produced an analysis which satisfactorily shows that these ills are inherent to contemporary American capitalism. Once again, then, the claimed inherent immorality of capitalism remains an open question.

3. Vested Interests

The third charge is that capitalism defends the vested interests of the few and prevents the vast productive forces of society from truly serving the masses. The natural tendency of the productive process is towards social ownership instead of private ownership of the means of production. Those in the capitalist class, however defend their own position and interests by preventing the transformation from private ownership to social ownership. In so doing, they delay the inevitable and prevent the people from enjoying the satisfaction of their needs which is possible given the great resources and productive capacity of our country. According to this critique, capitalism may not always have been inherently immoral. But it is immoral now, since it prevents the development of a morally better stage of social development. The analysis can be given a utilitarian interpretation. The consequences of protecting the vested interests of the rich at the expense of the workers produces less good on the whole than would the adoption of socialism or communism.

The reply of the defender of capitalism is to deny that the American system protects the rich at the expense of the worker. It protects and benefits all in the society, even if some people benefit more than others. The defender of the system then turns to socialism as it exists in the world today, whether it be democratic socialism such as that found in England or communistic socialism such as that found in the Soviet Union. Both are examples of highly productive societies. Yet neither society seems superior to American society either morally or materially. Hence, the reply continues, the claim that the American system prevents the development of a better society is a claim without adequate foundation. Moreover, the workers of the United States (the ones whom the Marxist critics say benefit most by a change to socialism) show no signs of developing a Marxist revolution.

The third class of inherent immorality, therefore, has also not been convincingly demonstrated. Capitalism may be inherently immoral; but the Marxists' attacks fail to prove this.

Non-Marxist Moral Critiques of American Capitalism

Though Marxists have tended to be the most vocal, systematic, and thorough critics of capitalism, they are not its only critics. The non-Marxist critics do not always speak with one voice. Nor is it always clear whether the ills to which they point are inherent evils of capitalism or remediable by-products. We will consider three criticisms which are symptomatic of others: capitalism creates waste and false needs; capitalism feeds the military–industrial complex at the expense of the general population; capitalism creates gross and unjust inequalities.

1. False Needs and Over-Production

The attack on American capitalism as wasteful takes a variety of forms. Americans have grown up with comparative abundance. We have had large expanses of land, a wealth of natural resources, and a high standard of living. As a result of our competitive system, we have worried little about conservation of our natural resources or about the resources of the rest of the world which we could buy. The waste is evident in many areas. Our use of energy and gasoline in particular is profligate. We have extended our cities into suburb after suburb without adequate public transportation, and then have had to rely on large fuel-inefficient automobiles which are rarely fully occupied. We have tended to build obsolescence into most of our products. We have preferred disposable products to ones with replaceable parts. The list is endless.

In many instances, the claim goes, we could have done much better. Competition has frequently led to duplication of wasteful effort. Manufacturers have built obsolescence into their products to protect their future markets, not to serve the consumer. Our cities and suburbs grew without plan or adequate forethought. Our waste is a national disgrace.

The attack is in large part true. We are paying the price for mistakes we made in the past. But our past waste was not the result of capitalism, nor is waste a necessary ingredient in capitalism. Many European countries with capitalist economies, for instance, have not fallen prety to the vice of waste. Nor is it clear that centralized planning eliminates waste, though that waste is frequently of a different kind. The chronic shortage of goods in some socialist countries is sometimes a result of producing a surplus of the wrong goods (e.g., too many pairs of size 13 shoes), rather than having too few materials for the production of goods. Duplication of effort is part of the price of competition. But its defenders claim with some justification that on the whole, it is more efficient than centralized planning.

The second part of the criticism strikes at the creation of false needs. Entrepreneurs create a product—e.g., an electric toothbrush—for which there was not an antecedent need or desire. Through a highpowered advertising campaign the manufacturer convinces people that they need the product to clean their teeth. The result is that a false need is created and filled, consuming resources that could be better used for other products.

Defenders of the free enterprise system have argued that the notion of false needs is an arbitrary one. Who is to say what is a real and what is a false need? Consumers, they claim, should   decide for themselves how they want to spend their money. They are not forced to buy one product rather than another. Nor is it true that manufacturers can sell anything they make simply by advertising it. Many products fail to gain a market because consumers resist the ads or ignore the product. The atack assumes that someone knows best what the people of the country should have. Their counterclaim is that people should be free both to produce and purchase what they wish without direction from some group with supposedly privileged knowledge.

The criticism, whatever its validity, is not central enough to render capitalism inherently immoral. It may, however, indicate an area in need of control, attention, or reform.

2. The Military-Industrial Complex

The second critique attacks the military–industrial complex and takes a variety of forms. One view claims that the government drains the people of the country through taxation in order to support industries which produce materials for war.

Another view claims that the system can in the long run exist only if it is periodically sustained by war and destruction and then the need for rebuilding which war produces. If this latter were the case, then the charge of an inherently immoral element could be sustained. A third claims that the military–industrial complex controls the government and has taken the power out of the hands of the people, if it did indeed ever reside there.

No easy answer is possible to such charges, but a few observations might be in order. First, war did not start with the appearance of capitalism. It has existed since the beginning of recorded history. Capitalism is not the only root of war, if it is a root at all. Second, the communist-run countries (such as the USSR) spend as much as and sometimes proportionately more on arms than the United States. Expenditure for war is not an exclusive characteristic of capitalism as found in the United States. Both the Soviet Union and the United States plausibly claim, moreover, that their major effort is in defense spending because of the threat posed by the other country. Each side has its hawks and doves. Third, the United States does spend large sums on its military establishment, but it is not clear that its economy would topple if its defense budget were reallocated to peaceful pursuits. There is even reason to believe that the opposite might be the case. Finally, the claim that the people have no voice in the political process because of the military-industrial complex is an overstatement. They may have less voice than many would like; however, they do have some voice and have achieved some gains at the expense of the military–industrial complex, and there is no inherent reason why they cannot make further strides in this direction within the system. The trick is to preserve democracy and prevent a slide towards a dictatorship.

3. Inequalities Inherent in the System

The third attack charges that capitalism creates gross and unjust inequalities. The disparity between the very rich and the very poor in the United States is enormous. A small percentage of the population controls a large proportion of the nation's wealth and income. The tax structure which is supposed to tax the rich is so full of loopholes that the tax burden is borne primarily by the middle class. Many of those with the largest incomes pay no or very little tax. No human being, the argument goes, is so much better off than another that the vast discrepancy in income among those who earn over $1,000,000 a year and those who earn $10,000 can be justified. According to Rawl's principles of justice, differences in income are justifiable if opportunities are open to all and if the least advantaged group benefits by the difference. It is not clear that the least advantaged group does benefit by the large differences in income; nor is it clear that even if they did, the benefit they receive is in any way proportional to the benefit that the rich receive. The poor not only obtain little improvement in their material conditions, but by comparison with the luxury of the wealthy they suffer a loss of self-respect. To compound the difficulties, many of the wealthiest families of our country amassed their fortunes in often questionable and unethical ways. The history of the robber barons is a notorious period in American history.

The drive toward greater equalization of wealth and income is one that has many supporters. The charge that the tax structure needs overhauling is widely recognized. The claim that the discrepancy between the wealth of the very rich and the poverty of the very poor is excessive carries a good deal of weight. Yet the question remains whether all of this, though a result of capitalism, is a necessary feature of capitalism. Differences in income are to be expected in a competitive system and in a system in which monetary reward is a prime incentive for creativity in production. Yet the overall system can reduce the differential between the highest and lowest paid, or it can equalize the two considerably more than it presently does through a different tax structure. Such injustices can be handled within the system. The charge, therefore, does not necessarily require a change in the system, although there is one way of achieving the equalization many seek.

Alternatives to Contemporary American Capitalism

Defenders of the American economic-political system feel there is no need for a change. Though they may admit the system is not perfect, they argue it is the best history has yet known. It has provided wealth for the masses, a great variety of goods, inventions, scientific and technological advances for all mankind, and a degree of human freedom unparalleled in previous history. Not everyone agrees, however, that ours is the best of all possible systems. Some look at American cities, at the poor, and at many business practices and see what might be improved and then suggest ways of improvement that vary dramatically. Others dream of radical change, of a new and better system, while still others fear the dreams of the radicals, of the right or of the left.

Neither Hitler's Germany nor Stalin's Soviet Union hold much appeal for most Americans. The dictatorial right is as much feared as the totalitarian left. From a moral point of view both involve a restraint on individual freedom incompatible with America's traditional value system. The moral arguments in support of our turning to either of these as real alternatives carry little, if any, weight. Rather, those two cases have become models of what most Americans feel we must guard against. They are imaginable alternatives to our present system, but models which are more feared and fought than pursued.

Nor is a radical revolution likely within the foreseeable future in the United States. The workers have not formed a proletariat of the type Marx thought would arise and have not seized the means of production. Modern-day Marxists have sought revolutionary forces in the intellectuals, students, unemployed, and in the outcasts of society. But none of these groups is sufficiently unified, numerous, or motivated to carry out the revolution in America of which some Marxists still dream.

There are three other alternatives to our present American system, championed by various groups. The three are not necessarily mutually exclusive. One is libertarianism, a movement of the right. A second is workers' democracy, a movement of the left. The third is piecemeal change whereever and however possible with no overall blueprint to be achieved. The first two are in some ways compatible with the third. Both the libertarians and the proponents of workers' democracy complain about the power and influence of government. The libertarians seek to diminish the role of government in business. The defenders of workers' democracy—whether or not they call themselves socialists—seek to end the collusion of big business and government, and to bring democracy into the marketplace. In the American context neither group seeks violent revolution; both pursue dramatic change within the system.

1. The Libertarian Alternative

The Libertarians, as their name indicates, put greater emphasis on liberty. They consider this the major virtue of the free enterprise system. They therefore complain that government has entered the marketplace with its laws, regulations, and taxes to the detriment of the freedom of the American citizen and businessman.

The attack takes several forms and involves not only a view of economics but also a view of government. The typical libertarian, while not an anarchist or someone who advocates the absence of government, is a minimalist concerning the role of government. The legitimate function of government, he maintains, consists of protecting people and property from foreign attack and internal violence, and consists of providing for the adjudication of disputes and the enforcement of contracts. Thus armed forces, police, and a legal and penal system are allowable. But governmental activity beyond these is inappropriate.

In particular, libertarians attack the redistributive function of government. Government, according to this position, should neither tax people nor redistribute income through welfare and other similar programs. The attack on taxes is especially vociferous. Taxation by government, they claim, is theft. If someone at gunpoint stopped you in the street and forced you to hand over 25 percent of your earnings so that he could give it to the poor, you would certainly protest that you were being robbed. Government does the same thing in taxation. Moreover, the libertarians continue, government does not simply turn over the money it takes in taxes to the poor. It uses a significant percentage of what it takes in taxes simply to keep its own machinery and giant bureaucracy operating. Not only does government take money from all of us, but it uses it in ways that many of us do not sanction. It wastes, squanders, and misspends enormous amounts. That it does so should come as no surprise. You and I are careful in how we spend our money because we have to make do on limited funds. Government spends not its own money, but yours and mine, and overspends with impunity—raising taxes if it needs more money, or printing or borrowing more. The resulting inflation further diminishes our real income, already cut by taxes.

The second strenuous attack of the libertarians is on government regulation of business. They see the capitalist system as one based on free competition. If allowed to operate as it could, they claim, there would be no need for government regulation. Competition would remedy the evils which government unsuccessfully and inefficiently tries to correct. Government has a penchant for overkill and over-regulation even when it operates with good intentions. Moreover, many regulations intended for big business slowly drive the small businessman out of business. Government regulations are so many and so complicated that the small businessman must spend more time and money keeping track of them and fulfilling their reporting requirements than he can afford. The government guarantees loans to giants such as Lockheed and Chrysler when they are faced with bankruptcy but provides no help for the small businessman. The libertarians do not claim that the government should help the small businessman; rather, the government should stay out of the business sector entirely, helping neither big nor small business.

The libertarian view is based on the notion of the sanctity of private property. Private property belongs to an individual. If he has worked for it, he deserves to keep what he has earned. If he has taken risks, if he has been lucky, if he has worked especially hard, if he has been innovative, the market will reward him. The rewards he fairly receives rightfully belong to him. They do not belong to government. The truly needly will be taken care of through charity and insurance plans; the lazy and unworthy poor will be forced to change their ways or suffer the consequences of their own actions.

The libertarian view thus has a moral thrust. It champions liberty as a moral virtue worthy of human beings. It faults government as acting immorally in view of taxation, welfare, and many of its other programs. It demands changes. Yet libertarians emphatically defend democracy in the political realm, just as they defend free enterprise in the economic realm.

The libertarian position has not received widespread support. But some of its claims have struck a responsive chord in a number of people. The contemporary American revolt against excessive taxation is one instance of this response. California's rebellion against unlimited property taxes has spread to other parts of the country. Rising inflation and an unreformed tax structure are leading more and more people to adopt the European practice of cutting their own taxes, gambling on not being caught.

Historically, business has not been libertarian. Businesses sought and received protection from government in the way of tariffs and limitations on certain types of imports. They argued that the United States had to be self-sufficient. Its industry had to be protected against the possibility that war might prevent imports. Farmers sought and received governmental support for the prices of their crops. They argued that such support was necessary if farming was to continue successfully. In these and other areas business accepted the protection and help of government. Libertarians maintain that business has paid the price in regulation.

Yet to be consistent, the libertarian cannot complain if people choose to be governed in certain ways (e.g., if they vote for taxes and for government spending) and if they freely choose security over freedom. He claims, however, that government is not truly responsive to the people, that people have not freely chosen that government act as it does, and that those who do not choose certain practices should not be bound by them. The practical matter of how to accomplish the ends libertarianism proposes is yet to be resolved. As an alternative to the present system, it is at best an indicator, an arrow pointing in a possible direction of change. It is not a ready-made alternative waiting in the wings as a panacea to the problems and immorality of the present system.

2. Workers' Democracy

The other alternative to the present system goes under a variety of names. It is sometimes called workers' democracy, sometimes socialism. But the kind of socialism advocated follows neither the Soviet model nor the British model. For the claim is not that government should take over and run industry. The position attacks government as strongly as do the libertarians, but for different reasons.

Workers' democracy sees government as inextricably intertwined with big business. Our elected leaders do not necessarily or consciously aim at supporting business interests at the expense of the interests of the ordinary citizen. But the structures of society are such that the interests of government and the interests of business are most often the same. Government has an enormous budget. Since it does not own industry it spends a good deal in contracts which it gives to private industry. America's interests abroad are predominantly business interests. We protect these interests in foreign countries and support them at home. We fight wars over natural resources in distant lands. Growing numbers of people move easily from the halls of government to the offices of big business, changing hats with little difficulty.

Capitalism has produced for the American worker a better life. He has more goods, comfort, and luxury than workers in any other part of the world and in any other period of history. But the American economic-political system has become more oppressive than liberating. Yet it can be liberated. True democracy is now possible, if we extend democracy to the economic realm and reverify it in the political realm.

Defenders of workers' democracy point out that many of the decisions made by the major corporations in America affect all of our lives more than the decisions made in Congress. We elect our representatives in Congress. We have no say at all in what the Board of Directors of GM or Gulf Oil or any other large corporation decides. The allocation of resources, the building and closing of plants, the creation and termination of jobs are all decisions that directly affect large numbers of people who have no voice in these decisions. Nor is government regulation the answer, since government is intertwined with big business.

The appropriate reply of the American people has been slow in coming. Consumer groups have grown up to protect their interests and to provide some sort of response to big business. Environmentalists have also organized to oppose business projects they consider harmful to the environment. Unions have, of course, represented workers vis-à-vis management and have fought for better wages and working conditions. But because they have been wed to their adversarial role with respect to management they have not typically sought worker participation in management, worker control of the productive process, or workers' democracy. It seems unlikely that workers' democracy will be anything other than a peripheral movement in the United States for a long time to come.

3. Piecemeal Change

If the basic aim of libertarianism is the liberty of the businessman, the basic aim of the workers' democracy is workers' control over their own destiny. In some ways the two positions are similar. Both wish greater freedom for members of society than they have today. Both attack government and the interrelation of government and business. But the means they advocate are dramatically different from one another.

The worker in a workers' democracy would have a say in what is produced and how it is produced. The division between workers and managers would give way. The workers would share in the profits of the firm directly. The adversary relation between employer and employee would be replaced by a cooperative effort of all those engaged in the same enterprise. An effective voice in business decisions would mean as much as an effective voice in government decisions. The democracy we have cherished in the political sector must be recouped and extended to the productive sector.

The division of management from ownership has already taken place in most large firms. Managers are as truly employers as assembly line workers. Peter Drucker has pointed to the unseen revolution in which workers through union pension funds and insurance funds are the largest owners of business. Management works for them in their role as shareholders. The reality of this relation should now be translated into fact. There should be an end to domination of the worker, his exploitation, and his alienation.

The movement toward workers' democracy has been slow in developing. Consumerism and environmentalism have grown. The demand for worker representation on boards of directors has been adopted in Germany, but such representation is rare in the United States. Ironically, the workers themselves have been slow to respond to the call for workers' democracy.

Both libertarianism and workers' democracy are straws in the wind. They are indicative of dissatisfaction with many aspects of big government and big business. They are rallying points for the expression of this dissatisfaction and for proposals for change. Both movements are wedded to change within the system, which may eventually lead to change of the system. They do not espouse violent revolution or sudden, drastic change. Their gradualism is consistent with a piecemeal approach to the correction of the immoral practices within the system.

A small minority claims that the American system is free of immorality, is sufficiently just, and should not be tinkered with. Most people realize that we do not yet have a completely just society, that our structures can be improved, that the war on poverty has not yet been won, that we still have to solve the problems of the appropriate use of energy, and that we have barely begun to face the moral demands made on us by the poor and underdeveloped countries of the world. Yet the consensus in America is that we do not need another system. No other system is morally preferable or waiting to be adopted. We can and should make the morally necessary changes in American capitalism, improve it, and work toward a yet unattained maximal mix of freedom and justice. The real alternative to our present American system does not consist in holistic change. What is most likely to succeed is piecemeal change, correcting ills where possible, outlawing immoral practices, and implementing structural changes that promote moral conduct. American capitalism can be made more moral than it is; the task before all of us is to make the required changes where and how we can.

Further Reading

Action, H.B. *The Morals of Markets; An Ethical Exploration.* London: Longman Group Ltd., 1971.

Arthur, John, and Shaw, William H., eds. *Justice and Economic Distribution.* Englewood Cliffs, N.J.: Prentice-Hall, Inc., 1978.

Boulding, Kenneth E. *Beyond Economics: Essays on Society, Religion and Ethics.* Ann Arbor: The University of Michigan Press, 1970.

Brandt, Richard, ed. *Social Justice.* Englewood Cliffs, N.J.: Prentice-Hall, Inc., 1962.

Chamberlin, John. *The Roots of Capitalism.* Indianapolis: Liberty Press, 1959.

Dalton, George. *Economic Systems & Society: Capitalism, Communism, and The Third World.* Harmondsworth: Penguin Books, 1974.

Drucker, Peter F. *The Unseen Revolution: How Pension Fund Socialism Came to America.* New York: Harper & Row, Publishers, Inc., 1976.

Edwards, Richard C.; Reich, Michael; and Weisskopf, Thomas E., eds. *The Capitalist System: A Radical Analysis of American Society.* 2nd ed. Englewood Cliffs, N.J.: Prentice-Hall, Inc., 1978.

Friedman, Milton. *Capitalism & Freedom.* Chicago: The University of Chicago Press, 1962.

Harrington, Michael. *The Twilight of Capitalism.* New York: Simon & Schuster, Inc., 1976.

Heilbroner, Robert L. *Between Capitalism and Socialism.* New York: Vintage Books, 1970.

Nozik, Robert. *Anarchy, State, and Utopia.* New York: Basic Books, Inc., 1974.

Olafson, Frederick A., ed. *Justice and Social Policy.* Englewood Cliffs, N.J.: Prentice-Hall, Inc., 1961.

Rothbard, Murray. *For a New Liberty.* New York: Macmillan, Inc., 1973.

Schumacher, E.F. *Small Is Beautiful.* New York: Harper & Row, Publishers, Inc., 1973.

Silk, Leonard. *Capitalism: The Moving Target.* New York: Quadrangle/The New York Times Book Co., Inc., 1974.

Sterba, James. *Justice: Alternative Political Perspectives.* Belmont, Ca.: Wadsworth Publishing Co., 1980.

8

Corporate Responsibility and the Moral Audit

At the heart of the American economic system lies the large, publicly owned corporate manufacturer of goods. Such corporations are a prime target for those who attack immorality in business. Any piecemeal approach to remedying immorality in our system must pay special attention to the role and functioning of the large corporation.

We have already seen that the corporation can be held morally liable for its actions and that within the corporation moral responsibility can be held collectively or individually in a variety of ways and on many levels. But we have not yet looked at what corporations and those within them are morally responsible for. Some of the topics will require detailed investigation and will be discussed in later chapters. This chapter will present an overview of the moral responsibility of the corporation as a whole and of the people within it, without trying to examine any particular aspect in great detail.

Businesses can be organized as proprietorships, partnerships, or as different types of corporations such as family, closely-held, not-for-profit, public, holding-company, conglomerate, and multinational. We shall focus on the publicly held, manufacturing type corporation, postponing for later discussion the complications that arise if it is part of a multinational operation. Often the focus of moral and social criticism, this is the kind of business that manufactures possibly dangerous products, that opens and closes plants employing large numbers of workers, that tends to become monopolistic, that creates products sold through high-pressure advertising campaigns, that pollutes the air, poisons the rivers, and harms people through its chemical and toxic effluents. At least this is the kind of enterprise that can do all of these things, and has done so in the past. Holding-companies pose special problems. Family-owned and closely-held businesses, even if incorporated, tend not to divide ownership from management, control, and responsibility. Service and retail corporations in part depend on manufacturers and often deal directly with consumers, posing particular moral problems but also subjecting them to more direct pressures. The large, publicly-owned manufacturing corporation is the typical target of moral critiques and is seen with some justification as a center of the capitalist system, a position it shares with banks and financial institutions.

In dealing with the corporation from a broad perspective I shall discuss four broad topics. I shall first consider the moral status of the corporation and its moral responsibility. Secondly, I shall outline the kinds of moral responsibility appropriate to each of the groups that make up the corporation. Thirdly, I shall investigate the structure of the corporation from a moral point of view. Lastly, I shall differentiate the social responsibilities from the moral responsibilities of the corporation and illustrate the difference by considering a problem of pollution and the environment.

The Moral Status of the Corporation

Defenders of the capitalist system emphasize the value of individual freedom and individual choice. Individuals are free under the system to act as they wish so long as they do not harm others. They may use their money as they choose and they register their preferences by their purchases. The freedom of choice and action on which the system is built requires that the freedom be exercised responsibly, i.e., that it not harm others. The second basic feature of the system is that each person entering into a transaction seeks thereby to achieve his own good or ends. A transaction is fair or just if both parties to it enter the transaction with appropriate knowledge and if they enter it freely. The basic moral components are thus freedom, absence of harm, and fairness of contracts where this involves appropriate knowledge and no force or coercion. It is in terms of these components that we can morally evaluate the corporation and its activities.

The corporation is a special kind of entity. It can act, hold property, and be sued. It not only has limited liability, but it also shelters its shareholders or owners from personal liability.

There are two views of the corporation. One—the legal-creator view—sees it entirely as a creature of law, existing only in contemplation of law. According to this view, the corporation is created by the state and does not exist without it. Since the state and the law are themselves creatures of society, the corporation is a creature of society. It has special qualities, privileges, and liabilities as a result of social decision and action. The corporation is made by society for its benefit. When the corporation no longer benefits society, society may modify or do away with it. Corporate structures vary from society to society and corporations are not necessary for society, even if industrial productive enterprises are necessary for modern societies. How they are structured, owned, and operated can vary greatly. According to this view, the corporation exists by public license. If and when corporations are found to harm the public good, they can be legitimately restricted, changed, and even, if necessary, eliminated.

The second view—the legal-recognition view—focuses not on the legal status of the corporation but on the corporation as a free, productive enterprise. Individuals have the moral right to do what they choose as long as they do not harm others thereby. They can, among other things, both produce goods and join together with others to produce goods. If they choose to organize their productive capacities, one of the ways open to them is incorporation. According to this view a corporation is formed by its members who organize themselves in certain ways. The state does not create the corporation. It simply registers and recognizes the existence of the corporation, similar to the way it registers a marriage or the birth of children for legal purposes. The corporation is a freely formed organization. Those who buy shares in the corporation provide money for its operation in the hope of increasing their capital through the productive success of the firm. They take the risk of losing the money they invest in a corporation, but their risk is limited to the amount of money they invest. Their gain is proportional to the percentage of the firm they own and to the profit of the corporation. The limitations of the liability of the corporation are set by law, but this again is simply an affirmation of an accepted practice freely entered into. Creditors know the status of the corporation and realize in dealing with it that they cannot attach the property of the shareholders and that their claims are limited to the assets of the corporation . . . .

The legal-recognition view emphasizes that the corporation is a result of a free activity on the part of those who form it and on the part of those who deal with it. It is not a creation of the state or of society. It may be limited by society if it harms society, just as an individual may be restrained in his actions if he harms society. But since it is not a creature of society, it sets its own ends and operates for its own purposes. It makes profit by serving society. But its end is not primarily to serve society. Its end is to produce and sell certain goods, thereby earning a desired return on its investment. Since its end is not directly to help society, in evaluating it from a moral or social point of view it is inappropriate to fault it for not helping society in any way other than by doing what it is formed to do.

The two views of the corporation lead to different approaches to its moral and social obligations. According to the legal-creator view, society can legitimately demand that it do certain kinds of activities, even if the corporation itself or those running it do not wish to do those things. According to the legal-recognition view the corporation is an autonomous entity, a being owned and run by a freely constituted group which has no special obligations simply because it is organized in a certain way. Since it is not the creation of society, society can regulate its free activity only to the extent that it rightly and justifiably regulates the free activity of individuals whose proper antecedent freedom the state should protect and who do not receive their freedom from the state. Proponents of both views must acknowledge, however, that there are activities in which the corporation is not allowed to participate because these activities harm others, and that the law provides a necessary backdrop without which the corporation could not function as it does. Since we need not settle the dispute between the two views here, I shall analyze the moral responsibilities of the corporation that are compatible with both of them. This involves a discussion of shareholders, the board of directors, management, and labor.

The relation of the corporation to its investors requires careful analysis. What is the relation of those who own stock in the corporation and the corporation itself? Why is their liability limited, and is this morally justifiable? For what, if anything, are the shareholders of a corporation morally responsible?

The moral status of the shareholder is an ambiguous one. Moral responsibility involves a causal connection to an action or result that is morally evaluated, and moral responsibility is properly ascribed and assumed only if the action in question was done knowingly and freely and if there were no excusing conditions. We have seen that the corporation can correctly be said to act, even if it acts only when those within it act. In a family-owned or closely-held corporation the owners of the corporation and the principal managers are typically the same people. Hence the owners, as managers, have responsibility for what the corporation does. Limited liability shields the personal property of the owners not only from creditors but also from those who file suit for damage of a negligent or criminal type. The shareholder of a large, publicly-held corporation is a part-owner of the corporation. He may own a very, very small part indeed. His ownership, moreover, is typically separated from management. He is in no sense a manager and has no voice in the management of the corporation. He has a vote proportional to the number of shares he owns—a vote which he can exercise at the annual shareholders meeting on the issues presented for a vote by management. But the small shareholder has no say in what gets on the agenda, nor does his vote carry much weight. Even large shareholders may own a very small percentage of the stock of a giant corporation.

Can the shareholder in such a situation be held responsible for what the firm does? According to our earlier analysis, the shareholder is in fact very distant from the causal relation between an action of the corporation and its effects. If a corporation is established for an immoral end, then no one can morally support its activities through the purchase of stock. But the ordinary public corporation does not have an immoral end. If those who hold stock in a corporation know that the corporation acts immorally, then they should do what they can to change the practices of the corporation, and failing that should sever their connection with the firm by selling their stock. The relation of stockholder and management, however, is a morally fuzzy one. The managers, strictly speaking, work for the shareholders, who are the owners of the corporation. The managers act as agents for the shareholders. Yet the shareholders in fact have little, if any, control over the managers. It is therefore farfetched to hold shareholders responsible for what the managers do according to the usual rule that responsibility falls on the person or persons who start a causal chain of agency.

Both the legal-creator and the legal-recognition views of the corporation fail to take into account the separation of ownership from management which is the rule for large corporations. It is not clear exactly what a shareholder of a large corporation contracts into by purchasing a share in a company. Frequently it is simply an investment made as a result of a broker's suggestion. The concept of owning a share of the company and of being responsible for what the company does is not part of the consciousness of many shareholders. The situation is magnified when someone owns stock through a pension or retirement plan, through a life insurance policy, or through a mutual fund. Though his money is invested in certain stocks and he owns a certain portion of these stocks, he frequently does not have any idea what stocks his money is invested in or how much he owns of each. Hence, he can hardly be responsible for what the corporation of which he is a part-owner does. The anomaly is that he is penalized for what the managers do and for which the corporation is sued. When the corporation pays a suit, the shareholders in effect pay it, even though they had nothing to do with the action in question. But they also gain by actions management takes which, even if immoral, add to the profit of the firm.

Corporations are the result of free agreements, even if owners do not know what management does. They purchase stock knowing that they will not have control and knowing that they will gain or lose depending on how effectively management runs the corporation. They know that the corporation may be sued, that it may make a profit or suffer losses, and they know in general how such things may happen. Shareholders agree to invest money and understand what this means. The corporation in turn acts under the direction of management. The corporation owns property, produces and sells goods, is liable for what it produces and for its commitments. Providing its actions do not harm anyone and providing its transactions are fair, the corporation as an institution is a morally acceptable kind of entity, a morally acceptable mode of organizing business, and a morally acceptable way of mediating the business relations among people.

Moral Responsibility Within the Corporation

We can outline the kinds of things for which the large, publicly-owned manufacturing corporation is responsible. There may be some things for which the corporation as a whole is responsible. But since the corporation acts only through the agency of those who work for it, we can also identify, at least in many cases, who has responsibility for what. In attempting to outline some of these obligations, we can start by considering the various groups that make up the corporation and the groups with which the corporation interacts. We have already mentioned the shareholders. They are the owners of the corporation. They are legally represented by the board of directors whose job it is, among other things, to look out for the interests of the shareholders. The board of directors oversees management. Management has the task of organizing the corporation in such a way that it can effect its end—profitably make and market a product. Management is responsible to the board for what it does. In a large firm there are, typically, levels of management. Top management sets policy; middle management implements the broad policies by breaking them down into components and devising a strategy for achieving them; lower management implements the decisions made by middle management by organizing and hiring the workers who actually engage in the production of the goods. Management is responsible for what is produced and for how it is produced. It is responsible to the workers for the conditions under which they work, and to the consumers for the quality of goods produced. The workers are responsible for doing the jobs for which they are paid.

The corporation as a whole is responsible to the other firms with which it deals for fulfilling its contracts—for delivering what was promised when and as promised, for paying the debts it incurs in its operation, and so on. The corporation is responsible to the consumer for the goods it sells. The corporation is also responsible to the general public, or to society, for the actions it takes which affect the public or society in general. All of these obligations can be deduced from the rule that every rational agent is responsible for his actions and is responsible to those whom his actions seriously affect. Each such agent is morally responsible for wrongful injury done to another. To the extent that the corporation acts, it is responsible for its actions, though it is the people within the corporation who must act in order for the corporation to fulfill its obligations. Let us look a little more closely at each level of the corporation and at the kinds of moral responsibility each has.

In a large corporation responsibility falls primarily on the representatives of the owners or shareholders, namely, the board of directors. They are the legal overseers of management. The members of the board are responsible to the shareholders for the selection of honest, effective managers, and especially for the selection of the president of the corporation. They may also be responsible for choosing the executive and other vice presidents. They are also morally responsible for the tone of the corporation and its major policies. They can set a moral tone or condone immoral practices. They can and should see that the company is managed honestly and that the interests of the shareholders are cared for and not ignored by management. They are also responsible for agreeing to major policy decisions and for the general well-being of the corporation. The members are morally responsible for the decisions they make, as well as for the decisions they should but fail to make. To be effective in their role as protectors of the interests of the shareholders and in their role as judges of the performance of management, they should be separate from management. They can hardly be objective in their evaluation of management if the members of the board are also members of management. When the president and the chairman of the board are the same person, for instance, we can hardly expect the board to fulfill its responsibility vis-à-vis management. Nor can we expect impartial evaluation of management if the board is composed of people appointed or recommended by management. We can also not expect a board to be effective if it is not informed by management of what management is doing, if it does not have access to any information about the firm it thinks necessary, and if it does not have the time to investigate what should be investigated.

Management is responsible to the board. It must inform the board of what it does, the decisions it makes or the decisions to be made, the financial condition of the firm, its successes and failures, and so on. Management is also responsible to the workers. It both hires them and provides for the conditions of work. In hiring workers it has the obligation to engage in what have become known as fair employment practices. These include following equitable guidelines and not discriminating on the basis of sex, race, religion or other non job-related characteristics. Once hired, there is a continuing obligation of fairness in evaluation, promotion, and equitable treatment. There are moral matters which may or may not be specified in contracts but which are implied in the hiring of one person by another. It is not moral for management to ignore the safety of working conditions. It should not endanger the workers by failing to provide screening from dangerous machines where appropriate and available, by not supplying goggles for work where fragments may cause blindness, by not supplying ventilation, and in general by ignoring the needs of workers as human beings.

Employers are not free to set any terms they wish as conditions of employment. They have a moral obligation to employees even if these are not spelled out in contracts or by government regulations. Government regulations, such as those imposed by the Occupational Safety and Health Act (OSHA) make explicit many of the conditions employers are morally as well as legally obliged to fulfill with respect to the safety and health of their employees. The OSHA regulations are sometimes inappropriate for certain firms, or are based on codes inappropriate to particular enterprises. But if employers had lived up to the moral obligation to provide adequate conditions of safety and health for their employees, there would have been no need for OSHA regulations.

The corporation is responsible to the consumer for its products. The goods produced should be reasonably safe when this means that the ordinary user is exposed only to a certain acceptable risk level when using the item in question. People do not expect to get electrocuted when they plug in an electrical appliance. They do not buy such appliances expecting to take that risk. A product which electrocutes them when plugged in is defective and causes harm to the consumer that is not part of the contract involved in the purchase of the product. Goods must be as advertised or labelled, and they should be adequately labelled so that the buyer knows what he is buying. Adequate knowledge is one of the ingredients of a fair transaction, and it is the obligation of the manufacturer to inform the purchaser of those significant qualities which the purchaser cannot observe for himself. For instance, the kind of material a garment is made of is pertinent, as is the horsepower of a vehicle. Goods should be reasonably durable. They should not fall apart on first use. Warranties should be clear and honored. The customer buys a product for a certain price. He should know what he is getting, and he has a moral right to have certain expectations fulfilled. Obviously there are grades of goods. Some are more expensive than others and may be correspondingly safer, more durable, more reliable, and more attractive than cheaper products and made of better quality components. For any transaction to be fair, however, the consumer must have adequate information and his reasonable expectations must be fulfilled by a product, or there must be adequate notice that the ordinary expectation in the given case will not be fulfilled. Damaged goods can be only sold if marked as damaged. "Seconds" can be sold as seconds but are not morally sold as "firsts." These few examples do not exhaust the responsibilities of corporations to consumers. We have not questioned the morality of built-in obsolescence, purposeful lack of standardization that ties a consumer into a certain line of products, failure to develop certain products or to prevent the production of items that would benefit the consumer but hurt a particular industry or manufacturer. But we have illustrated enough of the moral responsibilities of a corporation to consumers to indicate where its moral obligations in this area lie.

Finally, the corporation is morally responsible for its actions to the general public or society in general. In particular, it has the moral obligation not to harm those whom its actions affect. We can group these obligations under three major headings. The first can be called its responsibility not to harm the environment which it shares with its neighbors. It has the obligation not to pollute the air and water beyond socially acceptable levels and to control its noise pollution similarly. It is obliged to dispose of toxic and corrosive wastes so as not to endanger others. It must reclaim and restore the environment to a socially acceptable level if its operation despoils and ruins it.

The second group of moral obligations to the general public concerns the general safety of those who live in an area affected by a company's plant. A company has no right to expose those people living near it to a health risk from possible explosion or radiation. Some jobs involve high risk and those who take them are paid accordingly. But a plant has no right to expose its neighbors, even its distant neighbors, to dangers without their consent. Similarly, a corporation has an obligation to the general public for the safety of its products. For instance, substandard tires endanger not only those who purchase them unknowingly but those whom they may kill or injure in the accident the tires may cause.

The third set of responsibilities to the public concerns the location, opening, and closing of plants. These actions affect not only the corporation and its workers but also the communities in which the plants are located. Plant openings can affect a community positively or negatively just as closings can. A corporation must morally consider the impact of its actions in these matters on the community. This is not to say that plants can never morally be closed or opened. In both opening and closing a plant, a corporation has the obligation to minimize the harm and also to consider a variety of strategies to achieve this end.

The opening of a plant may involve a large commitment on the part of the community in which it is located. The community, for example, may have to add sewer lines, increase its fire and police department staff, and add to its social services personnel. Developers build houses for the increased employment the plant makes available. Businesses spring up to provide support services. Schools may be built to educate the children of the workers. The city or county begin to count on the increased tax base the plant represents. All of this may result from the new plant.

The corporation does not ask that all this happen; but it expects its workers will be provided housing and services in response to market demand.

The community nonetheless may be said to provide indirect support to the plant. The corporation should, therefore, not ignore the community's contribution to its operation when it considers closing the plant. It may have no legal duty to consider the community with which it has been associated. Morally it has an obligation to consider the effects of its action and to minimize the harm its closing will cause the community.

If we ask who has the obligation to do all this, the answer is the corporation. Management has the major role to play. Yet both the members of the board and individual workers may find on occasion that they have the moral responsibility to take certain actions to satisfy the corporation's responsibility to the general public.

Morality and Corporate Structure

Corporations should act morally. But knowing what is morally required of them is insufficient. Equally important from a moral point of view is restructuring many corporations so that they and the people who make them up are encouraged to act morally. Some structures encourage immoral behavior; others tend to preclude it. Organizational theory is only beginning to turn its attention in this direction. Yet a number of innovative organizational changes have been tried either in the United States or in Europe and deserve serious consideration.

We have already noted the tendency of moral responsibility to be ignored in corporations. Those at the top give orders and never see the specific results of the implementation of those orders on people far down the line. The managers tend to deny responsibility for results they never intended. Those near the end of the line execute orders given by those above them. They frequently feel they are simply doing their job when they obey orders, no matter what the results. They deny responsibility for the results because they did not set the policies, they simply obeyed orders. They did not will to do harm or evil; they willed only to do their jobs. The other structural aspect of many large corporations that undermines the acceptance of moral responsibility is that decisions are not made by individuals but by committees, or even worse, by sets of committees. A corporation's actions in some instances can be traced to no one. Many people had some input into a policy or decision. One person suggested it, another added something, a third person deleted a portion of it, a committee agreed to one version which was altered by another committee, and finally, a modified version of that was adopted, albeit slightly changed as it descended from organizational level to organizational level.

Structures are possible, however, for corporations that wish to be moral and to accept moral responsibility for their actions. The moral tone is set by those at the top. Unless those at the top insist on moral conduct, unless they punish immoral conduct and reward moral conduct, the corporation as a whole will tend to function without considering moral questions and the morality of its actions. It may by accident rather than by intent avoid immoral actions, though in the long run this is unlikely. We can list some specific suggestions for structurally implementing morality in a corporation.

1. If a board of directors is to be morally responsible it cannot simply rubber stamp management. The board members must be informed of the activities of the corporation and must have access to all the information they want concerning the corporation. They are responsible to the shareholders, the public, and to government. They can fulfill their responsibilities only if they spend adequate time investigating the company's activities and holding management accountable. Members of such boards will have to spend more than a few days a year on their board activities.

Management is responsible to the board. But it can obviously be held responsible only if management is different from the board. The second organizational suggestion is therefore:

2. More than half the board, as well as the chairman of the board, should not be from management.

Management can be held responsible only if management is different from the board. Executive compensation and perquisites, such as stock options, are notorious areas for conflict of interest. Management cannot be expected to evaluate its own performance objectively or to compensate itself without prejudice. The pattern of outside board members has been established in Europe and is a pattern followed by some corporations here. The board might include chief stockholders, workers, or people outside the corporation entirely. They must all, of course, be competent to fulfill their obligations as members of a board. There might be training courses run by the corporation or by schools of business to teach potential board members what they need to know. If the position of a board member is a demanding one, business executives will not be able to serve on more than one or two boards of other firms.

Responsibility on lower levels should be assigned; but assumption of responsibility should be not only required but taught by example.

Responsibility without accountability is empty. Here responsibility and responsiveness join together. Accountability requires not only a response to those to whom one is responsible, but it also requires access to information and the giving of reasons for decisions. One way to preserve one's power is to monopolize information so that others have to assume the decisions taken were proper in the light of all the information. Accountability under such conditions is impossible. Thus, accountability requires disclosure. There are certainly areas of legitimate trade secrets which should be protected by law. But these areas are probably fewer than most corporations are willing to admit. If people are to be held responsible for their decisions, those affected by a decision have a right to know at least something of the rationale for it. The supplying of information and reasons for a decision does not mean that the person who made the decision had no right to make it. But knowing that one may be called on to explain or defend decisions helps keep them from being made arbitrarily. Hence:

3. At each level a determination should be made about how much disclosure is appropriate and to whom. The determination should be made not unilaterally, but

through reasoned discourse with those seeking information and those to whom one is rightly accountable.

Accountability is not simply hierarchical. Management should be accountable to the workers as well as to the board, and the workers should be accountable to each other as well as to management. The board should be accountable to the stockholders and the public, but it should also be accountable to management, providing reasons for the decisions it takes. The rationale is that the corporation is composed of people and not simply of functions or positions on an organizational chart.

Accountability is the heart of both the demand for responsibility and for responsiveness, and it requires significant organizational modifications. Hence:

4. There should be channels and procedures for accountability up, down, and laterally.

There must be ways by which workers can make known their demands and concerns without fear or prejudice and receive explanations for decisions which affect them. Clearly, to speak of channels and procedures goes well beyond the suggestion box. The creation of a position of ombudsman has been tried in some corporations; special departments might be established in other corporations. Accountability to the public, moreover, gives the corporations the chance to tell their side of the story, to indicate what moral factors they have considered, and to present the reasons for the decisions they have made. The American public does not expect corporations to act from moral motives. It does expect them not to violate basic moral rules and to consider the social ramifications of their actions. If many corporations do meet these expectations, they fail to report it adequately or convincingly. Hence, corporations should:

5. Develop input lines whereby employees, consumers, stockholders, and the public can make known their concerns, demands and perceptions of a corporation's legitimate responsibilities.

6. Develop a mechanism (possibly a department) for anticipating the various demands, for seriously considering and weighing them, and for proposing appropriate action.

7. Develop techniques for disseminating to those interested the basis for decisions affecting the general good.

The mechanism for weighing various moral demands is crucial. Many of the demands cannot be handled in cost accounting terms. Where they cannot, then the arguments in defense of one set of actions and a consideration of the consequences are typically pitted against similar considerations for other sets of actions. But the only way to make the discussion fair is to have advocates for each side. The advocates should be within the corporation, even if they represent demands made by those outside the corporation. In at least some office or department it should be proper to ask not what can the corporation get away with but what is the right thing to do. That decision will have to be weighed against cost and other factors. But unless someone is paid to argue against the company's position, unless that person's position and advancement are dependent on his properly and strongly presenting the case of those outside the company, and unless he has some likelihood of winning, outside demands will not get an adequate hearing. A progressive company would demand even more, namely that some people within it be responsible for anticipating moral demands so that the company can respond to them before outside forces have to be marshalled. The development of a group, office or department within a corporation that argues against the company's short-term interest in the light of its larger responsibilities is a major organizational modification suggested by the proposed organizational restructuring.

Responsibility without sanctions, however, is empty. The demand for responsibility requires that sanctions be developed and enforced. If responsibility is personally assignable, then there is little difficulty in knowing whom to sanction. Kickbacks, foreign bribes, the use of insider information, and so on are everyday fare in newspapers and magazines. The deceit, deception, and dishonesty of a few tarnish the image of the many. Yet very few corporations have been willing to admit blame for their wrong-doing, fewer still take any effective measures against their managers or board members, and even fewer cast stones at fellow businessmen. It is difficult to believe that businessmen do not know when others are acting immorally, however that is defined. Yet rarely does any businessman publicly bring charges of impropriety or immorality; and even more rarely do any self-policing mechanisms result in the imposing of severe sanctions. Hence:

8. Responsibility should be enforced with sanctions both within an organization and, where compatible with antitrust laws, throughout an industry. The price for executive irresponsibility or immorality should be as severe as it is for lower-level employees.

A company policy or action may come into conflict with the moral obligation of the corporation.There should be some mechanism for dealing with a discrepancy of this type without endangering the position of the person raising the objection. There are a number of famous cases of whistle blowing in industry, and in most cases the whistle blowers have fared poorly for their moral stance. Hence:

9. A corporation that wishes to preclude the necessity of whistle blowing should provide procedures, mechanisms, and channels whereby any members of the organization can file moral concerns of the type that lead to whistle blowing and can get a fair hearing and possible action without fear of negative consequences.

To give this weight:

10. The corporation should hold some highly placed official in the corporation responsible if insufficient attention is paid to a legitimate claim of product safety and so on.

To have procedures for handling conflicts of corporate policy and employee morality does not mean that anything that someone claims to be immoral is immoral. But there should be organizational procedures so that such charges get a full and fair hearing from those who will ultimately be responsible. Those who raise such issues should be able to do so without threat of negative consequences. Contrary to the traditional model, people at every level should be held responsible for seeing and reporting such issues and should be penalized for failure to do so. If industry were responsive to legitimate complaints by those who see product dangers, employees would not have to go outside the company to get corporate action.

If a corporation is to face squarely its moral obligations, it must be able to learn clearly what they are and it must do so early enough to take most effective action. It must have the mechanism for weighing conflicting demands. And it must have the means not only for implementing its decisions but also for explaining and defending them to those whose demands could not be met.

The changes taken as a whole fall far short of socialism and workers' self-management. But there is no mandate yet to go very far in that direction. Because of this, some may construe the above suggestions as a means of defending the status quo. Others, enamoured of the traditional model and unwilling to give up any of the traditional privileges and autocracy of management, will argue that the suggestions call for an end to free enterprise and capitalism.

The changes outlined are not original and most have been tried somewhere in some way. But they do form a whole, come from a conception of what a moral corporation can be, and are in line with what is being legitimately demanded of business.

Morality, the Social Audit, and Pollution

In examining the moral responsibility of corporations we have seen the obligation not to produce harm and the necessity of adequate information and the absence of coercion if a transaction is to be fair. If pollution causes harm, then a corporation is morally required not to pollute. But the moral obligations that a corporation has can and should be distinguished from what have been called its "social obligations."

The growing literature on the social obligations of corporations includes a grab bag of obligations, some of them moral and some not. The social obligations which some people would like to have corporations undertake include taking care of the poor, rebuilding the inner city, fighting illicit drug traffic, giving to charity, endowing universities, and funding cultural programs. None of these is a moral obligation of corporations. The term "social obligation" suggests that society requires the corporations to act in these ways. The term also carries the hidden threat that unless corporations fulfill these obligations society will terminate their existence. The threat may be a real one. But the rebuilding of cities, caring for the poor, and the advancement of culture are social ends that should be socially implemented. Corporations may well donate money to such projects if they choose. They would do so presumably to enhance their public image, to gain free publicity, or for some other such reason. The government encourages such donations by making many of them tax-exempt. But social welfare and social projects are appropriately the end of government, not of business. Businesses are taxed, and such taxes may be used for social purposes. The end of the corporation, however, is profitable production and distribution, not social welfare. The manufacturing corporation is not structured to achieve social welfare. There is also great danger in allowing, much less expecting, such corporations to take upon themselves the production of public welfare. The corporation already has enormous power and it is not answerable for its use to the general public. Politicians are elected by the public and do not necessarily have the common good as their end. We should not expect corporations to do what they are neither competent nor organized to do. But we should insist that they fulfill their *moral* obligations.

If this analysis is correct, we should not impose on corporations a social audit, at least not a social audit that includes charity and social welfare. We should impose upon business a moral audit. The content of the two audits overlap. But the social audit in its broad sense suffers from including social obligations of charity and welfare which are not moral obligations and from lacking any principles for determining what the audit properly includes and what it does not. The moral audit includes only that portion of the social audit that can be generated from moral principles and listed as moral obligations.

Why should there be a moral audit and how can it be carried out? Morality governs the interaction of rational agents. The actions of corporations affect people. The general public as well as actual and potential investors have the right to know the moral as well as the financial position and record of a corporation. The techniques of reporting the moral quotient of a corporation are similar to techniques for carrying out the social audit. The attempts at formulating this with any precision are still rudimentary. But the government already requires reports on injuries, pollution levels, handling of toxic waste, and other data pertinent to a moral audit. The moral audit, however, would be restricted to what is morally required, rather than also including what environmentalists, conservationists, or other groups would like to have corporations do.

We have already seen that corporations have the moral obligation not to harm people. This obligation is reasonably clear when it comes to many products. If pollution causes harm, then corporations are morally obliged not to pollute. This is a moral, not a social obligation. It is a moral requirement, not a supererogatory act, i.e., an act that is morally commendable but not required. How the corporation is to fulfill this obligation, however, may be a social decision.

Consider the following case. Jason City, a town of 150,000 people has five factories in an industrially zoned section on the east side of the city. One of the factories is much older than the others and emits three times more sulphur into the atmosphere than the newer plants, each of which emits about the same amount of sulphur. The atmosphere can absorb a certain amount of pollution and carry it away without ill effects to either people or property. Therefore, the city has had no need to do anything about the emissions from the factories, and the factories have not invested in any pollution control equipment. A sixth factory is built. It emits the same amount of sulphur as the other new factories. But it adds just enough so that now a possibly dangerous level of sulphur is discharged into the air. The pollution may now cause harm. We have said that corporations have a moral responsibility not to cause harm to people or property. Who is morally responsible to do what? The oldest factory claims that it was in the town first and though it causes the most pollution it caused no harm until the sixth factory arrived. The other four claim that they are minor polluters and would cause no harm if either the sixth factory had not opened or if the first factory lowered its sulphur emissions to the same rate as the other factories. The sixth plant claims that it has as much right to emit sulphur into the atmosphere as the other plants and should not bear any special burden. By itself, it claims, it does no harm.

Clearly, the six plants together cause the harm, even though each one by itself would not cause harm. For purposes of a moral audit we would want to know how much sulphur each factory emits. But this information by itself tells us nothing about whether it is causing harm. We also have to know what procedures have been adopted for handling the sulphur pollution problem in Jason City and whether each factory is doing what, in its context, it is supposed to be doing.

There are many ways that Jason City can handle the problem of pollution. The city may decide that the pollution is small enough and the harm done to residents and property slight enough that nothing need be done about it. The city might decide that if anyone claims damage from the pollution, that individual should sue one or all the plants for compensation. There are many other ways the city might go. It could impose a limit on the amount of sulphur any plant can emit. It could prevent the construction of any future plants. It could allow future plants to be built only if they emit no sulphur whatsoever, keeping the emission level at its present rate. The city might even take it upon itself to supply emission control devices to the plants so that the pollution is controlled at the source by city expense. It might also tell the six companies that they are causing the pollution and that they must lower the level or face a series of fines, leaving it up to the plants to arrange among themselves how to lower the sulphur to an acceptable level.

There is no one right or best way for Jason City to solve the problem of sulphur pollution. There are many ways of approaching the problem. It is appropriate, however, for the plants emitting the sulphur to control their emissions because the sulphur belongs to them. They have been allowed to use the air to get rid of their wastes when doing so injured no one. But when such a procedure does threaten harm to others, then the action can be rightfully curtailed. The claim that the air belongs to all of us and so any of us can discharge what we want into it is a claim that cannot be successfully defended. Wastes belong to those who produce them. Just because they do not want their wastes does not release people or firms from the responsibility of disposing of them in a way that does not harm others. The principle is recognized with respect to garbage. Individual households in some cities pay to have their garbage disposed of; in other cities this is a service provided through tax funds; and in rural communities people are sometimes allowed to dispose of it by burning it or carrying it themselves to the town dump. Air and water pollution are industrial wastes which belong to the plants that produce them as truly as a household's garbage belongs to the household. The method of disposal of such wastes varies with communities. But the principle that the wastes belong to the producer and that producers have no right to harm others by their wastes is a sound moral basis for imposing limits on what pollutants are admissible, in what amounts, and how the rest is to be controlled or disposed of.

The moral audit with respect to pollution, therefore, would include information about emission levels, the levels allowed, and other pertinent information on the basis of which someone could tell whether the corporation was or was not fulfilling its obligations with respect to pollution. Its accident record would indicate whether it was providing adequate safety protection for its employees; its recall record would indicate its quality control and the safety of its products; its legal suits and its out-of-court settlements would indicate how it fulfills some of its moral obligations with respect to its customers. For each category of moral responsibility we could attempt to devise some method of reporting that would constitute an appropriate moral audit.

Corporations have moral responsibilities whether they wish to have them or not. Some firms attempt to fulfill these obligations. Other firms are better at evading them. The free market allows the consumer to cast its vote for a company by buying its product and to cast a vote against it by not buying its product. If the moral audit were part of the public record of each company, people could take this into account in casting such votes.

It may be, of course, that even if they know a company is immoral, people will buy its product if it is the best available. It is unlikely they will ignore the immorality of a company when such immorality hurts them. But even that is possible. Defenders of a free market, however, should have no reluctance about a moral audit. For the moral audit of a public firm would supply its potential customers with information that the latter may appropriately wish to have in making their decisions about whether or not to deal with any firm.

In the first chapter of this book we examined the Myth of Amoral Business. The myth tends to obscure the moral responsibilities that corporations have. The myth should be put to rest. Corporations not only have *moral* obligations, they *can* and *should* be held morally accountable for fulfilling them. The moral audit is an innovation whose time has come. If developed and applied to all large corporations it will go a long way toward replacing the Myth of Amoral Business with a clear and open approach to corporate moral responsibilities.

Further Reading

Ackerman, Robert W. *The Social Challenge to Business.* Cambridge, Mass.: Harvard University Press, 1975.

Anshen, M., ed. *Managing the Socially Responsible Corporation.* New York: Macmillan, Inc., 1974.

Bauer, R.A., and Fenn, D.H., Jr., *The Corporate Social Audit.* New York: Russell Sage Foundation, 1972.

Berle, A., and Means, G.C. *The Modern Corporation and Private Property.* New York: Macmillan, Inc., 1932. rev. ed., 1968.

Chamberlin, Neil. *The Limits of Corporate Responsibility.* New York: Basic Books, Inc., 1973.

Hessen, Robert. *In Defense of the Corporation.* Stanford: Hoover Institution Press, 1979.

Hurst, James Willard. *The Legitimacy of the Business Corporation.* Charlottesville: The University Press of Virginia, 1970.

Jacoby, N.H. *Corporate Power and Social Responsibility.* New York: Macmillan, Inc., 1973.

Luthans, Fred; Hodgetts, Richard M.; and Thompson, Kenneth R. *Social Issues in Business.* 3rd ed. New York: Macmillan, Inc., 1980.

Nader, Ralph, and Green, Mark J., eds. *Corporate Power in America.* New York: Grossman Publishers, 1973.

Sethi, S. Prakash. *Up Against the Corporate Wall.* 3rd ed. Englewood Cliffs, N.J.: Prentice-Hall, Inc., 1977.

Stone, Christopher D. *Where the Law Ends: The Social Control of Corporate Behavior.* New York: Harper & Row, Publishers, Inc., 1975.

Walton, Clarence, ed. *The Ethics of Corporate Conduct.* Englewood Cliffs, N.J.: Prentice-Hall, Inc., 1977.

Workers' Rights, Obedience, and Whistle Blowing

The gross annual income of such corporate giants as General Motors, American Telephone and Telegraph, Standard Oil and Ford is larger than the gross national product of Austria, Norway, Finland, and Greece, not to mention that of many Third World countries. An individual facing the corporate colossus is no David standing before Goliath. The individual who takes on a large corporation is more similar to David facing a whole army. What is the proper relation of corporation and worker? If the relation is an adversarial one, what chance does the worker have against so formidable a foe?

We have already seen several times that an agreement between two contracting parties is a fair one if each of the parties has adequate, appropriate information and if each enters into the transaction freely and without coercion. What of the transactions between worker and employer? Can we subsume these into a contract or agreement and treat them as we would any other contract? Can such a contract be fair and can the worker deal as an equal in negotiations with a giant corporation? Are there aspects of an employer-employee relationship that cannot be negotiated? Are there certain assumptions about workers' rights and obligations, and about employers' rights and obligations that form the background for worker-employer contracts, and are these assumptions justifiable? In this chapter we shall look in turn at the rights and duties of employees, at the obedience and loyalty appropriate for employees, and at justifications for corporate disobedience, including whistle blowing.

The Rights and Duties of Employees

A simple approach to the rights and duties of employees states that employees have all those, and only those, rights and duties which they negotiate with their employers as conditions of employment. This approach, however, is too simple and is seriously misleading. Employees and employers are not mere abstractions. A potential employee is first of all a human being and a rational agent—an end in himself worthy of respect. He is also a moral being and carries with him in all his endeavors and undertakings the moral obligation to do what is right and to avoid doing what is wrong. Neither on the job nor in any other aspect of his life is he free to do whatever he chooses. He remains bound by the moral law in all his activities. An employer, whether we mean the corporation as a moral entity or the actual person who is hired for the corporation, is also bound by the moral law. Hence neither side in the hiring process has the moral right to set whatever terms it wishes. Both sides are bound not only by morality but also by law. For instance, if I wish to sell myself into slavery to raise money to give to my family, I am morally and legally prohibited from doing so, and everyone else is morally and legally prohibited from making me a slave.

The background conditions for any contract between employer and employee are the conditions set by morality, law, local custom, and by the existing social circumstances in which the contract is made. Most people who start out in the employment market would like to earn as much as possible. Typically they have no work experience. If they also have no work skills, what they can offer is their time, their labor power, their ability to learn, and their intelligence, developed by however much schooling they have had. They offer these to the employer, who in turn has work of some kind available for which he promises a certain compensation. A wage laborer works for wages—a certain amount of money earned per hour, week, month, or per piece.

The development of industry in the nineteenth century taught us many lessons. The industrial employer was in a much stronger bargaining position than was the potential worker. The employer set the conditions of labor. The worker was not forced to accept any particular position. But if he wished to eat, feed his family, provide himself and them with shelter, clothing, and the other necessities of life, he had to work for someone. Since all the employers offered him conditions that were favorable only to themselves, the worker had to accept terms unfavorable to himself. Thus, one of the fairness conditions for a just contractual agreement was missing. Though a worker was not forced to work for Company Z rather than Company B or C or D, he was forced to work for one of them or starve. If they all offered him similar terms, he was forced to work for their terms. In time, workers found that by grouping together into unions they could bargain for better terms than they could individually. Employers could not pit workers against one another if they had to negotiate terms with all employees at once.

Not all workers belong to unions, but most workers below the management level in large industries do. Nonunion labor has also benefited from the conditions of work achieved by union workers which form an important backdrop for many negotiations between employers and nonunion employees. Workers have also fought for and secured legislation that protects them and their interests in many areas. Many workers in the past had to face the problem of how to live if they were laid off, fired, injured, or retired. Unemployment insurance, workman's compensation, and social security have helped alleviate the worst of those problems for large numbers of employees.

Employees have bargained collectively as well as individually for certain rights and privileges and have committed themselves to fulfilling certain obligations. Some employees have more to offer employers than others. Some people have special skills, much accumulated experience, and character or other traits that are in short supply and great demand. Such people can bargain better than those with no special skills, experience, or traits. Hollywood movie stars, stellar baseball, basketball or football players, and top executives of large corporations all command handsome salaries or compensation for their work. Teenagers often work at jobs that pay the minimum allowable by law, and they are happy to find even those jobs. The range of pay is enormous, as is the range of other types of compensation. The tasks required—from menial to professional and entrepreneurial—are also extremely diverse. Yet we can make some general statements about the rights and obligations of all workers.

1. Employee Rights

There are many kinds of rights. Civil rights are legal rights which entitle each person covered by them to certain kinds of treatment or to act in certain kinds of ways. The right to equal employment regardless of race or sex makes it illegal for employers to discriminate in their hiring practices with respect to these. The right to freedom of speech allows each citizen to express his views publicly and prevents others, especially government officials, from interfering in such expression. A moral right does not depend on positive law. A moral right might also be a civil right. But not every moral right is written into law; nor is the state the source of moral rights. People have such rights simply by virtue of being moral agents and worthy of respect. The rights to life, liberty, and the pursuit of happiness are among these moral rights. They were called natural rights by the Founding Fathers and are called human rights today.

Moral rights can be considered morally justifiable claims. Not everything claimed to be a moral right is a moral right. Not every claim is morally justifiable. But those that can be successfully supported by moral argument are moral rights. A right usually carries with it a correlative obligation on the part of others, assuming the good or benefit secured by the right is available. Some rights protect our freedom to act, and oblige others not to interfere in our actions. Other rights guarantee us goods or benefits and oblige others to provide them. My right to life not only prohibits others from killing me but also obliges society collectively and individually to feed me if I am starving to death when food is available.

By contract and position, I can secure other special rights. A business executive of a certain level may earn the right to eat in the executive restaurant; other employees have the right to eat in the company lunchroom. Those not employed by a firm have no general right to eat in the firm's lunchroom or restaurant or to use facilities of the firm. Special rights are not moral rights, though if they are extended under certain regular conditions and then denied some particular individual for no defensible reason, failure to extend them may be a violation of a moral right to equality of treatment.

The right of an employee to be treated like a human being is a moral right. It is an extremely broad and in many ways a vague right. But it is a central right. Its foundation is straightforwardly the fact that each person is a human being and a moral agent deserving of respect. We saw in our study of the Categorical Imperative that to treat a human being as a means only is immoral. Thus an employer who treats his workers only as a means to his profit, or as a way of getting done what he wants done treats them immorally. They are not machines or objects. What does this imply about their treatment? Can we translate the notion of respect for human beings into specific conditions of labor?

Since workers are human beings worthy of respect, they should not be treated like slaves, nor can they morally contract into such treatment. Their work should not be demeaning, nor the conditions of work unsafe, or unhealthy, and in general, conditions should be suitable for human beings. These vague statements will be translated into different work conditions depending on the country, the standard of living, the kind of work, and the availability of safety and other equipment. The right to be treated with respect also means that workers should not be made to work in stultifying jobs or be considered replaceable parts in the productive process.

In the United States, the right of workers to be treated with respect does not include the right to have employment. Workers deserve respect once they are employed; but the system of American capitalism does not guarantee labor for all those who want it and are able to work. Employers are not obliged to hire workers, nor are they obliged to keep them on once they have been hired. Nor does the government make up for the absence of the right to be employed—a right recognized in many socialist countries. The United States government has chosen to respect the right to life of the unemployed by supplying unemployment compensation and welfare, rather than competing with private industry by supplying employment. Many socialists claim that unemployment compensation and welfare payments for those able and willing to work is demeaning, and that the right to be employed is a right that stems from the right to be treated with respect. The unemployed tend to lose their own self-respect and the respect of others. Hence, through no fault of their own, they are not treated by society with the respect due all persons. Socialist countries, however, frequently also impose the obligation to work on all able to do so.

An employee carries with him into his employment his civil rights. Many disputes have arisen, however, about whether he is allowed to exercise his civil rights either on or off the job if the exercise of such rights is in some way perceived by his superiors as detrimental to the good of the corporation. Does a worker have the right to criticize his company, his company's management, or some of its decisions either on or off the job? Many managers complain that workers who criticize the company on the job sow disaffection, unrest, and discontent among other workers. This clearly hurts the company and affects its productivity. Hence, they argue, such people are rightly fired. Some companies go even so far as to claim that speaking or writing against the company and its policies during off-hours is disloyal, harmful to the company, and that people who so act are rightly open to censure and dismissal.

Two issues are involved in these situations. One is whether a worker forfeits his civil rights in areas concerning the corporation, its products, procedures, or personnel; the second is whether he has any right to continue his job, or whether he holds it at the pleasure of whoever hired him.

The right of an employee to freedom of expression on his own time is a civil right that his employer cannot morally deny him. Employers have the right to demand work of a specific kind from their employees. While they are working they can be expected to do certain tasks assigned to them. But no employer has the right to deprive his employees of their civil rights off the job. Employees, as members of society, have the moral right, moreover, to the most extensive liberty compatible with a like liberty for all. They have the right to belong to the church of their choosing, to live their private lives as they wish, and to engage in political or social activities as they desire. An employer violates these rights if he penalizes his employees for what they do on their own time. Employees are properly evaluated for their work on the job. This evaluation should not extend to their non-job-related activities as long as these do not adversely affect their job performance.

On the job, workers have the right to equality of treatment. They should receive equal pay for equal work, regardless of sex, race, or religion. They should all have equal opportunities for advancement. In general they should be evaluated only by job-related criteria, and treated accordingly. Whether they have the right to spread disaffection and employee unrest under the right of freedom of speech is not a clear-cut issue. It depends on how the right is exercised, on whether its exercise interferes with one's regularly assigned tasks, and other similar factors. Yet clearly, the workers should have the right to organize, unionize, complain about grievances, and so on, at least on their own time at work. In general they also have the right to strike to help them achieve their legitimate demands.

Employees have a moral right to privacy. They work for their employers for a certain period of time each day. But the rest of their time belongs not to the company but to themselves. They should be allowed to do what they want during that time, free from company interference. They do not surrender the right to privacy in their personal lives with employment. Nor does this privacy end when they enter the corporation's walls. Some aspects of their lives do not affect their capacity to do the work expected of them. Consequently, corporations have no right to inquire about such things nor to keep such information on record in personnel files. Workers have a concomitant right not to answer personal, non-job-related questions, and have a right to know that no such material is kept in their files.

Fairness requires procedures whereby workers can register their complaints against those above them and receive a fair hearing. They have a right not to be sexually harassed, and should have a right to get a hearing on such complaints. They also have a right not to be fired for non-job-related matters or for registering legitimate complaints. Established procedures for hiring, promotion, layoffs, and firing should guarantee that the worker's right to fair treatment is respected.

Employees, from the lowest paid in the corporation to the president, do not have the right to continuance in their jobs if they do not perform adequately or if the firm is not able to continue employing them. Yet those who give many years of acceptable service deserve more consideration than those who are new on a job, and therefore treatment with respect demands that some consideration be given to timely notice, to making an effort at transferring a worker or manager, to giving them severance pay or some other means of making the transition easier from one job to another. Some employers allow a manager who is let go because of financial exigency and not because of poor performance continued use of their company address as they look for a new position. Some companies, if able to do so, transfer workers who have been with the firm a long time to less demanding jobs as they get older. Few American companies go as far as Japanese firms that guarantee workers employment after a certain trial period, much as university teachers achieve tenure after six years and thereafter can be fired only for incompetence, moral turpitude, or financial exigency on the part of the institution.

We have noted that American workers do not have a recognized right to employment. Many suffer from constant fear of dismissal for petty reasons or even for no good reason. Such fear is incompatible with dignity and respect for persons. Every effort should be made to minimize such fear. But management has the right to fire people who are unproductive or whom they cannot afford to keep on. American capitalism has not yet solved the problem of how to weigh the right to employment against the right to fire those whom one chooses to fire for cause.

2. Employee Obligations

The list of a worker's obligations depends in part on his job or position.But we can generally specify some obligations that hold true for all employment.

Workers are morally obliged to obey the moral law, and they are legally obliged to obey the civil law at work just as during all other times. Hence, they should not steal from their companies, even in little ways—taking stamps or pencils, or paper, or other materials. If they feel they are underpaid, they should let this be known, bargain for more pay, or find other employment. They have no right to adjust their pay by taking things they want from the company.

They are obliged not to lie, not to spread false information, not to sexually or otherwise abuse or harass others. They are morally obliged to treat their fellow employees, whether above or below them, with respect.

They are also obliged to fulfill the terms of their contracts. If they are hired to work an eight-hour day, they should work that amount of time. They should work conscientiously at their jobs, and live up to the terms of their contracts. This is an obligation of justice.

Do they owe loyalty to their firm, as well as an honest day's work? The question is an ambiguous one. While they work for a particular firm, they should not subvert it or sabotage its activities. But loyalty to a firm does not require either that they not be willing to change employers or that they not criticize their employer.

The obligations of workers are sometimes spelled out in contracts and job descriptions. The latter are often extremely vague. Exactly what a person in a particular position is obliged to do may be unclear. A person in such a position has no obligation to do the maximum, though if he wants promotion and advancement he may choose to do more than expected or required of him. Workers have the obligation to perform adequately; they do not have the obligation to break records, work overtime, do jobs other than those that come with the position, and so on. Conversely, however, there is no moral objection—at least in most cases—to their doing more than can be legitimately expected of them.

The obligations of workers are more frequently insisted upon by management than are the rights of workers. It is often easier, therefore, to know what is expected of one than to know when one's rights are being unjustly ignored or violated.

Worker Loyalty and Obedience

Consider the following three hypothetical cases:

Case I: James Monroe works for ABC Construction Corporation. His immediate superior has drawn up an estimate for a project and on the basis of the resulting bid, the company has received the contract. Though the contract has already been signed, James' boss asks him to verify his calculations, which is part of James' job. In doing so James discovers an error. The result will be a slight loss for the company rather than the anticipated profit. James points this out to his superior, who tells James to forget the error and mention it to no one; otherwise James will be fired. His superior does not report the error in turn to his own superior.

Case II: Sam Jones works for XYZ Printing Company. He is in charge of ordering high quality paper for the firm. A salesman from O. Good Paper wishes to land a large contract from XYZ Printing and offers Sam a new Ford as a gift if he gives him the contract. Sam refuses the car. The next day he learns that Tom Brand, who is in charge of ordering lower quality paper for XYZ, placed an order with O. Good Paper; he also knows that Tom is driving a new Ford.

Case III: Lewis Cage is Director of Personnel at a large firm. He is in charge of hiring new personnel, keeping records, and issuing notices of dismissal. His firm has just hired a new president from a competitor. On his first visit to Cage's office he tells Cage that he (the president) is not prejudiced. He believes in hiring the best people for a job. But, he goes on, he does not like to work with Jews. He tells Cage that if there are any Jews working for the firm, he should keep his eyes open for any excuse to have them fired. Cage should also not consider Jewish people for any future opening in the firm. Cage, unbeknownst to the new president, is Jewish.

The three cases raise a variety of issues dealing with worker loyalty and obedience. Before analyzing the cases, we can state a few general principles. Many firms expect obedience, and in fact, many employers regard it as a prime virtue. Employees are to do what they are told, how they are told, and when they are told. They are frequently not asked to think originally or even inquire too deeply into the workings of the company. They need only follow orders. Some people are paid to be leaders; others are paid to be followers. When a worker accepts a position he agrees to do what the position requires, including what those above him tell him to do. This view of obedience makes it a blank check to be filled in by the employer.

Though obedience can be morally justified, there are clear moral limits to obedience. No one can be morally obliged to do what is immoral. This statement needs little defense and is essentially a statement of self-consistency. If we were morally obliged to do what is immoral, we would be morally obliged both to do and not to do the action in question. Every command by an employer to an employee has two parts. One is the fact that the employer tells the employee to do something or gives him an order which he expects to be obeyed. The second part constitutes the action he is told to do. If the action falls within the area of work of the employee and if it is not an immoral act, then the employee is rightly expected by the employer to obey the command. For instance, if the vice president for finance tells his secretary to type a letter to the auditors before typing the letter to the accounting department, he can rightly expect her to follow his instructions. If he hands her his personal Christmas shopping list and tells her to spend her weekend buying the items on the list for him, she may well protest that doing his shopping is not part of her job. If he tells her to come to his apartment that evening to spend the night with him, she clearly has no moral obligation to do so, and if she reads his intent correctly, she may have a moral obligation *not* to do as he commands.

Loyalty is also a quality expected and demanded by many firms. A worker for such a company does not merely give it minimal time and effort. He is part of the enterprise, a member of the team, and he is expected to show his loyalty to the company in a variety of ways. If the company has a vacancy in a branch office, company loyalty may demand one's being willing to move to the branch office. An offer by another company at somewhat higher pay is to be refused because of loyalty, even if the other offer is not matched. If the company is sued or maligned, the loyal worker defends the company. In these and many other ways an employee can show loyalty. Showing loyalty in these ways is morally permissible. But it is not morally obligatory. One has no general, moral obligation of loyalty to one's employer, even though employers would like to have loyal employees.

We can now turn to Case I. What, if anything, should James Monroe do in the situation described? He is told by his immediate superior not to say anything about the error to anyone. If he does as he is told, he will be obeying his immediate superior. Does he owe anything more to the company? Suppose that by going over his superior's head to the vice president he can bring the error to the company's attention and some adjustments can be made so that the company does not lose money on the project. Does he have an obligation to the company to do so? If he does go to the vice president, perhaps nothing can be done, and he will simply get himself fired. Sooner or later the company will find out that it is going to lose money on the project. Will James be made the scapegoat because he was supposed to verify the calculations? These and similar considerations are likely to come to James' mind. The approach he is implicitly taking is a utilitarian one. What are the consequences for all concerned if he does go over his superior's head? What are the results for all concerned if he does not?

Another approach is to try to weigh the obligation he has to obey his superior and the obligation he has to inform the company of facts which may adversely affect it. The latter is an obligation of loyalty. The former is one of obedience. Each is prima facie defensible. Which carries more weight in this situation?

The first thing James should do before going above his superior's head is attempt to reason with his superior. If there is a mistake, it will be found out sooner or later. Will it be better for all concerned to find out sooner rather than later? How will the superior try to remedy the situation, if at all? Will he take the blame when the error is found or will be put the blame on James?

The case is not a clear one; but since it is internal to the company it reflects a difficulty not only for James but also for the company. James can argue that he owes obedience to his superior and that in doing as he is told he also shows loyalty to the firm. He does not know what will happen and is not responsible for what does happen. If the firm suffers a small loss, the firm will not be ruined. He is not being asked to do anything immoral. If he had been asked to falsify a record or to sign that the figures were correct, he could not morally do so. But he is simply being told not to report a mistake, and unless it is his duty to report it (i.e., unless it is a part of his job to do so) he is not doing anything immoral.

Any company might learn from the above cases, however. A company should have a mechanism to protect those who have something to report to higher echelons of a firm and who are threatened with dismissal by those immediately above them if they do. A firm should also not tolerate attempts by anyone to cover up mistakes or immoral conduct by threatening to fire those subordinates who report the mistake or conduct.

Case II raises somewhat different problems. Sam Jones acted properly in refusing the car offered by the O. Good salesman. Does he have a further obligation to find out whether Tom Brand received his new Ford from the O. Good salesman? If he finds out that Tom did receive it from the salesman, should he report it to the appropriate person in the firm? Should he or should the firm also report it to O. Good paper?

In the absence of any written guidelines, does one have an obligation to investigate and report wrongdoings in one's firm? To what extent is one one's brother's keeper in a firm, and does loyalty require that one report wrongdoings in the firm by others? Does a company or its employees have an obligation to report the wrongdoings of employees of other firms to their employers?

Once again the situation could be clarified if XYZ Printing Company had a policy on these issues. If it were policy not to accept any gift or any gift worth more than $25.00, for example, Sam would have no difficulty knowing that he should not accept the car. But he did not accept it. Does he have an obligation to report that the salesman offered him a car? If there were a company policy that such offers be reported, then he should do so. Those to whom he reported could then watch other areas of the company dealing with that salesman; or they could stop dealing with that salesman altogether, letting the XYZ Printing Company know what they were doing and why.

In the absence of such guidelines, however, Sam is not morally obliged to investigate Tom's conduct. He is not Tom's supervisor and has no responsibility for his actions. If he does investigate, and finds out that Tom took the car, he is not morally obliged to report it to their superior. He might talk to Tom about it; or he might report that he was approached by the salesman and let those above determine whether Tom was similarly approached. If they choose not to investigate, that is their decision. Loyalty to one's firm does not imply that one should be on constant watch to make sure that those over whom one has no authority are acting morally.

Case III involves discrimination and injustice. One can never morally do what is immoral. Hence, the order to find a pretext to fire a group of people because of their religious beliefs and the order to practice discrimination based on religion in hiring are both orders that Lewis is morally prohibited from carrying out. The irony is that under the order Lewis should find some reason for having himself fired. That reason is easily found. Lewis should not follow the order of the president and since he disobeys the order to have Jews fired, Lewis gives the president grounds to fire him.

Does not a company have the right to hire whom it pleases? Can anyone rightly force a company to hire people it does not want working for it? Does the president not have the right to issue the order he gave Lewis? The answer is that although no one can force a company to hire certain people, companies are bound both by morality and by law (Title VII of the Civil Rights Act of 1964) to hire on the basis of job-related characteristics and not to discriminate on the basis of sex, race, color, religion, or national origin. Refusing to hire qualified people because of religion is discriminatory and firing people because of their religion is similarly discriminatory. Neither practice is morally justifiable.

Lewis could report the order to the board of directors of the company. If they agree that the president's policy should be followed, Lewis could then report the situation to the appropriate government agency.

Lewis could take another approach—tacitly ignore the order, and wait until he is called to task or fired for not obeying orders. This, however, puts an excessive burden on him—a burden that loyalty to the company cannot legitimately demand.

There are times when injustice within a company can be rectified only by forces outside a company and recourse to them is morally justifiable.

Whistle Blowing

We have seen that corporate disobedience is required when one is commanded to do what is immoral. We have also seen that loyalty to the corporation may morally allow or demand breaking the chain of command by going over the head of one's immediate superior. In many companies, breaking the chain of command is considered a form of corporate disobedience. Another form of corporate disobedience that has received much attention is whistle blowing.

By whistle blowing is meant making known to some governmental agency, news reporter, or media personnel actions or conditions within a firm that are either illegal or harmful to the public or to consumers of the firm's products. The only motivation for whistle blowing that we shall consider here is moral motivation. Those who blow the whistle to get revenge or out of spite, or for other similar reasons are not covered by this discussion. The questions we shall raise are when, if ever, is whistle blowing morally justifiable, and when, if ever, is whistle blowing morally obligatory?

Whistle blowing cases are different from the cases we have just considered. Typically the one who feels impelled to blow the whistle on his company is not commanded to do anything immoral. Breaking the hierarchical chain of command is not necessary for whistle blowing since one may go up the hierarchical ladder with the knowledge and permission of successively higher superiors.

The cases we shall consider illustrate the moral motivation and concern behind whistle blowing. Corporations are complex entities. Sometimes those at the top do not want to know in detail difficulties encountered by those below them. They wish lower management to handle difficulties as best they can. Those down below, on the other hand, frequently present only good news to those above them, even if those at the top want to know what is going wrong. They hope that things will be straightened out without letting their superiors know that anything has gone wrong. Sometimes production schedules are drawn up which many along the line know cannot be achieved. Each level cuts a few days off what he will actually need so that his projection will look better to those above. Since it happens at each level, the final projection is weeks, if not months, off. When difficulties develop in actual production, each level is further squeezed and is tempted to cut corners in order not to fall too far behind the overall schedule. In such times the cuts may consist of not correcting defects in a design, or of allowing a part to go through which a department head and the workers in that department know will cause trouble for the consumer. Sometimes these defects will be annoying. Sometimes they will be dangerous.

Producing goods which are known to be defective or that will break down after a short period of time is sometimes justified by producers who point out that the product is warrantied and that it will be repaired for consumers free of charge. It is better to have the product available for the Christmas market or for the new model season for cars, or for some other target date, even if it must later be recalled and fixed, than to have the product delayed beyond the target date.

When the product is defective in such a way as to be dangerous, the situation from a moral point of view is much more serious than when simple inconvenience is at stake. If the danger is such that people are likely to die from the defect, then clearly it should be repaired before being sold. There have been instances, however, in which a company, knowing that its product was dangerous, did a cost-benefit analysis. The managers of the company determined how many people were likely to be killed and what the cost to the company would be if a certain percentage of the deceased's families successfully sued the company. They then compared this figure with the cost of repairing the defect or of repairing it immediately rather than at a later date through a recall. The company might be not only sued but also fined. If the loss from immediate repair substantially exceeded the probable cost of suits and fines, they continued production.

Such a cost-benefit analysis may resemble a utilitarian calculation. What it fails to do that a utilitarian calculation would do is consider the effect on all parties. The cost-benefit analysis is made exclusively from the standpoint of the company. How much, we have to ask, is a human life worth? If a defective part will probably cause fifty or sixty deaths, can we simply calculate the probability of a certain number of people suing and weigh that against the cost of replacing the part? An adequate moral utilitarian calculation would include the deaths and the injuries, the inconvenience for all the purchasers, and weigh these factors against the dollars saved. The equation is not a difficult one to solve. For we know that we all have a moral obligation not to harm others when we are able to prevent it. In such cases the equation of deaths to dollars is an equation that from a moral point of view will always balance out in favor of lives saved.

The reply on the part of some defenders of the cost-benefit analysis described above is that every product carries some risk. In driving an automobile, for instance, there is some risk that people will die. We cannot make cars absolutely safe. Whenever we make any car we have to trade off some safety features against cost. Some very expensive cars are safer than many inexpensive cars. Everyone knows that. There is nothing immoral about making cars less safe than is technically possible. We all know that less expensive cars are frequently less safe than more expensive cars. But this is different from knowing that a part in a car is dangerously defective. A new car, for instance, is expected to have working brakes, even if it is an inexpensive car. If the brakes are defective and likely to give out under pressure when going down a steep incline, that is a danger that no one purchasing a car expects. If a car dealer stated what was wrong with the car and what might happen, it is unlikely that many people would purchase it; rather, they would go to some comparable competitor without the defect. Thus, even the argument that claims the immorality is not in selling a defective product but in selling a defective product without informing the purchaser must ultimately conclude that the sale is immoral.

The argument does not justify the cost-benefit analysis in which profits are compared with lives.

There are other corporate activities that have led people to disclose publicly the internal actions of their companies. In some cases, a company was dumping toxic wastes into a water supply, knowing that it would harm the people who lived near the supply. In other cases papers were signed certifying a dangerous defect had been repaired when in fact no repairs had been made. In the Bay Area Rapid Transit case, three engineers saw a dangerous defect in the system. When their warnings were systematically ignored and they were told to keep quiet, they felt the moral demand to make the danger public.

The whistle blower usually fares very poorly at the hands of his company. Most of them have been fired. In some instances they have been blackballed in the whole industry. When not fired, they are frequently shunted aside at promotion time and treated as pariahs. Company officials feel whistle blowers have violated the confidence of the company, have shown themselves disloyal, have washed the company's dirty linen in public, frequently have cost the company large sums of money, and they have opened it up to public abuse and criticism. Not only their superiors but frequently their coworkers feel the whistle blower has betrayed the company and they make their feelings known to him. Those who consider making a firm's wrongdoings public must therefore consider that they may be fired, ostracized, and condemned by others. They may ruin their chances of future promotion and security. They open themselves up to possible revenge. Only rarely have companies praised and promoted such people. Nor is this surprising since the whistle blower forces the company to do what it did not want to do, even if it was the morally right action. The scandal is not only that these employees get fired but that those guilty of endangering the lives of others—even of indirectly killing them—frequently get promoted by their companies for increasing profits.

Since the consequences for the whistle blower are often disastrous, such action is not to be undertaken lightly. Because the consequences are so serious for the employee, whistle blowing in a particular situation may be morally justifiable without being morally mandatory. The position we shall develop is a moderate one, and falls between two extremes: those who claim that whistle blowing is always morally justifiable; and those who say it is never morally justifiable.

The defenders of the first position claim that whistle blowing is always morally justifiable since it is simply the exercise of an individual's right to free speech. Outside the confines of the company, this position contends, an employee has the civil right of freedom of speech. His employer has no right to prevent his speaking or writing about the corporation, just as it has no right to prevent him from speaking about politics or religion or any other topic he chooses. The corporation has no special right to the employee's silence, and the employee owes no special obligation of silence to the employer. If the employer underpays his employees, if he fails to provide them with safety equipment where needed, or if he mistreats them in any way, there is no reason why the employee has to keep quiet about these things. Even more, therefore, he has no obligation to keep quiet about his employer's endangering the lives or health of others. If the firm is dumping toxic substances, emitting radiation, or not correcting defective parts in its product, the employee has every right to tell this to whomever he wishes. He may write about it to the newspapers, report it to government agencies, write his congressman, write articles in magazines, give lectures before interested groups and do any of the other things he is allowed to do by virtue of the First Amendment to the Constitution. An employer who penalizes a worker for exercising his right of free speech acts immorally. A worker may from prudence refrain from voicing complaints or bringing charges against his employer. But he needs no special moral justification for making such charges public. If the employee is mistaken in what he charges or if he maligns the company, then he can properly be sued.

The counterview claims that workers never have the moral right to blow the whistle on a company. The typical worker, the argument goes, does not know the whole operation of a plant. He is not privy to all the considerations that go into making decisions regarding many aspects of the company. If he sees something that he thinks is wrong, harmful, or illegal, then he fulfills his moral duty by reporting the discrepancy, his fear, or moral concern to his superior. His superior in turn should take the appropriate action. But what if what the superior thinks is the appropriate action may not be what the person who made the report thinks his superior should do? It is up to the superior to decide what action to take and whether any action should be taken. Those below him should not try to second-guess him. He knows the broader picture that they, because of their position, do not know. What may appear to be wrong, mistaken, or immoral from their point of view may in fact be perfectly acceptable, justifiable, and moral from the broader point of view. Workers are not paid to oversee their superiors and they are not expected to go over the heads of their superiors. If this is a policy of the firm, then the firm assumes the responsibility for the final product. All that a worker is responsible for is doing his job. It makes no difference, moreover, whether the worker in question is a blue collar worker or an engineer, an accountant, or a lawyer. They all report to those above them and have discharged their moral obligations once they have done so. It is improper, the argument continues, for workers to carry complaints to the newspapers, government agencies, or to other public bodies. The affairs of the company should be kept within the company. They are not the public's business. Workers should realize this. If they have complaints, they should be directed to the appropriate person within the company. Loyalty to the employer is an appropriate concomitant of the job they hold and the pay they receive. They, their fellow workers, and the company all benefit by keeping company problems within the company.

The first view is extreme because it allows no exceptions. There are cases of privileged information, as we shall discuss in another chapter. Not all the affairs of a company are open game for anyone to discuss publicly. It is also extreme insofar as it denies any obligation of loyalty on the part of an employee to the company that employs him. There is a special relation between employer and employee, a reciprocal relation that is violated if the employee feels no obligation to the firm of which he is a part. The second view, however, goes too far in the other direction. It maintains both that an employee discharges his moral obligation by reporting his concerns to his superior and that the bond of loyalty precludes an employee from ever making public the wrongdoings of the firm. This view, like the first, fails to allow justifiable exceptions.

Under what conditions does an employee both discharge his obligation of loyalty and still have the moral right to blow the whistle on his company? Whistle blowing is morally *justifiable* if the following conditions are fulfilled:

1. The issue on which an employee intends to disclose information to the public about the company concerns the infliction of serious harm on the public in general or on some members of it. For instance: the production of an unsafe tire which will be sold as first quality, a car with a dangerously placed gas tank which may explode on impact from the rear, a practice of dumping toxic waste into a river in metal drums which will eventually corrode and release their contents, failure to repair an airplane door which will come open during flight, failure to x-ray fittings for a nuclear reactor plant and substituting the same x-ray pictures for all the pictures required—these are matters which imperil the lives of people. In all these cases, the company can and should take action to prevent the harm which may be done. Other cases qualify as well. Firms that grossly overcharge their customers, routinely waste large sums of government money, falsify documents, and so on provide appropriate grounds for whistle blowing.

2. Once the employee identifies a serious threat to the public or a serious injustice perpetrated by the firm, he should report it to his immediate superior and make his moral concern known.

A firm that wishes to be moral will take such concerns and complaints seriously and do something about them.

3. If his immediate superior does nothing about the concern or complaint, the employee should take it higher up the managerial line, all the way to the board of directors, if necessary. If he still gets no action of the type that he thinks is mandatory, then he has exhausted the possible avenues within the firm. Once he has done this, he is morally justified in bringing his concerns to the attention of the public in whatever way he deems appropriate—reporting them to a governmental agency, leaking information to the newspapers, writing up a report for publication, trying to get concerned groups to apply pressure on the firm, and so on.

Though justifiable, his action may be unwise, ineffective, or even counterproductive. The above stated conditions are not sufficient to make it obligatory that he blow the whistle on the company's activities by going public. But they do justify his blowing the whistle.

For it to be *morally obligatory* that a person take action to try to stop the company from doing the wrong in which it is engaged:

1. The company must be engaged in a practice or about to release a product which does *serious* harm to individuals or to society in general. The more serious the harm, the more serious the obligation.

2. The employee should report his concern or complaint to his immediate superior. If no appropriate action is taken, then

3. The employee should take the matter up the managerial line. Before he is obliged to go public he should exhaust the resources for remedy within the company.

There may be times when it is sufficient that he be reasonably sure that no action will be taken within the company, even if he himself has not raised the issue to the board. Thus far, the requirements parallel those that justify but do not make it obligatory to blow the whistle. In addition,

4. The employee should have documentation of the practice or defect.

A fear that maybe some people will be hurt, without documentation and evidence to that effect, will not motivate action by outside groups, the press, or by government. Without adequate evidence his chances of being successful in his whistle blowing are slim. Difficulty or danger in getting adequate evidence may preclude his obligation to do so, if the chances of success are slim.

5. The employee must have good reason to believe that by going public he will be able to bring about the necessary changes. The chance of his being successful must be worth the risk he takes and the danger to which he exposes himself.

The whistle blower should know to whom he is going to make available the information, what the probable response of the corporation will be, and what the probable response of the public or of government will be. Unless he can know these, he has no obligation to blow the whistle.

The fourth and fifth conditions seem too strong to some people and too weak to others. They are too strong for those who wish everyone to be ready and willing to blow the whistle whenever the public may be harmed. But since blowing the whistle usually has serious adverse consequences for the whistle blower, it is an act of moral heroism. Moral heroism is rarely obligatory.

The conditions are too strong for those who feel that since whistle blowing is a kind of moral heroism, it is never morally obligatory. They argue further that whistle blowing involves preventing others from doing something immoral. Though we are never ourselves allowed to do what is immoral, we are not always obliged to prevent others from doing what is immoral. The principle of maximal freedom implies that we allow others to act immorally, at least insofar as the effects of their actions fall mainly on themselves. Moreover, we are not *obliged* to put ourselves at great risk in the hope of possibly preventing someone from doing harm to another.

The counter to these arguments maintains that we are morally obliged to prevent serious harm to others when we can prevent that without great harm to ourselves. The greater the harm to others, moreover, the more the harm to which we are obliged to expose ourselves, at least up to a certain limit. If we can save someone simply by extending our hand, we are obliged to do so. If we can save the inhabitants of a town by reporting a crack in a dam, we are obliged to do so even at some risk to ourselves. If we can save many lives by blowing the whistle on some defective part in an airplane or automobile, we are obliged to do so, even at some risk to ourselves. Exactly how much risk is a matter of debate. But the principle is applicable and will apply to at least some cases in which it becomes obligatory to blow the whistle. Conditions four and five state some plausible circumstances in which blowing the whistle is obligatory, providing the harm that will be done to others is sufficiently serious, and providing that harm is not overriden by especially great harm, e.g., threat of death, to the whistle blower.

We have not discussed *how* the whistle should be blown. It might be possible to do so anonymously. But anonymous tips or stories seldom get much attention. One can confide in a governmental agency or in a reporter on condition that one's name not be disclosed. But this approach, too, is frequently ineffective in achieving the results required. To be effective one must usually be willing to be identified, to testify publicly, to produce verifiable evidence, and put oneself at risk. As with civil disobedience, what captures the conscience of others is the willingness of the whistle blower to suffer harm for the benefit of others and for what he thinks is right.

The need for moral heroes, however, shows a defective society and a defective corporation. More important than convincing people to be moral heroes is changing the legal and corporate structures that make whistle blowing necessary.

Since it is easier to change the law than to change the practices of all corporations, it should be illegal for any employer to fire or to take any punitive measures at the time or later, against an employee who satisfies the first set of conditions above and blows the whistle on the company. Since satisfying those conditions makes the action morally justifiable, the law should protect the employee in acting in accordance with what his conscience demands. If the whistle is falsely blown, the company will have suffered no great harm. If it is appropriately blown, the company should suffer the consequences of its actions being made public. Protecting the whistle blower by law is no easy matter. Employers can make life difficult for whistle blowers without firing them. There are many ways of passing over an employee, of relegating him to the back room of the firm, or giving him the unpleasant jobs, of finding reasons not to promote him or give him raises. Not all of this can be prevented by law. But some of the more blatant practices can be prohibited.

Secondly, the law can mandate that the individuals responsible for the decision to proceed with a faulty product or engage in a harmful practice be penalized. The law has been reluctant to interfere with the operations of companies. As a result, those guilty of immoral and illegal practices have gone untouched while the corporation has been fined for its activity.

A third possibility is that every company of a certain size be required to have an inspector general or an internal operational auditor whose job it is to uncover immoral and illegal practices, and whose job it is to listen to the moral concerns of employees at every level about the firm's practices. He should be independent of management, and report to the audit committee of the board, which ideally should be a committee made up of independent board members. He should be charged with making public those complaints that should be made public if not changed from within. Failure on his part not to take proper action with respect to a worker complaint, such that the worker is forced to go public, should be prima facie evidence of an attempt to cover up a dangerous practice or product and should be subject to criminal charges.

The last suggestion places someone such as an inspector general within the company by law. A company that wishes to be moral, that does not wish to engage in harmful practices or to produce harmful products can take additional steps of its own to preclude the necessity of whistle blowing. It can establish channels whereby those employees who have moral concerns can get a fair hearing without danger to their position or standing in the company. Expressing such concerns, moreover, should be considered a demonstration of company loyalty and should be rewarded appropriately. The company might establish the position of ombudsman to hear such complaints or moral concerns. There might be an independent committee of the board established to hear such complaints and concerns. Someone might even be paid by the company to present the position of the would-be whistle blower, arguing what the company should do from a moral point of view rather than what those interested in meeting a schedule or making a profit would like to do. Such a person's success within the company could depend on his success in precluding whistle blowing and the conditions that lead to it.

In addition to government, unions and professional organizations should become concerned with the problem of whistle blowing. They can support their members who feel obligated to blow the whistle on a company, defending the member, supporting him in his endeavor, and protecting him from being fired or abused on the job. They can also establish channels of their own to which members can report concerns and take it upon themselves to follow up such situations and force appropriate action.

The moral concerns of workers as well as their moral rights and moral obligations have received little attention from corporations. A firm that takes morality seriously will set a moral tone from above, will pay close attention to the moral concerns of its employees, and will structure itself in a way appropriate both to respond to their concerns and to see that they receive the moral rights to which they are entitled.

Further Reading

Baum, Robert J., and Flores, Albert, eds. *Ethical Problems in Engineering.* Troy, N.Y.: Center for the Study of the Human Dimensions of Science and Technology, 1978.

Bendix, Reinhard. *Work and Authority in Industry.* Berkeley: University of California Press, 1974.

Eddy, Paul; Potter, Elaine; and Page, Bruce. *Destination Disaster. From the Tri-Motor to the DC-10: The Risk of Flying.* New York: Quadrangle/New York Times Book Co., 1976.

Ewing, David W. *Freedom Inside the Organization.* New York: McGraw-Hill, Inc., 1977.

Nader, Ralph; Green, Mark; and Seligman, Joel. *Taming the Giant Corporation.* New York: W.W. Norton & Co., Inc., 1976.

Nader, Ralph; Petkas, Peter J.; and Blackwell, Kate, eds. *Whistle Blowing: The Report of the Conference on Professional Responsibility.* New York: Grossman, Publishers, 1972.

O'Neil, Robert. *The Rights of Government Employees.* New York: Avon Books, 1978.

Peters, Charles, and Branch, Taylor. *Blowing the Whistle: Dissent in the Public Interest.* New York: Praeger Publishers, Inc., 1972.

Walters, Kenneth D. "Your Employee's Right to Blow the Whistle." In *Harvard Business Review,* July–August, 1975.

10   Discrimination, Affirmative Action, and Reverse Discrimination

Discrimination

Since workers have the right to equal treatment, discrimination on the basis of non-job-related characteristics in hiring, firing, or promoting people is immoral. Few dispute this statement, which is fairly easy to demonstrate using a utilitarian, a Kantian, or a Rawlsian approach.

Consider the practice of discrimination from a utilitarian point of view. We see immediately that harm is done to those who are discriminated against. If the practice is widespread and repeated in successive job situations, the harm done is serious and long-lasting. It affects not only the individuals but also their families. Those who get the positions and promotions they would not get under conditions of fair competition do benefit. The good done to them, however, is probably not as great as the harm done to those discriminated against. But let us assume that the good is equal to the harm. In this case the morality of the practice hinges on the results to others and to society in general. We can first consider the companies in which discrimination is practiced. If they did not discriminate but hired and promoted only on the basis of merit, they would undoubtedly hire and promote some of those they discriminate against. Hence they are not getting the best people possible.To that extent they suffer some harm and experience no benefit.

What about society as a whole? It also suffers. Systematic discrimination produces a class of people who are treated unjustly. They cannot help but feel anger against society, an anger that will show itself in many ways—from violence to seething ill will. Other groups in the society will also have cause to worry about whether they will be the next group to be discriminated against. On the whole, more harm than good is attained by following the practice of discrimination than by not following it. Discrimination is therefore an immoral practice.

We can reach the same result by a Kantian-type analysis. Can discrimination be made universal consistently? In fact, it can. People might not like the kind of society in which they live if discrimination were made universal; but the action is not self-contradictory. It passes the first of the three tests. But it fails the next two. Discrimination does not treat people as ends in themselves. They are not considered as persons at all but simply as members of a class with a certain characteristic. As a result of that characteristic they are not given equal treatment. They are not treated with respect. They are made means to the ends of the dominant class's desire to maintain its superiority and its class prerogatives. Nor, if we ask whether rational human beings would will to live in a society that discriminates rather than in one that does not, can we expect anything other than a negative answer.

Using a Rawlsian approach, we can consider the decision rational people would make behind the veil of ignorance. If they did not know where they would end up, would they prefer to live in a discriminatory society or in a nondiscriminatory one? Clearly, the least advantaged would be better off in a nondiscriminatory society than in one that discriminates. Hence the rational person, not knowing where he would end up, would see that the morally preferable, the morally just society is the one that does not practice discrimination.

Because it seems so clear that discrimination is immoral we should pause to consider why discrimination has been so widely practiced in our society. Part of the reply comes from historical circumstances. To understand why people discriminate is not to justify their doing so. But while condemning the practice, we can at least understand the human motivation for it.

Blacks have been one chief group against whom discrimination has been practiced for a long period of time, and, in a systematic way. The reason for the discrimination stems back to the fact that with but a few exceptions, the blacks in the United States were slaves until freed in 1861. Many whites did not even consider them human beings. This attitude toward blacks enabled the whites to live with the immoral institution of slavery. The Emancipation Proclamation could not instantly change the attitude of those who considered blacks slaves, inferior to whites, and nonhuman. Neither amendments to the Constitution nor legislation granting blacks the rights of citizens could change the views and attitudes of such Southerners. Attitudes are not easily or quickly changed. Moreover, the blacks were uneducated and were used to living in extremely poor conditions. When they were freed, they could leave the plantation and seek employment elsewhere. But they were not trained to work in factories or to run their own affairs. They were easy prey for entrepreneurs who hired them for a pittance. The standard of living of many blacks was little, if at all, improved over the slave days. Some even backslid. The whites in both the North and the South who had felt superior to the slaves continued to feel so—the well-to-do because they lived better, had more money, and could hire the blacks cheaply and even the poor whites simply because they were white. The color of skin was all they had to feel superior about, but it was enough. The blacks were forced to live in segregated areas and were discriminated against in schooling, opportunities to gain advancement, employment, and in almost every aspect of social life.

Women form another group of those against whom discrimination in employment has been practiced. The historical situation with respect to women is more complicated and more controversial than the above. During the nineteenth century and the early part of the twentieth century, other than the movement for women's suffrage, there was little cry concerning discrimination against women. The majority of women did not seek employment outside the home. The man in a household was considered the head of the family and the breadwinner. Frequently men were paid more than women for the same work. It was assumed that men had families to support whereas women either had to support only themselves or had to contribute to the support of a family in which the man already worked. The allocation of pay was based on need rather than equality only. In speaking of justice we saw that one view of it defends the distribution of income on the basis of need. The combination of both work and need in deciding upon a proper wage is not necessarily unjust. Many people in former times considered it appropriate. Women who did not work or who worked to supplement their husband's income benefitted from the fact that their husbands were paid more than women. With hindsight we can now see that the women who were underpaid for their work were actually being discriminated against. As women joined the work force in greater numbers, as divorce increased, as more women became heads of households, and as it became clear that single men were also paid more than single women, a movement gradually grew demanding equal pay for equal work, equal opportunity for women, and an end to discrimination against women. Old habits die hard, however, and much discrimination, often in subtle forms, continues to the present day. Its historical roots are nonetheless important to remember.

Ethnic and religious groups have also been the object of discrimination: the American Indian, Orientals, Hispanics, Italians, Irish, Poles, Czechs, all who arrived in great numbers with no money and frequently without knowledge of English; Jews, Catholics, Mormons, and members of other religious sects. In each case the people in question were different from the majority of Americans. They lived on reservations or in ghettos, or were migrant workers. Eventually some of them were assimilated, sometimes after two or three generations. But before assimilation they suffered discrimination in the job market as well as in other areas of life.

Discrimination is unjust and causes harm to those against whom it is practiced. Compensatory justice demands that restitution be made to those harmed. The compensation should be equivalent to the harm suffered, and it should be paid to the one harmed by the one who caused the harm.

If a black or a woman working for a company has been receiving less pay for the same work done by white males, then compensatory justice requires that the company pay the black or the woman the amount he or she did not receive during his or her tenure with the company. Few cases, however, are that simple. Those who were discriminated against and have since died cannot be compensated by payment. Should their children or their heirs be compensated? Those who were never hired by any of the firms to which they applied cannot easily say which ones turned them down because of discrimination. Even if they could say which firms were guilty of discrimination, for what amount should they be compensated? Should they be paid a certain sum by all the companies that turned them down, or by all the firms that would have turned them down had they applied to them? None of these questions is easy to answer.

Hence some people have urged that certain groups or classes of people who have been discriminated against should be identified. The members of that group deserve compensation of some form from the group of people and companies who have discriminated or who have been the beneficiaries of discrimination. In concrete terms, the class of all blacks, women, Chicanos, American Indians, and Orientals are considered to be the major bearers of the burdens of discrimination. If an individual in that group has not been personally discriminated against, it is very likely that his parents have been or that some other ancestor or relative has been. If by chance a few who bear no scars of discrimination receive compensation, that is better than large numbers never receiving any compensation.

Who is to pay the compensation? Those who have benefited from discrimination are said to be American corporations and American white males. Even if some individual white males did not benefit directly, they benefited indirectly as a result of the systematic discrimination which favored them throughout their lives. Similarly, even if some particular company did not discriminate, it took advantage of the climate of corporate life which discrimination fostered.

What should compensation consist of? It could not in justice consist of monetary payments, for there would be no way to determine these in any equitable way. The only sort of compensation possible, the argument goes, is for the class of people who were previously discriminated against to be given special privileges and opportunities to make up for the absence of such privileges and opportunities in the past. A variety of target goals has been proposed. Some urge that every firm have represented in it the same proportion of women, blacks, Chicanos, and Orientals as is found in the general population. Others favor proportions in each type of position equal to the proportion of each group in training for that position. But this is found unsatisfactory by those who feel that fewer women and blacks, for instance, are in engineering schools than should be because discrimination has steered them away from such professions.

At what rate should those previously discriminated against be taken into companies and given promotions? Some would set targets and quotas for each year until the proper proportion is reached. Some simply advocate an affirmative approach, making sure that places are open to those qualified. Others seek preferential hiring of women and minorities—a term which can be interpreted in several different ways.

Before we look into the specifics of some of these proposals we should examine carefully the approach to compensation in terms of classes. Is such an approach fair, just, and proper? In arguing that discrimination was immoral we saw that harm was done to the one discriminated against, that benefit was provided to the one chosen, and that harm was done to society and to the companies that engaged in the practice. Suppose we follow the suggested class or group approach. If people from the previously-discriminated-against groups were chosen in favor of more qualified white males, we would have an instance of discrimination, even though the discrimination was against white males and in favor of blacks and females. Less qualified people would still be chosen over more qualified people. Harm would be done to the group and individuals discriminated against, as well as to the companies and to society. If discrimination was wrong because of these results in the first instance, it cannot be right when the results are similar in the second instance. After years of this practice we would then have a group of white males who had suffered discrimination, and we would have to start the cycle all over again. The argument that white males are the group that had previously benefited will not be convincing to the individual white males discriminated against. They will rightly claim that they are not guilty of past discrimination and that it is unjust to punish sons for the sins of their fathers. The children of immigrants from Italy or Poland, or Ireland will cry out even louder for justice. Their parents were discriminated against just as blacks and women were. Do they not deserve compensation too? But under the proposed system they are the ones threatened with direct discrimination after having suffered indirectly the discrimination against their parents.

Other objections have been raised against the class approach to compensation. How much black blood is necessary for one to be considered black and therefore eligible to belong to the class of those to get recompense? How much Jewish blood, or Mexican blood, and so on, is necessary? This is not an insuperable obstacle since the number of borderline cases may be small in proportion to the number of clear cases. Yet it does raise some problems. Are those who have succeeded despite discrimination to receive compensation? There are, of course successful and prosperous blacks and women. Some are in the professions; some are in business. Some were born in middle class communities; some were born well-to-do. Some were born in the slums and worked their way up the ladder to success, however that is defined. Their children may not have suffered discrimination. Should they be recompensed? Many women now in college have lived their lives during the period of the rise of the women's movement. They have not been discriminated against in school. They frequently come from families supported by their fathers. If their fathers are white, they probably benefited from the discrimination against blacks which aided their fathers' success. Should these young women be compensated for discrimination?

The class approach to discrimination and recompense suffers from many forms of inequity. One assumption is that without discrimination no white male would have been successful in the competition of the marketplace. This seems unlikely. Further, it assumes that all white males somehow make up a class that can and should be penalized. Discrimination, however, was practiced by those now at the senior levels not by those who will suffer the cost of reparation. In our discussion of responsibility we saw that a causal connection is necessary for someone to be responsible and to be properly censurable and punished. But those being punished in the class approach to discrimination are not those who are causally responsible for discrimination; and those who benefitted most are not those who will suffer the major effects of this new discrimination.

The conclusion to which we are reluctantly brought is that the class approach to discrimination and compensation itself involves discrimination, produces harm to those who did not cause it, does not solve the social problems of discrimination, and is immoral. Yet we also saw that the individual approach is not sufficiently extensive and that it ignores many who still suffer indirectly from the discrimination practiced against their parents. Is there any way to satisfy the demands of compensatory justice and still not continue discrimination in another form—frequently called reverse discrimination?

Three answers suggest themselves. First, the problem is not simply one of individuals, classes, or groups. The problem involves all members of society. Past discrimination was a result of certain social structures. These have to be changed and some beneficial structures must be built that give at least some compensation for those still suffering from the effects of discrimination. Second, affirmative action can be taken to insure that members of those groups previously discriminated against are not further ignored by the system. Third, preferential hiring can be implemented to achieve affirmative action goals. Each of these deserves further discussion.

Changing Social Structures

Discrimination against women, blacks, and other minority groups was not necessarily done consciously or with personally malicious intentions. It was an effect of certain ways of doing business, certain patterns of thinking and acting, and certain social structures. These must be changed. A necessary first step has been the raising of the consciousness of the ordinary citizen and of those people holding responsible positions in business. Discrimination is now illegal. But legislation cannot change people's attitudes and their old habits. These have been changing slowly under constant pressure from minority associations and women's groups as well as from individuals who push for their rights, press suits when appropriate, and jostle those who tend to revert back to old habits.

People who have been individually discriminated against can bargain or sue for compensation; but those who suffer the effects of discrimination in a less specific manner cannot. In many ways society as a whole is to blame for past discrimination. So society should bear the burden of compensation when direct individual reparation by a business or individual is not available. Though the claim is plausible, its implementation raises questions. For instance, what is to count as evidence of suffering from past discrimination, either directly or indirectly? Similarly, what is to count as evidence of having profited from past discrimination either directly or indirectly? Who should bear the cost of compensation? What form should the compensation take? There are no easy answers to these questions. Yet we can suggest some approaches.

No specific condition is evidence of past discrimination: neither poverty, nor a poor education, nor failure to get and keep a good job, however that is defined. All of these are often the result of discrimination. But other causes also contribute to poverty, poor education, and failure to get a job of one's choosing. From a social point of view, need we distinguish between the help given to the poor or the poorly educated that is called compensation and the help we give to the poor and the poorly educated simply because they are poor and poorly educated? There is little to gain in attempting to make such fine distinctions. If one of the results of racial discrimination is poverty and poor schooling, then justice requires that attempts be made to get rid of poverty and to improve schooling. But it is also appropriate for society to do these things for all the poor and the poorly educated. Society should make available the opportunities for people to rise above the poverty level, to take part in the mainstream of social activity if they wish, and to have available the schooling and more advanced educational opportunities that allow them to better themselves and to compete on an equal footing with others.

The attempts at making black schools equal to white schools have not been successful. Obviously more must be done in this regard. The problem of how to achieve the desired end of equal educational opportunities for all has not been satisfactorily solved. It is a problem which requires more work, thought, experimentation, and money. Society should supply all of these in greater quantity than it has thus far.

Improving education for blacks by improving their schools is a slow approach. It will take several generations of people to produce any real effect. We first have to provide good basic schooling at the elementary level, then improve the junior high and high school levels so that blacks can compete on the college level and then go on to professional schools. The process is obviously long and drawn out. What of the blacks and other minority members who have had poor elementary school training and are now in high school, or those who have had poor high school training and are now having difficulty in college? Thus far the best that can be done is to provide remedial help wherever possible. Those who earn engineering or medical degrees must have mastered the requisite knowledge. They cannot be compassionately passed through because they are the victims of past discrimination. Nor do many advocate that they should be passed through. No one would want to consult a doctor who was not properly trained nor entrust his life to a building designed or built by an incompetent engineer.

Industry, however, can provide special training financed by business as well as by public funds. Business can appropriately be asked to take the lead in such programs and to make some contribution to them because businesses in the past have practiced discrimination and because businesses will benefit by the training they give such people once they hire them. Government can also appropriately be asked to contribute since such programs represent society's effort to make restitution for past social injustice.

The situation with respect to women is in some ways easier and in some ways more difficult because it is more subtle. It is easier because at least white women have in recent years gained access to as good schools as men and have had the opportunity to receive adequate education for a variety of jobs and professions. They have been discriminated against however in the hiring process and in the promotion process. But these are both remediable, and important first steps have already been taken. Obviously, however, not many women have made it to the top of their professions and firms, considering the number of women in them. Proportional representation at the top takes time, and women have to compete with men and have had the opportunity to do so for too short a time. Those impatient with this approach want more women at the top now. Those with more patience claim that promoting women to the "level of their incompetence" too soon will not help but hinder the cause of women in general. There are admittedly still too many barriers at the top which must come down, and which will come down with time and with steady pressure to bring them down.

On the other hand, the situation of women is more difficult than that of blacks and minorities because women are a majority. Some of them feel they are oppressed by language which gives dominance to men, and by culture which stereotypes them and forces them into certain roles. There is less agreement about whether there is such discrimination and oppression of women by men. Nor is it a matter of males against females on these issues—a significant number of women are unsympathetic to the radical position of the women's movement; there are men who sympathize with it. The social problem of stereotyping women and men in textbooks, in the media, and in business has been persuasively raised. Some change has been made; however, less change has been made than many think is appropriate. But change does continue and society is surely, if slowly, moving in the direction of greater equality of treatment for women.

Racial, sexual, religious, and other kinds of discrimination were always immoral. Discrimination is now illegal in many areas and is under attack in areas beyond the reach of the law. We must still provide equal access to all, making up for past discrimination by improved schooling for those who have suffered from poor schooling, improved training for those who have not had access to training, improved chances for advancement through affirmative action and preferential hiring. Changes in our social structures are essential.

What I have not suggested is that either businesses or individual white males be directly penalized unless they can be identified as perpetrators or direct beneficiaries of specific discrimination in the past. There are some who claim the above permits the guilty, or at least those who have benefited from discrimination, to remain without censure or penalty. The reply is that we cannot know, simply from the fact that a white male has been successful in business, for instance, that his success is due to discrimination. Presumably, if there had been no discrimination, some white males would nonetheless be successful. Unless we have evidence to determine which are which, we do some an injustice by condemning or seeking retribution from all. One solution may be for society to appropriately tax all people who do well financially in order to help those who need financial assistance. Society similarly taxes businesses for the social good. Such taxation can be defended as justifiable, even though we cannot say exactly which company benefited or to what precise extent it benefited from discrimination, or which company practiced it to what extent, wittingly or unwittingly.

Affirmative Action

The promise on the part of businesses not to engage in discrimination is not enough to offset the effects of past discrimination. Nor is it enough for them simply to refrain from discrimination. An active rather than a passive approach is required. An approach mandated by government and advocated by many groups has become known as affirmative action. Affirmative action can operate on four levels: (1) active recruiting of women and members of minority groups; (2) equalization of criteria so as not to give preference to any group; (3) adequate training for senior positions; and (4) promotion of women and members of minority groups to senior positions.

Who should practice affirmative action? Those firms and institutions that have a small number of minorities and women in proportion to the general population (or in proportion to the number of persons qualified for the positions in the firm or organization) are prime candidates for affirmative action. Though the small percentage of women and minority workers does not prove active discrimination in the past, it presents prima facie evidence either of active discrimination or of cooperation in discriminatory conditions in other parts of society. The head of a scientific laboratory that has no women may plead that he has never had good women candidates. The question then becomes why did so few women go into science? Is there any reason other than that sexual stereotyping took place from infancy on? Yet, if indeed there is a shortage of women in a certain field of science, it would be ridiculous to demand that all laboratories add women scientists within the next two or three years. The patterns that lead to women choosing scientific fields must be established if women are to be represented in adequate numbers in all laboratories.

Business has less excuse for not hiring women. Women are eligible for executive traineeships in large numbers, just as they are eligible for other kinds of work in business. The training is neither so long nor so specialized in many cases that it may justify long delays in hiring women in appreciable numbers. Though the same case cannot be made for all minority groups due to the fact that a smaller percentage of minorities go on to college, minority members are available for managerial jobs in ever-growing numbers. The problem here is why more minority members do not go on to college. What forces of discrimination have to be overcome to change that pattern? It seems justifiable to assume that more members of minority groups would choose college and the kinds of jobs it can lead to if they had the chance.

1. Active Recruitment

The first level of affirmative action involves the active recruiting of women and members of minority groups. This represents a change from the way many positions were filled in the past. Frequently, no woman or minority member was turned down in competition with a white male because no woman or minority member *knew* of the opening. Openings were filled by the "old boy" network. If one employer had an opening for a good job, he would call up his friends and ask whom they recommended. Or we would write to a few select universities and hire one of their best graduates. Affirmative action requires that jobs be advertised publicly and not simply by word of mouth to one's friends. It also requires adequate advertising in the outlets commonly used by those interested in certain kinds of positions. If in addition there are special publications that are more likely to be read by women and minority members, then the opening should be listed in them. Affirmative action should go even further if a reasonable number of applicants of women and minority groups do not apply. In such cases, active soliciting of applications from members of these groups may be in order. Affirmative action, as the name suggests, consists of actively seeking applicants from the previously discriminated against group rather than waiting for them to take the initiative. This is not too much to demand. Typically, those who have been discriminated against by a certain firm or kind of business tend not to apply on the assumption that the future will be like the past. Those who have discriminated or who give prima facie evidence of having participated in a discriminatory social syndrome should take the initiative to contact groups whom they have previously ignored. This may be more costly in time and money than the old way of hiring. The extra burden is part of the cost of compensation and an appropriate form of reparation.

2. Equalization of Criteria

Discrimination is often subtle. If one chooses criteria for a position in terms of what white males are typically good at, one can write a job description that can be filled only by white males. If standard tests are skewed in such a way that white males excel at them, and if these tests are used to screen candidates, then white males will appear as the most qualified. Hence we must ask: Are the criteria themselves free of bias and prejudice? Are they fair? Are they relevant to the position advertised?

The fairness of criteria and tests has taken many strange turns. Some claim that blacks should not be discriminated against for using "black English" and for not writing standard English fluently. This argument may hold if the command of standard English is not necessary for the job. But it does not hold true for a job in which a person must write memos, letters, and reports for a range of American readers. This does not constitute prejudice any more than not hiring a Mexican who cannot write English would be prejudice if the job called for such a skill. More plausible are the claims that many of the objective tests designed to test intelligence or work skills are culturally slanted in favor of middle class white males. The problem is a difficult one. Research has so far proven inconclusive, and even where the result seems to bear out the claim, it is not clear how to devise a test that will be fair to all, or how to weigh the built-in bias in favor of a certain group.

There are other sorts of bias built into job criteria. Frequently, a position calls for a college degree. The reason for demanding a college degree is not that one needs to know anything that was taught in college. Any degree in any major will do. The assumption is that anyone who had the discipline to work four years and get a degree is a better candidate than someone who does not have that sort of background. But in many cases a person who has worked for four years shows as much discipline as the person who attended college and perhaps even more.

Discrimination that is built into job criteria is difficult to root out by law. Employers are free to draw up their job descriptions and no government bureaucrat can assume to know better than an employer what qualifications an employer needs in an employee. But pressure can be brought to bear by those within a firm as well as by unions and professional associations to free job descriptions from built-in discrimination.

3. Adequate Training

We have already noted that many women and minority members have only in the past decade or two entered a large number of firms and institutions. They are still poorly represented in top positions. Affirmative action has been taken by a number of firms to remedy this situation. They have established training internships for women and members of minority groups in which they become apprenticed for six months or a year to a senior executive. They learn what executives do and how they do it. This firsthand apprenticeship has served as an effective means of advancing those who have taken part in them. This is affirmative action. Instead of letting the natural process work, this technique has advanced people faster. The internships are usually available only to women or minority members in the firm who have been there a certain length of time and who compete for the positions. Does this mean the internships are discriminatory against white males? The answer seems to be clearly so. When vacancies occur for regular positions, white males are eligible for them and compete with women and minority members. The best person for the job should be chosen. Women and minority members need such internships to compete adequately with many white males who for years had access to special privileges not available to them.

4. Promotion to Senior Positions

Affirmative action in hiring is not significant unless those hired have a chance to compete fairly for advancement and raises. In these areas, just as in hiring, many firms have had built-in prejudices and bias in favor of white males. The background assumptions have frequently favored the white male. Managers have usually assumed that married women would not accept a promotion that involved transfer to another city, whereas they have offered such positions to men and then found out whether they would accept the transfer. Managers have assumed single women would soon get married or leave to have and raise children. Minority members were stereotyped as blue collar workers, and racial prejudices about intelligence and ability were prevalent even when falsified by performance. These and other assumptions were not spelled out in promotion criteria.

Affirmative action in promotion means that higher level positions are truly open to competent women and minority members. It means searching through personnel records and inviting women and minority members to apply for positions that they may otherwise feel would not be open to them. It involves counseling them (if in fact they are passed over) as to how they can improve their chances for the next opening. Once again what may seem like favoritism is justifiable in order to equalize the predispositions in favor of the white male that still linger consciously or unconsciously in the system.

Affirmative action does not mandate quotas. If quotas mean hiring unqualified people, it is difficult to see how they can be morally mandatory. The unqualified will either be let go after a short while or will remain at their entry level indefinitely, be passed over by those qualified, and will eventually lose their self-respect in the process. Quotas will not supply role models for women and minority members nor improve their image among managers in general. Quotas, however, can be distinguished from the expectation that firms will make reasonable progress toward hiring members of those groups grossly underrepresented, if the pool of applicants is reasonably large. Making such progress is a reasonable moral expectation.

Hiring token women and members of minority groups is not affirmative action. Tokenism is not an adequate way to fulfill the moral responsibility to break the pattern and system of discrimination. The moral obligation to take affirmative action goes beyond satisfying the letter of the law.

Preferential Hiring

Preferential hiring is the hiring of one person rather than another on the basis of some non-job-related characteristic, such as sex, race or religion. Is preferential hiring a form of discrimination, and is it therefore immoral?

A standard way of seeking someone to fill a job is to announce the opening with a description indicating the qualifications necessary for the job. The implied agreement between those who advertise job openings and those who apply for them is that the best person for the job will be chosen. The criteria to be used in making the selection is understood to be job-related criteria. It is unfair to use non-job-related criteria, since use of such criteria breaks the implicit conditions of seeking and granting jobs. It is unfair to raise expectations when hidden criteria are being used, which, if known, would let some people know that they will not be seriously considered for the job. Using criteria other than those stated or those that are obviously job related is to mislead, deceive, raise false hopes, and violate an implied practice governing hiring. If a person is denied a job solely because of sex, race, or religion, that person is a victim of discrimination.

Does preferential hiring fall under this description? We can simplify our inquiry by rejecting two interpretations immediately. One could claim that preferential hiring does not fall under the description and is not a form of discrimination because it *chooses* someone on the basis of sex, race, or religion rather than *denying* someone a position for these reasons. The distinction, however, will not stand up to scrutiny. If a white male is hired because he is white and a black male is not hired, and we are told that the black male was not discriminated against, since the white male was simply preferred *because* of the color of his skin, we would certainly call the choice one of racial discrimination. The second interpretation would claim that it is permissible to use preferential hiring if the announcement indicates that preference will be given to women or minority members. This, the claim goes, would indicate the rules of the game, would not deceive, and hence would be morally permitted. Consider, however, an ad for a job that read: "Women and minority members need not apply" or that indicated preference would be given to white males, even though one need not be a white male to do the job described. Surely we would say such an ad was discriminatory, as would be the practice. The same can be said of the reverse situation—when preference is given to women or minorities. If employers use non-job-related criteria such as sex, race, or religion to hire people, they discriminate whether they announce openly that they are or whether they do so without making it public.

To clarify the moral status of preferential hiring, consider the following job announcement with respect to each of the situations listed below:

Wanted: Computer programmer. Must have knowledge of Fortran and Cobol, plus at least two years programming experience. Salary: open, depending on experience. An equal opportunity employer. Call 938-7625.

Situation 1. Sally Hanson and Tom Byers both apply for the job. Sally knows Fortran but does not know the program language Cobol. She has had only one year experience as a programmer. She applies, figuring she has nothing to lose. Tom knows Fortran and Cobol and has three years experience as a programmer. (a) Tom gets the job. He is the more qualified of the two. (b) Sally gets the job. The employer needs to add women to his work force to meet affirmative action goals.

Situation 2. Sue Jones and John Green apply for the job. Sue fulfills all the listed requirements. John knows Fortran and Cobol but has only one year programming experience. (a) Sue gets the job. She is the more qualified of the two. (b) John gets the job. The employer prefers to hire males.

Situation 3. Sandra Hopkins and Henry Thompson apply for the job. Sandra and Henry both know Fortran and Cobol and both have had two years of programming experience. (a) Sandra gets the job. The employer wants to add women to his work force to meet affirmative action goals. (b) Henry gets the job. Henry is a veteran and the employer gives extra credit to veterans. (c) Henry gets the job. The employer prefers to hire males.

Situation 4. Sarah Hall and Peter Brock apply for the job. Sarah knows Fortran and Cobol and has had two years of programming experience. Her former employers noted her to be only adequate on the job. Peter is a computer whiz. He knows Fortran, Cobol, and three other computer languages. He has had four years of programming experience and is rated as outstanding by his past employers. (a) Sarah gets the job. The employer wants to add women to his work force to meet affirmative action goals. (b) Peter gets the job. He is the better of the two applicants regarding job experience.

In Situation 1, it is appropriate that Tom rather than Sally get the job since he has the specified qualifications she does not have. If Sally gets the job because she is a woman and the employer wishes to meet his affirmative action goals, then the employer has achieved his purpose in a way that does an injustice to Tom. If the qualifications listed are not the qualifications required for the job, and if the employer is going to consider someone with lesser qualifications if that someone is female, then he should write the job description differently. Clearly, if the situation with respect to qualifications were reversed as they are in situation 2, we feel that it is inappropriate for John to be hired rather than Sue. Sue has all the stated qualifications. John has only one year of experience. The reason the employer gives in situation 2b is that he prefers to hire males. Hiring John who does not have the stipulated qualifications, rather than Sue who does is a classic case of discrimination. The employer's only criterion for choosing John over Sue is that John is male. Is there a difference between 2b and 1b? In both cases a person who does *not* meet the stated qualifications for the job is chosen over a person of the other sex who *does* meet the qualifications. In both cases the person is chosen on the basis of sex, a non-job-related characteristic. The difference in the two cases is that in 2b, the reason is personal preference while in case 1b, it is a desire to fulfill an affirmative action goal with or without personal preference for the hiring of women. Does the achieving of the goal outweigh the injustice done to Tom?

In order to answer this we might try a utilitarian approach to the question. Consider the following rule: Managers should hire women who do not meet stated job requirements rather than men who do, when the choice is between two such people and when the firm should make progress toward fulfilling affirmative action goals. If we calculate the good and bad effects of the rule on all concerned, we can decide whether the practice is morally justifiable.

The good effect for Sally, at least initially, is that she gets the job. The bad effect for Tom is that he does not get the job. Would the results be equal if Tom got the job rather than Sally? The answer is no. If Tom got the job rather than Sally, Sally would not feel that an injustice had been done since she knew she did not have the stated qualifications. Tom, however, would feel that an injustice had been done to him since, despite his qualifications, he did not get the job and someone who is unqualified did. Just by considering the two people directly affected in the first instance, therefore, more good overall would be done by hiring Tom than by hiring Sally. Consider next what happens after the person hired is on the job. If the job actually requires knowledge of Cobol, Sally will not be able to perform that portion of her job. She could, of course, learn it. But that takes time—sufficient time so that if it were really necessary for the job, she might even be fired for lacking this knowledge before she earned it. This would not happen if Tom were hired. How does the practice affect the company? Hiring Sally helps the company toward its affirmative action goal; but, if she cannot perform adequately in the job, her performance hurts the firm. Hiring Tom helps the firm do its work but does not help it achieve its affirmative action goal. What is the effect on the other workers? If they feel that Sally is hired only for affirmative action reasons, she will probably not be treated well or thought well of by her fellow workers. This will also have an effect on Sally. If she cannot do what the job calls for, the other workers are likely to resent her being hired. They would have no such feelings toward Tom.

The overall results of following the practice of hiring women who do not meet the stated requirements rather than men who do, therefore, turns out to produce more harm than good. Hence it is immoral and should not be adopted as a practice.

In the analysis, certain assumptions were made, one of them being that Sally could not learn Cobol in sufficient time to be able to carry out her job well. If she could learn Cobol quickly enough, then the job description was not an accurate statement of the qualifications needed for the position. The real qualifications would then be knowledge of Fortran and one year experience as a programmer, together with the ability to learn Cobol quickly. But if those were the real qualifications needed, we would have an entirely different situation—the kind described in situations 3 and 4.

In situation 3, both Sandra and Henry have all the required qualifications. Assuming that those are the only qualifications needed for the job, both candidates are equally qualified. Hence, there is no job-related criterion on the basis of which the employer can choose one of them rather than another. He could with justice make his decision in some random way—for instance, by tossing a coin. Situation 3c is puzzling. Is it an instance of discrimination? The employer chooses Henry only because Henry is a male. Is it proper for him to do so when he could choose either of them indiscriminately by tossing a coin? Is it wrong to choose one of them because of sex when it is right to choose either of them? The answer seems to be yes—to choose a male applicant over an equally qualified female applicant simply on the basis of sex is discriminatory. It would be better to choose between them by the toss of a coin rather than on the basis of sex, since the toss of the coin gives them each an equal chance at the job.

What of situations 3a and 3b? In each case the employer uses some criterion other than job-related qualifications. Is this fair? The answer is yes. But that answer requires some defense. Situation 3a is a classic case of justifiable preferential hiring. The reason it is justifiable is that in hiring Sandra rather than Henry, the employer is able to meet another need of his firm—namely, making progress toward its affirmative action goal. The need of the firm is not identical with a job-related qualification. But, in a broad way, it is an employment-related criterion. It does not spring from a prejudice. It does no injustice to Henry, since he is not being turned down in favor of someone unqualified. The job could properly go to either of them. If an employer can serve affirmative action goals by hiring a qualified woman over an equally qualified man, this is a step, even if a small one, in the direction of making up for past discrimination by the firm.

Governmental jobs allow a certain amount of credit to an applicant who has served in the armed forces and has been honorably discharged. This is considered both a reward for past service to the government and the country and perhaps an incentive for others to join the armed forces. Such service credit is not inappropriate in private employment, though not required by law. By giving government service credit, the employer helps the country achieve certain goals. But the fact that the company gives such credit should be made known in advance. It should not be used as a criterion after the fact. If the policy is to give government service credit, then it should be given consistently. If in situation 3b giving Henry credit for military service is part of the firm's policy, it is justifiable. If giving Henry credit for military service is just a device used to decide this case, then it is an inappropriate device. If the firm has the policy of giving military service credit, the problem then becomes how one is to balance military service credit against affirmative action goals. Both policies are governmentally and socially approved. Which takes precedence is not clear and requires more information to decide. How close, for instance, is the firm toward meeting its affirmative action goal? How much weight does it give for military service? Whatever way the manager finally makes that decision, he should be able to defend it, giving reasons for his weighting the various factors. If they are equally weighted, then we are back to tossing a coin.

Situation 4 demonstrates another aspect of preferential hiring. In 4a, Sarah gets the job. In 4b, Peter gets the job. Both outcomes are morally justifiable. Preferential hiring is morally justifiable to achieve affirmative action goals and to make up for past discrimination. But as long as a firm makes reasonable progress toward affirmative action goals., it is not required in any specific case to hire a woman or a minority member rather than a white male. In 4a, the company may properly decide to hire Sarah. She satisfies the job qualifications. The qualifications, we shall assume, are appropriate to the job she will fill. She will be able to handle the job and will in no way harm the company. The fact that someone else has stronger credentials in the field does not make her any less qualified for the job. By hiring her, the company gets a qualified person and helps achieve its affirmative action goal which is an employment-related criterion.

In 4b, the company hires an excellently qualified worker. He has more skillls than what the job requires. Even discounting his additional knowledge, his past ratings are higher than Sarah's. As far as job qualifications go, he can be shown to be the stronger candidate on the basis of job-related qualities. The firm cannot be blamed for choosing him, and no injustice is done to Sarah if he is chosen. No injustice is done to him, however, if Sarah is chosen.

We can generalize from our discussion of these varied situations.

1. Affirmative action does not justify hiring unqualified women or minority members in preference to qualified white males.

2. Qualified women and minority members can morally be given preference on the basis of sex or race over equally qualified white males in order to achieve affirmative action goals.

3. Qualified women and minority members can morally be given preference over better qualified white males in order to achieve affirmative action goals.

4. Preferential hiring is not mandatory in any given case, though overall a firm must make adequate progress toward achieving affirmative action goals.

The generalizations above can be applied to promotion as well as to initial hiring. Firing raises a special problem. Many companies use the rule: "last on, first off." Unions generally support this rule and often agree to it in contracts. The rule protects seniority rights. Senior people, under this rule, have more job security than junior people. Older people usually have a harder time finding a new job than younger people do. Older people have put down roots which are more difficult to pull up than newly planted roots. Older people usually make more than beginners and may be prime candidates for a firm that wants to save as much as possible by laying people off during a recession. This is why unions favor the rule. Supporters of the rule argue, moreover, that it does no injustice to the young, since in the natural course of events the young grow older. What they lose in their youth they gain in their older age.

The rule is compatible with the above four principles properly modified to apply to firing instead of hiring. Where two workers, for instance a woman and a man, have comparable jobs, have worked the same amount of time, and have performed equally well in their jobs, then the woman can be given preference to help the firm achieve affirmative action goals. But since affirmative action and preferential hiring are of recent vintage, many of the people most vulnerable to layoff under the seniority system are those hired under affirmative action guidelines. Hence, a period of recession and the resulting layoffs tend to undo most of the good done by affirmative action programs. Is the seniority rule sacrosanct or would more good be done by violating it and giving preference to achieving affirmative action goals, keeping on junior women and minority members while laying off white males senior to them? That question is still unresolved. An argument has not yet been mounted in support of a breach of seniority rules in favor of affirmative action adequate to convince union leaders and members of the general public.

The Supreme Court has moved very slowly and carefully in deciding cases that involve reverse discrimination. It has chosen to rule narrowly rather than broadly in such cases as Bakke, De Funis, and Weber. The issue, however, as this chapter has shown, is amenable to moral analysis and argument.

Further Reading

Bittker, Boris. *The Case for Black Reparations.* New York: Vintage Books, 1973.

Blackstone, William T., and Heslep, Robert, eds. *Social Justice and Preferential Treatment.* Athens, Ga.: University of Georgia Press, 1977.

Cohen, Marshall; Nagel, Thomas; and Scanlon, Thomas, eds. *Equality and Preferential Treatment.* Princeton: Princeton University Press, 1977.

Davidson, Kenneth M.; Ginsburg, Ruth B.; and Kay, Herman H., eds. *Sex-Based Discrimination: Text, Cases, and Materials.* Minneapolis: West Publishing Company, 1974.

Epstein, E.M., and Hampton, D.R. *Black America and White Business.* Belmont, Ca.: Dickenson Publishing Co., Inc., 1971.

Glazer, Nathan. *Affirmative Discrimination.* New York: Basic Books, Inc., 1975.

Goldman, Alan H. *Justice and Reverse Discrimination.* Princeton: Princeton University Press, 1979.

Gross, Barry R., ed. *Reverse Discrimination.* Buffalo: Prometheus Books, 1977.

Viteritti, Joseph P. *Bureaucracy and Social Justice: Allocation of Jobs and Services to Minority Groups.* Port Washington, N.Y.: Kennikat Press Corporation, 1979.

11

Truth and Advertising

Once products are made, they must be sold. Marketing covers this process. Some products are produced only when ordered; others are first produced and then sold. The techniques by which a market is determined and goods sold is frequently complex, and the specific means chosen depends on the nature of the product, the potential buyer, the cost, and so on. Some goods are sold primarily by salespersons, others through store displays. But advertising is the major method by which consumer goods are sold.

Moral issues arise in other aspects of marketing besides advertising. Salespeople frequently use techniques of questionable character. We have already discussed in passing the question of bribery and the giving of gifts. Some salespeople use what are called high-pressure techniques of salesmanship, sometimes of dubious moral quality. Goods sold to one company by another are advertised as well as being marketed through sales representatives. Yet public and governmental concern has tended to focus on the advertising of consumer products to the general public. Corporations are thought capable of handling their own wants and of being qualified to determine on their own what they need. Although they are legally protected against fraud, they are less likely than the ordinary consumer to be taken in by misleading advertising or to be sold what they do not want.

Advertising is not in itself immoral. Once a producer makes a commodity, his object is to sell it. To do so he must inform potential buyers that the product is available, what it does, and how it might be a product they want or need. Advertising provides this information to large numbers of people. A product might be advertised through a direct mail campaign or through use of the media—newspapers, magazines, TV. Advertising, therefore, is part of the process of selling one's products. Since any sale is a transaction between a buyer and a seller, the transaction is fair if both parties have adequate appropriate information about the product and if they enter into the transaction willingly and without coercion. From a moral point of view, since advertising helps achieve the goal of both seller and buyer, it is morally justifiable and permissible, providing it is not deceptive, misleading, or coercive. It can be abused, but it is not inherently immoral.

Before we examine in detail some of the abuses of advertising, we can put aside three morally irrelevant charges brought against advertising. The first charge that advertising is not necessary in a socialist economic system and that it is an immoral part of capitalism is vague and for the most part untrue. Any producer must make known that a product is available if people are to know that they can buy it. Displaying an item in a window so that people can see it is a form of advertising, as is displaying it on a shelf. In every economic system there must be some way of letting potential buyers know of the existence of goods. In a society of comparative scarcity, where only essentials are available, people may constantly be on the lookout for products they want, spotting them when they arrive on a shelf. They may then transmit the information that the product is available through word of mouth. Before long there are lines of people waiting to purchase the item, and soon it is sold out. Those who did not get the item then wait for it to appear again. Or if an item is a staple, and generally available, people know where it can be purchased and simply go to that store when they need it. In such a society advertising plays a comparatively small role.

American society is not a society of comparative scarcity but one of comparative wealth. There are many items available to the consumer. Competition, moreover, encourages producers to enter a market in which there is consumer demand. If a company had a monopoly on an item, then it would have little need for advertising once people knew of its availability. Competition, therefore, accounts for the amount of advertising we have in the United States as opposed to that in the Soviet Union. The American automobile industry, for instance, produces a great many different kinds of cars—different styles and makes, with different accessories, price ranges, and so on. If there were only one kind of car made, clearly there would be less advertising by the automobile industry. Would it be better if there were only one car manufacturer—perhaps the government? The typical American answer is no. Once we allow competition—which has not been shown to be immoral—then advertising is a reasonable concomitant, and as such it is not inherently immoral.

A second charge against advertising which we can dismiss from a moral point of view is its frequent poor taste, offensive to one's finer sensibilities. The charge can hardly be denied. But poor taste is not immoral. As members of society we can make known our displeasure at such advertising either by vocal or written protest or by not purchasing the item advertised. We should keep distinct, however, what is in poor taste from what is immoral.

A third charge claims that advertising takes advantage of people either by forcing them to buy what they do not want or, more plausibly, by psychologically manipulating them to buy what they do not need. According to this view, people are not able to resist the lure of the vast resources available to producers for advertising campaigns. Manipulation and coercion through advertising are immoral, as we shall see in detail. But the charge is clearly an overstatement if it asserts that all members of the public are gullible, unsophisticated, and manipulable by media advertising. Advertising would be immoral if it always and necessarily manipulated and coerced people. But it does not. The difficulty is deciding what is manipulative and what is not, who should be protected from certain kinds of advertising, and who does not need such protection. The notion of protection from advertising is closely linked to governmental paternalism. To what extent are people to be allowed to make their own decisions and to what extent should government protect them against themselves because of its superior knowledge of their real needs and wants? The Federal Trade Commission (FTC) and the Food and Drug Administration (FDA) are the two American agencies with major responsibility for policing advertising. The standards they adopt are frequently more restrictive and paternalistic than morality requires. They have sometimes ruled advertising misleading if only 5 percent of the population would be misled by it. Whether morality demands this much protection is among the topics we shall investigate.

We shall consider five areas in which the moral dimension of advertising is of central importance: (1) the immorality of untruthful, misleading, or deceptive advertising; (2) the immorality of manipulation and coercion through advertising, including the question of audience; (3) the morality of paternalism with respect to advertising; (4) the immorality of preventing some kinds of advertising; and (5) the allocation and distribution of moral responsibility with respect to advertising.

Truth and Advertising

A major function of advertising is to sell goods. But this is not its only purpose, nor does it accomplish this only by supplying information. Advertising may educate the public or mold public opinion. Propaganda might be considered a form of advertising for a political party, a religious sect, or some special social group. Let us, however, limit this discussion to advertising in business and to the aim of selling a product. Informing the public of an item's availability is only part of the task of advertising. A manufacturer also wants to influence people to buy the product. Hence, ads are not only informative but also persuasive. Through advertisements some companies wish to achieve public notice and recognition. They feel that people will tend to buy products with a familiar name. The purpose of some advertising is the building of goodwill for the producer, who assumes that public goodwill will eventually help sales.

The approach to advertising which sees its function only in terms of supplying information takes too narrow a view of the objectives of advertising and tends to evaluate it from too narrow a moral perspective. If its proper function were exclusively the giving of information, and if information were always given in declarative sentences, then we could concern ourselves exclusively with the questions of truth in advertising. If what an advertisement says is true, it is morally permissible; if what it says is false, it is immoral. We shall initially approach advertising in this way. In doing so, we shall also see the shortcomings of this approach.

Let us start with some distinctions that will be helpful in clarifying the complex question of truth in advertising. What is truth in advertising contrasted with? It can be contrasted either with falsehood or with lying. Lying is immoral; stating falsehoods is not necessarily immoral. Suppose, for instance, I were to tell a story. I could make a number of statements that were not factually true; yet I would not be lying.

The terms "true" and "false" are properly predicated of statements or propositions. Only a proposition can be true or false. An exclamation, a question, an interjection, cannot be true or false. A statement or a proposition contains a subject and a predicate. The subject has the property or is related to something else stated in the predicate. A statement or proposition is true, roughly speaking, if the relation stated to maintain between subject and predicate actually corresponds to the same relation in the world between what is designated or referred to by the subject and predicate. Hence the sentence, "This page of this book has words printed on it," is true if the page of this book does in fact have words printed on it. Obviously this page does have words printed on it. Therefore the sentence is true. The sentence, "This page is colored green," is false if in fact this page is not colored green. This rough characterization of truth and falsehood will suffice for our purposes.

Lying consists, however, not simply in making a false statement. From a moral point of view lying is an activity. Lying consists in making a statement which one believes is false to another person whom one has reason to think will believe the statement to be true. Lying consists both of my saying what I believe to be false and of my intending that another believe to be true what is actually false. I both say what I do not believe, and I intend to deceive or mislead the one to whom I make the statement.

Using this definition of lying, falsehood is not a necessary part of it. Suppose, for instance, that I believe there are four pints in a quart. A friend who is baking a cake asks me how many pints are in a quart. I reply, "There are four pints in a quart." Actually there are only two pints in a quart. What I have said is false. But I have not told a lie; I have made a mistake. Conversely, suppose I believe that there are four pints in a quart and the same person asks me the same question in the same situation. I want the cake to fail so that my friend will not spend any more of our time making cakes. So, intending to give false information, I say, "There are two pints in a quart." Morally speaking, I am guilty of telling a lie, even though, by accident, what I said was a true statement. It is a lie because I thought that what I was saying was false and I said it with the intent to deceive and the expectation that what I said would be believed.

Whether a statement or proposition is true or false depends on the world; whether a statement is an instance of lying depends on the intent of the speaker.

Not all statements that are false and that I state believing they are false, however, are lies. Suppose, for instance, I say during a chilling wintry day, "I'm as cold as an iceberg." What I say is literally false. My body temperature is about 98.6 degrees, even if I feel cold. But my statement is not a lie. I have no intention of deceiving anyone when I make that statement; nor is it likely anyone will be deceived by it. I use language in many ways. Part of the normal person's use of language enables him to distinguish by context, phrasing, intonation, and other subtle techniques the difference between a sentence that is literally true and one that is figurative, exaggerated, or not to be taken literally. Metaphor, simile, hyperbole are all accepted figures of speech. We do not speak only in declarative sentences, and when we speak in declarative sentences we do not always speak literally. When I say, "I'm so hungry I could eat a bear," I do not expect people to point out that an average bear weighs much more than I do, that I could not possibly eat a whole bear, or that I probably would not even like bear meat. All that is true but beside the point. I am simply saying in an expressive way that I am very hungry. There is no moral reason why I should not use expressive language when I do not intend to deceive and when there is little or no likelihood that I will deceive, even if my statements are not literally true.

We can now turn to advertising. Some advertisements contain sentences and hence express propositions which are appropriately evaluated in terms of truth and falsity. If an ad makes a false claim, which the advertiser knows to be false, for the purpose of misleading, misinforming, or deceiving potential customers, then the ad is immoral. It is immoral because the advertiser in the ad is lying, and lying is immoral. An advertiser might also be morally guilty of lying if what he said in an ad was accidentally true, but he believed it to be false and intended to deceive. This problem, however, need not concern us, since it is of only peripheral interest.

The problem of truth in advertising, however, does not end here. For it is possible to deceive and mislead without making any statements that are false; and it is also possible, as we have seen, not to deceive or mislead while making statements that are not literally true.

Consider the following slogan used by Esso a number of years ago: "Esso puts a tiger in your tank!" The statement, of course, is not literally true. But did anyone think it was literally true? Do we really wonder if, after some customer had put Esso gasoline into his car, he worried about whether it had turned into a tiger? Exactly what Esso meant to convey by its slogan is to some extent a matter of speculation. It clearly did not want its slogan to be taken literally, but rather figuratively. The semantics of advertising properly allow the use of figurative language. To restrict ads to statements that are literally true is to fail to understand the semantics of advertising or of language in general. There is, however, no neat line between allowable figurative language and lying. An obvious exaggeration is not likely to be taken literally. But what is obvious to me and to you may not be an obvious exaggeration to everyone. Must we protect those who might be deceived by exaggeration by forcing advertising to be literally true in the statements it makes?

From a moral point of view it seems sufficient that the vast majority of those at whom the ad is directed not be misled by it. In dealing with responsibility we used the rule that people are morally responsible for the foreseeable consequences of their actions. The test of what is foreseeable is what the ordinary person of good-will in those circumstances would foresee. A similar approach can be taken to advertising. An advertiser will know whether he intends his ad to deceive. If he does, then the advertiser acts immorally in placing the ad. But if he does not intend to deceive, and we are to judge the ad on its merits and not on the advertiser's intent, then the ad is morally permissible if the ordinary person at whom the ad is directed is not deceived. Some ads directed at car owners might be misunderstood by children. This is not a matter of moral concern, however, since the ad is not directed at them but at the car owners.

The Better Business Bureaus, the FTC, and the FDA are all concerned with accuracy in advertisements. Advertisers are not allowed to make false statements. Moreover, advertisers must be able to document statements which make factual claims that are taken literally, if challenged. These agencies sometimes go beyond what is morally necessary according to our analysis. Even if a very small percentage of people might be misled, the ad is not allowed. The action of government agencies in these cases, if morally justifiable, depends not on the question of lying, but on the legitimate extent of paternalism which a government can practice. We shall consider this question later.

Without making any false statements, an ad might be misleading or deceptive. A misleading ad is one in which the ad does not misrepresent or make false claims but makes claims in such a way that the normal person, or at least many ordinary people reading it quickly and without great attention and thought, will make a false inference or draw a false conclusion. Those who attempt to justify such ads claim that the mistake is made by the reader or viewer of the ad and that the responsibility for drawing the false conclusion rests with the reader or viewer and not with the advertiser. Strictly speaking, this is correct. But the intent in such ads is often clearly to mislead. They are written or presented that way, and their effect is predictable. Such ads are immoral because they intend to deceive even if they do not literally state what is false. The same is true of packaging. If a large box is only half filled, a consumer may erroneously think he will get more in a big box than in a smaller one. If no claim is made that the box is full, no false statement has been made. The mistake is the consumer's. But the maker of the product is morally at fault.

A deceptive ad is one which either makes a false statement and therefore lies, or which misrepresents the product without making any statement. Deception of the eye and mind may take place not only through sentences or propositions but also through pictures, through individual words, or through certain juxtapositions of objects. Such deception trades on a background of ordinary expectations. We are accustomed to having the contents of a box pictured on the box. We expect the pictures to be reasonably close to the product within. When this is not the case, the picture is deceptive. If an item is called "chicken soup" and it contains no chicken and was not made from chicken, the name is deceptive even if no statement is made that the soup contains chicken or is made from chicken. If an item is advertised as being at half price and the item was never sold at full price but is always sold at the price indicated, the ad is deceptive.

The semantics of advertising, however, allows a certain leeway in some products. The cosmetics field provides some examples. We expect cosmetics to be packaged in pretty bottles, boxes, or containers. Perfumes would smell just as sweet if they were packaged in mustard jars. But they would not sell as well. Face creams would cleanse and soften just as well without perfume; but they would not sell as well. Cosmetics are a luxury item. They are packaged as such. They are sold as much for their promise as for their chemicals. Shampoo, hair rinse, conditioners, and other hair products will not make the ordinary person's hair look like the hair of the models who claim in ads to use these products. Nor will the use of other beauty products make the average person look like the models pictured using them. Is this misleading advertising? Do people actually believe that a product will change their looks, their personalities, or their lives? Most people know that the semantics of cosmetic advertising is puffery and do not take the pictures or the implied claims literally. They hope the product will make them more attractive, and the products sometimes *do* make their users more self-confident. This is what the customer is paying for. Repeat sales for such products is an indication that the customer is not being deceived.

Advertisements not only make statements but also try to persuade people to purchase the product advertised. Persuasion may take the form of making statements. But it need not. Many ads simply create associations in the mind of the purchaser. An ad for an expensive scotch whiskey might simply show a couple in evening clothes sipping a drink in an elegant room, together with a picture of the bottle of scotch. The association of the scotch with elegance and class is all the ad wishes to convey.

Some ads simply show a picture of the product and aim only at recognition of the product when the consumer sees it on a supermarket shelf together with eight other brands of the same kind of item. Name recognition has an effect on purchasing. This is not inappropriate. A customer who knows little about the nine items on the shelf knows at least that one of the nine items is advertised. This is some information about it. An item which did not sell would not be advertised for very long. An item which depends on repeat purchases for success has a fairly large number of users if it is continuously advertised. That does not mean the product is the best of its kind. But it is information which makes the choice of products less than random.

The final aspect of truth in advertising that we will consider is the question of half-truths. A statement made about a product may be true, may not mislead, may not deceive, and still may be morally objectionable. What the ad does *not* say is as important as what the ad does say. A dangerous product cannot morally be advertised and sold without indicating its dangers. If the background assumption of a certain product on the part of the ordinary person is that products of that kind are safe, and in fact the given advertised product is not safe, then the ad and/or box should include the caution that is appropriate. We expect lye to be caustic, and ads for lye which depend on its caustic property may not have to specify that it burns the skin, though that information should be prominent on the can. But we do not usually expect hair dye to contain lye or to be caustic. An ad for such a product that does not indicate its unusual potential danger would be immoral.

Our general rules concerning truth in advertising can be summarized in the following way. It is immoral to lie, mislead, and deceive in advertising. It is immoral to fail to indicate dangers that are not normally expected. It is not immoral to use metaphors or other figures of speech if these will be normally understood as the figurative use of language; nor is it immoral to persuade as well as to inform.

Manipulation and Coercion

Advertising not only informs, it frequently also aims to persuade. Persuasion in itself is not immoral. We all attempt to persuade others to do what we want—to go with us to a movie, go out to dinner, and so on. If what we persuade another to do is not immoral, and if we do not use immoral means to persuade them, persuasion is not an immoral activity. Persuasion, however, is different from manipulation and coercion; these are all ways of getting others to do what we want. But manipulation and coercion are at least prima facie immoral. They are immoral in business and advertising. The reason is not difficult to state. In Kantian terms both coercion and manipulation treat another person only as a means to an end and deny respect for his freedom. Coercion involves force or the threat of force, either physical or psychological. Manipulation does not use force but involves playing upon a person's will by trickery or by devious, unfair, or insidious means. Both take unfair advantage of a person and the use of either renders a transaction between the two parties an unfair or unjust one. Coercion and manipulation in advertising are therefore immoral.

But what does constitute coercion or manipulation in advertising? Can an advertiser truly coerce or manipulate consumers?

The least controversial form of manipulative advertising is subliminal advertising. An advertiser can insert his message into music played in a store, into a film shown in a theatre, or on TV in such a way that the viewer is not consciously aware of the advertisement even though he is subconsciously picking it up. This is possible because a certain threshold of perception must be exceeded for us to consciously see a motion picture. The film must be run at a certain number of frames per minute. By inserting a message between the frames below the threshold of conscious perception, we do not consciously see the message. Despite the fact that we do not consciously see it, tests have shown that we do perceive the message without being conscious of it. Such ads are called subliminal because they are projected below the limit of our conscious perception.

Subliminal advertising is manipulative because it acts on us without our knowledge and hence, without our consent. If an ad appears on TV, we can tune it out or change stations if we do not want to be subject to it. If an ad appears in a magazine, we are not forced to look at it. In either case, if we do choose to look and listen, we can consciously evaluate what we see and hear. We can, if we wish, take a critical stance toward the advertisement. All of this is impossible with subliminal advertising since we do not even know we are being subjected to the message. The advertiser is imposing his message on us without our knowledge or consent. We cannot tune it out since we do not know it is there. Nor can we be at all critical of it. A subliminal advertisement may simply flash on the screen the name of a product or a simple message such as "Buy X brand of soap." The messages are not complex. Yet they have been shown to have an effect. They are manipulative and their use is immoral.

Some department stores and supermarkets have inserted in their music tracks the message "Don't shoplift" or "Don't steal." Studies have shown that stores which use this device have a lower rate of shoplifting than comparable stores which do not use it. Though the message is a moral one, the use of the subliminal technique is still immoral. Since we do not know what message we are being subjected to, there is no way of guaranteeing that the message is a moral one rather than one that is objectionable in some way or to some people. Since we have no control over the content when we do not know that we are being subjected to a subliminal message, the practice is manipulative, tends to produce more harm than good, and is from a moral point of view unjustifiable.

Advertisements aimed at preschool children are another fairly clear case of manipulation. Such children tend to be very impressionable, to believe most of what they hear and see, to be unable clearly to distinguish truth from fancy, and to have very little critical skill or experience. They are very susceptible, therefore, to TV advertisements. What is the point of advertisers aiming messages at preschool children? Clearly, they do not make purchases, but they can pressure, hound, and influence their parents in the purchases their parents do make. For instance, if a certain children's vitamin is successfully advertised to children on TV, they may be anxious to take that vitamin pill rather than any other. A parent interested in having a child take vitamins may find the job made easier by having the child anxious to take a certain brand, and may buy that brand for that reason. Children may also pester their mothers and fathers to buy certain sugar-coated cereals or other products advertised for children. Is this manipulation?

Two replies have been given. One reply is that the adults in the family make the purchases and if they feel that the product should not be purchased, they should exercise their best judgment. They, and not the children, make the final judgment. If they cannot stand up to their children's demands, that is not the problem of the advertiser but the problem of the parent. The other reply is that if the parents are the purchasers, the ads for children's products should be aimed at the parents and not at the children. Ads aimed at children are inappropriate since they build a desire in children for products they do not understand, e.g., vitamins. The intent of the ads is clearly to manipulate the children into applying pressure on their parents to make such purchases. Though the parents make the final decision, the children are still being manipulated for the advertiser's purposes. Such ads take advantage of children and those who advertise in this way are morally culpable of manipulation and of treating children only as a means to their ends.

The situation with respect to adolescents is more difficult. Many ads aimed at this group play on their social insecurity. They are told that unless their breath is sweetened by a certain product they will not be popular, or that if they want to attract a certain boy or girl they should use brand X deodorant, or that the key to making friends is using a certain shampoo or soap. Each of the products does something: reduces bad breath or body odor, or cleans hair and skin. And each of these may to some extent make one more attractive or less offensive. But it is extremely unlikely that any or all of them are the basis for a teenager to be popular or to have friends. Adolescents know this; yet they are frequently so insecure socially that the ads play on their fears, worries, hopes, and dreams. Do such ads coerce or manipulate? Only a case-by-case examination can answer this question. The potential for manipulation is present, though not all such ads are manipulative.

The question of audience also crops up in other ways. Certain products—alcohol and cigarettes, for instance—are restricted for sale to adults. These and similar items should not be advertised in children's magazines or in magazines aimed at young teenagers. A more difficult problem involves the small minority, such as those people who are gullible or those with a lower than average intelligence who may be manipulated by ads that are not manipulative to the average adult. From a moral point of view, a general rule would be that it is immoral to gear ads to such a group in order to manipulate them, but that for ads aimed at the general public, the appropriate moral criterion should be whether the ad is manipulative for the average reader or viewer. Society may take a stronger line; in fact, the FTC has done this. The arguments for a stronger line, however, have to do with paternalism.

Paternalism and Advertising

The United States Surgeon General has determined that smoking is dangerous to one's health. We know that drinking intoxicating alcoholic beverages can sometimes lead to alcoholism, to a large number of accidents while driving, and to other ills. Should the United States government and American society allow the spread of the use of these products through advertising? Should we prohibit the advertising of pornography? Should we allow the advertising of marijuana and other illegal drugs? What of "Saturday Night Specials" and other guns? Are there any limits to what can be morally advertised?

Although there are clear limits, there is much dispute about where to draw the line. Anything that it is illegal to manufacture and sell to the general public cannot legally be advertised to the general public. This poses no real problem since it would be self-defeating for anyone to advertise what is illegal. If someone is selling illegal drugs, for instance, to advertise would be to invite the police to arrest him. We have also seen that it would be immoral to advertise to children what they are prohibited by law from buying. Beyond these clear cases, however, there is little consensus. If an item can be legally sold, why can't it be advertised? What is the proper role of government in protecting people against what will harm them? The question is a political one. The answer in a democracy such as the United States is that the proper paternalistic role of government is to be decided by the people through their representatives and with a majority rule limited by the rights of individuals and minority groups.

The Food and Drug Administration (FDA) acts in the people's interests when it requires by law that packaged foods list on the package the ingredients in the order of decreasing quantity. Such information allows the purchaser to know what he is buying and makes the transaction a fair one. With respect to drugs, the FDA also acts to protect the consumer. It prohibits the sale of certain drugs, allows other drugs to be sold only with a doctor's prescription, demands a testing period before approving drugs, and so on. It sets high standards, standards which some people and some drug companies claim are too high.

The Federal Trade Commission has prohibited the advertising of tobacco and alcohol on TV. It has not prohibited the advertising of such items in journals and newspapers, though in the case of cigarette ads, the Surgeon General's warning must be included. Some people claim that drinking alcoholic beverages is immoral and that smoking, since it harms the health of the smoker, should be prohibited. They claim that even if such items can legally be sold, the producers of them should not be allowed through advertising to encourage people to smoke and drink.

The philosophy of liberalism, defended eloquently by John Stuart Mill in the nineteenth century in *On Liberty,* defends the principle that government should not interfere in the actions of individuals if the results of their actions fall mainly on themselves. In both smoking and drinking, the results fall mainly on the agent. Hence the government should not interfere with their use by individuals. The government does more than what is required by insisting that cigarette packages carry the Surgeon General's warning. The liberalist position can be extended to advertising these products as well—if they are legal and publicly sold, then those who wish to purchase them should be allowed to do so. Those who do not wish to purchase them are not forced to do so simply because they are advertised. Each person can weigh the good and bad effects for himself and make his own decision. If the smoker feels that he gets more enjoyment from smoking a pack of cigarettes a day for twenty-five or thirty years, even if it cuts four or five years off his life, the government cannot legitimately say he is mistaken. Others will consider the four or five years of extended life preferable to the enjoyment of smoking. Neither answer is right or wrong; each is simply a matter of choice or preference. The question allows for differences of opinion.

The extent to which the FTC has restricted advertising of any kind that might mislead even a very small percentage of the population goes beyond what morality requires of advertisers. The FTC perceives its mandate toward paternalism to extend that far. We have no indication yet that the general public feels the FTC has gone too far. Since the amount of paternalism government exercises is a political as well as a moral question, we can distinguish what is morally required from what is politically required without expecting that the two will always coincide.

One further attack on advertising should be discussed before we leave the role of government and paternalism. Some people claim that advertising creates false needs in people. Producers decide not what the people want or need, but what the *producers* want to produce based on which products will bring the most profit. The producers then make those items, create demand through a high-powered and expensive advertising campaign, and in effect, take advantage of the general population. Since we can correctly call this taking advantage of people, it is immoral.

The attack is not entirely without merit. American producers sometimes do choose to produce what they want instead of what the general public wants. When they do so, it is not always possible to convince people to buy what is produced. Sometimes it is. It is difficult to imagine that people really needed electric toothbrushes. It seems more likely that a manufacturer decided to produce them and then advertise the product. It is also doubtful that Americans really wanted large cars with built-in obsolescence. For many years they had little choice. Detroit decided what cars would be produced and Americans chose from what was available. Only when foreign manufacturers entered the market in significant quantity did American car manufacturers switch to producing smaller cars.

What conclusion can we draw from this? The conclusion that advertising can sell anything is much too strong. It cannot. But it can sell some products that people had not thought they needed or wanted before the item was produced. It is difficult to imagine, however, an appropriate solution to this type of problem —if it *is* a problem. People can purchase what they want. If they do not want to buy electric toothbrushes, advertisements do not force them to do so. If they do not want to buy Edsel cars, an expensive ad campaign will not make them buy one. But if they want small cars and only large cars are available, they may prefer to buy a large car rather than no car. Even here, however, the possibility of free entry into the market by foreign car makers seems to show that the system of the free market tends to correct itself in the long run. The alternative would be some type of centralized decision-making apparatus, either governmental or private.This body would presumably decide that electric toothbrushes should not be made, or that small cars rather than large cars should be produced. But how will this group know what should and should not be produced? Will they know better than the individual consumer what the consumer wants? It seems unlikely. In countries where there is such central planning the consumer is generally more poorly served than in the United States.

Our system may be wasteful to some extent. It may produce goods that are not necessary. It may needlessly duplicate effort. All this is true. But the system which is to replace the present one has not been sufficiently articulated or defended. Nor is advertising the culprit. We have seen that government can restrict advertising to some extent where harm to people will result. But the harm must be more clear and present than simply the advertising of what some people think is unnecessary. Decisions of this type go far beyond the kind and extent of paternalism mandated to government by the American people.

The Prevention of Advertising

The prevention of advertising in some cases comes up against the First Amendment's right of free speech. Although I have argued that in some instances the government can, with the consent of the people, exercise a certain amount of paternalism to protect them, can it do so by violating the rights of advertisers? Do advertisers have the right to advertise in virtue of the First Amendment? The question is again a legal and not a directly moral one. First Amendment rights, just as other civil rights, can be restricted under certain circumstances. Government restriction of advertising in the case of cigarettes and liquor however, has not been successfully challenged in the courts.

There is another area in which we find a different moral issue. Is it morally permissible for doctors, lawyers, and other professionals not to advertise? Obviously, no individual doctor or lawyer is morally obliged to advertise. But is it appropriate for the American Medical Association (AMA) or the American Bar Association (ABA) or other professional organizations to prohibit advertising by their members? Until recently many professionals were restricted from advertising by their professional associations. Advertising was considered to be in poor taste, vulgar, and unprofessional. Moreover, many professionals claimed, it was not possible to advertise adequately. The services professionals perform vary from client to client or patient to patient. The relations they develop are personal. They do not sell a product at a certain price.

The prohibition of advertising by doctors and lawyers, however, has been attacked as self-serving for the members of the profession and harmful to the general public. It has been determined to be a practice that tends to hinder competition and free trade. Recently, therefore, these portions of the AMA and ABA codes of professional conduct have been declared illegal and have been changed.

The arguments in favor of changing them were several. One can be put in utilitarian terms. Essentially, the good gained by lawyers and doctors and their respective professions was less than the evil suffered by their potential and actual clients and patients. The clients and patients were not able to compare doctors or lawyers the way they were able to compare plumbers and carpenters. The latter could compete through their ads, making known their specialties, rates, and other pertinent information. In order to choose a doctor or lawyer, one usually only had a list in the Yellow Pages. Storefront lawyers who wished to serve lower income groups at very low rates, frequently in ghetto areas, were prevented from advertising by the old code. This was not in the best interests of people who might be able to use their services but could not afford the services of the typical law firm.

Another argument rests on the right of the individual practitioner to make known his services and to compete, in price and in kinds of services provided, for the business of potential clients. Preventing the individual practitioner from advertising if he so chose was a violation of his right to free speech, restricted not by government but by his professional organization. The right of a professional organization to do this has been successfully challenged.

Under the new guidelines, lawyers are still supposed to insure that their ads are in good taste so as not to harm the reputation of the profession. "Good taste," however, is broad enough to include a wide range of ads.

The important principle underscored by the ruling on professional advertising is that to prevent advertising is in many instances both to harm the public by restricting information which it wants and can profitably use and to protect the interests of members of the professions at public expense. Monopolies do not have to advertise because they control the market. A market that allows free entry appropriately allows advertising so that each of the competitors can make known his product or service, inform the public of its availability, and attempt to persuade the public to purchase the product or service.

We therefore conclude that in some cases it is immoral to prevent advertising, just as in other cases, morality demands that certain advertising be restrained or prohibited.

The Allocation and Distribution of the Moral Responsibility Concerning Advertising

In each of the preceding sections we have seen that certain advertising practices are immoral. Who is morally responsible for advertising and who has moral responsibility with respect to it? We can identify five groups: (1) the producer or manufacturer; (2) the advertising agency; (3) the media in which or through which the advertisement appears; (4) the general public; and (5) government and governmental agencies.

1. Prime responsibility for advertising rests on the one who initiates and directs the advertising. In most cases this is the producer or manufacturer of a product. The manufacturer decides what and how to advertise. The decisions may be made by the chief executive officer, by the marketing, publicity, advertising, or public relations departments, or by some combination of these and others. In whatever way responsibility for the decision on advertising is made internally, the company is responsible for the advertising it does or commissions, its content and accuracy, the medium it chooses, and so on. If it aims ads at preschool children, it is responsible for doing so; if it misrepresents or misleads, it is responsible for doing so. Although primary responsibility is held by the producer or manufacturer, it does not hold exclusive moral responsibility.

2. Advertising agencies handle the promotion of a great many goods. They frequently produce ideas for advertising campaigns which are submitted to and

approved by their customers, the producing companies. What is their responsibility?

Since they do not manufacture the product, they are not responsible for the product as such. They must be informed of the product's qualities and selling points. But advertising people often work closely with their customers. They frequently know what is true about a product and what is not, what is misleading or deceptive. Sometimes it is the ad writer rather than the manufacturer who comes up with a promotion that is deceptive or misleading in such a way as to benefit the manufacturer. The temptation in such cases is for the ad writer to feel that responsibility for the ad rests with the manufacturer. The ad writer is simply an agent paid to do what the client asks. The manufacturer feels that the responsibility is that of the ad writer. He, after all, is the specialist. Both are responsible and neither party can escape moral responsibility.

Frequently both manufacturer and ad agency have no difficulty with the initial advertising of a product. A good product that serves a need will sell if attractively presented. The pressure builds, however, as competition increases. As a competitor's product resembles one's own more and more, the need to find something distinctive as a selling point becomes more difficult. If a company's number one position in the field is threatened or slips to number two, the temptation is to keep or regain first place by even more noticeable advertising. The temptation to exaggerate, write misleading copy, or consider immoral approaches becomes strong. One is tempted to think in terms of the good of the company, protecting the interests of the shareholders, keeping up profits, protecting one's job, and in these terms to justify practices that one would not ordinarily consider or condone.

Advertising agencies have the moral responsibility not to lie, mislead, or misrepresent products. They also have an obligation to investigate when they suspect that they are being asked to lie, mislead, or misrepresent products. Ignorance is no excuse if the typical advertising specialist would know something was amiss in what he or she was told about a product to be advertised. Admen and women should not take part in lying or misleading the public, and should try to convince their clients not to push that approach. If they cannot convince their clients, they still have the responsibility not to take part in lying or deception. A good ad agency should not have to resort to unethical practices to sell a product.

3. Once an advertisement or an advertising program has been produced, it can be presented to the public in a variety of forms. The major ones are TV and the print media (newspapers and magazines). Specialized products are usually advertised in specialized journals, trade journals, or through direct mail. General products are usually advertised through TV, magazines, and newspapers.

All TV stations, magazines, and newspapers have moral responsibility for what appears in their shows or in the pages of their publications. They receive copy or film submitted by the manufacturer or ad agency. Do they have the right to question, censor, or prohibit something they are paid to show or print? Yes, they do. Moreover, they have the moral responsibility not to show or print an advertisement that they know to be false, misleading or deceptive. They may go even further and choose not to air or print an advertisement they feel is offensive or in extremely bad taste. If they feel that running an ad will offend their readers, then they may morally refuse the ad, though they are not morally required to refuse it. They are morally required to refuse an immoral ad, however.

To show or print an immoral ad would be to take part in an immoral action. We are neither allowed to act immorally nor to take part in immoral conduct by acting as agents for others. Yet the obligation must be kept within the bounds of reason. We cannot expect every magazine editor to check up on every ad submitted for publication to see whether it is in fact false or misleading. The primary responsibility rests with the manufacturer and the advertising agency that produced the ad. But even if the ordinary professional working on the magazine would suspect that a given ad is false or misleading, then the ad should be questioned and some evidence sought to show its moral legitimacy. The general principle is that it is immoral for those in control of TV advertising or advertising in newspapers or magazines to air or print what they know to be immoral. Once again the temptation will be to claim the responsibility falls on the manufacturer or ad agency, especially when the account is a big one. But TV stations, newspapers, and magazines cannot morally cast aside their responsibility so lightly.

4. What of the public? Members of the general public do not act immorally when they look at misleading ads (how would they know they were misleading if they did not look at them?). They also have no moral obligation to take any positive action about them. But if they are concerned about the truthfulness or accuracy of an ad, if they feel an ad is misleading or deceptive, they can perform a public service by making their feelings and perceptions known. They can write to the producer to complain about the ad, or if they know the responsible ad agency, they can appropriately write to it. They can write to the TV station, newspaper, or magazine that carried the ad. They can write to the local or national Better Business Bureau, the FTC or FDA or to the National Advertising Review Board (NARB). The NARB was formed in 1971 and is sponsored by the American Association of Advertising Agencies, the American Advertising Federation, the Association of National Advertisers, and the Council of Better Business Bureaus. It aims at self-regulation by advertisers. It investigates complaints, asks advertisers for substantiation, and reports any results both to the one who files a complaint and in a monthly press release.

Public pressure can help keep advertising responsible. If advertisers know that the public would not only complain about misleading or immoral advertising, but would also cast their vote against a product so advertised by not purchasing it, they would then have a strong incentive to keep their advertising moral.

5. Government has taken an active role in regulating and monitoring advertising. The FTC and the FDA enforce only legal standards, however. They do not and should not enforce moral standards if these differ from legal ones. Government is not empowered in our political system to be the final arbiter of morality, but, through the law, it can sometimes legally settle issues about which there is moral controversy. But government does not make actions, policies, or practices moral or immoral by its legislation. Legislators and administrators can certainly listen to moral arguments. Moral arguments, as well as the prudential ones, and legal prece-

dents are all appropriately considered. Government and its agencies should not act immorally. But they are neither capable of, nor empowered to, legislate morality.

The role of government in the area of advertising is to protect the public interest. It does this in a variety of ways, some of which we have seen. To the extent that advertisers regulate their own behavior, legislation is not needed. When advertisers seek to achieve their own good at the expense of the general public, however, then the government should play a legitimate regulatory role.

The role of government as regulator is not without its moral temptations. Regulatory agencies have sometimes been staffed by people who have worked in the areas being regulated or who hope to work in the areas regulated. The conflict of interest possible here is fairly clear. Who regulates the regulators? Regulators also sometimes take it upon themselves to interpret legislation very broadly, even if this was not the legislative intent. Regulatory agencies can become minor legislators on their own through the writing of regulations implementing laws. They may, if so inclined, attempt to impose their own moral standards on an industry. They may misinterpret the degree to which the general public wishes or needs paternalistic protection. Regulators, Congress, the President, and the people should be aware of these dangers of governmental regulation.

Advertising is a pervasive activity in the United States. Most people learn the semantics of advertising as they grow up. They learn to discount certain claims as puffery; they learn to read fine print in ads and to see if an ad may be interpreted in more than one way. They learn that they make associations and that some associations tell us nothing about a product. Whether or not a movie star or baseball hero uses a beauty product or eats a breakfast cereal tells us more about the star and the hero than it does about the product. The semantics of advertising includes within it, however, the notions of lying, misrepresentation, deception, manipulation, and other questionable practices. Those that are immoral should be labeled as such. Public pressure even more than government regulation is likely to be effective in curbing the major excesses of advertising.

Further Reading

Baird, Charles W. *Advertising by Professionals.* International Institute for Economic Research. Green Hills Publishers, 1977.

Bok, Sissela. *Lying: Moral Choice in Public and Private Life.* New York: Pantheon Books, 1978.

Galbraith, John Kenneth. *The Affluent Society.* 3rd ed. New York: Houghton Mifflin Company, 1976.

Lucas, John T., and Gurman, Richard. *Truth in Advertising.* New York: American Management Association, Inc., 1972.

Preston, Ivan L. *The Great American Blow-up: Puffery in Advertising and Selling.* Madison: University of Wisconsin Press, 1975.

Sandage, C.H., and Fryburger, Vernon. *Advertising Theory and Practice.* 9th ed. Homewood, Ill.: Richard D. Irwin, Inc., 1975.

Stuart, Frederick, ed. *Consumer Protection from Deceptive Advertising.* Hempstead, N.Y.: Hofstra University, 1974.

Truth in Advertising: A Symposium of the Toronto School of Theology. Toronto, 1975.

12

Trade Secrets, Insider Information, and Corporate Disclosure

If one company were to hijack a truckload of TV sets from another company, or if an employee were to embezzle funds from his employer, we would have no hesitation about calling the acts immoral. We know what it means for a company to own TV sets or money and what it means for someone to take these wrongfully. When it comes to knowledge and information, however, our concept of proprietorship is clear. If I take information or knowledge from you, I do not physically deprive you of it. We may both have it and have it equally. Since my taking it from you does not leave you without it, knowledge and information are different from physical objects. If, furthermore, we lived in a society in which all goods were shared, knowledge and information would be among those items that would be shared most freely, since each person could enjoy the benefit of the knowledge and information without depriving anyone else of their use.

Information and knowledge are vital aspects of many businesses. They may give one business an advantage over another, and hence, in a competitive situation, one business may not wish to share its knowledge and information even if in doing so it would not lessen its own knowledge and information. Information and knowledge, moreover, often represent a financial investment by a firm. Some knowledge is costly to obtain or develop. Organizational knowledge may be the product of a long series of trial and error and may represent a great deal of experience; for instance, computer programs require special skill to develop. A company's desire to keep these programs secret is understandable.

To whom does the knowledge and information developed by people in a corporation belong? To whom does knowledge and information about a corporation belong? What may be morally kept secret and what must morally be disclosed? Trade secrets, insider information, and disclosure are three aspects of questions pertaining to knowledge and information in business. They have generated much discussion. For example, many people are demanding and receiving more and more disclosure of information from corporations at the same time that computer theft is rising and corporations are trying to devise ways of keeping corporate information both secret and secure.

Trade Secrets

Let us start our discussion of trade secrets by looking at three typical, though hypothetical cases.

Case 1: John Knosit was head of a research team of CDE Electric. His team was working on developing a cheaper and more effective filament for light bulbs. Six months ago, a rumor circulated in the industry that the team had made a breakthrough and all that was required was final testing. This would put CDE Electric far ahead of its competitors. Five months ago, X Electric hired John away from CDE, offering him $25,000 a year more than he had been getting. No mention was made of his work on the new filament. After being in his new position for three months, his superior approached him and said that X Electric had hired him because of his work on the filament and that he would have to develop the filament quickly for X Electric or be fired. John knows how to develop the filament. Is he morally justified in developing it for X Electric?

Case 2: Tom Berry works as Sales Manager for Pretty-Good Refrigeration. He is hired by Even-Better Refrigeration to fill a similar position in their firm, at a sizeable raise in salary. Before he leaves Pretty-Good Refrigeration, Tom makes a copy of the "customer book" which contains the list of Pretty-Good Refrigeration's customers, the contact person in other firms, the kind of equipment each purchased, when it is due for replacement, and other similar information. He brings the list with him and then systematically contacts the people on the list at the appropriate time promoting the products of Even-Better Refrigeration. He feels Even-Better Refrigeration products are superior to Pretty-Good Refrigeration, and since he knows both products, he is able to mount a convincing sales pitch. Does he act morally in doing so?

Case 3: Henry Mangel is Assistant Personnel Manager of Dirt-Brown Construction Company. He has worked for the company for five years. During that time he has learned a good deal about personnel management techniques which were implemented and which proved successful. Partly as a result of his innovations, the workers have been content and their productivity has increased. He is hired by Grass-Green Construction Company as their Personnel Manager. At his new job he immediately introduces a series of changes based on his experience at Dirt-Brown Construction, and uses some of the techniques he learned as well as those he introduced there. Is he morally justified in doing this?

The three cases share a common feature. In all three cases, a person goes from one company to another, bringing with him certain knowledge from the first company. He uses that knowledge in the second company. Is it appropriate to do so? Does the knowledge belong to him or to the firm at which he worked? What knowledge belongs to a company and how can it be protected?

Consider the first case. John Knosit was the head of a research team. He was appointed to that position, presumably because of his leadership ability and because of his knowledge and skill. These belong to him. He takes with him his own knowledge, skill, experience, and personal qualities wherever he goes. But while working for CDE Electric he works on a specific project. The company pays his salary while he works on the project. It also pays the salaries of his fellow teamworkers. The company provides the laboratory in which they conduct their experiments; it supplies all the materials they need. When they develop the new filament, the company will take out a patent on it. Clearly the filament belongs to the company. But John knows how to develop the filament. Is that knowledge his?

To get some perspective on the question, suppose that while working for CDE Electric John went to X Electric and offered to sell them the process he had developed for $50,000. Most people would readily admit that to do so would be immoral. The reason it is immoral is that the process belongs to CDE Electric. Even though John knows the process, it does not belong to him. He is morally restricted in what he can do with that information, and giving it or selling it to others is not morally allowable. His being hired by X Electric does not change the status of his knowledge of the filament. That still belongs to CDE Electric. Hence, he cannot morally develop the filament for X Electric as he is commanded to do. X Electric Acts immorally in commanding it, and if he does what they command, he acts immorally.

A short utilitarian analysis will help us see why it is immoral to develop the filament for X Electric. Consider the consequences for all those involved. John benefits because he gets to keep his job and handsome increase in salary. X Electric benefits because they get the filament quickly and cheaply. They will therefore be able to compete easily with CDE Electric. In order to get around patent laws, they may have to make minor modifications so that the filament is not identical. But the cost of doing that will not be anything like the cost of developing the original filament. Since they do not have to recoup research and development costs, they will even be able to market the new bulbs more cheaply than CDE Electric. CDE

Electric is the loser. It still has the filament. But it has lost its competitive edge. Moreover, since it has to cover its research and development costs, it will not be able to sell the new bulbs as cheaply as X Electric, and will lose part of the market it would otherwise have had to itself. It will make less profit than it otherwise would have.

The harm that CDE suffers, however, seems to be offset by the benefit that X Electric reaps. If we then add in the benefit John receives, John's action seems morally justifiable. This, however, is not the case. For we have not yet considered the result of the practice on the rest of society. Suppose that the practice of hiring away team leaders in order to gain trade secrets from them becomes a practice. Any firm that spent money—perhaps millions of dollars—to develop a new product or idea would expect to lose that investment to a competitor who would obtain the information by hiring away its developer. The second company would benefit in each case at the expense of the first. Clearly every company would see that it is not in its best interest to develop any product or idea. They would all be better off waiting for someone else to develop a product or idea. In the end, no one would develop any product or idea. The result of the practice in the long run, therefore, would be very serious not only for society as a whole but also for the companies— all companies—that now benefit from research and development. Taking the broad consequences into account, we see that the practice is an immoral one.

What can we draw from this consideration? If the analysis is correct, we can legitimately claim that at least some trade secrets are justifiable. A company is allowed to protect the products and ideas it develops in its research and develop- ment programs for at least a certain amount of time.

The analysis, however, though plausible is not universally accepted. There are some who argue that John Knosit is the real inventor and the product, since it is the result of his genius or ingenuity, rightfully belongs to him. Since he developed it while working for the company, the company has the "shop right" to it, i.e., it has the right to use the invention for its own ends. But it has no right, this view main- tains, to prevent John from taking that knowledge with him and using it for the benefit of his new employer, if he so chooses.

Because of controversies of this type, certain practices have become more or less standard in industry and laws have been developed to help regulate the use of information and inventions. Patent laws are one obvious device that help com- panies achieve some protection in the use of products developed by those in their employ. A company can protect its interests in other ways as well. It can, for instance, fragment its projects so that very few people know the total project. A firm will also typically require that people who work for it in development areas keep sensitive information they acquire as employees of the firm (including infor- mation on products the employees themselves develop) confidential for a certain length of time, even if they leave the company. This is specified in a contract that details what an employee may and may not reveal. Employees must often sign such agreements before they are given access to the company's research and devel- opment. Should an employee break this contract, he can be sued for the damages incurred. The contract itself in such cases sets not only the legal but also the moral framework within which to decide the morality of a given act of disclosure. In general, the practice is a morally defensible one even though some companies abuse the practice. They do so when the contract violates an employee's rights by imposing unreasonable limitation on what the employee assigns to them in terms of his knowledge. Firms sometimes will subtly coerce the employee to sign unreasonable agreements by making him sign a condition of employment *only after* he has left his other position and has agreed to work for the new firm.

The right of the company to be the first to use and profit from its research is nonetheless in general morally defensible. This does not mean, however, that it has the exclusive right to what it develops forever, nor that if it develops a product which would benefit society, it can for its own reasons indefinitely prevent it from ever becoming known. Knowledge is not an object whch one can keep locked up as long as one likes. Patents appropriately expire. Long before they expire, any new idea that can be reverse engineered may be so engineered and copied with just sufficient changes so as not to infringe on the patent laws. Competition thus enters the field. The delay, however, that such copying requires after the original item appears is sufficient for the originator to recoup his research expenses. Interestingly, the formula for Coca-Cola has never been patented precisely in order to keep it secret. Chemical analysis has not yielded the formula. The formula for Coca-Cola is one of the best kept trade secrets in history. From a moral point of view, there is no objection to that secret remaining a secret of the company indefinitely and no demonstrable harm would befall society even if it were a secret that eventually died with its keepers.

If a cheap substitute for gasoline were developed, however, oil companies might find it in their own interests to keep such a product from being developed. If the find were made in their laboratories, they might prefer to lock up the process in their company safe until it was necessary to use it, rather than compete with their own oil interests.'Could they morally do so and could they morally keep those employees who developed it from divulging the formula *forever?* No. The good that society would reap from the oil substitute would far exceed the damage done to the oil company by the substitute's appearing on the market. The developer has the right to market the product first and to protect its investment in development so as to recover its cost. But this right is a limited one.

The argument necessary to show why the right is a limited one hinges on the nature of knowledge. Whatever knowledge a company produces is always an increment to the knowledge developed by society or by previous people in society and passed from one generation to another. Any new invention is made by people who learned a great deal from a general store of knowledge before they could bring what they knew to bear on a particular problem. Though we can attribute them to particular efforts of individuals or teams, therefore, inventions and discoveries also are the result of those people who developed them and passed on their knowledge to others. In this way every advance in knowledge is social and belongs ultimately to society, even though for practical purposes we can assign it temporarily to a given individual or firm.

Case 2 raises a somewhat different issue. Tom Berry makes a copy of the customer list of Pretty-Good Refrigeration. Since he does not take the original, the information is still available to Pretty-Good Refrigeration. To whom does the list belong? The list is in the company's book. It does not simply contain a list of purchasers such as might be obtained from an industry trade list. It was generated by employees of the company and they were paid for their services while it was generated. The list therefore belongs to Pretty-Good Refrigeration. By taking the list with him, Tom is stealing information that does not belong to him. He uses it, moreover, for his own ends at the expense of his former employer. As in the previous case, the information rightfully belongs to the company and Tom acts immorally in taking it.

What if instead of taking a copy of the customer book Tom goes to his new employer with the list imprinted in his memory? Does this make a difference? The answer is clearly no. What is immoral is not the fact that he took a certain amount of paper from Pretty-Good Refrigeration but that he took its annotated customer list. That list belongs to the company. Whether he takes it in his head or on photocopied paper does not matter. The information is not his and he uses it immorally when he uses it to take away the customers from his former employer.

Case 3, however, is different from the other two. In Case 3, Henry does not take what does not belong to him. He steals no secrets from the company. What managerial skill he learns while working for the company belongs to him. It is not patentable information and is not guaranteed by copyright or any other law. A person who works for a firm earns his pay by discharging the duties of whatever position he holds in the firm. As Personnel Manager, Henry carried out his duties. In doing so, he gained experience. He had ideas for improvement and these were implemented in the firm to the firm's advantage. But managerial techniques and organizational structures that one develops do not belong to the firm for which one works.

Let us test this claim. Suppose that while working for Dirty-Brown Construction, Henry went to Grass-Green Construction and offered to sell them his managerial ideas for $50 thousand. What would we say about the morality of that action? A proper first reply is that it is unlikely Grass-Green Construction would be interested. Managerial ideas are not the kinds of things one can simply take and implement. Each firm has a certain structure and dynamism. A consultant might come in and do a study of how to increase the efficiency of a firm. No consultant would simply offer some managerial idea and expect to receive much for it.

If Henry's ideas are good, could he legitimately consult on the side? The answer, of course, depends on the firm he is working for and the nature of his agreement with the firm. His employer could make it a condition of his employment that he not consult, or that he not consult with the company's competitors. His consulting, however, is different from his selling information that belongs to the firm. The skill that one develops and the experience that one attains on a job belongs to the employee, not to the firm. If he can sell his experience and skill for more to another employer, the employee is entitled to do so. Each company, in fact, unless it hires only unskilled labor and does all its training and hiring from its own ranks, hires people who have acquired knowledge, skill, and experience under other employers.

The distinction between the information and knowledge that belong appropriately to the employer and the information and knowledge that belong appropriately to the employee is not always an easy one to draw. Certain guidelines can help in the determination of what is appropriately secret. Information that is independently available in the public domain is not secret. Even if some firm independently develops identical information in its own laboratory, it cannot claim proprietary rights to what is accessible in technical or popular journals. If such material is publicly available, an employee violates no trust or obligation of loyalty if he uses that knowledge in a position with his new employer. Similarly, if the information can be easily generated by those competent to do so, then the restriction on an employee using such information in his new position is minimal, if it exists at all.

Three indicators are useful in determining what information is appropriately secret, what information belongs to a given firm, and hence what information an employee has a moral obligation not to reveal to his original firm's competitors. A first indication of the secrecy of the information is the amount of security the company employs to maintain the secrecy of the information. If a company treats the information—be it techniques, inventions, or consumer and/or supplier lists—as highly confidential, if it takes measures to insure that the information is not available routinely, if it restricts access and takes other comparable measures, then the employees with access to that information know that it is considered secret by the firm. Typically the employees are not only cautioned about the secrecy of the data or information to which they are given access, but they must also sign an agreement not to divulge the information. A second criterion is the amount of money that a firm has invested or spends in developing the information. Strict security regulations for information that is in the public domain or that can be easily developed make no sense. Safeguards of an elaborate nature make sense only where the information is costly to produce and important to the financial future of the firm. A third criterion is the value of the information to a competitor. Again, it is unlikely that a firm will initiate great security to protect information valuable only to the firm itself. If, however, the information could be used by a competitor to gain a competitive edge, then it is reasonable that the originating firm be permitted to protect its investment.

From the above analysis we can conclude that firms have the right to protect certain kinds of information that belong appropriately to them, and that they can legitimately impose restrictions on their employees not to divulge such information. The analysis provided some rough guidelines. But the conclusion should not be taken as stronger than it is. In particular, we should note two points. First, the obligation on the part of an employee not to sell or give to another person what properly belongs to the firm is a moral obligation. Attempts to reinforce the moral obligation through law have been only minimally effective. Some employers have attempted to restrain their employees from working for competing firms for a period of two years after they leave. Such agreements, even if signed, have generally not held up in court. They violate the right of the employee to change jobs. The attempts of firms to issue injunctions against competitors pursuing research with the help of a former employee have usually not been successful. Firms have tended to emphasize the ethical obligations of employees both before they begin work on certain projects and just prior to their leaving the service of the company. They have also attempted to keep them loyal by offering consulting fees for a period of one or two years, and by giving them retirement benefits, or other benefits that they would not normally receive, in return for not revealing trade secrets.

The second point concerns the information that a firm can appropriately keep secret. Some firms, it seems, would prefer to keep all aspects of their operation secret. They have been reluctant to disclose any information at all, unless forced to do so by law. The guidelines listed above concern only certain kinds of information, namely that which is closely guarded, expensive, and which if divulged to a competitor, would cause serious competitive harm to the firm. A great deal of information in a firm is not of this type. There are some interesting borderline cases. Many firms claimed, for instance, that the salaries of their top executives were trade secrets. If the competition knew what these salaries were, they could more easily lure top executives than otherwise. But clearly what a top executive makes is not something he is required to keep secret from those who might want to employ him. His total compensation is also of interest to stockholders. Such information is now a matter of public record. Claims to secrecy have to be balanced against claims of the employees to freedom of speech and movement, against claims of the government, stockholders, and the public to information that properly concerns them and that they have a right to know, and against the right of society in general to benefit from information and knowledge developed by a company which the company would rather not divulge despite the information's great social usefulness.

Insider Information

Insider information is information that someone within a company has that is not available to those outside the company. These include not only trade secrets, which we have already discussed, but also company strategy and plans. The moral problems connected with insider information concern the use that individuals may make of such information while they are still members of a firm. There are two aspects of the question that raise special problems. One is the use of information by someone within the firm for his own private gain at the expense of the firm. This is an instance of conflict of interest. The other is the use of insider information by someone within a firm to secure personal advantage over those not in the firm. In both cases the individual seeks his own and not the firm's benefit through the use of his information. Is this morally justifiable?

We have seen that some information belongs to a company and some information belongs to the employee who can appropriately use it in another firm. In our discussion of the corporation and of the responsibility of employees within it, we distinguished between an employee and the role he plays or the function he fills within a corporation. In the same way we can distinguish between information belonging to an individual that he can use as he wishes and that which does not belong to him and which he cannot use as he wishes.

An employee of a firm fills a certain position within the firm. We saw that no employee can morally do what is immoral, even if he is expected or commanded to do so as part of his job. An individual remains a moral being while filling any position in a firm. He cannot compartmentalize himself into person and employee. Hence, any information he receives or absorbs in his capacity as an employee, he retains in his capacity as a human being. As a human being he has certain interests and a private life. He is interested in advancing his own good as well as advancing the good of the firm for which he works. What information and knowledge he receives in his capacity as an employee can he morally use for his own benefit?

Consider the following fairly obvious case. A vice-president of a railroad company is involved in planning the expansion of the railroad. He and others work on the most desirable route for the railroad to take. He has access to the plans of the company and knows well in advance where the railroad expects to put its new line. The company does not disclose its plans publicly. It tries to keep the route secret until it can purchase or negotiate the right of way. If it were to divulge its intent, the price of the land would rise significantly. The vice-president, knowing the route, purchases as much of the land along the projected route as he can. He intends to buy the land as cheaply as possible from its present owners who do not know the railroad's plans, and then sell the land to the railroad at as high a price as he can get. He knows in advance the amount of money that the railroad has projected for purchase of the land and hence knows how much he can hold out for. Does he act morally in doing this?

The company will certainly not look kindly on his action. He is increasing the cost of the land to the company and profiting at the company's expense. Such action will probably result in his being fired. But is he not free to exercise his private right to buy and sell land, to look after his personal finances and to invest as he wishes? What, if anything, is wrong with his action? The crux of the situation is that he used information which he received in his corporate capacity—in his position as the company's vice-president—for his personal gain in a private capacity. The information was not available to him in his capacity as a private individual. It was not public knowledge nor available except to a few within the company. The basis for calling this immoral is that he used information that was not his. He used it for his private gain at the expense of the company. The company might call that a breach of loyalty. More serious is his use of information to which as a private individual he had no right.

The distinction between what the information one has as occupant of a certain position in a firm and what one has as a private individual has wide application. In casual conversation, employees frequently emphasize their importance by dropping information they have because of their position in a firm. They do so to impress their importance on the people to whom they are speaking. They can exercise one-upmanship in this way. Frequently no harm is done by this practice. But sometimes great harm is done. Those who have access to personnel files, for instance, have no right to divulge what they know about employees if the information is learned only through their work and is not otherwise available. Morality demands confidentiality of records whether or not one signs a contract not to divulge such information. Similarly, many plans, discussions, or memos which pertain to a company's business and to which the employee has official access do not belong to him in his private capacity. He is not morally free to divulge such information casually for personal profit, monetary gain, or to feel self-important.

The second general case of the illegitimate use of insider information is personal gain not at the company's expense but at the expense of those not connected with the company. This typically occurs in trading the stock of the company for which one works. What is morally allowable in this respect and what is not?

Those who work for a company are in a position to know it better than those who do not. They can judge the efficiency of management on a daily basis. They can estimate worker satisfaction and productivity. They can sense whether the company is developing and whether management is dynamic and anxious for expansion and growth. On the basis of this information, they may be in a better position than others to decide whether or not to invest in the company by buying its stock. But such information is not privileged. It is at least generally available and lacks the specificity of insider information that makes it immoral to use such knowledge in buying the company's stock.

Consider the following two cases, however. The management of Company A in its private planning sessions decides that buying Company B as a subsidiary would be a profitable move. Such takeovers frequently result in the stock of Company B rising to the price that Company A will offer for the stock in its purchase offer. Adam Agile of Company A buys stock in Company B before any news or rumor of the takeover gets out. He makes a handsome profit. In the second case, Nick Nimble, an officer in Company B, buys a large block of stock in his own company as soon as he sees that the takeover is likely to occur. He too acts prior to any news or leak of the takeover and reaps the reward of a sizable profit. Are their actions morally justifiable?

In both cases the two men act on inside information. Neither harms his own company nor the other in any way. If their action is inappropriate, it must be because it harms someone. Whom do they hurt? As a result of their inside information they are able to act with knowledge not available to the general public or to other traders in the stock market. Any charge of immorality must be based on the fact that to buy and sell stock, both parties to the transaction must have access to the appropriate information. Their interpretation of that information, or their diligence in analyzing the information available, as well as their personal situations, make some people buyers at the time others are sellers. But the use of inside information makes the transaction an unequal one, and hence an unfair one.

In the above cases, Adam purchased stock in a company other than his own. Construed strictly, his action was not insider information, when this is taken to mean knowledge of the actions of one's own company and the purchase of that company's stock. But in a broad sense it was insider information. Nick used the same information to purchase stock in Company *B*. The law differentiates the two cases. Officers, board members, and large shareholders of publicly-owned corporations must disclose the purchase of stock in their own company. They do not have to disclose the purchase of stock for their portfolios which they make in other companies. Yet from a moral point of view the two cases are similar. If one of the two acted immorally, so did the other. Both took advantage of special knowledge to make a profit which they would not have been able to do without inside information.

In the above cases, however, there was no manipulation of the stock and no other unjust practice. Corporations are required to disclose or release information promptly to avoid special privilege to an insider. But clearly those on the inside frequently have access to the information before it is disclosed. Since they have that information in their capacity as corporate agents and not as private individuals, they inappropriately use it to achieve personal gain at the expense of members of the general public. This, of course, does not mean that they cannot buy and sell stock in their own companies. It simply means they cannot morally take unfair advantage of their special insider information.

Corporate Disclosure

Trade secrets cover those items of information and knowledge to which a firm has proprietary right and which it can legally and morally protect and refuse to reveal. At the other end of the information spectrum is a large amount of information which a public corporation must reveal by law. The information that a corporation is morally obliged to disclose coincides with much that is legally required, though pressures for increased disclosure are based for the most part on moral arguments.

The moral basis for disclosure of corporate information rests primarily on two second-order, substantive moral principles: (1) each person has the right to the information he needs to enter into a transaction fairly; and (2) each person has the right to know those actions of others that will seriously and adversely affect him or her. Each of these principles demands some defense.

We have discussed the first of these principles several times. A transaction is fair if those who are a party to it have the appropriate information and freely enter into it. They cannot fairly participate in a transaction if they are denied pertinent information. On the other hand, it is not necessary for each party to make sure that the other party is properly informed. What is necessary is that each party have access to the appropriate information. A transaction is fair even if one of the parties does not take advantage of information that is available to him and that he could profitably use. This principle probably requires no more explanation here even though it can be defended using a utilitarian, Kantian, or Rawlsian approach.

The second principle can be derived from our earlier analysis of moral responsibility. We saw that each person is morally responsible for his actions and their effects. He is responsible to those whom his actions affect, and he is morally bound not to harm others unless there is some overriding reason for doing so. Respect for persons, a contract formed behind a veil of ignorance, and a utilitarian calculation all lead to the conclusion that if we are going to engage in some action which endangers others, then we are morally bound to warn them or not to perform the action. Though we are not morally permitted to harm others, we are permitted to do some things that would cause others harm if we take the precautions necessary to prevent harm to them, including warning them. If a road crew is authorized to dynamite a pass, it is morally allowed to do so only if it takes proper precautions to assure that no one gets hurt. The obligation not to hurt others involves the potential victim's right not to be hurt and his right to be warned of actions that could hurt him, even if they are legitimate. If a company intends to build a nuclear power plant in a certain location, those in the vicinity of the site have a right to know this. If such a plant potentially endangers them, they have the right to this information. They may have further rights as well. But a basic right, and the one with which they can rationally take other action and exercise other rights, is the right to be informed.

In our discussion of disclosure we shall deal with three questions: to whom must disclosure be made available; what must morally be disclosed; and what form should disclosure take?

1. Based on the two principles stated before, a corporation has the moral obligation to disclose appropriate information to those with whom it enters into transactions, and those whom its actions affect seriously and adversely. In broad terms these can be designated as: (a) the shareholders and potential shareholders of the corporation; (b) the board of directors; (c) the workers; (d) government; (e) the corporation's suppliers and agents; (f) the consumer of the corporation's product; and (g) the general public, whether or not they are consumers of the product. A different kind of disclosure is appropriate for each of these groups.

The actions of a corporation may seriously and adversely affect its competitors. Yet if the results stem from legal and moral means—such as the production of a better product, a technological breakthrough, an aggressive marketing strategy, or increased efficiency—then the corporation owes the competitor no special information. If a competitor's plant is adjacent to that of another corporation, however, and an explosion may cause harm to the competitor's plant, then the competitor has the right to be informed of the danger just as every other neighbor does.

2. What morally must be disclosed? Since each group relates differently to the corporation, what is to be disclosed will vary from group to group. In each case the two principles apply.

(a) Disclosure of information to stockholders and to potential stockholders has caused a great deal of debate. Corporations argued that in disclosing information to these groups they were making information available to their competitors—information which by right the corporation should be allowed to keep secret. The argument in favor of secrecy, however, conflicts with the right of these groups to information. A partial solution has been effected by the Securities and Exchange Commission (SEC). It requires the disclosure of certain information by all corporations to shareholders and to potential shareholders. The latter group in effect means disclosure to the general public. Since the same information is required from all competing corporations, the conditions of competition are kept fair.

Those who own stock in a corporation are its legal owners. It would seem that they have the right to know everything about a corporation that they choose to know. Yet since disclosure of trade secrets, for instance, would compromise those secrets to the detriment of the owners, they neither have the right to be informed of everything, nor should they be routinely informed of everything. What they have a right to know includes information on the management of the corporation, its financial position, and its general plans for the future. They are routinely informed in some detail of these matters through the corporation's annual report to the shareholders given during the annual shareholders meeting. They are informed of the net sales of the company, net earnings, return on shareholder's equity, earnings per share, dividends, working capital, and the assets and liabilities of the corporation. The annual report usually includes an overview of the corporation's activities, possibly something about its research and development, a list of the members of the board of directors and the corporate officers, a financial balance sheet, and information on the corporation's debts, taxes, possibly some information on its retirement plan and similar pertinent information. This information is necessary for a shareholder to evaluate how his investment is being managed. Since he has a right to vote for members of the corporation's board of directors, he is also informed about them: who they are, what position they hold either in the corporation or in other companies, and how many shares of the corporation's stock they each own. If new members of the board are to be elected, shareholders are informed of who they are. For many years the salaries of the corporation's top officers were considered a trade secret. This information is now by law reported to the shareholders, as is appropriate since the shareholders are the owners of the corporation.

Once information of this type is disclosed to the shareholders, it also becomes a matter of public record with the SEC. The information is therefore available to a corporation's competitors. More important, it is available to potential purchasers of the corporation's stock. Before someone invests his money in a corporation and if the transaction is to be a fair one, he has the right to know something about the company he is investing in: its assets, the dividends it pays, its growth or lack of growth, the price/earnings ratio of the company's stock, its assets and liabilities, and its management.

The information disclosed to shareholders and potential shareholders has for the most part been financial. Those who defned this policy argue that the financial details of the corporation are the pieces of information that are necessary to judge management and also to judge whether one is making a sound investment. But there are some who feel that other kinds of information are of interest to shareholders and potential shareholders. The proposed "Corporate Democracy Act," for instance, desires "To increase the flow of information to consumers, shareholders and workers about employment patterns, environmental matters, job health and safety, foreign production, directorial performance, shareholder ownership, tax rates and legal and auditing fees." (*The Big Business Reader: Essays on Corporate America,* ed. by Mark Green & Robert Massie, Jr. New York, the Pilgrim Press, 1980, p. 592.) The Act spells out in detail a great deal of information about distribution of the work force by sex and race, of records submitted to the Environmental Protection Agency, and about overseas operations. In some cases it would require such information in the annual report; in others, it would require only that a corporation make such information available on demand to its shareholders.

The right of shareholders to information about the company is a right which no one denies. But exactly what they have the right to, in addition to what is already required by law, is a matter of debate. Corporations have argued that investors are interested only in financial information and claim that they already supply much more information than the vast majority of investors are interested in having. They also argue that beyond a certain point the increase of information results in a decrease in understanding on the part of all except the expert in accounting. An investor who is interested in whether the corporation is acting morally, however, may well be appropriately interested in how the corporation operates from the viewpoint of hiring women and minorities, how often its employees have blown the whistle, and whether if the corporation is operating in South Africa it practices apartheid. These and other issues are not irrelevant if one wishes to evaluate the corporation from a moral point of view. If shareholders and potential shareholders demand such information, they have a right to it. Uniform disclosure by all large corporations, however, can only be achieved by making such disclosures legally mandatory.

Shareholders are legally represented by members of the board of directors of a corporation. Shareholders, therefore, should be informed of the operation of the board and the actions of its members. Shareholders have a right to know not only for whom they are voting but how the nomination procedure for board members works, how the board functions, who sets agendas, how often the board meets, what the committees of the board are and who serves on them, the number of meetings each board member has attended in the previous year, and the reasons for the resignation of any board members. If a board member resigns in protest to board or corporation action, such information is of direct and pertinent interest to shareholders. At the present time, this information is generally not disclosed.

(b) Since the members of the board of directors are the legal representatives of the shareholders, they owe the shareholders appropriate information as well as honest service in their interests. Yet board members need not make public everything they learn. Since they are legally and morally bound to look after the interests of the corporation and to evaluate the corporation's activities and the performance of management, they have the right to independent access to the information they desire. The owners' right of access is exercised through the members of the board, and this access cannot be appropriately restricted by a decision of management.

(c) What must be disclosed to the workers? We have already seen that they have a right to know the conditions of work, including their rights, benefits, and obligations. This follows simply from the fact that this information is necessary if the contract between employer and employee is to be fair. The worker must know in advance what he is contracting into. He must also be informed of any danger to his health the work he performs might produce. If a corporation learns that a certain substance with which employees have been working is dangerous to them, it must morally inform the workers of this. Such information not only directly affects them but also changes the background conditions of their employment. Workers may choose to work in a dangerous or unhealthy environment for extra pay; but they must be informed of such conditions.

Workers also have a right to know the general policy of the corporation in the areas in which they have moral concerns. If they do not wish to work for a company that practices discrimination, they should be able to find out whether their company does engage in such practices. The other items of moral concern that we listed above may all be of moral concern to workers. If so, they have a right to such information.

Workers also have the right to know in ample time decisions made by management which directly and adversely affect them. The decision to close a plant and to dismiss all the employees working there, for example, is a decision which they have the right to know about in sufficient enough time to make alternative plans, especially if the corporation does not intend to help them relocate or find other jobs.

(d) Government has the right to know that corporations are complying with the law. Despite the fact that government receives a great deal of information from corporations concerning their activities, it is still very difficult for the Federal government to obtain adequate information on the activities of mammoth conglomerates. The information required of small and middle-sized corporations raises few problems from the point of view of adequate disclosure. The information reported by the large conglomerates and multinational corporations tends to be aggregative rather than broken down into the activities of each of the subsidiary units. The difficulty of mandating adequate reporting from these giants makes control difficult. In some cases the government needs more information than it has before it can even get a grasp on what specific additional information it must have. Ralph Nader, among others, has proposed federal chartering of corporations, rather than the present system of state chartering, as a means of gaining greater governmental control over large corporations and their operations. Information of their operations is a necessary prerequisite to adequate control, and adequate information is not now available to government.

(e) The corporation from a moral point of view should disclose to its suppliers whatever is necessary to make the contracts between them fair. The same general principle applies to a corporation's disclosure to its agents. They should know enough to fulfill in turn their responsibilities of disclosure to their customers.

(f) The consumer should be informed of any dangers posed by the use of the product he purchases. He properly expects that the item he buys will be reasonably safe if properly used. If a product is caustic, he should be so informed. If it is poisonous, he should be warned. If it is defective, he should be notified in some way before he purchases it. He should know what a food or a drug contains, what an article of clothing or upholstery is made of, and so on. Governmental regulations have been passed, frequently as a result of consumer pressures, mandating the disclosure of information about consumer products—for example, from the estimated gas mileage of a new car to the efficiency of air conditioners.

A customer cannot generally obtain information on such things as the morality of the corporation's employment practices or its overseas operations. Such information, of course, should not be carried on every box of cereal a company sells. But if customers wish to vote through their purchases for companies that behave morally, and wish to vote through withholding purchases against companies that engage in immoral practices, customers should have some way of determining a company's policy. Obviously we cannot expect any company to assert that it is engaging in an immoral practice. We can expect that customers have access to information about a company's employment policies, overseas operations, suits successfully brought against it, governmental fines it has paid, and similar details from which one can draw his own moral conclusions.

(g) The general public is broader than simply a corporation's customers or potential customers. The potential customers of an airplane manufacturer, for instance, would be airlines, governments, and possibly individual firms. Yet the location of an airplane manufacturing plant, the closing of such a plant, and its operation have a large impact on the area in which it is located. Those directly affected by such a plant include not only those employed by it but also those who live near it.

The closing of a plant may seriously and adversely affect not only the workers in the plant but also the shops and stores that have risen to serve the workers of the plant. Communities frequently have zoning regulations and negotiate the terms under which a plant can locate in a community. They rarely negotiate any conditions for the plant's closing. Such conditions, such as a certain amount of advance warning of a closing as well as specifications about closing procedures similar to opening procedures, would be appropriate.

Information concerning environmental impact, pollution, and safety of the operation to the surrounding population would also be of interest to the general public. The building of nuclear powered electric plants pose particular problems. The dangers of radiation are greatest to those nearest the plant. Such plants cannot morally be built without informing those in the vicinity of the danger. But if the dangers are considered low enough by the licensing authorities, information is all that is required. The consent on the part of those who will be directly affected in case of an accident is not presently required. Nor is there agreement on whether it is possible to state meaningfully what the chances of an accident occurring are. The moral issues here go beyond the question of appropriate disclosure. But it is agreed that public disclosure is appropriate where the actions of a corporation seriously and adversely affect the general public.

3. What form should disclosure take? We have already touched indirectly on some of the appropriate forms of disclosure. Shareholders are informed of a corpo-

ration's activities through the annual report and the annual shareholders' meeting; government is informed of a company's activities through legally mandated reports, and where appropriate, through on-site investigations and inspections; workers are informed of the conditions of employment prior to their employment. In some of these cases the information required is disclosed routinely through reports. In other cases it is supplied only on direct request from a party authorized to receive it. Information that is a matter of public record is available to the general population. If some action will directly endanger certain people, then that information must be conveyed directly to them.

The appropriate channels for reporting information concerning the moral dimensions of some of a corporation's actions have yet to be decided upon, much less standardized. The moral audit to which we referred in an earlier chapter fits into the question of disclosure at this point and will, if developed, be an appropriate vehicle for such information.

Problems arise when the corporation engages in some activity that is immoral, illegal, or dangerous to the public. We cannot expect the people engaged in such activities to disclose the fact that they are acting in that way. We have already seen the conditions under which an employee is morally allowed and morally required to inform the public of conditions which will seriously injure people. But some questions still remain concerning disclosure of such activities.

Problems arise with respect to members of the professions who work in one way or another for a corporation. Lawyers, engineers, accountants, and sometimes doctors and nurses fall into this category. They owe a certain loyalty to the corporation that employs them or pays them. They are also professionals, however. As such they are expected to maintain certain standards of conduct in the exercise of their profession. Suppose an accounting firm conducting an independent audit turns up a discrepancy in the company's books. It reports it to the president and perhaps to the chairman of the board. Suppose the discrepancy involves bribery or embezzlement, and the company decides simply to take the loss. Should this be reported to the shareholders? If the company does nothing about it, does the accounting firm or the individual accountant have any obligation to make known the facts of the case?

Suppose the corporation's lawyers are asked how to cover up some illegal procedure or act. Do they have any responsibility to make that fact known and also the procedure or act? Should they go to the board, and if the board does not take action, should they go to the shareholders or the government? If health measures are enforced only when there is danger of governmental inspection, or if the company doctor finds that more and more workers show signs of a work-related disease, does he fulfill his responsibilities in simply reporting this to management? If management takes no remedial action and does not inform the workers, does the doctor have any obligation to inform them?

These questions are related to disclosure within the firm to shareholders, management, the board, and the workers. Some of the questions are covered by codes of professional conduct of the individual professions, some are covered in individual firms by the firms' policy statement of its ethical code of conduct. Where neither is the case, then the rules that apply to whistle blowing can be modified to handle these questions as well.

Confidentiality raises another set of problems. Some of what a professional learns about his client or patient is confidential and is not proper matter for disclosure. The rule with respect to lawyers was once so severe that even if a lawyer learned in his professional relation with a client that the client was going to commit a felony, it was considered improper for the lawyer to disclose that information. That rule has recently and appropriately been changed. Journalists claim the right not to have to disclose their sources. This does not prevent them from having to document their stories. Investigative reporters often seek information about the wrongdoings of a firm, a group, or an individual and make this information public. They have no right to lie, but they do have the right to make known wrongdoings where they discover them, especially if they involve a cover-up by those who should appropriately disclose them.

Not all wrongdoings by members of a firm need to be publicly disclosed. But if members of a corporation have engaged in bribery, taken kickbacks, or covered up defects in a product, such information should be reported to the board of directors and possibly to the shareholders, together with a report of any action taken against such persons. A moral firm does not reward immorality with raises and promotions. One way shareholders can judge the morality of a firm is by knowing how it deals with those who are guilty of wrongdoing, even if done in the name of and for the sake of the company.

Corporations have typically been reluctant to disclose information about their activities. If left to themselves some of them would consider all their internal operations trade secrets. However, if they wish to remain within the law, they must disclose what is legally required. Should they disclose more, and if so, how much more? The analysis we have given indicates the basis for deciding what should be disclosed. Corporations frequently see the issue of disclosure in an adversarial context—a struggle between their desire not to disclose information and the unreasonable demands of environmentalists, consumer activists, and the enemies of capitalism. The relation need not be an adversarial one. A corporation that wishes to act morally and to fulfill its moral obligations will be amenable to discussion of the demands made upon it. It will, moreover, establish channels to hear those who have claims to press and demands to make. This does not mean that every claim for information is justifiable. Either the board, the officers of a corporation, or both must in the final analysis decide what disclosure is appropriate beyond what is legally required. But they should base this decision on what the corporation's customers, shareholders, or the general public wish and the arguments they give in defense of their demands. Shareholders' meetings are only one forum for raising and discussing these questions. It is more and more frequently used often because it is the only channel available to those who have concerns about corporations, their policies, and their activities. Other channels are possible and needed; they are certainly not beyond the organizational capacities of most large corporations.

Information plays a central role in modern business. Information is vital for adequate evaluation of business activities from the point of view of law, economics, and morality. The tension between the corporate urge for secrecy and the right to know by those affected or involved can strain a corporation's relations with the public. But if a corporation responds to this tension creatively and openly, it can lead to the exercise of more responsibility on the part of a corporation and to greater acceptance of corporations on the part of the general public.

Further Reading

Benston, George James. *Corporate Financial Disclosure in the UK and the USA.* Farnborough, Hants, Eng.: Saxon House, 1976.

DeMott, Deborah A., ed. *Corporations at the Crossroads: Governance and Reform.* New York: McGraw-Hill, Inc., 1980.

Executive Disclosure Guide: SEC Compliance:Corporations, Directors, Officers, Insiders. Chicago: Commerce Clearing House, Inc., 1976.

Flom, Joseph H.; Garfinkel, Barry H.; and Freund, James C. *Disclosure Requirements of Public Companies and Insiders.* Practicing Law Institute, 1967.

Goldschmidt, Harvey J., ed. *Business Disclosure: Government's Need to Know.* New York: McGraw-Hill, Inc., 1979.

Kintner, E.W., and Lahr, J.L. *Intellectual Property Law Primer: A Survey of the Law of Patents, Trade Secrets, Trademarks, Franchises, Copyrights, Personality, and Entertainment Rights.* New York: Macmillan, Inc., 1974.

Kripke, Homer. *The SEC and Corporate Disclosure: Regulation in Search of a Purpose.* New York: Law & Business, Inc., 1979.

Lieberstein, Stanley. *Who Owns What Is in Your Head?: Trade Secrets and the Mobile Employee.* New York: Hawthorn Books, Inc., 1979.

Nader, Ralph, and Green, Mark J., eds. *Corporate Power in America.* New York: Grossman Publishers, 1973.

13

Professionalism, Ethical Codes of Conduct, and Unions

The professions are inextricably intertwined with business. Corporations, for example, in 1977 spent $24 billion on legal services. Lawyers sometimes are employed directly by corporations; others form partnerships and sell their services. Still others have independent practices. The health professions form an important part of social life. Drug companies are among the corporate giants; hospitals, doctors' bills, and medical insurance take a significant part of the average worker's salary. Engineers build our roads and skyscrapers, bridges, and plants. They are hired in great number by corporations to design cars and airplanes, washing machines, electric toothbrushes, and the other many mechanical and electronic objects that form part of our daily life.

As modern society becomes more complex, it requires greater specialization and specialized knowledge. In the United States, automation has taken over many of the routine jobs formerly performed by unskilled labor. The need for advanced training and the growth of the service professions have encouraged more people to go to college and to professional schools. Schooling has in turn provided business and industry with a pool of trained workers to take on the jobs that require communication skills, computer programming knowledge, engineering expertise, and command of accounting procedures, legal practices, and a variety of specialized and arcane information.

The trend toward specialization has led groups to identify themselves as a profession, and to seek the prestige and wealth that have become identified with professions. Professionalism and the professions raise special problems from the point of view of ethics. Their growth makes the problems more pressing.

In dealing with the professions and professionalism, the first problem is to identify what we mean by a profession or by professionals. What is a profession? Typically, professions have been self-governing, and society has allowed them a large amount of autonomy. Is such autonomy justifiable and does it carry with it special moral or ethical responsibilities? A second topic for investigation follows from these questions: professional ethical codes. The codes in turn make demands on members of the professions, demands that are not always compatible with the loyalty and obedience expected by many employers. The role of the professions in business therefore requires examination, as do the activities of professional organizations. Since the members of many professions are self-employed, we should also look at the professions as businesses. Our discussion of the professions and professionalism will be in part applicable to unions, insofar as unions control entry into a field of work and protect the interests of their members. Our discussion of professional codes can also supply a basis from which to evaluate other ethical codes, for instance, those issued by some corporations to their employees.

Professionalism and the Professions

The history of the professions is still being written. How it is written depends on whether one identifies the professions first and then writes their history, or whether one specifies certain criteria that must be met for a group or field to qualify as a profession and then investigate which groups or fields have met those criteria.

The witch doctor has been proposed as the paradigm of a profession. A witch doctor has arcane, secret knowledge; he controls access to that knowledge and initiates his successor to his role; he performs an important service to his society; he commands respect and prestige. In the West, two occupations have served as exemplars of the professions. The doctor, from ancient times to the present, has performed a needed service for society, has controlled and had access to specialized knowledge, and has been given status and prestige, though not necessarily wealth. In the Middle Ages, priests made up an acknowledged profession. They had special powers and knowledge, controlled entry into their ranks, exercised a large degree of autonomy, and served an important social function. They were the educated members of society and professed the faith from the pulpit. By extension, other scholars came to be considered members of the scholarly professions. They too had access to and controlled knowledge, performed a service to society, and had something to profess. They were called professors and formed a profession.

Two other groups that had some early claim to being members of a profession were professional soldiers, especially officers, and engineers—those who designed and built aqueducts, cathedrals, palaces, and roads. The distinction between a professional soldier and the other occupations mentioned suggests a distinction we currently make.

A professional is someone, typically, who earns his living by practicing some skill or engaging in some activity that requires expertise but that others may do as hobbies, for pleasure, or in their spare time. Members of the various trades are professionals. There are professional carpenters, plumbers, auto mechanics, brick-layers, barbers, and so on. A professional knows his craft, devotes his full working time to it, usually is paid for what he does, and takes a certain pride in doing his job well. We speak of professional actors and actresses, writers, painters, gardeners, and athletes—people who do professionally what many other people do at an amateur level. Many activities are professional activities in this sense. But not all these activities constitute professions.

In the contemporary world, the paradigms of the professions are the medical and legal professions. Other occupations that often are considered professions are engineering, pharmacy, architecture, and nursing. Some people consider journalism a profession, as well as accounting. University teaching is probably a profession, though high school and grade school teaching are probably not. Many other groups claim professional status: actuaries, insurance underwriters, school administrators, public administrators, social workers, paramedics, and so on. The professions traditionally carry with them prestige, respect, social status, and autonomy. In recent times they have also been regarded as well-paid occupations. Hence, the desire of more and more groups to have their activity recognized as a profession is understandable.

Does it make any difference whether or not society recognizes a group as a profession? Would plumbers do better work if they were a profession instead of a trade? Would doctors perform less well if they were a trade rather than a profession? The answer depends on what society allows members of a profession that it does not allow others, and what it expects from members of a profession that it does not expect from others. Traditionally, society has allowed professions greater autonomy than it allows the trades, arts, or business. Members of a profession set their own standards, regulate entry into the profession, discipline their own members, and function with fewer restraints than others. In return for such increased autonomy, they are expected to serve the public good, set higher standards of conduct for their members than those required of others, and enforce a higher discipline. The trade-off for society is less social control on the condition that the profession be self-regulating and self-disciplinary. The standards to which members of a profession are to hold themselves is usually expressed in a professional code—most often called an ethical code—of conduct promulgated and enforced by a professional organization. Those groups wishing to gain the status of a profession frequently organize into a professional association and promulgate a code of professional ethical conduct.

Professional Ethical Codes

The argument in favor of allowing a profession to govern itself is based on two claims. The first is that the knowledge that members of the profession control is specialized, useful to society, and not easily mastered by the layman. The second is that the members of the profession set higher standards for themselves than society requires of its citizens, workers, and business men and women. The profession, therefore, is in the appropriate position to know how its members should behave, to be alert to violations of the standards it sets, and to censure or dismiss from its ranks those who do not live up to the profession's standards.

Doctors and lawyers are two groups that plausibly make both claims. Doctors have a large body of specialized knowledge. They study for four years beyond college, do an internship, and then sometimes go on to further specialized study. The knowledge that they have is clearly useful to society, and though some knowledge of health care is accessible to the layman, much is not. The medical profession has developed a specialized vocabulary and an impressive technical jargon. Mastering the vocabulary and jargon is part of a doctor's knowledge and expertise. Doctors perform a service that laymen need and want. Moreover, people want to be able to trust their doctors. They wish to be assured that those to whom they entrust their health and lives are competent. Hence it is reasonable for society to demand that only those competent should be allowed to practice medicine. Society reasonably requires proof of training, knowledge, and competence, and identifies those qualified to perform medical services by a licensing procedure.

Who does the licensing? The state does. But the state is not competent to decide what a doctor must know, nor to grade the tests of those who wish certification. Since the knowledge is technical, only those already trained—i.e., doctors or representative doctors—make up the medical examinations, set requirements for entry into the profession and certify those who pass. The profession, therefore, decides what knowledge a person must have to practice medicine legally; it sets the curriculum of medical schools. Since doctors decide how many students the medical school can handle, they control entry into the market. They decide not only how many people will be trained, but also who will be admitted to medical school, what these people must learn, who will be allowed to practice medicine. They set the standards for the practice of medicine. Lawyers similarly control legal education, bar examinations, and the standards of the legal profession. Since both groups control entry to the field and set policy for remaining in the field, both groups act in many ways like monopolies. Why should society allow such power to these groups when it denies the same power to business?

The reply is based on the second claim; namely, that the professions set higher standards for themselves than society sets for other groups. What exactly does this mean? Though originally the claim was best understood in moral terms, its present meaning is no longer clearly moral. What would it mean for members of a profession to hold themselves to higher moral norms than those applied to other members of society? Obviously, it will not suffice for members of the profession merely to refrain from cheating their clients or to refrain from lying to their patients. Honesty is a moral requirement of everyone, as is telling the truth. The higher moral norms to which members of a profession were to adhere were norms that go beyond the requirements of minimal morality. Doctors, for instance, were expected not to work only for the money, but to serve patients even if they could not pay for medical services. Lawyers, too, were expected to put their thirst for justice above the desire for fees. They were expected, therefore, to be willing to defend some people who could not afford to pay for their services. Tradesmen, shopkeepers, and businesspeople are not expected to work without pay. To expect members of a profession to do so is to expect more of them than society demands of others.

Members of a profession were also expected to take a different approach to their time and commitments than ordinary workers. Doctors and lawyers were not expected to punch a time clock. They were expected to work as many hours as their professional duties required, which frequently amounted to more than the standard workweek of others. Doctors, especially, were expected to be ready to provide their services at inconvenient times of the day or night when necessary.

A third way in which members of a profession were expected to follow a higher standard was in their personal as well as professional conduct. They were expected to set an example of proper conduct and be above suspicion. They were expected not only to refrain from improper conduct but also to be known to refrain. This is more than is expected of others.

In these and other ways the professions, at least in earlier times, were expected to adhere to higher moral standards than other people. They were in turn given more respect. It is no longer clear that the professions set higher moral standards for themselves. But they do set professional standards, sometimes called ethical standards. These, to a large extent, have become substitutes for higher moral standards, and though not immoral, frequently have little to do with moral standards at all. The second claim, therefore, has become an extension of the first claim of expertise rather than a distinctive claim concerning higher standards. The standards are now professional, but not necessarily higher from a moral point of view. Thus, the argument now goes, doctors and lawyers know the proper role members of their profession should play in society. They should set high professional standards to protect society against incompetent practitioners, frauds, and quacks. They know the subterfuges to which members of their profession are prone, the means by which doctors or lawyers can be immoral or unethical without public awareness of their activities. Since they have virtually exclusive access to specialized knowledge, they can use it to achieve their own ends at the expense of the public. They can best be restrained by those within the field who have comparable knowledge. Doctors and lawyers, the argument claims, should be given autonomy and be allowed to be self-regulating because they are best equipped to know how their peers should act and best able to judge when they act improperly.

These arguments in favor of self-regulation by the professions are plausible. If they are accepted by society, then society can allow these and other professions more autonomy than others. The standards to which members of the profession hold themselves are stated in their professional ethical codes.

Before we look at professional codes of conduct, however, we should note that the two arguments in defense of autonomy present some difficulties. The ordinary person does not spend four years learning medicine. But he or she can learn something about medicine. The ordinary person can also tell to some extent when a doctor seems to be unsure of him or herself, when the patient is not being given all the facts, when a diagnosis turns out to be wrong or a treatment inappropriate. It is not true that only doctors can judge other doctors. The ordinary people who make up society can judge certain aspects of medical practice and the results of some medical activities. The doctor's expertise is not as exclusive as some doctors would like people to believe. The same observation is true of lawyers.

Nor is it always the case that doctors are better judges of doctors and lawyers of lawyers than are the laypersons untrained in these professions. Ordinary citizens serve on juries to judge evidence of crimes. The evidence, when technical, is made intelligible to the jury members. Similarly, laypersons could serve on trial boards judging the charges of unethical or immoral conduct on the part of doctors and lawyers. Laypersons could either master the knowledge necessary for a particular case or could have the case explained in a nontechnical manner so that they could make an intelligent judgment on the issue.

Members of a profession know the pitfalls of the profession from the inside. But self-regulation by a profession is justifiable only if the general public is satisfied that a given profession is effectively policing itself, that its code requires higher standards than nonprofessional occupations, that its members are living up to the code, and that the profession is promoting the general good.

Difficulties sometimes arise. The extent to which doctors restrict entry to the profession, for instance, may be justified by the absence of facilities for training more doctors. By restricting entry, however, they can protect their own position. A potential conflict of interest clearly exists. The more doctors restrict entry, the fewer doctors there are and the more money they can demand for their services. Doctors were not always well paid. The old-time country doctor and the general practitioner received modest pay, worked long hours, were frequently called out at night, and did not complain loudly when someone could not pay. They were a service profession (somewhat like priests and ministers) and it was considered improper for them to charge or receive high fees. As the profession changes, so should society's view of the profession and of its autonomy.

Though professional codes of conduct were once expected to state high standards, they now serve a variety of purposes. Some codes are simply used to indicate that the group is a profession. The code is brought out and referred to on ceremonial occasions and is sometimes read by new members upon initiation to the profession. Some codes state a set of ideals that members of the profession should try to attain and by which they should guide their practice. But failure to attain the ideals is expected, and few members of the profession actually achieve the goals stated. Other codes or parts thereof are disciplinary. They state the minimum conditions that a member of the profession must satisfy. If he or she falls below that minimum, he or she is subject to sanction by the profession, the most serious of which is expulsion. Still other codes spell out the etiquette of the profession. A single code may include a statement of ideals, a set of disciplinary rules, and standards of professional etiquette.

If a professional code is to serve as a basis upon which a profession claims autonomy from nonprofessional social control to which other groups are subject, the code should have the following characteristics:

1. The code should be regulative. The inclusion of ideals is not necessarily inappropriate. But the code should make clear which of its statements are ideals and which are punitively regulative. Unless a code actually regulates the conduct of the members of a profession, the profession has no public statement by which society can hold the profession bound. Since society allows a profession autonomy on condition that it hold its members to higher norms than those to which others are held, these norms must be publicly available and must be perceived as being higher than other norms.

2. The code should protect the public interest and the interests of those served by the profession. Unless the public benefits by granting the profession autonomy, it should withdraw this privilege.

3. The code should not be self-serving. Codes can be used to serve the interests of the profession at the expense of the public. Certain regulations (for instance, those concerning the setting of fees or the restricting of advertising) protect the profession and are not in the public interest. Code provisions that prevent competition within the profession are generally not in the public's interest and tend to emphasize the negative monopoly aspects of the profession.

4. The code should be specific and honest. A code which simply says that its members should not lie, steal, or cheat requires nothing of them that is not required of all others. If a code is honest, then it deals with those aspects of the profession that pose particular and specialized temptations to its members. The profession is allowed autonomy because it knows the special pitfalls of the profession, its shady areas, and its unethical though not quite illegal practices. Unless these are addressed, the profession is not truly regulating itself.

5. The cost must be both policeable and policed. Unless the code has provisions in it for bringing charges and applying penalties, it is no more than a set of ideals. Unless a profession can demonstrate by its record that it does police its own ranks, society has little reason to believe that it is doing so. In such cases, it has no justification for allowing special privileges to the profession. Society then appropriately should legislate concerning the members of the profession and control its activities, as it does those of other occupations.

Recently the codes of both the medical and legal professions have come under attack. The provision that prevents advertising by doctors and lawyers has been successfully challenged as restricting trade and preventing competition. The setting of fees for professional work by the respective organizations has also been successfully attacked as artificially setting rates, serving the profession at the expense of the public, and preventing competition. Neither the American Bar Association nor the American Medical Association have been especially anxious to discipline their members. Frequently they act only after a lawyer or a doctor has been found guilty of a felony. Such limited action hardly justifies special privileges.

Ethical codes have proliferated in recent years. Not only are they issued by professions, but they have often been adopted by corporations, businesses, and by industries across corporate lines. Not all such ethical codes are moral codes. Some simply specify the legal requirements of which employees may not but should be aware. Some of these have reflected specific concerns, such as bribery and illegal political contributions. Some firms have drawn up codes that serve as guidelines to what is accepted practice within the organization. Thus some companies feel that no gift from a supplier should be accepted, while others allow accepting gifts of up to $25 or $50. Some firms prohibit giving gifts to suppliers or customers. Others limit contributions to political parties, the purchase of stock from companies with which the firm does business, and other practices that may cause or give the appearance of causing conflict of interest.

The proliferation of codes has raised a number of difficulties. Professional codes are supposed to govern the professional activity of all members of the profession, whether working for oneself or for an employer. The codes may set higher standards than the employer wishes his employees to adopt or than the company code allows. Industry-wide codes attempt to set standards of fair competition within an industry. Though sometimes effective, they are limited in what they can control, for they must not restrict trade or competition. Codes that place a lower limit on the price of a good, for instance, violate the anti-trust act, as do industry policies that standardize the hours of work. Though professions, industries, and firms can enforce their codes, they are not courts of law and cannot act as such. Violations of a code are subject to limited discipline. Expulsion from the professional association or from the industrial association are typically the severest penalties that can be enforced, together with public exposure of the act and expulsion. Censure is a more frequent penalty.

Codes can nonetheless serve an important function and can help in resolving specific issues faced by members of a profession or by workers within a firm. If there is a company policy, for instance, about how large a gift can be accepted, then an employee knows not only that bribery is immoral and to be avoided, but also what his employer considers a bribe.

We have noted that not all ethical codes are moral codes. Even when intended to set moral standards, however, a typical defect of codes is that they give the professional or workers no insight into how the code was formulated, what moral principles it exemplifies, or how to resolve issues of interpretation or of conflicts not covered by the code. The codes are usually promulgated by some board or committee of the profession or of the company in question, and seem to take the form of the Ten Commandments. The Ten Commandments, however, came from God, Who many people thought and still do think has either the knowledge or the authority to dictate what is morally right and wrong. Are ethical committees or boards of directors similarly placed and gifted? Most people think not. The difficulty with many codes is not that they prescribe what is immoral, but that they fail to be truly effective in helping members of the profession or company act morally. To be moral means not only doing what someone says is right, but also knowing why what one does is right, and assuming moral responsibility for the action. How were the provisions of the code arrived at? What moral basis do the injunctions stand on? Faced with a serious moral problem, how can the code help a member of a profession or of a firm truly sort out issues? Instructions are sometimes given in corporate codes that any difficulties or uncertainties should be discussed with the corporation's legal office. The legal office, presumably, can give advice about the law and what is legally permitted or forbidden. Not every legal office is competent to give advice about the morality of an action insofar as this may differ from the law.

Although moral codes cannot be expected to contain a detailed presentation of moral reasoning, they can make reference to general moral principles. The injunction, found in one code, to act in such a way that you would not be ashamed to have your actions exposed to the public—for instance, in the headlines of the local newspaper—is a step in the right direction. A code could appropriately and helpfully refer to the moral principles from which the code flows, to principles of justice and fairness. It could also refer to the moral principles of objectively weighing the consequences of all those affected by one's actions, respecting the rights of others, and so on.

It might be objected that this is asking too much of a code. It cannot and should not provide general moral principles since these are assumed to be held by all those who aspire to belong to the profession. People should learn these from their parents, ethics teachers, churches, and not from their professional organizations or from their employers. There is some truth to the objection. But unless the code is understood in terms of moral principles, it will tend simply to be the expression of rules learned by rote, or even worse, of ideals never to be attained. If the member of a profession is to internalize the rules of his profession, he must understand how they are derived, how they implement moral principles, and how he can use similar reasoning to cover situations of conflict and those situations not handled explicitly by the code. Ideally each member of the profession should understand the moral principles and the nature of the profession so that rather than needing to memorize a code, each person could derive the same code by thinking clearly and objectively about the moral issues typically faced by members of the profession.

A second general difficulty with codes is that they avoid significant problems which at least some members of a profession face. Professional codes often specify obligations to the client or patient, the employer (if there happens to be one), the public, and the profession. What is a professional to do when he finds that the obligations conflict? What if, for instance, a company's doctor is told not to release information of mounting evidence that the workers are suffering from an employment-related health hazard? Does his obligation to public health and his patients (the workers) take precedence over his obligation to his employer?

The professional codes give no indication of what action to take when the profession itself acts inappropriately. Professional codes do not often consider this possibility. Nor do company codes.

Professional and company ethical codes have a certain, limited usefulness. However, they are frequently better than nothing at all. But they are usually inadequate as guides to moral conduct or as guarantees that a profession is serving the public and preventing its members from taking advantage of the profession's privileged position.

Professional Organizations

Members of a profession tend to gather and organize into professional organizations and associations. The role of the professional association is to promote the profession's interest and to provide a forum for discussion of topics and dissemination of information concerning the profession. Professional associations also tend to be both the promulgators and the enforcers of professional codes. Although this is appropriate, some professional associations themselves need policing.

A professional association has the *de facto* (if not always the legal) power to control entry into the field, blackball certain practitioners in the field, set policy for its members, and restrict access to publication by those whom it does not approve. Such organizations are sometimes turned to by the government for advice, publishers for definitive texts, and by others for consultants and recommended experts. The power is often uncontrolled and excessive and can be damaging to some members of the profession who disagree with the organization's leadership or policies. Professional organizations are often able to silence opposition to the organization's policies and prevent minority views from being heard on public as well as professional issues. Such cases have led to the suggestion that professional organizations be subject to independent review by those outside the profession, that there be lay participation in hearing cases under the code, that an independent group serve as the recipient of complaints made by the public against members of the profession and follow the handling of the complaint by the profession.

Professional associations have tended both to monopolize power in the area of the profession's prestige and to safeguard the vested interests of its members. The failure of those in the professions and professional associations to police their ranks erodes the basis for society's trust of the profession and its autonomy. Provisions for reprimand, censure, and expulsion are usually pharased in professional codes so as to preserve secrecy rather than to publicize immoral activities by members of the profession. If a profession has higher moral standards than those required by law, the professional organization should not only make these standards generally known but also reveal infractions of these standards by members of the profession.

Since the professions have access to and control over specialized knowledge, the public is dependent on them for the effective use of this knowledge. The members of the profession are in the best position to know how their fellow professionals can abuse this knowledge and can take advantage of the public. Yet professional organizations rarely inform the ordinary person of the ways to protect him or herself against malpractice or unethical or immoral behavior by a member of the profession. Nor do professional societies ask for increased competition within professional ranks, greater disclosure on the part of their members, lower rates, or for any number of other changes in professional practice that would benefit the public. Yet if the professions have a higher code of ethics, if they respond to a higher morality than the ordinary workers, then greater disclosure of their activities, active demystification of their jargon and simplification of their language would be actions in the public interest.

Professional associations should also provide the forum within the profession or industry to raise ethical issues, face them, and provide solutions or work toward solutions that can be morally justified to the general public. To ask the professionals in an industry to help the public achieve more disclosure about a profession or industry might seem like asking them to go against their own best interests. But it is in the general interest of the professions and of industry to foster and develop public trust, and there is no better way to do so than by full, understandable, and proper disclosure.

Professional societies have in general failed to fulfill their obligations in the defense of members of the profession who lose their jobs or are otherwise penalized for following and living up to the code of the profession. Those who work for an employer, e.g., a corporation, are sometimes asked or required to perform some action that violates their professional code. The typical engineering code claims that the safety, health, and welfare of the public shall be held paramount in the performance of professional duties. Suppose an engineer for a tire company sees that the tires being produced are unsafe, reports this to his superiors, including the board, and gets no reaction except being told to keep quiet and mind his own business. He feels that the code requires him to hold the safety of the public paramount and accordingly informs the newspapers that the tires are unsafe. This leads to an investigation, a recall of the tires, and to a penalty for the tire manufacturer. Typically, such an engineer would be fired; perhaps he would be blackballed in the industry. And typically, no professional engineering organization would come to his defense for upholding its code. Yet such a defense seems professionally and morally mandatory if professional organizations expect their members to take their codes seriously and to live by them.

The Professions in Businesses

The case of the whistle blower in the tire factory is a classic instance of a professional conflict between the demands of a professional code and the demands of an employer. Though any employee may have blown the whistle, the engineering code placed a special and more stringent obligation on engineers to be concerned with public safety.

A professional code of conduct may demand more of professionals than of ordinary workers. If a professional is self-employed he may be able to live according to a higher standard of conduct. But what if he is employed by a corporation that demands he conform to the letter of the law? Does he carry with him special obligations and does a company act immorally if it does not respect these higher obligations?

The situation is especially difficult for engineers, nurses, and others who work for large corporations, hospitals, or firms. Engineers and nurses are treated as if their only duty is to obey orders and do what they are told. What does the nurse do when hospital rules require a doctor to scrub before an operation but he refuses to do so and tells her to mind her own business? What does an engineer do who feels the safety of some design is questionable and is told that for cost reasons the company refuses to change the design? What if an actuary sees that what he has produced is used in a way that he did not intend or that may be misleading, even though in his report he took pains to make sure his methods and assumptions were clear? In none of these cases may the danger to the public be serious enough to mandate whistle blowing. But in each case a professional would rightly feel his or her professional code demands that he or she take some action. Does loyalty to one's professional code take precedence over loyalty to one's employer?

There is no agreement on the appropriate answer. The typical professional code is not written to handle this problem, nor do the professional societies insist that employers respect the right of professionals in their employ to follow the letter and the spirit of the professional codes.

Members of the professions, just as everyone else who works for a firm, have the obligation not to do what is immoral. They have the obligation to employ their knowledge as they deem appropriate, to warn of unsafe products, illegal activities, and dangerous work conditions. But they do not have the responsibility to make final judgments that appropriately belong to management. Typically, an engineering judgment, a legal judgment, and a medical judgment is only part of the relevant information that goes into a managerial judgment. Professionals should make their professional views and concerns known. They should insist that public safety be protected when it is clearly threatened. But they have no obligation to insist that their way of doing things be observed or that their fears carry the day in a disputed area. The special obligations of those in professions require them to do more than others, be more sensitive to how their work is used, and be more alert to violations of ethical standards in their firms. Yet even here we can distinguish between what they are morally required to do as individuals from what they are required to do by their professional codes and hence, what they are professionally required to do. The limits on what they are professionally required to do are set not only by the code but also by the extent to which the profession as a whole is willing to support them.

Journalists have long fought for the right to preserve the secrecy of their sources. In their fight against courts and employers, they have generally been supported by their fellow journalists, their newspapers or TV stations, and the news media. Such support is an indication of a profession's commitment to a principle. The right to preserve the confidentiality of one's sources is a right that the profession has insisted on and convincingly defended. A similar right to confidentiality is claimed and generally given to priests in the confessional, lawyers and their clients, and to doctors and their patients.

Members of the various professions may have special rights and duties that outweigh their obligations to corporate loyalty and obedience. But until the profession as a whole—its members and its professional organizations—stand up and defend those professionals who strive to live up to the higher code by which they are supposed to live, neither the public nor most employers will take such rights and duties very seriously.

The Professions as Business

To contrast the professions and business is to give only a partial picture, for many members of the professions are also businessmen. Lawyers and engineers frequently move up the corporate ladder to management positions. Lawyers, doctors, accountants, consulting engineers, and members of many other professions are in business for themselves. As more and more groups claim the status of professions, the line between the professions and business blurs even more.

In considering the professions as businesses we shall focus only on a few aspects that tend to distinguish them from other businesses: restriction of entry to the field, restrictions on competition, and service to the public.

We have already seen that the medical profession has practical control of most aspects of the health industry. For many years there has been a shortage of doctors —at least in certain areas of the country. Rural areas and ghettos, for instance, are poorly served. Doctors as a profession set the standards that must be attained to practice medicine. They control the degree requirements for the M.D., they also decide how many doctors should be trained in their medical schools, and how large the medical schools should be. They also set up testing and other procedures required before one is allowed to practice medicine. All of these practices can be justified. Yet when doctors trained abroad have difficulty becoming licensed and when the shortage remains chronic despite a large pool of applicants for medical school, the profession is open to the charge of restricting entry. The charge gains strength as we notice that doctors are now typically among the more affluent members of society, whereas in previous eras they were among the less affluent. The responsibility for supplying doctors to all sectors of society is a responsibility held collectively by the professional.

Entry into the legal profession has also become more difficult than it once was, though the supply has tended to keep up with and at times even to exceed the demand.

Would society be better off if it were deprofessionalized? Have the professions become too strong? Have they won protective legislation that makes their services necessary without reason? Could midwives and paraprofessionals perform some of the services that are now the exclusive right of doctors? Are lawyers really needed to draw up wills, file for divorce, and to defend those charged with minor offenses? Can the law be simplified so that the intelligent layman could adequately handle these and similar tasks? The answer is not clear and is still hotly debated. Yet a comparative study of the United States and other countries shows evidence that we are overlegalized and overdoctored.

What of the other professions? The techniques of licensing and claims to specialized knowledge have made entry into certain areas more difficult. When used to keep fees up and to keep competition out, such techniques are clearly not in the public's interest.

Restrictions on competition among those already in a profession affect two areas in particular: professional limitations on advertising and the setting of fees.

The prohibition on advertising by doctors, lawyers, architects, and members of other professions has a long history not restricted to the United States. The prohibition, moreover, has frequently been included in codes of professional conduct and backed up by law. Many reasons are given for the prohibition. Some point to the outrageous claims made by quacks and peddlers of patent remedies for diseases ranging from the plague to cancer. Others claim that if doctors, lawyers, and others could advertise, the public would be poorly served. The best advertisers rather than the best practitioners would probably get the most patients and clients. Furthermore, the personal relation of doctor to patient and lawyer to client is developed and not just promoted. They are neither attracted nor established by advertising. A third claim is that advertising undermines the dignity of the professional. Clearly, though the arguments carry some weight with respect to some advertising, they do not make a very strong case for the total prohibition of it.

The prohibition against advertising by the professions has been found to be unconstitutional—an abridgement of First Amendment rights of freedom of speech and the press. The professional codes have been changed to reflect this. Yet we have not seen a rash of advertising by doctors, lawyers, architects, and others. Why not? Two answers suggest themselves. One is that the members of these professions have been raised on the prohibition against advertising, are unaccustomed to advertising, and are therefore not advertising from past habit. The other is that the absence of advertising has always benefited the professions and not the public. A lack of advertising reflects a lack of competition. By restricting entry, doctors have all the patients they can handle. Why seek more through advertising? Removing the law against advertising and removing the statement in the codes against advertising has had little effect on actual practice.

The second area of concern is the setting of fees by the professions. Is this unfair restraint of trade? Members of the professions, it is claimed, should not haggle over fees. To do so would be demeaning, undignified, and in a word, unprofessional. A second argument claims that a sliding fee schedule would give the professional an upper hand when faced with a desperate individual who needs his help, but put a professional in a poor bargaining position vis-à-vis a large firm. The same service would cost the individual who could least afford it more than it would the rich corporation. The setting of fees assures equal access. It guarantees equal fees for equal work. But it does not justify the reluctance to reveal fees or the lack of competition in setting professional fees. The ordinary person rarely shops around and inquires how much the various doctors in a town charge; nor is this part of general knowledge. The ordinary person's approach to medical and legal service is strangely removed from consideration of the fees that members of the profession charge. There is no obvious competition on the basis of fees. Some professions have even recommended minimum fees to be charged for certain services, a practice clearly in the interest of the profession and not in the interest of the public.

The practice of payment by results further protects the self-interest of the professional at the expense of the public. It is rarely practiced by doctors. They do not charge only if the patient gets better or only if the patient survives the operation. They charge for the use of their skill and time. The practice of charging by results is more common in civil suits in which lawyers take a certain percentage of the amount awarded their clients if they win the suit and nothing if they do not; however, the temptation is to sue for a larger amount than otherwise justifiable so as to collect higher fees.

The dual role of businessman and professional involves many potential conflicts of interest in which making money is opposed to serving the client or patient as best one can. Such conflicts make disclosure all the more necessary. Those professions that prefer to work under a veil of tacit secrecy must be more open to the public scrutiny of their business practices.

Unions

The role of unions and of labor union leaders in some ways parallels that of professional associations and members of the professions. In fact, some people include labor union leaders among the professions.

Unions have a specific constituency—their members. They do not claim to serve the larger society or to have the good of society as their aim. Their goal is to protect and promote the interests of their members. They typically take management as their adversary. Unions have championed the right to strike and have used it as an effective weapon. They engage in collective bargaining and press the demands of the workers as forcefully and fully as possible. They have achieved a good deal of success.

We have spoken at length about the immoral practices of business and management. We have spoken about the responsibilities and rights of workers. We can also evaluate unions from a moral point of view; and not just a few moral stones have been cast at them.

The right to strike has been widely accepted. The discrepancy between the power and resources of big business and the resources of the individual workers put the latter at the mercy of the former. Workers have had to unite to gain a position of equality from which to bargain with management about higher wages, shorter hours, vacations with pay, safer working conditions, retirement plans, and other similar benefits. Management has frequently passed on some of the cost of these benefits to their customers in the form of higher prices. But increased productivity has made it possible for companies to retain the same rate of profit despite paying higher wages to workers. The unions have also helped the plight of nonunion workers by bargaining for standards that become the norm for all.

Charges of corruption within unions need not delay us long. If union leaders use union money illegally or for their own private purposes, such actions are clearly immoral. They do not require discussion.

Three issues are of current concern: public service strikes, restriction of entry by unions and the establishing of closed shops, and the failure of unions to consider the results of their actions on society as a whole.

Public service strikes are strikes by federal, state, and municipal employees. Should teachers, firemen, policemen, municipal hospital employees, and members of the armed forces be allowed to strike? Enough strikes by public school teachers have taken place that a precedent for the right to strike has been established. The claimed harm to children has not been as great as feared. Firemen, policemen, and municipal hospital employees have also gone on strike in various parts of the country. When they do, they harm not only those who hire them—namely, the city, state, or federal bureaucracies, or departments that hire them, but also endanger the lives and safety of ordinary citizens who have no say in the settlement and no responsibility for the negotiations. Is this fair? A strike by employees against an employer aims at forcing him to suffer greater demage by failure of the workers to work than he would by giving in to their demands. Is the same true of public service strikes? Fireman, policemen, and municipal hospital workers work for the city, state, or nation. They are paid from money raised by public taxes. If their demands are not totally unreasonable, if the wages or other benefits they seek are in line with what others in the private sector are making, then by striking they apply pressure on the members of society to bear an increase in taxes or make cuts elsewhere in the services they receive. The pressure is appropriately placed on the public, since they work for the public. But what of the lives threatened by such strikes? The problem is a difficult one, and one that has been handled in a variety of ways. Sometimes the supervisory personnel in the organization take over the basic jobs; sometimes police are called upon to man the firehouses; sometimes the state reserves or the army are called in to handle the jobs of those on strike. Sometimes, also, if a true emergency arises, those on strike—or at least some of them—pitch in to help out.

America has not adopted the practice of the general strike in which all government employees leave at the same time for a set period—usually twenty-four or forty-eight hours. Such strikes are common in some European countries and make an effective point for a short period of time.

The justification for public sector strikes is that strikes are the only effective way such workers can make their plight known and can apply pressure to achieve some of the benefits enjoyed by the workers in the private sector.

Members of the armed forces have recently raised the question of their right to strike, but they have won little support. The qualities that are important in battle are immediate response to authority and trust in one's commanders. Soldiers are no more permitted to do what is immoral than anyone else. Yet within those bounds obedience is essential to their survival and their effectiveness. Is such obedience undermined by the development of a strike mentality? Some people argue that it is. When, after all, would a strike by the military be most effective? When the military is most needed, is the reply. Yet that is precisely the time when a strike is most inappropriate from the point of view of those who wish to be defended by the military. What about strikes in peacetime by a peactime army? The case justifying the military's use of the strike technique has yet to be forcefully and convincingly made; but that does not mean it cannot or will not some day be made.

The second charge to which unions have been subject is that they artificially restrict entry into their ranks and prevent those who do not wish to join the union from obtaining employment through the use of the closed shop technique. Unions set the conditions of entry and frequently have a monopoly of the labor force within an industry. In order to be employed by a certain industry, one must belong to the appropriate union. A policy according to which only union members are employed in an enterprise is called a closed shop policy.

Is it fair for unions to restrict membership in certain trades so that the number of members will be kept lower than the demand for them? Such a device obviously makes each member more valuable and able to command a higher wage. But he is able to do so at the expense of those who would wish to enter the marketplace and are prevented from doing so. If it is unfair for business to restrict trade and gain monopolies, it is unfair for some workers to restrict other workers from pursuing their interests and engaging in the type of work they prefer. Both are attempts to curtail competition for the benefit of the one restricting entry.

Is the same argument true of closed shops? The argument here is somewhat different. In a closed shop situation, the union typically does not restrict union membership. Often the point of a closed shop is to encourage membership. But the closed shop allows only union members to work in the plant or industry. The argument given in defense of a closed shop is twofold. If a plant is allowed to hire nonunion labor, then it can hire such labor at nonunion rates. Once a plant is able to hire people at cheaper than union rates, it will find it to its advantage to do so. As a result it will tend to replace union labor with nonunion labor. The success that unions have achieved will thus be undercut. The second argument claims that if a plant hires both union and nonunion labor and treats them both equally, workers will have little incentive to join the union. Why should they, if they receive the same benefits without having to pay union dues? The result in this case is once again to undercut and weaken the union, deplete its coffers, and make it financially impossible to fund a strike.

Both arguments carry a good deal of weight. They must be balanced against the right of an individual worker to seek a job and to have the option of not joining a union. He should not be forced to do so if he does not wish to do so. He should not be prevented from working or have his options narrowly restricted because he prefers not to join a union. The issue in some states has been decided at the polls. Right-to-work laws have been proposed that guarantee the right of a worker to seek employment without joining a union. If this means breaking up the closed shop, it robs unions of one of their key implements. The last word on this controversy has not yet been spoken.

The last charge we shall look at concerning unions is that they tend to ignore the public good and are willing to sacrifice it in order to achieve their own ends. The union practice of featherbedding, for example, preserves the jobs of those employees who would otherwise be laid off due to technological improvements. A frequently cited case was the requirement, during the transition from steam to electric trains, that each train have a fireman even though the train was run by electricity and did not need a fireman. The fireman was carried on each run, though he had no work to do. He continued to be paid and this pay eventually came out of the pockets of those who used the train. Unions have also been accused of fueling inflation by seeking higher wages in an unending spiral—each demand fueling other demands that in turn raise the demands of the first group. Each raise increases the cost of the products produced and in the long run, may even lead to unemployment and recession.

Unions, like businesses, sometimes act in terms of vested interests to the detriment of the general good. Union leaders claim, however, that in the long run (even in the particular instances cited), their actions lead to more good than harm, not only for their own workers but also for all workers and for society in general. Such claims should not be taken at face value. The argument is a shorthand version of a utilitarian argument and can properly be evaluated only by considering particular cases and by attempting to trace out the good and bad done to all those affected by the action.

Unions and the professions are important aspects of the American business scene. But we should watch and weigh their actions from a moral point of view as objectively and critically as we do the actions of businesses.

Further Reading

American Bar Association. *Code of Professional Responsibility and Code of Judicial Conduct*. Chicago: American Bar Association, 1977.

Ashley, Jo Ann. *Hospitals, Paternalism, and the Role of the Nurse*. New York: Teachers College Press, 1976.

Baum, Robert J., and Flores, Albert, eds. *Ethical Problems in Engineering*. Troy, N.Y.: Center for the Study of the Human Dimensions of Science and Technology, 1978.

Bennion, F.A.R. *Professional Ethics: The Consultant Professions and Their Code*. London: Charles Knight & Co. Ltd., 1969.

Clapp, Jane. *Professional Ethics and Insignia*. Metuchen, N.J.: Scarecrow Press, Inc., 1974.

Freidson, Eliot. *Profession of Medicine: A Study of the Sociology of Applied Knowledge*. New York: Dodd, Mead & Company, 1977.

Hazard, Geoffrey C., Jr. *Ethics in the Practice of Law*. New Haven: Yale University Press, 1978.

Larson, Magali Sarfatti. *The Rise of Professionalism: A Sociological Analysis*. Berkeley: University of California Press, 1977.

Layton, Edwin. *The Revolt of the Engineers*. Cleveland: Case Western Reserve University, 1971.

Morre, Wilbert. *The Professions: Roles and Rules.* New York: Russell Sage Foundation, 1970.

Pirsig, Maynard E. *Cases and Materials on Professional Responsibility.* St. Paul: West Publishing Co., 1970.

Public Employee Unions: A Study of the Crisis in Public Sector Labor Relations. San Francisco: Institute for Contemporary Studies, 1976.

14

Multinationals and Morality

Multinationals are corporations that operate extensively in more than one country, usually through branches or subsidiaries engaged in production, marketing, or both. They pose special moral problems. Since their activities are not confined to a single nation, no one nation can effectively control them. National law can circumscribe the activities of national firms and government action can offset the ill effects of certain activities of a firm. But no supernational state exists to confine or control the many varied activities of multinationals. Some agreements exist among nations that restrict to a limited extent the activities of such firms. But the control is far short of what is possible for firms operating in only one country. Critics of multinationals loudly proclaim that the multinational corporations operate to benefit themselves and their interests with no moral or legal constraints on their activities.

When we analyzed the capitalist system in the United States, we noted that government fulfills many necessary functions, such as keeping competition fair and protecting the interests of workers and consumers. There is no effective way to prevent firms on the international level, however, from forming cartels and controlling prices and production. We see this clearly in the case of the OPEC nations. Critics charge that the large international oil corporations (the seven largest have been called The Seven

Sisters) have conspired to limit the production of oil, creating false shortages, and driving up the price without any regard to whom they hurt by such action. Since these companies operate internationally, it is not possible for any government to check their books or to prevent such collusion. Other multinationals are charged with supporting repressive governments that serve their interests, exploiting workers in underdeveloped countries, marketing dangerous drugs and unsafe equipment, and disrupting the culture and traditions of other nations.

Multinational corporations have their parent headquarters not only in the United States, but increasingly in Japan, Germany, and other industrialized countries as well. We shall, however, concentrate on American based firms. The moral issues involved in the above charges are many and complex. We can illustrate the difficulties and sort out some of the complexities by discussing three controversial situations: (1) the marketing of drugs abroad which are prohibited in the United States; (2) the transfer of dangerous industries to underdeveloped countries; and (3) the operation of U.S. firms in South Africa.

Multinational Drug Companies

The control of drugs in the United States is probably more restrictive than in any other country in the world. The Food and Drug Administration (FDA) has adopted stringent requirements for testing drugs, and any drug allowed on the market in the United States must pass long and comprehensive testing. The FDA also determines which drugs require a doctor's prescription.

The argument in defense of the FDA's actions is that lives and health are at risk in the taking of any drug. Unless a drug is found to be safe it should not be sold. If a drug is known to have certain dangerous side effects, it should be sold only under certain conditions for people under a doctor's care. If the drug is known to cause cancer or some other serious illness, it should not be sold at all, or only under rigidly controlled conditions. The drug thalidomide was not authorized for sale in the United States but was prescribed by doctors in Europe. Its use by pregnant women resulted in large numbers of seriously deformed babies. Such disasters explain the FDA's insistence on high standards.

American drug companies, however, often feel that the FDA standards are too rigid, the testing required is too expensive, cumbersome, and long, and that it is inappropriate to impose U.S. standards on the operation of these companies in other countries. They claim that as long as they do not act illegally in those countries, there is no reason why they should not market whatever is allowed.

The morality of the action of these companies is not settled by determining whether what they do in other countries is legal. But the morality of their actions is also not settled simply by determining whether they live up to American standards abroad. The standards may be appropriate for Americans but inappropriate for people of some other countries because of special circumstances in those countries.

We can distinguish several typical kinds of cases and investigate them from a moral point of view. Consider the following three hypothetical cases.

Case 1: Drug Company XYZ produces a drug that relieves the symptoms of migraine headaches. It is marketed in the United States and initially thought to be safe enough for sale over the counter. After it is widely used, however, it is determined that one of the side effects in a significant number of patients is severe depression, sometimes leading to suicide. The drug is therefore considered too dangerous for sale over the counter in the United States, and is allowed only for use by those under a doctor's care. Doctors are warned of the dangerous side effects and cautioned to be alert to signs of depression in their patients. The drug is sold in many countries besides the United States. After the U.S. action, some other countries take similar action. Others do not. Drug Company XYZ continues to market the product in these other countries. It is sold over the counter and no information is provided about its possible dangerous side effects.

Case 2: Drug Company MNO develops and tests a drug that is slightly more effective than insulin for diabetics. After some use the drug is found to produce cancer. Its continued use is forbidden in the United States. Drug Company MNO continues to market it where it is not forbidden to do so.

Case 3: Drug Company ABC develops a drug which helps cure glaucoma. There is no other effective drug for this ailment on the market. After some extended use the drug is found to produce cancer in a significant number of cases. The drug is taken off the market in the United States. The drug company continues to market it in those countries in which it is legal to do so.

The three cases raise a number of different issues.

Is the action of Company XYZ morally justifiable, and if not, why not? In trying to decide, let us consider two substantive second-order principles which might apply. Principle 1: A drug company should not sell any drug that it knows to be harmful in any way. Principle 2: A drug company should not sell any drug which it knows to be harmful without informing the purchaser of the harmful effects.

The first of the principles is too strong. In Case 1, Drug Company XYZ was allowed to sell the drug in the United States to those who had a doctor's prescription for it. It is morally justifiable for the FDA to allow some drugs to be sold which have possibly harmful side effects. The reason is that the side effects are usually less serious than the illness that is being treated; the risks involved are worth taking, providing the patient and the doctor know about them and decide to take the risks, exercising due catuion. The second principle is morally sound. We can justify it in a number of ways. If we consider the purchase of the drug as a free transaction, such transactions are justifiable if both parties have the relevant knowledge concerning the transaction and freely enter into it. If the drug company knows of the drug's ill effects but does not disclose these to the purchaser, the latter does not have information necessary for him to make a competent decision concerning the transaction. To keep this information from the buyer is morally inappropriate, since the buyer will assume that the product is safe. The transaction is thus not morally justifiable. We can reach the same conclusion by asking whether the drug company is treating the purchaser as an end rather than simply as a means of earning profit. Since it does not warn him of the dangers of the drug the company treats him only as a means, and hence is treating him immorally.

Adopting the second principle, therefore, Drug Company XYZ can be morally faulted not for selling the drug but for selling it without informing the potential purchaser of the dangers of its use. Note that if this analysis is correct, it is morally permissible for Drug Company XYZ to market the drug as an over-the-counter product in the countries where this is allowed, even though it is not allowed to do so in the United States and other countries. The argument does not claim that the U.S. standards are the only appropriate ones, that all countries must adopt them, or that drug companies must adhere to them wherever they operate. This is not morally required. Standards other than those adopted by the FDA may be appropriate in other countries. But some standards are necessary. It would clearly be wrong to sell drugs that did little good and were known to be harmful, even if the selling of such drugs were legally permitted in some countries. Drug companies are morally bound not to inflict harm on others knowingly. To the extent that they do, drug companies act immorally even if they are acting legally.

In Case 3 there is no other drug for the disease, whereas in Case 2, an alternative drug is available. The argument for marketing the drug (in Case 2) which is only slightly more effective but also more dangerous than insulin is difficult to make. We might argue that if the company makes the risks known to the public, then it may sell the drug to those who wish to buy it. But why anyone would wish to buy it is not clear for the harm significantly outweighs the benefit of using it instead of insulin. Thus, if we assume that only those who really do not know what they are doing would use the alternative drug instead of insulin, we can conclude that despite its issuing a warning, the drug company is trading on the ignorance of the consumer. To so trade at the consumer's expense is to take unfair advantage and hence to act immorally. The case, however, is not as clearly immoral as it would be if the drug were marketed without any warning of its dangers.

The drug in Case 3 helps cure glaucoma but tends to produce cancer in some people. There is no other drug for this ailment on the market. Once again, the drug can be morally sold only if those who buy and use it are informed of its dangers. But even when informed of the risks, people may choose to use it, preferring to chance getting cancer rather than suffering blindness. That the drug is not allowed in the United States indicates that the FDA does not think the risk worth the cure. But others may feel differently and weigh the odds differently. If a person is relatively old and if the drug takes many years to produce cancer, he may feel the risk is worth taking. His doctor may agree.

One principle being argued for here is essentially the principle of informed consent. In order for the transaction to be morally permissible, the purchaser of the drug must be truly informed. For instance, a warning sentence in small print on page three of a technical information sheet inside the box is hardly adequate notice of the danger. The purchaser should be informed of any danger before purchasing the drug, and the information (e.g., on the box) should be readily visible and understandable.

If adequate information about the ill effects of the drug is not supplied to the potential purchaser, the practice is immoral. If adequate information is supplied, there is no alternative drug, and the risk is reasonable, the sale of the drug is still justifiable. However, if there is a similar or better product available that does not have the ill effects of the drug, the latter should not be marketed at all.

Some countries are unable to fund the extensive testing operations conducted by the United States government or required by it. These countries have passed laws, however, which prohibit a drug compnay from marketing a drug which has been prohibited for sale in the country of its origin. Some drug companies, wishing to market their drugs but also wishing to abide by the law, have adopted a number of practices for which they have been morally condemned. Some have added an inert substance to a drug so that technically it is not the same item, even though it has all the same effects. Then the drug has been marketed under a different name in the foreign country. Other countries have produced the drug that has been out-lawed in the United States in a third country where it is not outlawed, and then they have shipped it elsewhere. Both of these practices are within the letter of the law in the countries where the drugs are finally sold, even if they are clearly outside the spirit of those laws. The morality of these practices depends not on whether the law has been circumvented but rather on whether the companies acting in this way are doing harm to the people who take the drug and whether they are supplying the adequate and appropriate information. Their critics frequently claim otherwise. If this is so, then the companies act immorally. The cases illustrate the difficulty of dealing with multinationals. How laws can be rewritten to prohibit the sale of drugs outlawed in the country of its origin is an unsolved problem. One answer could be for all nations to adopt similar rules and standards; or an agency such as WHO or UNESCO could set minimal standards. Some nations might then adopt more stringent regulations. Until international standards are adopted, the tempta-tion of drug companies to abide only by the legal minimum in each country will remain. Succumbing to the temptation will benefit the drug companies mainly at the expense of the poorer and less developed countries—those who in the long run will be least able to cope with the negative effects of such drugs on their people.

The Transfer of Dangerous Industries to Underdeveloped Countries

Consider the following case: Asbestos USA (a fictitious name) produces asbestos products for the United States market. It competes with asbestos products made in Mexico. It is able to compete, despite the fact that Mexican labor is so much cheaper than labor in the United States, because it operates more efficiently and with more advanced equipment than do the Mexican companies. Recently the United States government determined that asbestos caused cancer. Those exposed to it for long periods had a significantly higher rate of cancer than others. The rate was especially high for those who worked in asbestos plants. The United States therefore passed legislation requiring the introduction of a series of safeguards for people working in asbestos plants. Asbestos USA calculated the cost of implementing the safeguards and decided it could not implement them and still stay in business. Rather than close down completely, however, it moved its plant to Mexico which has not passed comparable safety legislation. Asbestos USA continues to market its product in the United States though it manufactures its products in Mexico. There it operates its equipment the same way as it previously did in the United States; however, it only has to pay its workers the going wage for the industry in Mexico.

This situation involves several moral issues. Since Asbestos USA knows that working with asbestos without the proper safeguards will produce cancer in the Mexican workers, critics claim that the company acts immorally if it does not protect the Mexican workers the way it would have to protect its American workers. A second charge is that Asbestos USA exploits Mexican workers since it pays them less than what it would pay American workers. A third complaint is that companies such as Asbestos USA exploit Mexico by producing items to be marketed not in Mexico but in the United States. Is Asbestos USA acting immorally in moving its plant as indicated?

(a) Exposure to asbestos tends to produce cancer in a significant number of people. This is the overriding consideration to which the American government has reacted. No company, it has ruled, has the right to expose its workers to cancer if this can be prevented. The ruling is a defensible one. It applies to all industries and to all asbestos manufacturers. But obviously the U.S. rule applies only in the United States. It does not apply to asbestos factories in other countries. The United States government could protect its home industries by passing duties on imported asbestos products sufficient to make it possible for U.S. companies both to produce asbestos products under safe conditions and also to compete with foreign industries. If Asbestos USA's imports were subject to an import duty, it would have little incentive to move to Mexico. But since the safety requirements were passed without the concomitant protection against imports, it moved its plant. It serves its shareholders better this way than it does by going out of business. Since the asbestos products would be bought from Mexican firms anyway, why not have an American company serving the United States as well as Mexican companies? These considerations, however, fail to respond to the major issue—Is it moral to expose employees to the danger of cancer when this can be prevented? If the answer is no, then it is not moral to so expose Mexican workers.

Which second-order principle is applicable to this case? One candidate might be: It is immoral to hire anyone to do work that is in some way dangerous to his or her life or health. But the principle, as stated, is too strong. Any job may be dangerous in some way; therefore, it if it were immoral to hire someone to do work that was in any way dangerous, no one could be hired to do many jobs that seem perfectly acceptable. We also acknowledge that some jobs are more dangerous than others. A fireman is highly paid to put out fires, but he knows he risks his life in doing so. Policemen are also highly paid to risk their lives. Yet most people would be reluctant to say that hiring people to do these jobs is immoral. The immorality, therefore, does not come from hiring people to do work that involves risk to life or health. But we can defend the principle that it is immoral to hire someone to do work that is known to the employer to involve significant risk without informing the prospective employee of that risk. This principle of informed consent is comparable to the one we developed in discussing the selling of dangerous drugs, and is defensible in similar ways.

If we adopt this principle, then Asbestos USA could be morally right to hire workers in Mexico with working conditions that would not be allowed in the United States if the potential workers were warned of the dangers. We can assume that once warned of the dangers, the workers would agree to work in the plant only if they received more pay than they would for comparable work in a factory in which they were not exposed to the danger of cancer. If this were not the case, it would be an indication that the people who were hired were in some way being forced into the jobs and were not free agents contracting freely and knowingly to do dangerous work at pay they considered appropriate to make up for the increased risk. A contract between employer and employee is fair if both parties enter into the contract with adequate appropriate knowledge and if both freely agree to the terms of the contract.

The critics of Asbestos USA contend that the Mexican workers, even if informed of the dangers and paid somewhat higher wages than other workers are paid (Brazil requires triple pay for dangerous work), are forced because of the lack of work in Mexico to accept employment in asbestos plants at less than adequate pay. Hence, the critics contend, despite protestations of informed consent, the workers are forced to take such jobs and are exploited in them.

Informed consent is *necessary* for the action to be moral, but it is not *sufficient*. There are some things (e.g., selling oneself into slavery) to which no one can morally consent. There are also some conditions which are immoral for an employer to impose on his workers, even if the latter agree to work under those conditions. Consent is not enough because people who desperately need money may agree to work under almost any conditions. Built into capitalism is the tendency of employers to pay workers as little as possible and to spend as little as possible on a safe work environment. In the United States this tendency has been offset by unionization and government legislation. In countries where it is not offset, employers can take unfair advantage of workers and engage in immoral practices. If Asbestos USA wishes to operate its plant in Mexico, it can morally do so only if it informs the workers of the risk in terms they can understand, if it pays them more for undertaking the risk, and if it lowers the risk to some acceptable level. It need not be the level demanded by the Occupational Safety and Health Act (OSHA) in the United States, but it cannot morally be a level so low that risk is maximized rather than minimized. It would also be immoral not to eliminate risks which could be removed without extravagant cost. Mexican plants in which asbestos floats freely through the air, collecting like cobwebs, and in which workers do not even have paper masks, are clear examples of minimum safety standards not being observed.

Why does the Mexican government not pass laws similar to those in the United States concerning safeguards for workers? Why do not all nations pass such laws, making a move such as that by Asbestos USA unprofitable? The answer is that not all countries are as affluent as the United States. A wealthy country can afford to spend more to protect the health of its people than can a much poorer country. The standards of cleanliness and safety that the United States can enforce by law are much higher than businesses in many countries could afford. Traditions also vary from country to country. There is no reason to think that the traditions of the United States are the only right ones and that all the world must become like us. This attitude is itself condemned by many as a form of U.S. imperialism. We are a democratic country and our people enjoy a large measure of freedom. Some other countries are not democratic, or are much less so. The literacy rate and the level of education of the average person is much higher in the United States than in many other countries. We must be careful not to set our standards as the model of what every nation should do if it wishes to be moral. Our standards do not constitute the moral norm. Morality is universal and does not differ from country to country. But since conditions do differ from country to country, what morality demands in different countries may well vary. What may be required by the principle of utility in one country may not be required by the same principle in another country because the consequences of adopting the practice in each of the two countries may differ significantly. What may be prima facie right in both countries may be the proper thing to do in one country but not in the other because of conflicts with other duties or rights due to differing circumstances.

If we return to our example of Asbestos USA, the Mexican government sometimes passes different laws concerning health and safety from those passed in the United States. We cannot conclude that the Mexican government cares less for the welfare of its people than does the American government for its citizens. United States industry is more technologically developed than Mexican industry. Mexican industry is more labor intensive on the whole than is U.S. industry. Mexico seeks to attract foreign industry to help develop its potential, to train its people in work skills, and to bring in tax and other revenue. Imported industry also provides work for Mexicans who would otherwise be unemployed. Suppose that for these and similar reasons the Mexican government decides that it gains more by allowing somewhat unsafe factory conditions than by setting standards that would preclude the development of industry in the country. Suppose that the workers prefer to work in Asbestos USA than not to work at all. We can complain that it is unfair for people not to have work or that the contract of employment with such people is not free and hence morally marred. But granting all of this, it might still be true that Mexico and the Mexican people benefit more by Asbestos USA locating its plant in Mexico than by not being there. If this were the case, then the move of Asbestos USA would not be immoral, providing it fulfilled the above conditions.

Does this mean that it is moral to export cancer producing industries to Mexico and other countries where the regulations are more lenient than in the United

States? The argument so far considers Asbestos USA an isolated case. What will be the effect on Mexico and its people twenty years hence, if such industries move there in significant numbers? Are the country and people better off without such industries? Companies that wish to act morally must consider and attempt to answer this question. How will the cancer cases be treated? What will happen to families of workers who get cancer? Are health provisions and pension plans provided for the workers?

Ideally there should be international agreements on minimally acceptable standards of safety in industry. In the absence of such standards moral sense and pressure must function until law can equalize the position of the worker vis-à-vis the employer. But moral sense and pressure seem to play little role in the policies of many international corporations. Paradoxically, some underdeveloped countries see the conditions for moral action that have been discussed as impediments to the development of their countries, as requirements that keep them underdeveloped, and as the moralizing of Americans who are basically well off and do not understand other situations and the aspirations of other people. The difficulty of knowing what will benefit the people in such countries most, and of knowing what the people truly want—as opposed to what some governmental leaders say—is enormous. The difficulty forces us to be careful not to confuse what is morally right with what is proper for Americans. But American companies operating abroad that wish to be moral should not ignore the moral dimension of their actions and should not simply follow the letter of the law in the countries in which they operate.

(b) Is Asbestos USA immoral if it does not pay its Mexican employees the same wages that it paid its U.S. employees? The claim that it is immoral if it does not is a difficult one to sustain. Justice requires that people who do the same work should receive comparable pay. A woman can rightly complain of injustice if she is paid less than a man for doing comparable work. A Mexican could similarly and rightly complain of injustice if he were paid less than an American for doing comparable work. But the principle applies only within the same factory, plant, or office. Within the United States, for instance, the cost of living is higher in some parts of the country than in others. People who work for the same firm and do comparable work may receive a higher wage if they work in New York than if they work in Mobile, Alabama, assuming that living in New York is more expensive than living in Mobile. People who work for one company, moreover, may receive more or less pay than people who do similar work for another company. Assuming the freedom of workers to move from job to job and assuming differences in cost of living in different parts of the country, wage differences are justifiable.

If we apply this to the operation of Asbestos USA in Mexico, we can argue that it would be unfair to pay Mexicans less than U.S. nationals for the same work in the Mexican plant. The principle of comparable pay for comparable work applies in Mexico just as it does in the United States. But the claim that Mexicans working in a U.S.-owned plant in Mexico must be paid the same as Americans working in a comparable plant in the U.S. does not follow from the principle of comparable pay for comparable work.

We saw that within the United States people doing comparable work in different cities for the same company might receive different salaries. If the cost of living is lower in Mexico, then the pay can legitimately be lower. In Mexico, industry is more labor intensive. More people are required to produce the same number of goods than in a machine intensive form of production. To be competitive, the wages in labor intensive situations must be lower than in the machine intensive situation. Thus several factors enter into calculating comparative wages. Cost of living is one differential factor. Standard of living is a second. Mexican workers may work for lower wages because their standard of living is lower than that of American workers. A third factor is the competition for labor. A fourth is the productivity of the labor employed.

If Asbestos USA competes with Mexican asbestos firms in selling its product, then it cannot compete effectively if it pays its workers more than Mexican firms simply because it is an American-owned company. It might pay them more if it is more efficient. Or it might charge less for its products than the competition, thus seeking to capture more of the market. If it needed more skilled labor than the Mexican firms, it would have to pay more for such labor and make up for it in efficiency. The point is that though Asbestos USA *may* exploit its Mexican workers, it does not engage in exploitation simply because it does not pay Mexican workers the same wages it paid its American employees in the United States. But this does not mean that it is morally permissible to pay its Mexican workers as little as the firm can get away with. Just as it is immoral to fail to protect the workers from blatant exposure to harm and risk, so it is immoral to pay them as little as possible, trading on their need.

The desirability of some minimal international standards is obvious. But there is no visible movement in this direction, and multinational corporations on the whole have not attempted to promote such standards.

(c) The third charge is that Asbestos USA exploits Mexico because it produces products there for sale in the United States. Is it immoral to do so? Suppose a German company made cars in the United States exclusively for export to Germany. Would we similarly claim that the German company was exploiting the United States? It is difficult to supply a principle under which we would make such a determination. We might try to defend the principle that unless a foreign company benefits the country in which it operates, it exploits that country for its own advantage, and so acts immorally. The principle is plausible. But it does not specify to what extent and in what way the host country must benefit. It rules out as immoral exploitation of one country by another that dominates the first in such a way that it can force it to act contrary to its own best interests. But if we consider the building of plants in sovereign states by firms from other countries, the former are able to prevent and prohibit such exploitation. There are many ways Asbestos USA might help the economy other than by producing its products for the Mexican market. Among other things, it supplies work for its Mexican employees, teaches skills to the people it employs, pays taxes to the government, provides work for those who must build the plant in the first place, purchases materials it needs locally to the advantage of the local economy, and so on.

Although some companies may exploit the countries in which they are located, it is not necessarily the case that all multinationals do so. Nor is it necessarily the case that unless a firm produces its goods for local consumption it is exploiting the country in which it is located.

The above analysis has not exonerated Asbestos USA on all counts. But it has argued that Asbestos USA is not automatically guilty of the immoral practices attributed to it by typical critics. Asbestos USA may exploit its workers; it may exploit the country; and the production practice in which it engages endangers its workers.

Though morality is universal, what is morally demanded is a function not only of moral principles but also of the particular circumstances to which they are applied. We have not touched on the question of what the moral obligations of a multinational are in a country in which the government is repressive and in which the leaders care more for their own good and benefit than for the good of their people. If a government itself exploits its people and encourages foreign exploitation of its people by foreign firms that pay taxes to the government or pays government officials directly, the government acts immorally. If a firm knowingly and willingly exploits its workers, even if it is legal to do so, it also acts immorally. But whether a particular firm is exploiting its workers is often a matter of considerable debate, not easily settled.

The critics of multinationals will have little patience with the analysis we have given. Even if multinationals *can* operate morally, they would assert that multinationals typically do not act morally. By outlining the conditions under which multinationals might act morally, the critics would maintain, we have given the impression that multinationals do act morally, and that attacks on them are unfounded. Such was not the intent. The temptations to act immorally are great in the international arena, and it would be surprising if many, even most companies did not succumb. The restraints on such activity must be international restraints, and the abuses of multinationals underscore the need for effective international controls—controls, however, that the present international climate has not strongly fostered.

U.S. Firms in South Africa

The situation in South Africa illustrates one of the major difficulties in multinational operations. The Union of South Africa practices a policy of racial segregation, discrimination, and oppression known as apartheid. It is condemned as immoral by many in the United States and in other countries throughout the world. It is justified and defended by many whites in South Africa as the morally allowable lesser of two evils.

Under apartheid the blacks in South Africa suffer extreme repression. Although they constitute the overwhelming majority of the population, they are allowed to live on only 13 percent of the land. The other 87 percent is reserved for the whites, who constitute only 17 percent of the population. The whites control the gold and diamond mines, the harbors, and the industrial areas. Blacks who wish to work in these areas are required to live in townships outside of the major cities. Since only males are allowed in the townships, the workers are separated from their families for the major part of the year. The blacks cannot vote, own property, politically organize, or join unions. They are systematically paid less than whites for the same work. They are not allowed to hold managerial positions of even the lowest kind. They are forced to use segregated eating, dressing, and toilet facilities.

United States companies began moving into South Africa as early as the 1880's. At that time they employed only whites and sold their products almost exclusively to the white community. The white community was the economically advanced and productive sector of the country and supplied the market for goods. The blacks lived in their own sections of the country in their traditional tribal ways. The whites set up and controlled the government. The blacks did not take part in any governmental activities, were not educated, and were not considered able to run the government or to have any impact on it. A colonial type of paternalism was exercised by the whites over the blacks.

Whatever one considers the morality of such colonial paternalism, it is understandable how and why companies from the United States initially saw their market as the white community and their employees as coming from that same community. The intent of these companies was to expand their markets and make a profit, and South Africa was a ripe market to develop. With time and the changes of over half a century, colonialism fell out of favor in Africa, the native inhabitants took over the reins of power in country after country and ran their own affairs. In South Africa, however, blacks did not succeed in gaining power and have been kept from doing so by the legal enforcement of apartheid. Some changes, however, did take place finally. Factories, as they expanded, found that there were not enough white people to fill the jobs available, and blacks were found able and willing to work in these factories. Fear of their achieving control in part motivated the government to draw up and enforce the apartheid laws. But as blacks entered the labor market, they also had money to buy goods and so represented a potential and as yet untapped market for goods.

American-controlled multinationals moved into South Africa in greater numbers to take advantage of the low wages they could pay blacks and the large market which South Africa represented. The profits earned by South African subsidiaries were often twice as much as the profits earned by the home-based mother company. Many black-dominated countries in Africa have placed embargoes on goods manufactured by U.S. companies operating in South Africa. But the local market is sufficient to make operation of subsidiaries in South Africa profitable for IBM, Ford, General Motors, Goodyear, Firestone, Exxon, Mobil, Kellogg's, Eli Lilly, Kodak, Control Data, and over 300 other U.S. companies.

Despite the protestations of the whites in South Africa, most people acknowledge that apartheid is immoral. It is blatant racial segregation, discrimination, and oppression. Let us assume the majority view. The moral issues that have surfaced have been of two kinds, related though separable. One is the question of whether U.S. multinationals can morally operate in South Africa. The other is whether U.S.

investors, especially university endowment associations and churches, should invest in companies that operate in South Africa.

1. U.S. Multinationals in South Africa

U.S. multinationals would not open subsidiaries in South Africa unless it were profitable to do so. South Africa has four conditions that make it attractive to U.S. companies. First, it has a stable government. U.S. companies are reluctant to open plants in countries with unstable governments for fear of losing their investments through nationalization or constant domestic turmoil. U.S. companies therefore have an interest in helping preserve stable governments. They tend not to care whether the government is repressive or dictatorial. That, they claim, is a local, political matter. But from a business point of view, a strong stable government is a guarantee of the safety of their investment. Second, South Africa has a large potential market. Its population is 28 million people. Even though only 17 percent of the population is white, that represents a market of close to 5 million people; the other 23 million people form a pool that can be increasingly tapped. The U.S. companies are the chief suppliers of consumer goods and of advanced technology. Third, South Africa has a large and cheap supply of labor. The standard of living of the blacks is extremely low and the scale paid them by South African firms is about one-fourth the wages paid to white workers. As more blacks are brought into the work force, the market for manufactured goods grows. Fourth, South Africa is rich in minerals. It can provide the materials necessary for manufacturing within its own borders, as well as shipping to the parent companies raw materials needed for production in the United States.

All four conditions supply both the reasons for multinationals to locate subsidiaries in South Africa and the reasons why critics of such firms charge them with immoral exploitation and with supporting repressive regimes.

United States firms have not been unaware of the charges of immorality. A few of them have responded to the charges by withdrawal. Polaroid is one such company. Citibank and the First Pennsylvania Bank no longer give loans to the South African government. But most of the other companies have not moved out. They have felt the moral pressure from stockholders and vocal groups in the United States, however, and have responded in a number of cases by adopting a set of principles drawn up in 1977 by Leon Sullivan, a black Philadelphia minister and a director of General Motors. The principles, known as the Sullivan Code, aim to end apartheid in the companies that adopt it. The code calls for desegregation of eating, toilet, and work facilities; equal pay for all people doing comparable jobs within the plant; equal opportunity for advancement regardless of race; apprenticeships and training of nonwhites; promotion of blacks and coloreds to supervisory positions; improvement of living conditions; and support of unionization by nonwhites.

The Sullivan Code, its supporters argue, works to break down apartheid from within and so is more effective than simply casting moral stones at the system from outside the country. It helps train nonwhites who would not get such training without the multinationals. It increases the pay of the nonwhites to that of the whites doing similar work. All of this is illegal. It violates South African law. But the South African government has not complained or sought to prevent the adoption of the Sullivan Code by American companies.

The critics of the Sullivan Code claim that it is not an effective way of breaking down apartheid. If it were, it would not be allowed by the South African government. The American firms pay taxes, and so provide revenue essential to the government to support and enforce its practice of repression throughout the country. The Sullivan Code, its critics claim, serves as a smoke screen behind which American companies can hide. They can sign the Code and claim to adhere to it, while in fact not doing so, or doing so only in token fashion. The Code, moreover, takes pressure off the companies to withdraw from the country, and gives them a moral excuse for continuing their profitable and exploitative operations.

The Sullivan Code was proposed in 1977 and has been adopted by a significant number of American-owned firms operating in South Africa. These facts alone throw into question the morality of the practices of these firms prior to 1977. Apartheid, we have acknowledged, is immoral. Consequently, firms that observe apartheid laws follow immoral practices. The arguments of the South Africans that they (South Africans) must enforce apartheid for the benefit of all cannot apply to the American-owned companies. The U.S. companies do not need their South African affiliates or subsidiaries in order to exist. The proportion of the assets of Ford or of IBM tied up in South Africa is relatively small in comparison with their total operation. They have a live option, which is withdrawal from South Africa. The fact that many U.S. firms adopted the Sullivan Code so readily, at least in principle, indicates both that such companies respond to some extent to moral pressure applied in the United States, and that they can still operate profitably (even if less profitably) while observing the Code.

If we admit that U.S. companies act immorally when following the apartheid laws, are they morally permitted to operate in South Africa if they follow the Sullivan principles? The question is not whether any American company follows the Sullivan principles completely, but rather, *if* a company diligently enforced the Sullivan Code in all its detail, would its continued operation in South Africa be morally justifiable? If we assume that the Sullivan Code negates all of the immoral aspects of apartheid, then a company that implements the Code would not be guilty of racial segregation, discrimination, or exploitation unless white employees were also exploited. To that extent its operation would not be immoral. But that is not the end of the matter. Through its taxes the company helps support the government, which in turn enforces apartheid in South African firms and in all other aspects of life within the country. Is such support of a repressive government morally justifiable?

The arguments here are not conclusive. Suppose we attempt to analyze the question from a utilitarian point of view. What are the consequences of the American firms operating within the country as opposed to withdrawing from the country? The critics of the American firms claim that if the firms left South Africa, much of the revenue needed to support the government would disappear. Furthermore, a wholesale withdrawal of American firms would leave the country in chaos. The government would not be able to keep the peace or run the economy. Because of the subsequent turmoil, blacks would have the opportunity to stage an effective revolution, seize control of the government, and put an end to apartheid. As a result, they claim, the repression of the blacks would be ended. The 23 million nonwhites would benefit incomparably more than the 5 million whites would suffer. The whites would suffer loss of their special position. But the blacks would gain respect as persons which they have been denied for a century. The American firms would not be substantially harmed by withdrawal, and after the revolution they might even return to the country to operate within a moral rather than an immoral context.

The scenario of the critics, however, is disputed by defenders of continuing American operations in South Africa. In the first place, they say, consider the benefits to the South African blacks and coloreds. The U.S. firms are the only places where they can get work at wages comparable to whites. They are the only firms at which they can learn skills and rise to supervisory positions. Hence those who work for American companies that follow the Sullivan Code gain much more by working in U.S.-owned plants than they would if these firms left South Africa. Second, a wholesale U.S. withdrawal would not bring the results claimed by the critics of the U.S. companies. As the U.S. left the country, its presence would be replaced by firms from other countries, most likely Japanese or German firms. It is less likely that these firms will follow the Sullivan Code than U.S. firms will. The South African government will continue to receive the revenue it needs from these firms. Hence the government will not be affected and the workers will be harmed. Less good will be achieved on the whole, therefore, by U.S. withdrawal than by continued U.S. presence. Third, the violation of the apartheid laws by U.S. companies is the first step, in the process of abolishing these laws. It is admittedly a small step, but it sets the stage for a gradual change in the laws. Breaking down the laws from within the country is more effective than simply condemning the laws from outside the country. Finally, the spokesmen for an American presence claim that if (counter to what they predict) a revolution does take place, there is little reason to believe such a revolution will produce more good on the whole than a continuation of the present system. The blacks have not been educated or trained in the skills required to run the economy or government of the country. There is little reason to believe that a stable black government will be formed or that whatever government is formed will be less repressive than the present government, even though the repression may express itself differently. Many black leaders fear what might happen if American companies were to leave. The conclusion on utilitarian grounds, defenders of a continued American presence argue, is that more good is achieved by the U.S. firms remaining in South Africa and following the Sullivan Code than would be achieved by their departure.

Which scenario is more likely? Which side's predictions of what would happen as a result of U.S. withdrawal should be believed? The evidence is not sufficiently clear to make a dogmatic judgment of the morality of American companies in

South Africa. What is clear, however, is that any company operating in South Africa without adopting and fully enforcing the Sullivan Code directly practices apartheid and hence acts immorally.

2. Investing in Multinationals

Thus far we have focused on the morality of practices of multinationals that fall outside of the control of the United States government. But American-controlled multinationals do not fall outside of the control of the American parent company. And such companies are controlled by their respective boards of directors, which are in turn subject to the interests of the shareholders. American shareholders could, at least in theory, determine the practices of the U.S. multinationals.

Concerning those U.S. multinationals that operate in South Africa we can raise two moral issues. (a) Is it morally permissible for people or groups to hold stock in corporations that engage in immoral practices? (b) Should churches and universities in particular divest themselves of the stock of corporations that operate in South Africa?

(a) Every person has a moral obligation not to help others engage in immoral practices. Is it immoral for anyone to own stock in a company that engages in immoral practices? The simplest answer would be a flat yes. By owning part of a firm, a shareholder supplies the capital for its operation. If it operates immorally, the shareholder is helping it to do so. The answer to the above question would apply clearly in a company that had as its end some immoral purpose. For instance, no one could morally invest in Murders, Inc., if its purpose was to provide excellent hit men for those who wished to kill people they did not like. But few if any companies have as their purpose something that is outrightly immoral and the typical investor would not invest in such a firm if it did exist.

What makes a firm immoral? Is it enough that someone within the firm acts immorally? Is a firm immoral only if it habitually acts immorally? Is a firm immoral if it has one practice that is immoral? These questions cannot be answered with a simple yes or no. Clearly a firm is not immoral simply because someone within the firm acts immorally. If an employee of a firm, for instance, were to embezzle funds from the company, we would say that the employee and not the company was immoral. If a company made it a practice to exploit its workers, to discriminate against women and blacks, to overcharge its customers—and if it did all these things as a matter of ordinary practice—we could well say the company was immoral. It would therefore be immoral to invest in such a company, since such an investment would help promote the company's immoral practices.

But what are the moral responsibilities of an investor? Must he investigate from a moral point of view the activities of a company in which he is interested in investing? Is such a rule practical and reasonable, or does it ask too much of the typical, small investor? It is not always easy to obtain information about the immoral activities of companies. If the activities are questionable, it is unlikely the companies will publicize or publish them in their annual reports. Nor is there any guide to the moral index of companies for potential investors. There are many guides to the performance of companies from a financial and even from a management point of view. But there is no guide to the moral index of companies. Such a guide would be helpful to the morally conscientious investor. But in the absence of such information, an investor must make do with information that is available to him through the newspapers, any information on legal suits and charges brought against the company, and so on. Most scandals that reach the newspapers, however, bring about changes in corporate policy or personnel to reverse the scandalous practice. Yet despite all these difficulties we can assert that a moral investor should not support a firm that engages in immoral practices.

(b) Since individuals should not support firms that engage in immoral practices it follows that institutions also should not invest in such firms. Since corporate bodies usually make larger investments than individuals, they have a correspondingly greater responsibility concerning the investments they make. Critics have claimed that churches and universities should take the lead in ethical investment practices since they are appropriate models for moral behavior.

The critics of multinationals operating in South Africa have focused primarily on church and university investments. They have attempted to persuade these groups to divest themselves of their investments in American companies operating in South Africa. Their arguments are based on two premises. One is that companies operating in South Africa are engaged in immoral practices, even if they follow the Sullivan principles, since they help the government through their taxes. Secondly, they argue that the churches and universities can force the U.S. companies out of South Africa by selling their stock in protest.

We have already seen that those firms that do not follow the Sullivan principles act immorally. Since it is immoral to support such activity, those institutional as well as private investors who own stock in such companies should divest themselves of it. Many universities have followed this practice, for instance, with respect to banks that grant loans to the government of South Africa. Such banks do not help break down apartheid by hiring blacks, promoting them, or doing any of the things the Sullivan principles require. The banks help the government without attacking apartheid in any way. They thereby help support apartheid. Since this is immoral, many universities have protested this action by divestiture of their stock.

Two arguments that oppose such action have been raised but neither is very convincing. One argument claims that no investor can be sure that some company in which he is investing is not engaged in immoral practices. Since no one can investigate all companies, it is unreasonable to expect corporate investors to be guided in their investments by moral considerations. The argument is not convincing because we can grant that no one is required to find out what he cannot in practice determine. But when it is clear that a company is engaging in an immoral practice, and when this is brought to one's attention, then he should act on that information. To refuse to act on that information concerning company *A* simply because he may not know whether company *B* is acting immorally is to choose knowingly to participate in an immoral practice. As stated before, the second argument is that South African operations for most American companies constitute a very small part of their total activities. Hence, if on the whole companies operate morally, a small immorality in a minor portion of their operations should not be blown out of proportion. The companies are on the whole moral. The corporate investors claim that they have obligations to their respective institutions to invest their funds to produce the greatest return. They must weigh this obligation against the obligation not to support a company that engages in an immoral practice in some small portion of its total operation. The equation, they claim, often comes out in favor of retaining their invested shares. The counterclaim, however, is that they would lose so little if they did divest themselves of the shares of those companies that not to do so is to condone the immoral practice.

The situation is far less clear, however, when we consider those firms that follow the Sullivan Code. Nor is it clear that the universities and churches could effect the withdrawal of these companies from South Africa by selling their stock in protest. If they were to sell their stock and drive the price of the stock down, it would simply be purchased by traders who would be delighted to get it at a lower price, confident that it will soon rise again in accordance with its actual worth. Some of the institutional shareholders claim that they are more effective voting from within the company than they would be voicing disapproval as outsiders. But they have not been effective insiders when they have sought to force a company to leave South Africa.

During the 1970s and the early part of 1980, groups on campuses around the country have sought to get their local endowment associations to divest themselves of companies operating in South Africa. These groups have in some cases been successful and in others unsuccessful. They show how pressure might be brought to bear on university endowment associations. But they have not accomplished much in the way of effecting withdrawal of companies from South Africa. One reason is that their protest has been in some ways too broad and in others too narrow. It has been too broad because they have tarred all U.S. corporations operating in South Africa with the same brush, instead of concentrating on those corporations that do not even adopt the Sullivan principles. Their protest has been too narrow because it has focused only on divestment by university endowment associations, groups which even together could not force a change in policy. But if Ford Motor Company and IBM are immoral, then the attack should not stop with refusal by a university to own stock in the company. Ford is helped more by millions of students and their families buying Ford cars than by some endowment associations owning Ford stock. IBM is helped more by universities buying or renting IBM computers, and by offices and individuals buying IBM typewriters than by endowment associations owning stock. If a practice is immoral, there are more effective ways to influence a company than by symbolic divestiture. But what are we to do if all the major carmakers operate in South Africa or if we prefer IBM computers or typewriters to those of other companies? This question gets to the crux of the issue. Those seriously interested in stopping immorality and who wish to protest the immoral practice of a company should not only want other people to make sacrifices and take action, but they should also be willing themselves to sacrifice and act accordingly.

Multinationals can be held accountable by their stockholders if the stockholders are truly interested in holding them accountable. Stockholders can demand to know what practices the companies follow in their subsidiaries abroad. If immoral practices are discovered in an operation abroad and enough people in the United States refuse to purchase the product of the manufacturer in question until the immoral practice is stopped, then it is safe to assume that the practice will be changed when the economics of the situation demand it.

The structures for controlling multinationals and for preventing practices that harm people have been slow in coming. They require international cooperation both on the part of governments and people—organized either as workers or as consumers. Multinationals are helping bind the world closer together. As they do so, they help prepare the way for collective efforts by those affected by their actions.

Further Reading

Angel, J.L. *Directory of American Firms Operating in Foreign Countries.* New York: World Trade Academy Press, 1969.

Barnet, Richard, and Mueller, Ronald. *Global Reach: The Power of Multinational Corporations.* New York: Simon & Schuster, Inc., 1974.

Barratt-Brown, Michael. *The Economies of Imperialism.* London: Penguin Books Ltd., 1969.

Kindleberger, Charles. *American Business Abroad.* New Haven: Yale University Press, 1969.

Powers, Charles W. *The Ethical Investor.* New Haven: Yale University Press, 1972.

Schwamm, Henri, and Germidis, Dimitri. *Codes of Conduct for Multinational Companies: Issues and Positions.* Brussels: European Centre for Study and Information on Multinational Corporations, 1977.

Tugendhat, Christopher. *The Multinationals.* New York: Random House, Inc., 1972.

Turner, Louis. *Multinational Companies and the Third World.* New York: Hill & Wang, 1973.

United Nations Department of Economic and Social Affairs. *Multinational Corporations in World Development.* New York: United Nations, 1973.

Wilber, Charles, ed. *The Political Economy of Development and Underdevelopment.* New York: Random House, Inc., 1973.

15

Famine, Oil, and Intergenerational Obligations

In our analysis of the morality of American capitalism, we looked at capitalism primarily as it operates within the borders of the United States. In America, government supplements the capitalistic system to provide care for those unable to contribute to the economy and unable to care for themselves. Unless it did so, the total system would be immoral. A wealthy society that allowed some of its members to die of starvation could hardly be a moral society.

When we move beyond our borders and look at the rest of the world, however, we see that people frequently do die of starvation and that millions of people in the world suffer from chronic malnutrition. America, as a nation, possesses great material wealth while some other countries of the world are pitifully poor. By what right do some countries and people have so much wealth and use so much of the world's resources while others have so little? Is it just or moral for Americans to stockpile surplus food or to cut back on the acreage planted while people in other countries starve or live on the edge of starvation? Do our moral obligations stop at our borders? Since it is immoral to let people in our own country die of starvation, is it not immoral to let people in other countries die of starvation? Can our society be a moral society if it does not respond to the needs of others?

To whom do the natural resources of the earth belong? The sun, moon, and ocean belong to no one. By what right does land and the natural resources on or under it belong to those who happen to inhabit the land or who happen to find the resources? People born in an arid, barren country are doomed by an accident of birth. They have no free access to better land, no equal opportunity for improvement, and no real chance for a decent life. Is it fair for others, who happen to be born in lands rich in soil and minerals, oil, and gold to enjoy the exclusive use of these natural resources? The people of "have-not" nations are saying more clearly and more often that it is not fair. They are calling more and more strongly for an international plan of redistribution. Former colonies are seeking restitution for the exploitation they claim to have suffered from their imperialist colonizers.

If there seemed at one time to be an inexhaustible supply of land and natural resources, this is now known not to be the case. We can foresee the complete depletion of the world's oil supply, and we know other minerals are exhaustible. Do we have the right to use as much of these as we wish in any way we desire? Do we have an obligation to save any of these resources for future generations? Do Americans owe more to the poor of other countries or to our own descendants, if we must choose between them?

All of these questions are extremely complex, controversial, and difficult to answer. The moral intuitions of most people falter when they are faced with questions of this scope. It is easier to ignore them than to face them. But both as a nation and as individuals we would be immoral if we chose to ignore our moral obligations simply because they were difficult and new or because they concerned people far away in space or time. Since businesses, firms, and corporations are the major users of resources, the claimed perpetrators of exploitation, and the chief mediators between the economies of rich and poor nations, they are centrally involved in the moral issues.

Famine, Malnutrition, and Moral Obligation

The basic approaches of utilitarianism and deontology can be used to handle any type of moral problem. But it is also possible, using these approaches, to develop second-order principles or rules. These rules, we saw, are typically substantive rather than formal and thus have specific moral content. We can use them in solving complex moral problems. Frequently their application is clearer than is the application of the general and basic first-order moral rules or principles.

The most fruitful approach to complex moral problems is to divide them up into smaller, more manageable parts. As we develop clarity in each of the parts, we develop greater clarity with respect to the problem as a whole. In dealing with the general problems of famine and malnutrition, therefore, we should see if we can break them up into manageable pieces. We should also see if we can find some appropriate second-order moral principles that are applicable. Questions of famine and malnutrition concern our relations to food and to other human beings. We can start with ourselves. Each of us needs food in order to live. We need a certain amount and quality of food to do more than just survive—i.e., to develop fully, maintain our health, and work and act efficiently. When there is enough food for all, it is morally permissible for me to satisfy my need for food. It is moreover a prima facie moral duty for me to preserve my health under normal conditions, and so it is a prima facie moral duty for me to eat adequately.

What about an obligation to others with respect to food? Most people would readily agree that parents are morally obliged to feed their children if they are able to do so. Parents have a special responsibility with respect to their children because the children are theirs. It would be inappropriate in a family of meager means for the parents to eat well and let the children starve. They are not required, however, to feed the children well and starve themselves. How in the long run would the parents' resulting death benefit the children? As a general principle, no one is obliged to sacrifice himself for others. To do so may be morally praiseworthy, but it is not morally required because each person as a moral agent is an end in himself, equally worthy of respect as any other person. We can also argue that each person has a greater obligation to feed those for whom he is responsible because of a special relationship than those for whom he is not so responsible.

We can push this a step further. In general, everyone is obliged to help others in serious need, if he can do so at little cost to himself. Suppose I am in a boat when I see another boat turn over. I see that the occupant of the other boat is drowning. I could easily extend my oar, let him grab onto it, and he could thereby climb to safety in my boat. Most people would readily admit I have the moral obligation to do so. To adopt this rule would be to promote the greatest good of all concerned, since the good the drowning man gains is weighed against minimal effort required for me to extend my oar. Equally clearly we could all rationally will such a principle to be a universal law; it can be universalized without contradiction, and would show respect to people as valuable ends in themselves. Applying the same principle, if I have plenty of food and see someone starving whom I can save at little cost to myself, I am obliged to do so.

We can use a similar reasoning to arrive at our collective obligation to help those in our society who are in serious need. We each have an obligation to help if we can do so at little cost to ourselves. If all those able to do so contribute a little, those in dire need can be helped. As a society, we collectively organize to fulfill this as well as other common ends. We achieve the redistribution of income through taxation and welfare programs.

But why help the needy in our own society rather than those in other societies? Are they not all people and do they not therefore each have equal claim on us? By following a line of reasoning analogous to that which we used above, we find that we have a special relation to those with whom we form a society. We are bound to each other by common laws, share common burdens, and jointly pursue common goods within our society. Just as we have a greater obligation to feed those for whom we are responsible than to feed others in need, so we have a greater obligation to feed the hungry in our own society than we do the hungry of other societies, if the need of each group is equal.

Suppose that as a nation all of us are adequately fed and that we have surplus food left over or resources for producing it. There are starving people in other countries. Do we have a moral obligation to feed them? We saw that we each have an obligation to help another in serious need if we can do so at little cost to ourselves. Is the principle applicable here? Starvation constitutes dire need. Individually, someone in the United States cannot by himself help someone starving in a remote area of Africa. But collectively—i.e., through a united effort, or through governmental action—he may be able to do so. If this is the case, then the principle applies and the person has a moral obligation. He discharges this obligation by paying his taxes or by donating to Care, the Red Cross, or some other relief fund. Obviously those within our country who have barely enough for themselves cannot help others without significant cost and sacrifice to themselves. But those who can do so have the obligation to help others. They can discharge their obligation through the government which acts for them and uses the money they pay in taxes in the way they authorize. The obligation of the government is to act as the people authorize. The obligation of the people is to help those in need. The distinction is an important one.

Thus far we have argued using a weak second-order moral principle. Can we justify a stronger principle, e.g., each person has an obligation to help another seriously in need, even at considerable cost to himself? We argued that no one is morally obliged to sacrifice himself for another. But if we consider that principle at one end of a continuum bounded at the other end by the obligation of helping another at little cost to oneself, we see there are many alternatives between the extremes. Where do we draw the line of obligation? How much cost must we bear to help others in dire need? Rather than attempting to answer that question directly, we can answer it indirectly. We can join our weak principle with the principle that we owe more to those for whom we are directly responsible for than others, and we owe more to those with whom we have a special relation than we do to those with whom we have no special relation. Wherever we draw the line concerning the trade-off of the other's good and one's own cost, we have greater obligations and should be willing to suffer a greater loss to benefit those with whom we have a special relation and ties than others.

Up to now, we have been dealing with the responsibility of Americans, assuming that on the whole Americans have enough to eat and the wherewithal to help others. The argument, however, can be applied equally to all other people. It can apply to the Japanese, the Germans, the people of the Soviet Union, and many others as well. This consideration leads to two questions. Do we each individually have an obligation to help up to a certain point, or do we each have an obligation only equal to the total amount necessary to relieve starvation divided by the total number of people on earth able to help? Are people in countries who are not organized for such purposes relieved of their responsibility?

In answer to the first question, our principle assigns an obligation to help if we can do so at little cost. What is considered little cost to someone who is rich is different than for someone of very modest means and income. Hence the obligation is proportional. If we chose to have the government discharge our obligations, we equalize the burden if we tax people in proportion to their income. But if the people of some countries of the world do not fulfill their obligations, with respect to starving peoples of other countries, does that affect our obligations? The first obligation is to help if it costs us little. The amount is initially determined by dividing what is required by all those capable of giving. The failure of some to give what they ought increases the amount the others must give if the lives of those in need are to be saved. We are obliged to give that greater amount if we are able to give it at little cost.

The reply to the second question is that people are not relieved of their responsibility if their countries are not organized to serve these ends. The obligation remains, even if it cannot be directly discharged. It then leads to the obligation to so organize that they can discharge their obligations. But the situation is by no means simple. People who do not know of the starvation of others may be excused from fulfilling their obligation to the starving if they are invincibly ignorant or can satisfy some other excusing condition. They may not, for instance, be able with little cost to themselves to organize the country to satisfy this obligation.

How moral responsibility and blame for failure to fulfill one's responsibility should be assigned in all these cases is far from clear. The starving people of other countries are to us unknown, unseen people whose presence and plight do not impress themselves upon us as do the needs of our own society. If we feel an obligation to help the starving in other lands, it is usually not an obligation first and foremost on the list of other pressing obligations we have. If the share of each of us is ten cents, it does not seem to be a major moral obligation, even if the ten cents is part of the $2 million required to save the lives of the people in question. If no one helps and thousands die, is each of us responsible for the death of all these people or only for a very small part of the death of one person? In the latter case, is a small part of the death of one person a reasonable concept or is each of us, together with some others, fully responsible for that one death? The answer, though not clear, is worth pondering.

There is a difference between a country suffering from a temporary famine due to an unusual and devastating drought and a country whose people suffer from chronic malnutrition. Are the obligations of those able to help the same in both cases? Many argue they are not, and we can consider the cases separately.

People live in countries and are organized into societies within certain geographical boundaries. These nation-states each have governments that, with only periodic exceptions, other governments recognize as exercising sovereignty within their domain. Recognition of sovereignty demands that no state physically violate the territorial integrity of another state. Each government rules its own people and represents them in the international arena. This in some ways simplifies and in some ways complicates our problem. If the people of one country are starving, the system of nation-states makes it possible for other countries to make the plight known to other countries. The governments of these other countries can in turn respond with food or aid.

Suppose, however, that some people in a country are starving. The government of the country does not wish foreign aid and would prefer to have some of its people die; or suppose the starving people are a dissident, rebellious sect, being starved into submission by the government; or suppose food delivered free to the government of a country is not freely given to the starving but sold by the government to those able to purchase it. Suppose, finally, that the government wishes to distribute the food it received from abroad to the starving, but due to inefficiency on its part, it is unable to deliver the food to those who need it, and the food rots on the docks.

Is the moral obligation to help the starving greater than the obligation to respect national sovereignty? As with many instances which involve the clash of prima facie obligations, the question cannot be answered a priori. Since we are using the weak principle of little cost, if the violation of sovereignty might lead to war or to a break in diplomatic relations or to something else which may be viewed as more than a little cost, the principle does not apply. The fact that such difficulties frequently arise, moreover, makes it difficult for individuals to know what the actual situation is and whether they actually have a moral obligation to supply aid.

What is the difference between cases of famine and chronic malnutrition? We can distinguish cases of famine through no fault of the people vs. famine through the fault of the people and malnutrition through no fault of the people vs. malnutrition through fault of the people. Does it make any difference whether people starve through no fault of their own or through their own fault? We might get a better perspective by making the fault vs. no-fault distinction with respect to people in our own country. Suppose someone is able to work, work is available, but he prefers not to work; he chooses to sleep and idle away the hours. He runs out of money and still refuses to work. He comes close to starvation, announces that he is starving, and claims it is the obligation of others to feed him. Do they have this obligation? Each person has the obligation to care for himself if he is able to do so. If he does not, must others care for him? Several principles seem to apply here in addition to the one concerning help of others. One is that it is not unjust to let people suffer the evil consequences of their freely chosen deliberate actions. A solution to the problem which can satisfy both principles would consist not of feeding the person indefinitely but of making it possible for him to work and of making his receiving food contingent on his working. Suppose he has children? Assuming they are starving through the fault of their father and no fault of their own, theirs is a no-fault case governed by our weak principle concerning aid to the needy.

We can now return to a starving country. Suppose a people were warned not to denude their forests. They did so nonetheless. This resulted in floods, loss of topsoil, and destruction of their farmlands. They are now starving and ask for help. By analogy with the case above only some of the people are at fault—namely, those who cut the forests. The others suffer the results of the actions of a few. Help should be given in accordance with earlier principles. But since the land is barren, help might appropriately include not only food but also fertilizer, saplings for planting, and technical aid necessary to prevent future failure. As in the case of the individual, willingness of a country to help itself is an appropriate condition for continued aid.

The cases of malnutrition are in some ways parallel to the cases of starvation and in some ways different. Let us assume the malnutrition is serious and so the harm to those who suffer it is serious. Though the harm is less than in the cases of starvation, the same principles seem to apply. We have not yet considered one principle, however, that some people claim is applicable, viz., we should not help others if giving such help will produce more harm than not giving it. This is a simple application of the general principle of utility. It can also be defended from a deontological perspective.

Suppose that by supplying food to a country whose people chronically suffer from malnutrition we alleviate that malnutrition for a given year. If we did not supply them with food, some of them would die from their inability to fight off disease, but some children would still be born and the population would remain on the whole stable. If we supply them with food one year, fewer people would die. Let us further suppose that because it is healthier, the population increases faster than it would otherwise. The result is a larger population than before. If there was not enough food for the smaller population, there will be even less food per person with the increase in population. By giving aid we thus render a larger number worse off than the number of people who would originally suffer without our help. Our help in fact therefore produces more harm than good. If we alleviate the harm that would follow by helping them a second year, we postpone but multiply the harm of helping them the third year, and so on. If they can be helped to become nutritionally self-sufficient through technological aid, then that should be our moral obligation. But if despite advanced agricultural techniques the land is unable to support their numbers, then the numbers must be reduced by decreasing the fertility rate. This, however, may not be what they choose to do. Then the principle of accepting the consequences of their freely chosen actions is applicable. A difficulty, of course, is that frequently the people involved do not freely and knowingly choose a course of action and the resulting situation becomes unclear.

We have argued thus far from the weak principle of help at little cost. We did not attempt to draw the line at some greater cost, except that it is higher for those for whom we are responsible and with whom we have special relations. If we defend and adopt a stronger principle, the analysis will proceed in much the same way as above; our moral responsibility for helping those in need will increase in direct proportion to the increase in cost we are to bear and inversely as the need of the other is less serious.

We did not claim that governments have the obligation to help people in foreign countries except insofar as government is the medium through which the people of a country discharge their obligations. The reason for making this distinction is that the government of a country has obligations to the people of the country which it governs. Its obligations to feed the hungry of its own country are a result of the structure of the society. The members of the society contribute to the government and as members of the same society, receive benefits and bear obligations. We are not subject to governments other than our own. We owe no duties to them and deserve no benefits from them. Our government properly takes the initiative in helping the starving in other countries to the extent that that action is one authorized by the people through their representatives.

Nation-states are not moral beings. The international arena is not one of total anarchy, since there is cooperation and there are some agreed upon rules of interaction. But the arena is not one of genuine human community and the nations of the world do not form a moral community. Although each of us has the obligation to help people in dire need, governments and national boundaries come and go. Agreements may obligate one nation to help another. Nations do not starve, however. People do. The moral obligation to help the starving is an obligation to people and so the obligation is not dependent on the type of government under which a people live. Nonetheless, since we have a special relation to the people of other countries with which our country forms a community, we have a greater obligation to help them than to help those with whom we do not form a community. The absence of a world government precludes the kind of redistribution possible within a nation-state. This often makes it difficult to give effective and equitable aid to people in need in other countries.

What of businesses? Do they have obligations with respect to starving people in other lands? Do farmers and those in the food industry have special obligations? On the basis of the second-order principles we have been using, the answer is that businesses, through taxes, help provide the income necessary for people in the society to discharge their obligations collectively. Businesses, in this regard, have no special obligations providing they have no special relations to the country in question. But a multinational corporation which operates in the starving country would have different obligations from a corporation that operates entirely in America.

Farmers and businesses in the food industry do not have greater obligations to feed the starving simply because they are food producers or processors. Since the food for starving people in other lands is paid for by the people of the nation giving the food, the burden should be equitably borne. No special responsibility falls on any group. The decision to increase crop production or to grow enough to produce a surplus for the needy of other countries is a decision within our system. Production can be increased in response to the government's placing orders for food. Farmers have no special obligation to help others, though it would be immoral for them purposely to hinder others from providing such help by refusing to increase production. Hindering others from doing what they ought is wrong for everyone, and farmers in this instance fall under the general rule.

The above analysis of starvation and malnutrition has assumed certain background conditions. It has assumed, for instance, that it is possible to feed all the people of the world at a level above that of malnutrition, and that each country is capable of doing so. If we change these background assumptions, we shall have to modify the analysis accordingly. Assume, for instance, that the world is not capable of supporting the number of people in it at a decent level of life. We might then either argue that the number of people should be reduced or that those with more than enough should change their diet, sharing more of what is available with others. Some aspects of this question are already pressing issues with respect to the depletion of nonrenewable resources.

Oil and the Depletion of Natural Resources

For many centuries the goods of the earth seemed inexhaustible. Only in recent times have people come to realize that at our present rate of consumption and growth we can conceivably use up certain nonrenewable resources within the foreseeable future. This realization has raised a large number of questions related to the use of resources, to growth, alternative means of producing energy, and to other similar issues. For purposes of simplicity and illustration, only a few of the moral issues involved in our use of oil shall be addressed. How can we determine what use is morally justifiable? What do we owe, if anything, to developing nations with respect to their need for oil? How do we balance the present need for oil against that of future generations?

1. The Morally Justifiable Use of Oil

The United States today has approximately 6 percent of the world's population. Collectively we use approximately 30 percent of the world's refined oil production. Is our use of it just? The answer is based in part on two prior questions: To whom do the resources of the world belong? Does each person, present and future, have a proper share?

If the resources of the world belong to mankind as a whole, then we shall get one answer to the proper use of oil. If the resources belong to those who find and develop them, and to those who in turn purchase them, our answer to the proper use of oil will be different. The latter is the assumption upon which the world presently operates.

Until very recent times mankind lived without oil. Oil is not necessary for life as such. But it is essential to many aspects of modern life. Oil is used in the manufacture of gas for our automobiles and fuel for our airplanes. Oil is widely used to heat our homes and to run our factories. Oil produces 43 percent of our energy. In a modern society such as ours oil is a present and practical necessity. Oil is also the key for underdeveloped nations to achieve a standard of living that will approach our own. And countries that produce no oil, such as Japan, are heavily dependent on it.

If we take the view that oil belongs to those who happen to own the oil fields, or to those who produce the oil, a number of questions arise. Can those who own the oil do with it whatever they choose? Can they morally choose to produce it or not? Can they morally refuse either to pump it out of the ground or to sell it? Can they morally charge any price they wish for it? The traditional free market approach to all these questions would be yes, providing that the market is truly free. The oil belongs to those who find and develop it. They can do with it what they choose. They will be induced to develop and sell it by others who wish it, and it will be in the interests of both parties for them to do so. Competition and the market mechanism will determine the price of oil and its use. When the price becomes too high, alternatives will be used. The answer is straightforward and simple. The transaction is fair, providing both parties enter into it freely and with adequate knowledge.

Many people will object, however, that the situation is not that simple. Saudi Arabia is one of the largest oil producers in the world. Suppose that tomorrow it decided to terminate its oil production. Even worse, suppose that all the Oil Producing and Exporting Countries (OPEC) decided to stop producing oil. The effect would be devastating on the oil importing countries. It would be devastating to many of the highly industrialized countries; but it would also be devastating to oil-poor Third World countries. Can a producer morally terminate its production in this way? It cannot if it has contracts that it has an obligation to honor. But suppose it honors those contracts but does not renew them and does not sell what it has not contracted to sell? The results will still be devastating. A scenario that will have almost as serious consequences involves the OPEC countries raising their prices so that the importing nations cannot afford to import the oil they need. Is this moral?

A defender of free enterprise might argue that it is moral, but that neither scenario is likely to develop because both of them fail to take into account that it is in the interest of the oil producing countries to produce and sell oil. This is their chief source of wealth and income. If they do not produce and sell oil, they deprive themselves of the wealth they can use to modernize their countries and improve the standard of living of their people. If they wreck the economies of the industrialized countries, they kill off their markets to their own detriment. But the assumption of this reply is that the oil proceeds go to the country and not to individuals within the country who may have more wealth than they know what to do with and who hence have no incentive to continue to produce and get more money. If they have reasons of their own for not producing oil, are they morally obliged to?

A utilitarian approach to this question considers the action and its consequences. Since the stopping of oil would produce very damaging results on large numbers of people, the action can be morally justified only if the damage is outweighed in the long run by advantages. One of the consequences to consider is the reaction of the industrialized countries to such a shutoff of oil. They would undoubtedly see the action as seriously detrimental to their life and not merely to their lifestyle. If this were in fact so, they could argue that in self-defense they are justified in taking military action to preserve themselves and to secure for themselves the oil they need to survive. It is difficult to imagine the positive benefits of terminating the production of oil, or to imagine them so great as to outweigh the evils which would result from such termination. To the extent that the action produces more harm than good, it is immoral.

Does the same line of reasoning hold true with respect to raising the price of oil? Or to one country rather than all of the OPEC countries terminating the production of oil? Clearly the consequences of one country's terminating its oil production will not be as serious as all of them doing so. Utilitarianism would require that we investigate the consequences of that particular action, or if it is an action based on principle, investigating that principle in terms of its consequences.

The free market approach to prices depends on the market being truly free. Within the confines of the United States, the political mechanism operates to preclude collusion and monopoly action. Internationally we have no such mechanism. Hence, the setting of prices by an international cartel is possible. If users are dependent on the product, they are forced to purchase it on the terms of the seller or not to purchase it at all.

Within the United States the price of oil is dependent not only on the cost of oil imported into the country but also on the cost of domestically produced oil. If the free market is allowed to operate, American oil companies would find it profitable to charge the prices of foreign producers. American producers could compete against one another. But if the supply is less than the demand, they have no incentive to do so. One result of letting the market set the price of oil is that it may price oil out of the reach of the poor. For instance, if the poor need oil to heat their homes but cannot afford fuel, they suffer extreme consequences. Our earlier principle of helping those in our society through taxes and governmental redistribution of income would have to come into play. The money that is redistributed might come from the well-to-do; or, many argue, it should come from the profits of the oil producers, if they reap unusually high profits as a result of the operation of OPEC.

What of the poor countries of the world? We have no international mechanism to protect them from the effects of the rise in prices of oil due to cartel action. While it is not likely that they will starve or suffer greatly, especially if they are just beginning industrialization, they will be precluded from developing industrially and will be condemned to being poor and underdeveloped for the indefinite future. There is a mechanism for redistribution from the oil companies to the poor in the United States; there is no similar mechanism for redistribution from the oil producers to the poor countries in the world. To the extent that their continued plight is a result of the cost of oil, they have a moral claim on the oil producers, a claim that the producers should weigh against the uses to which they put their profits. The moral claim of the poor countries is one, however, that they cannot presently press either by law, war, or economic sanctions.

If we start from the moral legitimacy of certain people owning and controlling the production of oil, then those who have a right to it are those who are able to purchase it. We adopt this general approach with nonessential as well as with essential resources. Since the people of the industrialized countries are dependent for their well-being on a continuing supply of oil, it would cause serious harm, and so be morally improper, for all oil producers to suddenly stop producing and selling oil. The proper price for oil is determined, up to the present, by the market, just as the proper price for other goods is determined. But when oil becomes very expensive, then those who depend on it and cannot afford it must be taken care of by others.

2. The Needs of Developing Countries

The solution suggested above for the use of oil is plausible if oil is inexhaustible. We did not consider the fact, however, that the world's oil supply is not inexhaustible. Does this throw some special light on the fact that 6 percent of the people of the world use 30 percent of the oil? Does the fact that a portion of the human race can afford to buy up nonrenewable resources make it morally permissible to do so? The answer is to be found not in looking at statistics but in attempting to uncover the relevant second-order moral principles. Is there any reason to think that the principle which says that *n* percent of the people of the world should use *n* percent of the nonrenewable resources of the world is a principle? Might we derive it from a principle of equity, and might we defend that principle by saying that everyone has a right to an equal amount of the resources of the world? Is such a principle of equity reasonable? Suppose, for instance, we consider people in the sixteenth century. Did they have the right to the oil in the ground? It would have been a vacuous right. For they did not know about the vast deposits of oil, nor did they know what to do with it. They had no need or use for it, given their knowledge and technological development. It only makes sense to talk about the equal right of people to oil if we mean by it equal right of access to the oil they need. If someone does not need oil, it is hard to understand what his right to it means.

Suppose we adopt the principle that each person has equal right of access to the oil that he needs. Suppose, further, that Americans for a variety of historical reasons, have built their houses in the suburbs, have not developed their public transportation systems, and hence need far more gasoline than do their German or Japanese counterparts. They also need much more gasoline than do countries with very few roads and automobiles, or small countries in which the need to travel great distances is much less than in the United States. People who live in cold climates and need fuel oil to heat their homes also need more oil than do people who live in warm climates. There are a great many variables. If we consider need, therefore, the simple quotation of statistics is not necessarily morally significant.

There are several other principles, however, that are appropriate and that we can apply to the case of the use of oil. The amount of oil is limited. Oil is a natural resource available for the good of people. Approaching the use of oil either from a utilitarian point of view or from a deontological one, we can defend the principle that other things being equal we should not waste natural resources and hence should not waste oil. Put positively this is a principle of conversation. We should conserve natural resources to the extent possible consistent with our needs.

Had we known that oil was limited and that we might exhaust it in the foreseeable future, we should not have built our cities as we did. But we did not and perhaps could not foresee the consequences of our actions. Hence we can plausibly, as a nation, argue nonculpable ignorance. If we could do so before, however, we can no longer make the same excuse. We are now morally obliged to conserve oil. This is a prima facie obligation to be weighed against our other obligations. It is an obligation not only of individuals but also of those in a position to make it possible to conserve oil—automobile manufacturers, those who build factories, and others appropriately placed.

If this argument so far has been correct, then there is no set amount of oil which has to be saved in principle for some particular people. If Americans use up more oil per capita than other nations, this is justifiable providing they do not waste it. They should make efforts to conserve it. They are now becoming motivated to save it as the cost grows higher. They are now also motivated to develop alternative energy sources.

Poor countries according to this analysis have as much right to the available oil to satisfy their needs as do industrialized countries. As underdeveloped countries develop they will need more and more oil. This fact does not justify the industrialized nations preventing the development of the underdeveloped countries. Nor does it justify any arbitrary limit being placed on the use of oil by industrialized nations on the grounds that a certain amount must be saved for use by developing countries after they develop. Once oil is no longer available, no one has any right to it. To have a right to what does not exist is to have a vacuous right.

3. The Needs of Future Generations

I have argued that people have a right to equal access to the oil they need. But how are we to deal with the needs of future generations? Do they have a right to oil, and should we morally consider their future needs against our present needs? The argument that claims that future peoples have an equal right in some strong sense can be reduced to an absurdity. Consider the amount of oil actually in the ground. Call it x. If each person has a right to a certain amount of oil, then the amount to which I have proper claim is x divided by the number of people with a basic claim, however that is measured. The question, then, is how many people in the future we wish to count. The denominator of the equation increases as we add more and more generations. The amount each person has a right to gets proportionately smaller as the number we consider increases. Pushed far enough into the future, each of us has a right to a barrel, a gallon, or to a thimblefull of gasoline.

We do not know the needs of all generations in the future. But there are some things we know, assuming there will be future generations. They will have certain needs, some of which will be similar to our own. We also know that generations overlap. One obligation that every generation has to the next generation is to pass on to it the common goods that it has received. The goods of knowledge, virtue, and culture do not belong to individuals, they are not used up, and they should be passed along, if possible, at a higher level than that at which they were received. The passage takes place normally by one generation teaching the next. In this way each generation maximizes good, and each fulfills an obligation to the next generation.

What of goods that can be used up? There is no similar obligation to pass on these goods at the same level at which they were received. Such an obligation could not be discharged. Since each generation uses part of the nonrenewable resources available, it necessarily leaves less to later generations than was available to it. If such resources are needed by one generation, the people of that generation have the right to use them. They have an obligation not to waste them. They have no obligation to make sure that those who come after them will enjoy a higher standard of living than they enjoy. Since the good of each person is as important as the good of any other, no sacrifice of one's good for another is required. No particular generation has to sacrifice so that the next generation will have a higher standard of living than it had. It may do so out of love; but it is not morally required to do so.

Yet this does not mean that generations have no obligations to take into consideration the needs of those who come after them. No generation has the right to endanger future people any more than it has the right to endanger present people. It should not, for instance, bury nuclear waste in such a way that it will not affect people of the present, but will be dangerous five hundred years from now to people who live where it is buried. This obligation is one that applies not only to generations but to individuals, governments, and businesses, since it is through the agency of individuals, governments, and business that generations act.

Optimally, each generation should make it possible for all succeeding generations to live at a decent level of life, well above that of subsistence. But practically we can only foresee a certain distance into the future, and can only provide for a few generations beyond us, if that far. Nor can we guarantee that some later generation will not selfishly endanger the good of later generations.

How does this relate to oil? A suggestion is that we collectively have no obligation to save oil that we can profitably use. Our resources are not so low as to demand that; nor are alternative sources of energy unimaginable. They are already possible and likely to be developed. Nor would there be any justification for Americans, for instance, to try to guarantee future Americans access to oil by preventing developing countries from developing and using more oil than they presently do.

People are sometimes spoken of as stewards of the earth. If we are stewards, we should use the resources of the earth wisely. But such stewardship cannot justify any group preventing any other group from legitimate access to fulfill its needs. Nor does it demand that we not use what we need in order to pass it on to those who come after us.

In discussing these broad questions the moral obligations of each individual are difficult to pinpoint. Individuals should not waste resources on the theory that they each use so little; their combined waste mounts up to a great deal. Businesses also should not waste, even if they can afford to do so. Nor should government. The difficulty, of course, comes in trying to specify exactly what constitutes waste and what constitutes need. There are clear cases of each, and there is also a grey area. People may genuinely differ on these questions. But rational debate and discussion of the issues can help us gain clarity, and organized effort in these areas will make an important difference. Circumstances may force us to conserve. By trying to think through the issues in moral terms we may arrive at a course of action that will be just and maximally beneficial.

The problems of famine, our obligations to people in foreign countries, and our obligations to future generations fall outside of the socio-economic structures of our country. Future generations of Americans are represented in our political process only through those living in the present who have an interest in representing and planning for them. The problems relating to people outside our system are difficult to analyze because of the absence of international structures necessary to make all the people of the world a true community. Without such a community and without structures for redistributing wealth, such redistribution is haphazard, inequitably assigned, and skewed by a host of barriers. A truly worldwide application of moral principles requires a truly worldwide community.

Whether such a community can be formed while preserving national sovereignty and differing economic systems is a basic question to which we have no clear answer. Without a true international community, however, it is difficult to get clear the extent of our duty—individually or collectively—to people of other countries, and even more difficult to fulfill those obligations. Paradoxically, the rise of multinational corporations, the targets of so much moral condemnation, may pave the way for increased contact and community, and so lay the basis for developing structures we can jointly use in relating morally to people throughout the world. We should be aware of this possibility at the same time that we help prevent such companies from exploiting other people. We have argued that our government has no obligation to other peoples. But we as individuals do. It is up to us to make known to government our desire to fulfill these obligations collectively through government action. We can come up with many rationalizations to ignore our moral obligations to the people of other nations. But we have no valid excuse for not attempting to determine our obligations in this area and doing what we can to fulfill these obligations.

Further Reading

Aiken, William, and La Follette, Hugh, eds. *World Hunger and Moral Obligation.* Englewood Cliffs, N.J.: Prentice-Hall, Inc., 1977.

Arthur, John, and Shaw, William H., eds. *Justice and Economic Distribution.* Englewood Cliffs, N.J.: Prentice-Hall, Inc., 1978.

Blackstone, William T., ed. *Philosophy and Environmental Crisis.* Athens, Ga.: University of Georgia Press, 1974.

Goodpaster, K.E., and Sayre, K.M., eds. *Ethics and Problems of the 21st Century.* Notre Dame: University of Notre Dame Press, 1979.

Heilbroner, Robert L. *An Inquiry Into the Human Prospect.* New York: W.W. Norton & Co., Inc., 1975.

Narveson, Jan. "Moral Problems of Population," In *Monist,* LVII (1973), pp. 69–78.

Passmore, John. *Man's Responsibility for Nature.* New York: Charles Scribner's Sons, 1974.

Reutlinger, S. and Selowsky, M. *Malnutrition and Poverty.* Baltimore: The Johns Hopkins University Press, 1976.

Schumacher, E.G. *Small is Beautiful.* New York: Harper & Row, Inc., 1973.

Sikora, R.I., and Barry, Brian, eds. *Obligations to Future Generations.* Philadelphia: Temple University Press, 1978.

Conclusion

16

The New Moral Imperative for Business

"There is no free lunch." This adage often quoted in certain business circles means that for everything we get, we have to pay a certain price. The price is sometimes in money, sometimes in time, sometimes in convenience, sometimes in other opportunities lost.

The original mandate of the American people to business was to grow, produce a rich variety of goods at as low a price as possible, provide employment, and help society achieve the good life. Business met this mandate but at a certain cost that has varied with the times. As the service industries came to employ more people than factories, the possibility of expanding output to cover increased wages diminished. Wage increases without increased productivity led to inflation. America's use of oil was profligate. People counted on this cheap energy source for inexpensive transportation, heating in winter, and industrial use. As the cost of oil has risen relentlessly, Americans have had to face and will continue to face decisions about the use of oil and energy in general. Cost must be traded off against comfort.

As times and conditions have changed, so has the original American mandate to business. The change has been gradual and it has not been sufficiently articulated. Many businesses still do not realize there is a new mandate, and struggle to maintain their old ways of doing things. They see increasing legislative controls on business not as a part of a changing mandate but as a personal affront and attack by antibusiness factions and minorities. The national concern with pollution provides an index of the new mandate. When industry was starting, a certain amount of pollution was tolerated as a necessary evil. As automobiles came into popular use, again a certain level of pollution and smog was tolerated. But as industrial waste became more toxic, as lakes and rivers were threatened, as the air became dangerous to plants and humans, the general population came to see that something had to be done. Business was reluctant to change its ways, and was slowly forced to do so by the Environmental Protection Agency. Car manufacturers were ordered to find ways to lower the pollution caused from car fumes. Once ordered, the industry responded. Unless ordered, it is unlikely any manufacturer would have spent the money necessary to modify its engines since the increased cost would tend to make its cars uncompetitive. The cost of cleaner engines, of course, is ultimately borne by the consumer who breathes the cleaner air, and pays for it through increased car costs. Electric power plants pay for antipollution devices and pass the costs on to their customers. But manufacturers are reluctant to incur expenses that force them to raise their prices for fear of losing some customers who are no longer able to afford their products. Though the cost of controlling pollution might be handled through taxes, our society has favored the technique of making the user of the product bear the additional cost.

The American people have not operated according to some plan in changing the mandate to business. It has been changed through legislation, through collective bargaining, and through the rise of a powerful new force—consumerism.

The development of American business started with the businessman in the dominant position. He set the pace, took the risks, invested his capital, and sometimes made a financial killing. The marketplace provided an opportunity for the poor to improve their lot. Social mobility was possible in the marketplace, and the stories of Horato Alger inspired many workers to try to strike it rich. Some succeeded. Most did not. Capitalism put the workers into a situation of inequality with respect to employers. They organized into unions to defend themselves and to advance their interests. Big labor soon matched big business with big government as the third component of the system. A fourth component, the consumer, was long ignored and has only recently gained the self-consciousness necessary to organize. Consumers now fight for their rights, lobby government, and force management and labor to consider their interests.

The result is a new mix on the economic scene. Decisions are not as easy to make as they once were. Instead of aiming only at profits or at increasing production, managers must now weigh many factors and many interests. The rights of employees, consumers, and of society in general must be respected. Respecting these rights has a moral and not just an economic dimension. Faced with conflicting demands by different groups, some of which seem to be counter to the interests of business, many corporations have not known how to respond. Many of them have evidently decided to ride out the storm, doing what legislation forces them to do, but hoping that such things as consumerism and demands for social accounting will go away. A few corporations have indicated that they would like to comply with the new demands placed on them, if only they knew how. They complain that the demands made on them by diverse groups are vague, sometimes at odds with one another, and no one except government spells them out clearly. Even fewer corporations have attempted to reply either by taking positive action to preempt harsh legislation or by mounting public counterattacks explaining and defending their views of the situation to all interested parties.

Standing in the way of an effective response is frequently an outdated image of the corporation as an independent entity responding to the simple mandate of a former time. We have seen that the attacks on the system of American free enterprise have not proven that capitalism is inherently immoral. But we have also seen that moral issues pervade business and society, and that they cannot be ignored or dismissed as irrelevant to business.

The new moral mandate to business can be found not only in such movements as consumerism, environmentalism, and conservationism but in public outcries over bribery and windfall profits as well as in legislation. Business has opposed legislation dealing with environmental protection, worker safety, consumer protection, social welfare, affirmative action, truth in lending, fair packaging and labeling, truth in advertising, child labor, workmen's compensation, minimum wages, pension reform, and so on. Legislation has been passed in all these areas over the objections of business. Why has business been opposed to such legislation—legislation that in most instances seems progressive, socially desirable, and in the public good? In each case business decried the encroachment of government and claimed that it was protecting profits. Yet all this legislation has not prevented business from prospering and making profits. The legislation has expressed social demands and it embodies a view of business that, when taken as a whole, is clearly different from the eighteenth century view found in the writings of John Locke or in the Constitution, and different from the simplistic mandate given to business in an earlier time.

The negative response of business to each such piece of legislation shows that it is less sensitive to popular demands than many people think it should be. As a result the general public has labeled it as self-seeking, narrowly self-interested, and socially blind. Books such as Silk and Vogel's *Ethics and Profits* show that even businessmen tend to have a low image of themselves. The fact that business has prospered despite such legislation shows that it is more resilient and more able to face social demands than many of its leaders believe or would have us believe. There may be a limit beyond which business cannot respond. But as long as the costs of such demands can be shifted to the consumer who is the ultimate beneficiary, the costs represent social decisions. If airbags in cars increase passenger safety, and if the degree of safety that such bags represent are desired by the general population, then the car buyer will have to pay the cost. It is difficult to know whether legislation represents the will of the people. If airbags were an optional extra that car buyers could order or not, people would have a choice. Americans in large numbers did not want to wear seat belts. Do they want air bags? The issue has not been left up to public choice. Should it be? The new mandate to business is more complex than it was in the past; but exactly what it includes and what it does not is still not completely clear.

What is clear in the new mandate is that business must now consider the worker, consumer, and the general public as well as the shareholder—and the views and demands of all four—in making decisions. The good of all must be considered. The key to responding positively to this moral requirement is developing a mechanism for assuming moral responsibility. Business must find structures for doing so.

The solution to handling competing demands is not to be found in ethical codes, important though these may be. Nor is it to be found in any other substantive set of guidelines. Sometimes the demands of workers will carry greater weight than the interests of shareholders; sometimes the opposite will be the case; and sometimes both will have to give way to environmental needs. The demands cannot all be expressed in cost-accounting terms. The solution to handling these sometimes conflicting demands lies not so much in substantive as in procedural guidelines. This approach leaves the ultimate decisions concerning a business in the hands of management. But management can and should be held responsible for the decisions it makes and for its mistakes, making it more vulnerable than under an older view of the corporation and business. More importantly, this approach requires a restructuring of business and the corporate organization itself. Codes and substantive guidelines superimposed on an organization will not significantly change the way the organization functions. Procedural guidelines call for internal modifications so that in some ways the corporation will no longer function as it did before.

By what right can anyone require such changes? The reply is that only organizational changes can enable the corporation to handle the many demands placed upon it and survive in anything like its present form. To adhere to the traditional model, refuse to consider the social dimensions of a corporation's activities and to take positive action only when forced invites increasingly harsh and restrictive legislation that will eventually replace the corporation with governmental control, planning, and finally ownership. The creative genius of American business, if put to the test, can undoubtedly come up with better solutions to many problems than those forced upon it in procrustean legislation. But business must both be willing to respond and willing to change.

In the preceding chapters we have seen a variety of suggestions for change, ways of increasing input by those employees with moral reservations about a company's policy or product, ways of making the board more responsive to the shareholders whom it represents, and ways of assigning responsibility. For instance, in the past consumers have not been given the opportunity to vote on how much styling they wanted to pay for as opposed to safety. Car manufacturers assumed that the public was interested in the former. The automobile industry decided what would sell and what would not, and how much emphasis to put on safety. American car dealers have not typically emphasized safety features in selling their cars. Despite market surveys, American drivers have had little voice in the decisions; for instance, the surveys typically test consumer preferences among what the manufacturers wished to offer rather than attempting to find out what consumers want so the manufacturers can offer it.

Engineers are in a better position than anyone else to figure costs and risks. But they are not better equipped to figure the acceptability of risk or the amount that people should be willing to pay to eliminate such risk. Neither, however, are the managers of automobile corporations. The amount of acceptable risk is a public decision that can and should be made by representatives of the public or by the public itself.

What should be the roles of the manufacturers, government, and the public with respect to automobile safety? A proper role of government is to ascertain the minimum level of risk compatible with the state of the art of automobile manufacturing. Such a standard can be arrived at by an independent body of engineers. The engineers should be kept free from lobbying by the automobile manufacturers, but the engineers need not be government employees. A broad representation from engineers at automotive engineering departments at universities, perhaps some from industry, and some from government might be an appropriate mix. The automobile manufacturers should be informed of the minimum standards they must meet in reasonable time for them to make the required changes.Thus far the National Highway Traffic Safety Administration (NHTSA) has established and implemented only a few major safety standards, the two most important being the 1972 side impact standard and the 1977 gasoline tank safety standard. The NHTSA appropriately allows each manufacturer to determine how it will meet the set standard. The next appropriate step is for the automobile manufacturers to exceed the set safety standard and market the additional safety of their cars the way they market options and new models. Safety could become as much a feature of competition among car makers as style now is. To enhance this feature of cars, the NHTSA might require auto manufacturers to inform the public about the safety quotient of each car, just as it now requires each car to specify the miles per gallon it is capable of achieving. Such an approach would put the onus for basic safety on the manufacturers, but it would also make additional safety a feature of consumer interest, competition, and choice. It is puzzling that manufacturers have not taken the initiative in this respect. It seems that the auto industry for years has preferred to follow the patterns of the past rather than respond to the changing views of the public.

A bill was recently proposed in Congress requiring managers to disclose the existence of life-threatening defects to the appropriate federal agency. Failure to do so and attempts to conceal defects could result in fines of $50,000 or imprisonment for a minimum of two years, or both. The fine in corporate terms is negligible. But a prison term for corporate managers is not. The possibility of going to jail for one's corporate actions would make each manager more careful of his decisions. The president of a corporation could be held criminally responsible for life-threatening defects unless he could give evidence of the person causally responsible for the decision to proceed with a product known to be dangerous. This would supply strong outside pressure to reorganize the corporation so that responsibility would be individually assigned and assumed. Such a law would provide an outside incentive for corporations to listen to complaints by their employees of the dangers of defective and dangerous products.

We must have moral persons if we are to have moral businesses. But that is only half the truth. We must also have structures that reinforce rather than place obstacles in the way of moral action.

Business ethics has as much to do with business as with ethics. The Myth of Amoral Business with which we began this book has not yet been put to rest in the business world. Many still believe business has no moral responsibility. The myth stands in the way of changes suggested to reinforce moral action. Showing it to be a myth is not enough. Corporate organization must be changed so that it can respond to moral mandates and so that those in business can act morally by design rather than by accident.

We can briefly consider the role of government in this process, the suggestion of corporate democracy, and the relation of business ethics to the building of a good society.

The Role of Government

The government is involved with business at many levels. It is itself an employer and a purchaser of goods. It controls interest rates, regulates the money supply, and performs a great many other functions. Our central concern with respect to the new moral mandate is in government's relation to business through its regulatory agencies or through legislation. It may therefore be asked what is the proper role of government?

From a moral point of view, no government has the right to demand through legislation what is immoral. But neither is its proper function the legislation of morality. Through its courts it settles disputes. Through its tax structure and social welfare programs it provides for a redistribution of wealth and takes care of those whom the market system does not provide for. In supplementing the economic system of free enterprise, we see that it fulfills a moral need.

A prime requisite for a moral government is that it act justly. It should treat its citizens equally before the law, provide the conditions in which they can interact safely, and prevent gross injury by any individual or group against any other individual or group. It does this through its laws and law enforcement system. Beyond this its primary moral obligation is not to harm or cause harm to any of its citizens. This obligation is stronger and more important than the moral obligation to provide for the welfare of its citizens. The first is a demand of justice. The second is a demand of welfare. A government has no right to harm its citizens. It has an obligation to help them to the extent possible. The first is an imperative by which it is bound; the second a task which it should try to fulfill. As a result, it should not attempt to weigh the harm it does to some and the benefits it brings to others—it should simply act so as to produce the greatest amount of good on the whole. The government is not an individual. It is a servant of all the people, who have equal rights before it and all who have the right not to be harmed by it. Its laws, then, cannot be morally justified on utilitarian grounds if they do harm or are unjust to any citizen.

What then of such things as income tax, which some say is stealing from the rich for the benefit of the poor? If it were stealing, it would indeed be immoral. We have already seen the moral obligation for people within the same society to help those in need. The justification for taxation, moreover, goes beyond that. It is the result of legislation representing majority will. The government has the moral as well as the legal right to do those actions that it is empowered to do under the Constitution with the consent of the majority, providing it violates no one's rights. The practice of majority rule is bounded by respect for the rights of the minority. But within that restriction, it can be justified as productive of the greatest amount of good for all—even for those in the minority, assuming that it is not always the same group that is in the minority on all issues.

Following this line of reasoning, the American government can protect the consumer through truth in advertising and labeling laws, through actions of the FDA and the FTC, and in many other ways, some of which we have discussed. The government is not morally obliged to interfere or protect people in their transactions. But it is entitled to do so to the extent that it is authorized by the people. Hence, legislation that controls various aspects of business and places demands of one kind or another on it is morally justifiable providing the laws represent the will of the people and do not violate the rights of any citizen. In this sense, legislation represents the people's mandate to business. A tendency for legislation to move in the direction of greater free enterprise is in itself no more or less moral than the tendency for it to move in the direction of socialism. Both are morally justifiable, providing that neither violates the rights of any citizen or infringes on any norms of justice. We have seen no argument that satisfactorily concludes that one direction rather than another is morally preferable. How far we should go in either direction is therefore a matter for public debate.

Since the direction that government takes with respect to the control or lack of control of business is a matter for the public to decide, it is called a public policy issue. Such issues should be fully and publicly debated even though frequently they are not. One of the difficulties of big government, however, is that decisions are often taken by agencies with limited vision. No one takes the time or has the capacity to see how all the different regulations impinge on those affected by them. Many small businesses, for instance, claim that there are so many government regulations with which they must now contend that they must hire more people than they can afford simply to fill out the required government forms and keep up with the government requirements. When requirements become so burdensome that they force people out of business, there should be some mechanism by which government and the people can see if legislation and regulation are becoming counterproductive. The tendency of Congress to form administrative units to carry out supervision has also led to such administrations passing regulations that seem to some people to go well beyond what Congress originally intended. Yet they are not carefully overseen and turn into self-perpetuating bureaucracies.

The complaints about inefficient government regulation, regulators being partial to the industries they regulate, people moving back and forth between the regulating agencies and the industries that are to be regulated, and about overregulation point to issues that deserve careful scrutiny. To the extent that these points are well-founded, government tends to harm some of its citizens or to treat some of them unjustly, and thereby violate its primary obligation.

Immoral practices in business can be eliminated if those involved in it wanted to change. Governmental regulation and legislation have been used more and more frequently, and now have become the favorite and usual means of reform. Self-regulation and self-reform are possible alternatives. But unless they are used, increased governmental control is the direction in which the public mandate will continue to move.

Corporate Democracy

We have already seen that workers own a large part of industry through their pension plans and insurance policies and we have argued that workers have rights that should be respected. We have also discussed the need for greater disclosure to shareholders by and about the boards of directors. The corporation is now being looked at in a fresh light—there is more public debate about its future and concern about its power than in any previous decade. But we are still a very long way from corporate democracy.

Worker self-management is an experiment that is being tried with some success in Yugoslavia. Other forms of it have succeeded in Sweden. A few experiments in the direction of informing employees about a whole firm's operation and the use of teams instead of individual stations on an assembly line have proven moderately successful. They deserve careful study as possible models for future development. But most American workers do not want to take over management or to run their own corporations. Legislation has been suggested that would require a company to offer to sell to its employees a plant it intended to close. But the point of the legislation is not clear. If the corporation feels the plant is unprofitable, why should the workers in most cases feel any differently, or why should anyone assume that the workers could run it successfully when management could not? Workers have even been reluctant to have union representatives sit on the boards of directors of corporations, feeling that their representatives would then assume management's view rather than that of the worker's. Yet the placing of union leaders on corporate boards has already taken place and may presage a direction that will be followed in the future. The practice of naming outside members to boards of directors is also growing in popularity.

The claim that political democracy demands economic democracy is an ambiguous one. In one sense freedom of individuals to form productive or service units and to work together to carry out an enterprise is democracy in the marketplace. The existence of private corporations, therefore, can be seen as an exercise of freedom in the economic realm. But when those corporations become giants with a gross income as large as the GNP of some nations, critics claim that they should be subject to the same kinds of controls citizens have over governments. The argument is a reasonable one if the shareholder is considered comparable to the citizen. It is less clear if the claim is that each person should have the right to some say in the operation of large corporations because they influence all of our lives.

The movement toward some form of corporate democracy may be taking place. But if it is, it is taking place slowly and in a piecemeal fashion. There is no head-on movement for corporate democracy that has yet caught the conscience or the consciousness of the public at large. In a typically American way the corporation is changing slowly as it meets new situations and encounters new problems. If our earlier analysis is correct and if it perceived the new moral mandate more clearly, the corporation could move more quickly to accommodate itself to that mandate. But where there is still too little consensus and articulation of the mandate, the corporation will develop together with the mandate until one day, some observer will bring to public consciousness what will then be readily perceived: that business has changed and that it has responded willy-nilly to a new mandate.

Building a Good Society

A society without justice, at least without justice in its basic institutions, cannot be a good society. A good society must also have a sufficient amount of wealth distributed in such a way that all its people have their basic needs satisfied and enough in addition for them to enjoy some of the goods of life. Beyond this there is no single morally preferable mix of other goods in a good society.

One good society may have a certain amount of security for its people, together with a large amount of freedom of economic activity. Another good society may have less economic freedom and more security. Any good society probably has both freedom and security. But there is no one proper place to draw the line between them. Some societies desire and require a great deal of paternalism on the part of its leaders and government; some prosper with less.

Nor need a good society have no evil in it. A society that tolerated a limited amount of drunkenness among its citizens, for instance, might be preferable to one that had no drunkenness but at the price of a lack of privacy and periodic governmental searches. The totalitarian society depicted in the book *1984* is hardly the notion of a good society most Americans have. But neither is the society portrayed in More's *Utopia* or Plato's *Republic*.

The freedom of the individual to choose his or her own lifestyle, develop those talents the individual wishes, engage in one type of labor or occupation rather than another—all of these are part of what most Americans would expect to be available in a good society. A welfare state is not the kind of society that Americans want; nor is a society run by and for big business. Equality of opportunity has long been treasured rather than equality of results. But the opportunity must be truly equal and truly available to all.

There is no one best society that we can describe. For each one we imagine we can always add more happiness, virtue, beauty, or more knowledge. One of the tasks of ethics is to describe the goods worth seeking in life. Paramount among them is virtue, but it is not the only good. Happiness ranks a close second and may be the same as virtue for some people. A society whose people value virtue, respect each human individual, and think not only of themselves but of all whom their actions affect is a good society even if it does not enjoy luxury and ease. One of the greatest gifts any generation can give to the next generation is the wisdom to make the best of what is available and the fortitude to overcome adversity.

Business is an activity by which human beings associate with one another to exchange goods and services for their mutual advantage. It is not an end in itself. It is a means by which people endeavor to attain a good life for themselves and their loved ones. Business is a central activity of society and a type of human association. Too often it is seen in terms of dollars and cents instead of in terms of people. Although a firm may be established for profit, the profit earned is simply a means to an end and not an end in itself. When this fact is obscured and profit becomes an end, then people are poorly served because they are forgotten and ignored in the business process.

This volume has been a long argument in defense of the thesis that the Myth of Amoral Business should be seen for what it truly is—a myth. Ethics and morality have an important part to play in business. If morality is to pervade the marketplace, management must come to acknowledge the role of ethics and morality openly and vocally. The central moral obligation of business is not to cause harm to any of those affected by its actions. This is the heart of the new moral mandate. It is not the obligation of business to reform society but rather to reform that part of society which is business. Business has no mandate to take on government's responsibility for promoting the general good, welfare programs, or for redistributing income. These are properly public policy matters to be decided by the people. Business does have the obligation, however, to treat its workers and customers fairly, to give them adequate information, to control its toxic wastes, to provide reasonable safety in its products commensurate with the state of the engineering art, and in the other ways we have discussed to give due weight to those with whom it interacts.

There are three stages in the process of overcoming the Myth of Amoral Business. The first is to see it as a myth. The second is to raise the moral consciousness of those engaged in business in any of its aspects—as managers, workers, shareholders, consumers, or simply people affected by what happens generally in business. The third is to change the structures that have been built under the guise of being value-neutral. The processes of business are all value-laden. The need for moral heroes in business is an indication of immoral structures in business. Moral heroes will appear from time to time. They are to be applauded. But we cannot and should not expect ordinary people to be moral heroes. They cannot be trained in school or made heroic by courses in business ethics.

In recent years we have had more moral heroes in the marketplace than we have had for many decades. Their appearance is an indication both of the changing times and the need to change some of our social and corporate structures. Business ethics should take as its goal not only the teaching of moral reasoning and the presenting of moral arguments in defense of moral practices. It should also encourage thought among those in business as well as among legislators and the general public about the changes that are needed to promote morality. We have no moral blueprint of what has to be done, no panacea waiting in the wings, and no full-blown alternative system waiting to be adopted. But we are faced every day with moral problems, immoral and unethical conduct, and injustice. If we look carefully, we can see what needs change and improvement, what will increase justice and fairness, and what will motivate people to act so as to benefit rather than harm others. This requires moral imagination. A better life, better society, and a more moral society will not be achieved by some few people developing and presenting it to others—it is a joint endeavor that can be achieved only jointly.

Business can cling tenaciously to the Myth of Amoral Business, and can refuse to respond to the new moral mandate. If it does, it will convince the public that business is business, that it condones and fosters immorality and injustice, and that it puts profit above people. Some businesses and business people act this way, but not all businesses do. Business will enjoy the moral respect of society only when it earns it. It can show that businss ethics is not a contradiction in terms, not a myth, and not merely a body of theory. Ethics and morality can be a part of business. When they are built into its structure, when business lives up to its new moral mandate, it will deserve the public respect it will once again enjoy.

Further Reading

Ackerman, Robert, and Bauer, Raymond. *Corporate Social Responsiveness: The Modern Dilemma.* Reston, Va.: Reston Publishing Co., 1976.

Bell, Daniel. *The Cultural Contradictions of Capitalism.* New York: Basic Books, Inc., 1976.

Heilbroner, Robert L. *Business Civilization in Decline.* New York: W.W. Norton & Co., Inc., 1976.

Hill, Ivan, ed. *The Ethical Basis of Economic Freedom.* Chapel Hill: American Viewpoint, Inc., 1976.

Kahn, Herman; Martel, William; and Brown, William. *The Next 200 Years.* New York: William Morrow & Co., Inc., 1976.

Luthans, Fred; Hodgetts, Richard M.; and Thompson, Kenneth R. *Social Issues in Business.* 3rd ed. New York: Macmillan, Inc., 1980.

Nader, Ralph; Green, Mark; and Seligman, Joel. *Taming the Giant Corporation.* New York: W.W. Norton & Co., Inc., 1976.

Palusek, John L. *Will the Corporation Survive?* Reston, Va.: Reston Publishing Co., Inc., 1977.

Silk, Leonard, and Vogel, David. *Ethics and Profits: The Crisis of Confidence in American Business.* New York: Simon & Schuster, Inc., 1976.

Stone, Christopher. *Where the Law Ends: The Social Control of Corporate Behavior.* New York: Harper & Row, Publishers, Inc., 1975.

Walton, Clarence C. *Corporate Social Responsibilities.* Belmont, CA.: Wadsworth Publishing Co., 1967.

Index